F

SEL
ZIONISM, PROPAGANDA, AND THE USES OF HASBARA
BY HARRIET MALINOWITZ

"Deeply informative and carefully nuanced, *Selling Israel* shines a clear light on patterns of distortions and outright lies that remain grimly powerful. Harriet Malinowitz deftly refutes timeworn myths and provides a cogent analysis of how propaganda about Israel has continued to defend the indefensible."
— **Norman Solomon, author of** *War Made Invisible*

"As Israel has continued its pathological genocide in full view of the world, many have wondered why the so-called civilized west would allow it to continue unabated. More than that, why would they offer it full-throated support in terms of diplomacy and military supplies. In this splendid, wide-ranging, and exhaustively researched book, Harriet Malinowitz provides an answer to how the cult of messianic Zionism, starting in the 19th century, conquered the minds of generations of western elites. As the full-scope of Israel's brutality is now revealed, the spell cast over western public opinion has been lifted. The only people parroting the propaganda are western elites. Read this invaluable book to understand why."
— **Sut Jhally, professor of communication, University of Massachusetts Amherst**

"A systematic dissecting of how the Zionist movement and Israeli state have 'sold' us that which we as a society claim to loathe, all the way to genocide—a task that Harriet Malinowitz has tackled brilliantly. She examines the techniques through which Zionism and the Israeli state enlisted the fanatical support of the 'western' nations, better equipping us with the tools to break our addiction to Zionism's 'product.'"
— **Thomas Suárez, author of** *Palestine Hijacked: How Zionism Forged an Apartheid State from River to Sea*

"Lies sold displacement settler colonialism projects globally, but here in Palestine it is unique and far more devastating ... This eminently readable book shows a consistent pattern of lies and distortions feeding horrendous atrocities since the foundation of the Zionist project. Exposing the lies begins the needed process of reckoning that is a key to peace and justice for all people."
— **Mazin Qumsiyeh, professor and director of the Palestine Institute for Biodiversity and Sustainability, and author of *Sharing the Land of Canaan* and *Popular Resistance in Palestine***

"Now, more than ever, it is urgent to understand how Israel remains impervious to international law? How has it managed to promote its narrative of victimhood and self-righteousness through decades of occupation and violence? This book provides a thorough and very clear historical analysis of the Zionist narrative, its evolution and pervasive impact both within and outside of Israel. Multiple historical factors, institutions, and agencies have cooperated to cultivate a 'collective memory' as well as a 'collective amnesia'; to reduce history to a storyline that promotes the political requirements of Zionism. Today as unspeakable horrors are committed daily in Gaza and the truth is spun by pundits on all sides who know so little, *Selling Israel* disentangles many of the ubiquitous narrative distortions and is indispensable reading for any serious understanding of the Palestine/Israel wars."
— **Daphna Levit, author of *Wrestling with Zionism***

"An eye-opener ... Global in approach and powerfully comprehensive in scope, *Selling Israel* traces the history, the strategies, the institutions, the cultural figures, the lobbies, and the money that continue to empower Israel's *hasbara*, or international propaganda campaigns, ensuring access to billions in US taxpayer dollars and guarantees of US diplomatic protection at the UN and beyond."
— **Phyllis Bennis, author of *Understanding Palestine and Israel***

"In this incisive study, English literature scholar Malinowitz examines foundational myths of Israeli history ... [she] writes persuasively of the strength of hasbara, recalling how, as a Jewish American, she grew up with 'stories, aphorisms, and creeds' that 'recirculated' and self-reinforced within her community. It makes for an impressive and meticulous challenge to established narratives."
— **Publishers Weekly**

HARRIET MALINOWITZ

SELLING ISRAEL

ZIONISM, PROPAGANDA, AND THE USES OF HASBARA

OLIVE
BRANCH
PRESS

An imprint of Interlink Publishing Group, Inc.
Northampton, Massachusetts

First published in 2025 by

Olive Branch Press
An imprint of Interlink Publishing Group, Inc.
46 Crosby Street, Northampton, MA 01060
www.interlinkbooks.com

Library of Congress Cataloging-in-Publication data available
ISBN-13: 978-1-62371-580-9

Printed and bound in the United States of America

This book is dedicated to my beloved, wise and perceptive brother, Stan Malinowitz, who has accompanied me in decrypting hoary, smarmy shibboleths since the beginning of our time

and to those whose awe-inspiring *sumud* will lead everyone along the path to a free Palestine.

"The pursuit of balance can create imbalance,
because sometimes something is true."

—Dan Okrent, first public editor of the *New York Times,*
in what became known as Okrent's Law

CONTENTS

CHAPTER 1:
INTRODUCTION

Propaganda includes, but goes far beyond, the telling and selling of lies. It is used to induce people to think, and consequently act, in ways that may run counter to their own value systems or even their own interests—without them noticing or being perturbed by it. "Israel has a right to defend itself" may surely ring true for honest people who know little of how and why or even what it means for Israel to have been "attacked," who has done the attacking, who has enabled Israel to carry out acts that it calls "defense," and what that "defense" actually consists of. Many—including international legal experts—would argue that burning and starving civilian populations, maiming children to the point where their limbs must be amputated, destroying hospitals (along with their patients and personnel), and attacking media and humanitarian aid workers do not count as any sort of "defense." However, with those contexts occluded, the "true" statement may wield enormous deceptive power and enlist widespread support for the erroneous claim.

Even outright lies are far more easily sold when they are encrypted in appeals to an audience's own deeply held beliefs. These beliefs may even run counter to that audience's empirically derived perceptions. In a confounding phenomenon that George Orwell made famous as "doublethink" in his novel *1984*,[1] people routinely accept versions of reality that defy logic and their lived experience. For example, many accept that the United States has always been a democracy, despite its long history of slavery, disenfranchisement of women, genocide of Native Americans and theft of their lands, Jim Crow laws, and an electoral college that can produce a "winner" who has actually lost the majority vote. Many believe that certain groups or persons are "terrorists" and others are not, even when their behaviors are identical. Complex systems of social indoctrination that the theorist Jacques Ellul[2] has called "the propaganda of integration" and that another French theorist, Louis Althusser, has called "ideological state apparatuses"[3] instill these beliefs so that they seem self-evident and nonnegotiable. In both cases, this is manifested through mechanisms of civil society such as schools, religious institutions, media, charitable organizations, even the family.

Certain lies that underwrote the Zionist version of its own history have long enjoyed acceptance in the Western world. Of course, the existence of social media in the twenty-first century has radically altered audiences' access to events as they unfold in the present, so that what CNN tells us is happening in Jenin may easily be challenged with streamed video footage from a resident of the refugee camp there. Yet at least as far back as the 1980s, older, pre-Internet lies have been widely called out by historians, journalists, activists, artists, academics, and public intellectuals. These include, for instance, the claims that Palestine was "a land without a people," that the Jewish "pioneers" who migrated from Eastern Europe to Palestine "made the desert bloom," that Israel's wars have been waged only when there was "no choice," and that the Palestinian refugee phenomenon of 1948 was brought about because Arab leaders urged the residents to flee.

A number of circumstances together assisted the refutation of these oft-told tales, most notably the surfacing of previously inaccessible empirical evidence. Related factors include the opening up of archives that had been previously sealed and the historical scholarship that resulted; major changes in the way colonial ventures are studied and understood; the expanded reach of the concept of "multiculturalism" and the resulting transformation of the ways that the truth-claims of dominant groups and the authorship of historical accounts are evaluated; the decentering of the European gaze in our notions of history and culture; and, resulting from all of these, the salubrious skepticism that has penetrated our consumption of canonical national narratives.

Yet despite the fact that artifacts have emerged that contravene the truisms enshrined in nationalist lore, many of the old canards have not lost their grip on the Zionist imagination. Some sorts of myths—for example, that early Zionists opposed the transfer of Arab residents of Palestine to other countries and simply wanted to create a society inclusive of all—can be rendered demonstrably false via extant documents, although others are not so tangibly subject to "proof" or "disproof." As discussed above, rationalizations for occupation or genocide via nostrums such as "Israel has a right to defend itself," which involve complex acts of rhetorical acrobatics, require for their dismantling a much greater degree of rhetorical proficiency. And this, unfortunately, is not a capability that the above-mentioned "state ideological apparatuses" are always eager to instill in their citizenry. Therefore, finding ways to cultivate a more widespread critical literacy, very much including media literacy, is a crucial component in any fight against propaganda.

At the same time, what does it mean to assert that, as my epigraph avers, "sometimes something is true" even while intellectuals have lost confidence in the notion of absolute truth? It is my contention that people will continue to agree or disagree with the "truths" that Zionism, colonialism, racism, the "civilizing mission," and the legitimacy of a demeaned people seeking salvation in a sovereign ethno-nation-state are Good or Bad. Nonetheless, certain moves can bring reasonable people to reach some common recognition, even if grudging, about the more basic or underlying truths that lead us to those conclusions. I am here referring to the ability of primary sources to lend credibility—or not—to the secondary accounts and oral lore that purport to represent them. The documentary evidence that reveals who actually said, or declaimed, or sold, or did what, and to whom, and under what circumstances—as opposed to what their enemies or supporters said they said—must be considered the most dependable gauge of "what happened." By this I do not mean that because, for example, a leader declared something in a document their statement was necessarily "true." But it does mean that it's "true" that that's what the leader said. When the first prime minister of Israel, David Ben-Gurion, said, "The Bible is our mandate,"[4] this may very well not be evidence of genuine religious faith on his part—he was, after all, an avowed secularist, which opens up serious questions about the veracity of the statement. But it *is* evidence that he publicly *claimed* divine guidance steered Zionist policy. We can then go on to investigate *why* he deemed such a strategy useful, and *how* he deployed it to achieve his goals.

Rather than averaging out or "balancing" opposing views to arrive at an absurdly quantified picture of reality, we need to rely on the humble tools of critical inquiry into relevant documents, which may reveal that some things have actually transpired and that others have, at the very least, left not the faintest trace.

This is not a radical suggestion. In modern American universities, certain skills—evaluating sources, mounting persuasive evidence, scrutinizing the logic of an argument and recognizing logical fallacies, checking the accuracy of paraphrases, summaries, and quotations—are taught from the outset. These same skills are crucially exercised in the legal realm, where they are essential to weighing divergent testimonies against one another, or where a primary document may validate or belie the claim of a witness. Yet anyone who has ingested the day's news, or been urged to consume products or experiences, or heard election campaign speeches, or served on a jury knows that many of the college graduates who staff these enterprises are wont to discard what they learned as freshmen. The convenient assumption, often borne out, is that their audiences will have forgotten these lessons as well.

Professionals in the fields of public relations, media, and politics have, over many decades, exploited this cognitive deficiency to create a uniquely Israeli manifestation of public diplomacy called *hasbara*. It is most benignly described as "explanation," most bluntly described as "propaganda," but in fact comprises a huge network of government ministries, nongovernmental organizations (NGOs), nonprofit agencies and charities, campus organizations, volunteer groups, watchdog bodies, professional associations, media networks, fundraising operations, and educational programs that aim to fortify a Zionist-defined notion of Jewishness in persons within Israel, the United States, and other countries. The main purpose of foreign-aimed *hasbara* is to build support for Israel and its policies abroad. The main purpose of domestically focused *hasbara* is to shore up nationalist, patriotic feelings and attitudes that will render citizens compliant with their leaders' desired policies. *Hasbara* will be discussed in detail in Chapter 9, but for the moment suffice it to say that it is not a secret from the public or private consciousness of Israelis (though some of its elements may be). Rather, it is an apparatus that Israelis feel is essential for ensuring their legitimacy on the global stage and modifying their pariah status—which itself is believed to be the result of the world's "misunderstanding" of Israel's policies and behaviors. Their main complaint about it is that it is not executed proficiently enough to be as efficacious as they would desire. In Israel, *hasbara* is a word in everyday use.

CRITICAL INQUIRY AND PRIMARY SOURCES

In 2004, the Israeli writer and educator Dan Porat published a fascinating account of the ways the Holocaust had been taught in Israeli's centralized educational system over many decades—and how for a brief moment, a curriculum grounded in primary sources took hold. From the 1950s to the twenty-first century, the representation of the Holocaust in the national curriculum was tailored, in dramatically different fashions, to the national identity requirements of the moment. In the post-war period, writes Porat, the Holocaust "was ignored so that Israeli students could overcome what was perceived as a national humiliation."[5] Ghetto resistance fighters and Jewish paratroopers, models for the "New Jews" who would grow a muscular Israel, were valorized, but those who were said to "go like sheep to the slaughter" in the gas chambers were scorned as emblems of diaspora abjection and the catastrophic powerlessness of Jews who didn't have a state of their own. After the wars of 1967 and 1973, when the fear of vulnerability and "a second Holocaust" were used to mobilize Israelis' militaristic determination to stave off further victimhood, "a new and unfamiliar empathy with Holocaust victims emerged from the newly-published textbooks."[6]

In the 1970s studying the Holocaust was still an elective, and few chose it. However, those who did choose to study it encountered an interesting new pedagogy, based on American educational models:

> This approach demanded that students analyse historical sources them-selves, interpret them and form their own historical accounts of events.... Adopting such an approach to history-teaching meant that no consistent account of the Holocaust would be communicated to students and that one could not formulate a single authoritative Holocaust memory among all students."[7]

Students confronted primary documents and were asked open-ended questions about them that required analysis and problem-solving methods, so that "history became a bundle of complex considerations and alternatives."[8] But this presentation of data, leaving students to draw their own conclusions rather than imbibe inexorable "lessons" about the Holocaust's meaning, "frustrated some people," with some arguing that "Holocaust education is of 'extreme national-educational significance'" and should be both expanded and centrally controlled.[9] After 1977, when Menachem Begin and his right-wing, territori-ally maximalist Likud Party came to power, the Holocaust became a required subject of study for high school students and a "Holocaust memory law" was passed. Porat explains that members of the Knesset were induced to adopt this new legislation because it "aimed to transform students' personal memory and perception, to turn the Holocaust into the cornerstone of Israeli students' day-to-day identity"[10]—furnishing a "causal link" between the Holocaust and the establishment of the state. To this end, a new generation of textbooks highlighting the centrality of the Holocaust to the character of the Israeli state materialized. The "causal" connection was further bolstered by a new tradition: Israeli high schoolers ritually traveled to Poland to visit the remains of concentration camps and ghettos, and the international March of the Living program expanded on this so that Jewish youth worldwide could have the "once-in-a-lifetime experience" of marching from Auschwitz to Birkenau—before flying to Israel to celebrate Israel's Independence Day.[11]

I contend that teaching practices such as the short-lived "open-ended" curriculum that Porat describes are most helpful in resisting the force of propagandistic, indoctrinating education. This extends, too, beyond the school system. As the work of Israel's "New Historians" has shown, the power of wielding primary sources has already changed perceptions of Zionism and its fabrications. Particularly noteworthy is the case of Benny Morris, whose 1988 work, *The Birth of the Palestinian Refugee Problem, 1947–1949*, harvested the fruits of previously sealed archival resources. He and other committed Zionist historians of that era—including Ilan Pappe, Tom Segev, and Avi Shlaim—were shocked at what they found in documents that had long been kept from public view. These documents supported what Israelis had long discounted as "Arab propaganda" about the Nakba—the 1948 "catastrophe" of ethnic cleansing and mass destruction of Palestinian communities by Zionist militias (and later the Israeli army itself). "Like most Israelis, I had always been under the influence of certain myths that had become accepted as historical truth," wrote one of this cohort, Simha Flapan. "Israel's myths are located at the core of the nation's self-perception.... Yet...the documents at hand not only failed to substantiate them, they openly contradicted them."[12] Morris himself, in a subsequent essay, wrote that the discoveries of this generation revealed the "simplistic and consciously pro-Israeli interpretation of the past" that had saturated the "old" history. "*Raisons d'état* often took precedence over telling the truth."[13]

Morris, a dogged researcher and an ardent positivist, had revealed artifacts that, he felt, ought to speak for themselves. However, assailed by criticisms about his stance regarding those artifacts, he backpedaled on the very conclusions they clearly suggested. In a February 2002 article in the *Guardian*[14] he wrote of "the rumour that I have undergone a brain transplant." Now, thanks in large part to him, the cat was out of the bag: he had produced proof that the roots of the Palestinian refugee catastrophe lay in brutal Zionist attacks and fear of more of them, not, as Israeli leaders had long alleged, Arab radio broadcasts urging the residents to leave to clear the path for invading Arab armies. Dismayed by the implications of his own research (and that of others) for Israel's "legitimacy," and unable to mop up the flood of further substantiating information he had unloosed, he resorted instead to changing the subject. It was no longer *what had happened* that was under debate or of significance, he maintained, but *why it was justified.*

"If you recognize the responsibility," he said in a December 2001 interview with the Israeli newspaper *Yediot Ahronot,* "millions will demand their lands in return immediately thereafter . . . and that will be the end of the State of Israel." He did not deny the facts he had uncovered: "I revealed to the Israelis the truth of what happened in 1948, the historic facts." But he rued the Pandora's box he had opened because its contents legitimated Palestinian claims and aims and thus, in his estimation, threatened the very existence of Israel. "In the heart of every Palestinian exists a desire that the State of Israel will not be here anymore," he averred. "As far as they are concerned, all of their misfortunes are a consequence of our deeds, and our destruction will bring about their salvation. Their salvation is the whole of Palestine."[15] No longer the sober bearer of rock-solid information, he refrained to cite any evidence of this calculation or other vague accusations—such as that the Palestinians "cheer for bin Laden."[16]

All this said, I strongly contend that Morris's retracted conclusion and his rationalization of atrocities are of less consequence than the fact that he has provided us, irrefutably, with the incriminating words of David Ben-Gurion and other leaders of the Zionist conquest to begin with. As the Palestinian historian Nur Masalha wrote in response to Morris's turnabout, Morris has documented what was long denied by Israel and its supporters. His putatively explosive revelations echoed countless oral history testimonies and the work of highly respected Palestinian scholars such as Walid Khalidi. What was different was that, in Aristotelian terms, the message, now conveyed directly from the annals of Israel's most iconic figures, was imbued with an unimpeachable *ethos*—a persuasive power emanating from the character or position of the speaker—that finally could not be gainsaid, even as much of its audience reeled under its naked, counterintuitive force. "Morris's findings," says Masalha, "constitute a landmark and are now a major contribution to our knowledge because they show that the evacuation of hundreds of thousands of Palestinians was a result of direct attacks, fear of attacks, intimidation, psychological warfare (e.g., the whispering campaign) and sometimes outright expulsions ordered by the Haganah/IDF leadership." Yet, he is critiquing Benny Morris, not apologizing for him, and his ultimate point is that Morris's latter-day thinking stalls in the face of his own evidence. Masalha concludes that "a wider explanatory and theoretical framework within which the Palestinian catastrophe can be properly understood must be sought elsewhere."[17]

Those propelled by nationalist or messianic passions may well continue to assert that brutal means justify transcendent ends. But they are not the intended audience of this book or the objects of my principal claim—which is that *some* contentions are verifiable, their veracity not hopelessly lost in the fog of indeterminacy; and if we really want to we can achieve some clarity by using the means that are available to dig for and gauge evidence that supports or refutes them. We learn more, I argue, from an analysis of the methods and motives of those who spin facts into ideologically compelling master narratives than we do from ping-pong arguments over the accuracy of disembodied mantras and slogans (e.g., "Anti-Zionism is antisemitism." "No, it isn't."). I am interested, furthermore, in intervening in the escapism of those who imagine that because they haven't heard of something, whether by happenstance or by choice, it doesn't exist (and by extension has no impact on anything else); or that because an act they are engaged in may clash with what they believe to be their "values," a sort of lobotomy is in order to keep the inner peace. This is often accomplished by resorting to the "balance" argument: something may or may not be true, the jury is still out, there are strong views and compelling arguments on *both sides,* our thinking must be *nuanced,* and conclusions and action must necessarily be forestalled until the day comes when the disparity is resolved. Through the convolutions of propaganda, that day may be postponed indefinitely.

THE OPPOSITE OF "SINGLING ISRAEL OUT" IS GIVING IT A CONTEXT

Another overarching aim of this book is to extract Zionism's use of propaganda from the pigeonhole of exceptionalism and examine it in a broader context, both spatially and historically. Zionism's tools have not been tools of Zionism alone; much of the vitality of Zionists' techniques has been amply tested and proven elsewhere. For example, throughout Zionism's history, Zionists have influenced the opinion of various publics by creating cultural imagery that tugs at the sentiments and delineates chimerical contours of reality—a staple project of romantic nationalist movements. Like many other conquerors, occupiers, and dominant castes, Zionists have promulgated archetypal notions of the heroic subject and the debased Other. Zionists hardly invented—though they resurrected at a rather late date—the practice of deploying images of the civilizing mission of Europeans in the primitive backwaters of the world. Masterfully inverting notions of who is "indigenous" and who is a threatening "invader" had already been tried in the Americas before the Zionists began to arrive in Palestine. The art of disseminating catchy refrains that persuasively rework history in short declaratory sentences or exhortations—such as "Columbus discovered America" and "Remember the Alamo!"—obviously did not originate with "a land without a people for a people without a land" or *Never compare* Israelis with Nazis!" In addition, the Zionists were beneficiaries of a long tradition, going back to ancient Athens, of wielding the rhetorical appeals of classical persuasive argument. These practices, it should be said, were not always as forthright and exacting as Aristotle—who maintained that the cheap tricks of relativist argument lay solely in the province of the Sophists—might have hoped.

The State of Israel, in tandem with many other countries, has also utilized tools of the public relations industry—from wielding "soft power" and "nation branding" to "greenwashing" and the spin machinery of think tanks, from blurring the boundaries between NGOs and governments to exploiting the powers of new media—which can conceal or fabricate the identity of a speaker in a discourse. Therefore, understanding the ways that these tools have been perfected in myriad conditions can help us better comprehend the ways they have been applied with such massive success in the Zionist enterprise.

It is important to note that having a well-honed sense of "audience" is always central to the effective rhetorical act of propaganda. At least since Israeli statehood came into being in the mid-twentieth century, Zionist propagandists have had to simultaneously aim their declarations toward two primary audiences whose interests sometimes clash. First, there is the Jewish Israeli populace, whose foundational tenet is that the Jewish state must have a powerful military so that antisemitic victimization can never happen again, and whose citizens are groomed to be compliant when they are called up repeatedly for army service. But second, also enormously important, is the American public, whose leaders' ongoing financial, diplomatic, and ideological cover is essential to Israel's wellbeing—yet whose expressed idea of a positive outcome to the conflict is more apt to revolve around diplomacy leading to "peace" and the ever-hazy "two-state solution," and whose citizens will be called upon repeatedly for fundraising. The American audience, which prominently features an interconnected web of Jewish membership and lobbying associations, also includes a vast number of fundamentalist Christian Zionist groups and congregations who support Israel insofar as they see Jews as instrumental to the second coming of Christ.

In the Jewish diaspora, identification and loyalty are cultivated through a complex network of Jewish centers with synagogues, Hebrew schools, and programs tailored to a variety of age and gender groupings; Zionist summer camps; religious events such as bar and bat mitzvahs that have taken on a cultural cachet of their own; customized rituals such as LGBTQ-friendly or Black Lives Matter-focused seders that link the ancient Hebrews with other oppressed communities in their righteous quests for freedom; trips to Israel; membership in Zionist clubs and youth movements; the recreational practice of Israeli music and dance; and a coordinated system of Israel-affiliated organizations such as Hillel and StandWithUs on college campuses.

THE PROPAGANDA OF INTEGRATION LAYS THE FOUNDATION

In Israel, what Jacques Ellul calls the "propaganda of integration" takes a number of forms, some of which spill over into diaspora consciousness and some of which reflect values that non-Israeli Jews, as well as non-Jewish Israelis, are unlikely to share. This entrenching of core beliefs lays the foundation for popular acceptance of more specifically situational forms of propaganda—what Ellul calls the "propaganda of agitation"—triggered by varying immediate national needs.

As with virtually every society, a key site in which normative values are instilled in Israel is the school curriculum, reflecting the perspectives of the society's ruling class. We saw this earlier in Porat's discussion of how scholastic narratives about the Holocaust were adjusted to reflect different ideological moments in Israel's social-psychological climate. Nurit Peled-Elhanan, an Israeli scholar of education at the Hebrew University of Jerusalem, did a major study in which she examined Israeli history, geography, and civics school books published between 1996 and 2009. She concluded that the texts "inculcate collective memory in the populace grounded in state approved civic truth" via techniques that resembled those employed in Soviet textbooks—for example, "unchallenged narratives, especially tragic and heroic ones"; events reduced to "mythic archetypes"; and a preference for "a usable past over accuracy," with the past often represented in ways that afford "justification of the present."[18]

In these texts, she finds, the disciplinary discourses of history and geography mingle with politics, ideology, and military concerns, and are reinforced by "biblical prophecies, patriotic songs, and heroic poetry," all "designed to immortalize Jewish dominance through its presentation as legitimate from the dawn of civilization."[19] The depiction of Palestinian life, meanwhile, "enhances ignorance," presenting images of people engaged in primitive activity rather than modern pursuits such as attending universities or practicing professions. When Palestinian people are not rendered altogether invisible or irrelevant to modernity, they are portrayed as terrorists or a demographic threat (if they become a majority, it is said, it will deal an existential blow to the "Jewishness" of the state). Thorny topics are simply omitted from the discussion. For example, there is no mention of what happened to the 1948 refugees after their exodus, the first Intifada, or the ways that Israeli laws discriminate against and impoverish Palestinian citizens as well as noncitizens under occupation. Massacres of Palestinian villages are "legitimated" based on "effect and utility"—that is, the extent to which their outcomes "are compatible with Zionist goals and Jewish convictions."[20] This was the key criterion, as we saw, in Benny Morris's turnabout in his appraisal of the Nakba. It can also be seen in this statement Peled-Elhanan quotes from a textbook: "The escape of the Arabs solved a horrifying demographic problem."[21]

Other modes of consolidating an ostensibly stable Jewish group identity are found across the academic disciplines. Again, the knowledge produced tends to dovetail with the needs of the state. Somewhat paradoxically in the perspective of most Western democracies, according to Israel's Nation-State Law of 2018, Israel is the declared homeland and state of the Jewish people (including its diasporic citizens of other nations) rather than of its own citizens (many of whom are not Jewish).[22] This means that all (and only) Jews have the right, among other things, to immigrate, develop settlements, and have their heritage, customs, and religion officially honored. For this highly unusual proposition to be persuasive, there need to be ways of confirming that the world's Jews indeed constitute One People and are thus the collective heirs to the property. That, in turn, involves pronouncing a legitimate basis for confirming that someone is a Jew.

For the rabbinate, Jewishness has traditionally derived from having a Jewish birth mother—though this is more complicated than it once was, as contemporary reproductive practices and technologies have made it possible for a child, say, to be born with the DNA of a Jewish mother and father, yet to emerge from the womb of a non-Jewish surrogate mother. (Is that baby Jewish?)[23] Inevitably, as with much else in the twenty-first century, the discussion of Jewishness has shifted to the field of genetics. Numerous studies have been conducted to support the argument that there are biological markers of Jewishness, though they have employed disparate methodologies (e.g., blood studies, mitochondrial studies, Y-chromosome studies, studies that blurred the distinction between *phenotypes* and *genotypes,* studies of "Cohanim" —the priestly line said to descend father-to-son from Moses's brother Aaron)—and thus yield inconsistent results, with no "Jewish gene" having been identified.[24] According to anthropologist Nadia Abu El-Haj:

> In the case of Jewish origins, researchers ask: Is the story of a Jewish population originating in ancient Palestine, from which it was exiled, plausible?.... Are the various Jewish communities of the Jewish diaspora phylogenically related to one another? Do they descend from a common ancient stock? How much have Jewish communities mixed with their "host" communities over the centuries?[25]

Numerous "legitimating" issues are at stake here. For one, Israel seeks to increase the number of Jews among its populace to maintain its "demographic majority," enabling it to continue winning electoral and legal contests in a way that that will seem "democratically" legible to other Western nations. Meanwhile, major Jewish organizations have declared that any doubts about the Jewish lineage reaching directly back to ancient Israel are evidence of antisemitism. For instance, in February 2024 the Anti-Defamation League had this on its website: "One of the most insidious claims used to discredit both Jews and Israel is that Ashkenazi Jews (i.e., Jews who trace their ancestry to Northern and Eastern Europe) have no historical or genetic relationship to Jewish antiquity in the land of Israel—making Jews 'colonizers' with no legitimate claim to the land that makes up the Jewish state."[26] Or one can find this news item on the website of the World Jewish Congress: Bennett Greenspan, founder and president of Family Tree DNA, hotly disputed the findings of Israeli historian Shlomo Sand, who maintained that Jewish continuity was a myth sustained by conversions over the ages. "'We are not interlopers who came here from Eastern Europe, and we're not Serbs or Kazars. You can use whatever polemic you want to discredit the Jews or discredit the nation, but saying that we weren't here is a lie,' Greenspan was quoted by 'Haaretz' as saying."[27]

Part of demonstrating the singularity of the Jewish people and the exclusion of others from the lineage involves unearthing an umbilical cord stretching from the alleged Iron Age kingdom of David and Solomon to the purportedly "revived" Zionist nation of Israel in the twentieth century. The field of Bible studies, in which authorship, provenance of information, and ideological stimulus for the narratives have long been matters of contention, became entangled with archaeological and cartographic work from the founding of the Palestine Exploration Fund (PEF) in London in 1865. The hope was that, in the words of Nadia Abu El-Haj, their "search for observable truths" via surveying, mapping, and excavating the Holy Land would ultimately "establish the veracity of the historical texts on which the tenets of the Christian faith were based" and thus serve to "recuperate" Ancient Palestine as "the foundation of…modern European (Christian) civilization."[28] Decades later, in the early twentieth century, the Jewish Palestine Exploration Society (later the Israel Exploration Society) plumbed the remains of tombs and synagogues to locate traces of Jewishness across the land, firming up the sense of connection between "then" and "now." In 1949, some of their principal members served on Prime Minister David Ben-Gurion's Governmental Names Committee, where they further fortified the umbilical cord by "reviving" ancient [Hebrew] place names in the Negev. Their mission was to replace, in the words of one committee report, Arabic names through which "a foreign spirit blows," bearing "negative, sad or degrading connotations" that "evoke[] fear" with "original [Hebrew] names close to the heart of the Jewish defender and settler in the Negev."[29]

Noted religious studies scholar (and critic of the methods and assumptions of traditional Biblical archaeology) Keith W. Whitelam has argued that the focus on "ancient Israel" in the fields of archaeology and biblical studies has speciously discounted all else that transpired in that region over millennia. These disciplines promote, he contends, a selective, retrojective attention that has served to bolster the contemporary preferred identity requirements of Israel—as well as the political ideals of the West, which sees the Holy Land as the bedrock of its civilization. In both cases, the notion of the European nation-state supplies the *only* frame through which the entire past is to be viewed and interpreted. As a result, the histories of neighboring peoples in the region have been disregarded—a critical factor in the denial that Palestinian history has existed. *Left out* of the purview of biblical studies, Whitelam says, is "a broad-based thematic conception of history concerned with the economy, demography, settlement, religions and ideologies of Palestine as a whole." This erases even the notion of Palestinian *people*: "It is possible to refer to the 'Palestinian coastline,' 'Palestinian agriculture,' or the 'Palestinian economy'…, but the inhabitants are never described as Palestinians." Though "the land might be called Palestine…its inhabitants are Amorites, Canaanites, or Israelites." Whitelam asks, "If we have a land called 'Palestine,' why are its inhabitants not called Palestinians?" They are "nameless except for designation by archaeological period: Neolithic," etc. "Those inhabitants who are acknowledged before the beginning of the Iron Age are only temporary, mostly anonymous, awaiting Israel's arrival to claim its national heritage." In effect, within this template, no one except the ancient "Israelites" count as antecedents to present-day inhabitants of the region, thus giving the "Jewish people" sole entitlement to the legacy and the land.[30]

Abu El-Haj describes some of the archaeological practices that mold the image of Palestine as a "new/old land" (which happened to be the title of a 1902 utopian novel by Theodor Herzl extolling the Zionist cause), in which modern Israelis emerge as the only true heirs to the land because their ancestors were the only "people" who resided there. She explains, for instance, the common

Israeli use of bulldozers in site excavation—"the ultimate sign of 'bad science' and of nationalist politics guiding research agendas…in order to get down to the earlier strata, which are saturated with national significance, as quickly as possible (Iron Age through early-Roman)," while remains in layers above them (sometimes referred to as "debris") are destroyed or discarded. This is true despite the fact that more sensitive tools and techniques are available in order to find and record "very small remains: artifactual, animal, seeds, and so forth," which "are seen as essential to the reconstruction of aspects of ancient daily life," to say nothing of information-laden artifacts of cultures that Israeli archaeologists may deem "insignificant."[31] It is notable that bulldozers have become a broader emblem of Israeli destruction—of houses, streets and alleys, infrastructure, vegetation, and of human beings such as 23-year-old American activist Rachel Corrie, on March 16, 2003.

In June 1967, with Israel's victory in the Six-Day War barely established, the Moroccan Quarter of Jerusalem's Old City (dating to 1193) was bulldozed, an act of "destruction and expulsion" that "launched the process of reconfiguring the identity of the place itself…." Abu El-Haj writes that the "leveling of this neighborhood was the first step in Israel's policy of unification, which was to claim and seize the entire city as rightfully and exclusively, at the level of national sovereignty, its own…. [O]ne thing was already clear: Jerusalem would never again be divided."[32] The "new" Jewish quarter, in which "modern buildings overlook or are built on top of archaeological remains," invests the quarter with "a general aura of historical continuity and longevity, exemplifying an '"old-new' (Jewish) place and the symbolic center of the unified capital of the Israeli state."[33]

Outside the bounds of formal education and accepted scholarship, "integrative propaganda" is enshrouded in myriad customs, rituals, monuments, tourist sites, and holidays. Jewish studies scholar Yael Zerubavel argues that many of these contribute to the cultivation of "collective memory"—which, she says, "reduces complex historical events to basic plot structures"—and also to "collective amnesia" about past realities that conflict with the society's preferred master narrative about itself. Zionist historiography has challenged traditional Jewish (religious) collective memory and superimposed upon it a "countermemory" in which the past is divided simply into two parts.[34]

The first recognized period is "Antiquity," which "begins with the Israelites' conquest of ancient Canaan and extends over centuries of collective experience there" and "ends with a series of revolts that fail—the Great Revolt against the Romans during the first century, followed by the failure of the Bar Kokhba revolt in the second century." The roughly two thousand-year period of "Exile" that follows "covers the many centuries when Jews lived as a religious minority dispersed among other peoples," a condition Zionists view as extremely abject and dishonorable. The cure for the ignominy of Exile was said to lie in the mass "return" to Zion in the twentieth century and the "restoration" of Israelite culture in its "ancient homeland."[35]

The "revived" modern Israeli society implanted the message of what Zerubavel calls "the Zionist binary model of Jewish history" through numerous newly invented traditions. For example, the key values promoted by the new society involved muscular activities such as military service and agricultural work rather than sedentary Talmudic scholarship in dimly lit yeshivas. "The New Hebrew," writes Zerubavel, "was "expected to be closer to his ancient forebears [who engaged valiantly in battle] than to his exilic parents" and was "portrayed as a man of action, not a man of words." Furthermore, the "holiday cycle," she says, "has a major role in shaping our basic views of the past," and to that end, "[l]earning about the holidays often occupies an important place in early childhood curriculum."[36] She stresses that

> [t]he Zionist collective memory did not invent new mythical structures. Rather, it promoted a closer association between existing Jewish myth plot structures and certain periods in Jewish history and reinterpreted their meaning…. Furthermore, it shifted from the traditional, religious framework of attributing historical developments to divine help and punishment, to a secular national framework that emphasizes sociopolitical explanations.[37]

For example, she says, in commemorating Hanukah, "the Maccabees' success in liberating their people from foreign oppressors has become the focal point of the celebration, rather than the divine miracle of the flask of oil and the renewal of services at the Temple." Other holidays, as well, came to be infused with themes of national-political import, and, as Zerubavel says, "accentuated the pattern of besiegement, confrontation, and survival throughout Jewish history."[38]

Practices were institutionalized that emphasized the way Israelis deeply "knew" their land in a way that others did not. The *tiyul,* a hike in nature that was said to promote intimacy with the homeland, has been "considered a sacred activity" for Hebrew youth and, in Zerubavel's words, "established a sense of ownership over the land...."[39] Pilgrimages to sites emblematic of legendary "heroic" Jewish behavior have been carried out by youth movements, school groups, soldiers, and tourists to inspire awe for the past and for renewed heroic Jewish acts in the present. In particular, treks to the remains of Masada—a fortress built by King Herod in the first century BCE and perched on a remote hilltop in the Judean Hills overlooking the Dead Sea—have been particularly laden with symbolic meanings. However, those "meanings," as well as the facts they are purportedly derived from (none of which are verifiable), conflict sharply with one another.

A CASE IN POINT: THE MUTATED MASADA STORY

The legend of Masada is a curious one to be mythologized for the supposed heroism of its protagonists, since their distinguishing act was to commit a mass murder-suicide—among them 960 men, women, and children. Having fled the Roman general Titus's conquest of Jerusalem in 70 CE and escaped the devastation following the destruction of the Second Temple, this surviving cohort of free Jews who remained in Palestine had sought refuge in the barricaded mountaintop stronghold. The mass suicide (as it is usually described, the "murder" dimension discreetly omitted) was said to be a choice they deemed preferable to surrender or enslavement to the Roman army that finally breached their fortress wall in 72 CE. Yet, as some have noted, the concept of "choice" hardly seems apt here, consensus being impossible as women and surely children would not have had equal decision-making input and even dissident men would likely have been overpowered by others.

As explained in detail by Israeli sociologist Nachman Ben-Yehuda, there really is no "primary" source available for what happened, as the only eyewitnesses were two women and five children who had hidden in a cave during the massacre and told the Romans (that is, the conquerors who they now had to face alone) what had happened. It is unknown what game of "telephone" may have relayed the story and how that may have affected its particulars before it came to the ear of Josephus Flavius (36–100 CE), a former leader of the Jewish Great Revolt against the Romans in the Galilee. After surrendering, he became a Roman citizen and, within that environment and with the largesse of that patronage, a noted historian of Jewish life.[40] The Biblical Archaeological Society calls him the author of "arguably the most consequential ancient writings in the West after the Bible...."[41] It was Josephus's account of Masada that became the urtext of the story that, many iterations later, came to take on a very different— and ideologically resonant—life of its own.

Ben-Yehuda emphasizes that, while even Josephus's report is a secondary source (as he had not been there to witness the events themselves), it is the *only* account from that time that we know of: "Without Josephus," he says, "there is not much we know about Masada." However, that reality did not preclude a wealth of latter-day embellishments that better suited the needs of the "revived" state of Israel. Very significantly, the cast of characters was altered. The mountaintop "defenders" of Josephus's story were of a Jewish sect called the Sicarii. "The Sicarii's distinct feature," writes Ben-Yehuda, "was their use of political assassinations against both Romans and Jews. The Sicarii were disliked and were driven out of Jerusalem not by Romans but by other Jews a long time before the Roman army put the city under siege and destroyed it. The Sicarii fled to Masada." Once there, they "raided nearby (Jewish) villages, killed the inhabitants, and took their food to Masada. They were responsible for a terrible massacre of presumably innocent women and children at Ein Gedi."[42]

Yet in the account of Yigal Yadin, the Hebrew University archaeologist who led two famous excavations of Masada between 1963 and 1965, the "defenders" on the mountaintop—those who made "their heroic stand" in their "choice of death over slavery," who "elevated Masada to an undying symbol of desperate courage, a symbol which has stirred hearts throughout the last nineteen centuries" and which "brings the recruits of the armoured units of the Defence Forces of modern Israel to swear the oath of allegiance on Masada's heights: 'Masada shall not fall again!'"[43]—were not the Sicarii at all. Rather, they were a sect called the Zealots, who were *not* disagreeably tainted by what we might now call terrorist acts against their fellow Jews. Yadin, though he acknowledges Josephus's earlier version, calling it "detailed" and "compelling," makes no attempt to clarify or justify this perplexing switch in the warriors' identity.[44]

This fabrication did not actually originate with Yadin, though he popularized it. The unbridled mythologizing had been put into motion in the 1930s via a young Zionist immigrant to Palestine named Shmaria Guttman, who invented it, packaged it for youth groups, and then in a series of seminars "educated" guides who themselves went on to instill the fiction in generations to come.[45] He did it, he said, because "I wanted to bring ourselves, the young adolescents, to the point where they would have the willingness to fight to the end. Not to die, but to fight to the end."[46]

Why, then, choose a story of collective suicide without a fight? Ben-Yehuda offers his opinion on the matter:

> The biggest advantage of the Masada story is the site itself. The narrative was problematic. So it was overhauled and constructed in such a way as to "fit" a heroic narrative. The technique was simple: emphasize and magnify the heroic elements; add if necessary; ignore and discount the more problematic aspects....This technique was precedent-setting....[T]he creation of the Masada myth was *based* on its effective manipulation."[47]

To that end, Guttman and others who went on to enshrine the story in patriotic lore tweaked other key facts, as well. Most notably, rather than having the Jewish corpses confront the invading Romans with an awe-inspiring fait accompli of mass death, the defenders were said to have engaged in protracted battle "to the end." Further omitted from the narrative is the fact that Eleazar ben Yair, the Sicarii leader, had to use all his rhetorical prowess and make *two* speeches before he could convince all the men to participate in the murder/suicide scheme. (Also lost in the present version is the fact that ben Yair professed that those who demurred lacked courage because they were "effeminate.")[48]

When Ben-Yehuda interviewed IDF officers about Masada in preparation for his book, he found that they believed that the myth *was* the true story. When unpleasant dimensions of the story such as the suicide surfaced, he says, they tended to be "explained" or dismissed as moot because "we now have a state."[49] In recent decades, Masada has become more of a tourist site than a prototype of counterintuitively intrepid conduct. Yet Ben-Yehuda found tour guides still delivering the mythical plotline. When he inquired what they believed to be the source of the narrative, they replied Yadin, not Josephus Flavius.[50]

The tortuous route of the Masada story over the past century is germane to the study of Zionism and propaganda in two key ways. First, as we have seen, certain well-positioned figures have fashioned it as a heuristic that is vital to the construction of an Israeli national identity. This is an identity that prizes "fighting to the end" and the valor of "the few against the many" (though as Ben-Yehuda points out, 960 people isn't really "few")[51] as well as the righteousness of resorting to drastic action when the available choices (enslavement or murder, rape, and torture by the enemy) really amount to "no choice." Creating a template for national character folklorically is emblematic of what Jacques Ellul calls "integrative propaganda," and instills the values and worldview on which myriad other forms of propaganda depend.

The Masada story—or, more accurately, the story of the story—is also pertinent for our study in that it affords a unique perspective on the use (and misuse) of primary and secondary sources. As we see here, the earliest source available (that is, Josephus Flavius's account) doesn't necessarily reveal "what really happened"—which may remain forever unknowable. But unless or until further primary material is discovered, it does provide a ground zero for understanding *how* the tale has shape-shifted, and for analyzing *why* it has been made to do so, and for considering the motives behind the *meanings* and *plots* that have subsequently been constructed regarding this event. It *does* provide evidence, at the very least, of *what Josephus Flavius claimed*. Electing to ignore this itself becomes an essential chapter of the "story of the story," in that it conceals possible ideological incentives for the redactions. These themselves merit critical scrutiny because they can tell us volumes about how a society wants to present itself—and how it may want to disguise itself.

Though we lack solid evidence telling us what transpired that day on Masada, we can easily point to the fact that there is *no evidence* for some of the claims made later on—for instance, that the defenders were Zealots, that they fought a long, brave battle against the Romans, and so on. Similarly, other (newer) old debates continue to be aired: whether there *really was* an ancient Israelite kingdom that granted Zionists the deed to the land millennia later; whether there *really were* radio broadcasts by Arab leaders encouraging Palestinians to flee during the Nakba; whether the Jews of Iraq *really were* victims of a rabid, age-old form of antisemitism that was not triggered by Zionism and colonialism. To such claims, we can apply these same tools of research and critical inquiry. Sometimes, something is true. But sometimes, more obviously, something is demonstrably *not* true.

THE ORGANIZATION OF THIS BOOK

This book is organized thematically, not according to a historical chronology. Its structure reflects various aims and methods of propaganda that have been used by Zionists but have also, as we shall see, been used by many others—though its focus is decidedly how these have been manifested by Zionists.

Chapter 1: Introduction explains the purposes of this book and some of its underlying principles.

Chapter 2: Foundations provides crucial background information on the phenomenon of propaganda as well as the phenomenon of Zionism.

Chapter 3: "Balance" and the Manufacture of Doubt examines the idea of "balance" and the doctrine of objectivity in a debate, particularly insofar as they are used to inculcate *doubt* that any conclusive findings have been made—or perhaps, even, *can* be made—on a subject. It traces the uses of the "tobacco strategy"—that is, generating doubt as a way to undermine the carefully researched findings of experts. For the tobacco industry, those experts were scientists, and their subject was the toxicity of certain products and practices. This strategy, which long delayed regulations mitigating the harms of smoking, was replicated in a number of other realms: the debates over pesticides, acid rain, and climate change; contested hearings for Supreme Court justices; the denial of the Armenian genocide; and the obfuscation of harsh realities brought about by Zionists before and after the creation of the State of Israel. The imperative to always provide "balance" in any argument challenging Israel's legality or integrity implies that a controversial matter is still in dispute, and any resolution must wait until the day (which may never come) when the two "sides" are reconciled in an "objective" conclusion.

Chapter 4: "The Pictures in Our Heads" and the Manufacture of Denial draws on the work of Pulitzer Prize-winning journalist Walter Lippmann, who wrote of the ways propagandists can exploit "stock images" of realities beyond people's immediate experience to instill particular convictions. This chapter looks at Israeli control of pro-Palestinian media, including refusing journalists' access to sites of carnage and destruction, the direct targeting of media workers and facilities, repressive social media measures engaged in by the Israeli government, and the uses of technology platforms such as Google and Venmo in suppressing Palestinians' freedoms. Also explored is how semantic acrobatics and speech acts—such as "designating" a person or an organization as "terrorist"—can invest claims with effective credibility and foreclose on the possibility of negotiating with or allowing those so designated the protection of international law.

Chapter 5: Jewish Nationalism and the Manufacture of Consent draws on the work of Edward Bernays, Walter Lippmann, Noam Chomsky, and Edward Herman on the engineering of public opinion to examine the task of consolidating a sense of "peoplehood" or "nationhood" among the world's disparate Jews. Romantic nationalism, the "negation of the diaspora," the settler's claim of indigeneity, and the instrumental use of the Bible are some of the paradigms that were invoked to bring this about. Concepts of the "Jewish nation" by key Zionist theorists such as Moses Hess and Leo Pinsker are discussed, leading up to an analysis of the thought and galvanizing activities of Theodor Herzl. Ideas about "the crowd," "the public," "the herd," and "the leader" from Gustave Le Bon, Gabriel Tarde, Wilfred Trotter, and Sigmund Freud underpin this part of the discussion to explain how Jewish nationalism was aroused and the ways that Herzl's performances as the "leader" were germane to this process. Also examined is the apocryphal nature of Herzl's famous and pivotal claim that it was the Dreyfus Affair that made him embrace Zionism.

Chapter 6: "We Bought It": Ersatz Narratives and the Manufacture of Ownership looks at land sales in Palestine from absentee landlords to Russian Jewish immigrants during and after the Ottoman period and how these transactions have been framed, according to conventional colonial logic, as a "fair deal." The politics of definition and categorization are analyzed for their ability to alter perceptions of reality, including, for example, the claim that Palestine was a desolate wasteland awaiting Jewish reclamation. The "land without a people for a people without a land" slogan has been frequently invoked (beginning with nineteenth-century Christian Zionists) and thoroughly debunked. My interest here is not in the fact that it wasn't true (which it quite evidently wasn't) but rather what methods were used to make it *seem* true. One focus here is the use (or deliberate misuse) that Zionists have made of Mark Twain's satirical novel *The Innocents Abroad* to prove the "barren land" point. Also in this chapter, the public claims made by Zionist leaders that their program would be to the enormous benefit of the Arabs of Palestine are juxtaposed against their secretive plans to expel the indigenous population in order to create a Jewish demographic majority. This chapter considers how these contradictory plans were managed—and how the contradiction was not, ultimately, impervious to deconstruction by Palestinian Arabs witnessing facts on the ground.

Chapter 7: The Jewish National Fund and the Manufacture of Environmental Stewardship traces the history and work of the JNF from the beginning of the twentieth century to the present. The organization has long relied on what is now known as "greenwashing." That is, it has used the notions of the "redemption of the land" and, more currently, "environmental sustainability" to disguise the erasure of Palestinians and the physical artifacts of their culture. For example, the JNF's much-vaunted work on "draining the swamps" to create agricultural land has turned out to be, rather, "destroying the wetlands." This chapter also looks at JNF's fundraising activities as cover for its propaganda—most notably through the "Blue Box" used to collect coins from children. The JNF's twentieth-first century programs, such as Blueprint Negev, Go North, and Israel 2040 are assessed for the ways they attempt to "Judaize" the Negev and Galilee by bolstering these regions' development as technology and hospitality hubs. Middle-class Jews are drawn to relocate there in gated, segregated communities with plentiful amenities that in reality replace intentionally destroyed Arab communities. At the same time, the fact that only Jewish families are allowed entrance via admissions committees is skillfully camouflaged.

Chapter 8: The "Causal Nexus": The Holocaust and Israel considers two of the key, related ways in which Zionists have instrumentalized the Holocaust: by using it as a vehicle for shoring up the Zionist project, and by positing the tragedy and abjection of the Holocaust and its victims as the supreme counter-point to the safety and security of a Jewish state. There is an extended section on *Exodus* that I call "a propaganda spectacle in three acts"—that is, first, the real ship and its drama, then the novel, and then the movie. Also discussed is the rivalry between Zionist political parties and how issues such as the German reparations debate and the threat of a "second Holocaust" created advantages for some. The "lessons" of the Holocaust are appraised, including the ways they are embedded in Holocaust memorials and the annual March of the Living odyssey established by the Israeli Ministry of Education.

Chapter 9: Great Explanations: The Arts and Craftiness of *Hasbara* reviews the concept and history of this well-known Israeli phenomenon, which has alternately been described as public diplomacy, propaganda, "explaining," or persuading others of the righteousness of Israel's actions. Public diplomacy techniques of marshalling "soft power" and "nation branding" are described, as is the trajectory of the Zionist movement's *hasbara* apparatus from the pre-state period in the early twentieth century onward. The *hasbara* departments of various Israeli government ministries and agencies, as well as the "network approach" that connects them to NGOs, nonprofits, and campus groups in the US, are explored. This network is particularly vigorous in response to what Israel perceives as its "delegitimization" by the Boycott, Divestment, and Sanctions (BDS) movement. The chapter also portrays special *hasbara* initiatives such as *Masbirim Israel,* Taglit Birthright Israel, Canary Mission, and Concert, as well as influence campaigns such as the "Wikipedia wars." Lastly, it describes the many complaints Israelis continually voice about *hasbara*, insisting that its deficiencies, rather than Israel's policies and actions, render Israel such a sustained object of criticism in the global sphere.

Epilogue: "What They Said They Said about October 7, 2023." Due to the timing of writing this book—the very last parts overlapped with the events of October 7, 2023, and the subsequent wars on Gaza and Lebanon—those phenomena are not a substantial part of my discussion. However, an epilogue briefly addresses propaganda in the post-October 7 world.

CHAPTER 2:
FOUNDATIONS

"[I]f a patent forgery like the 'Protocols of the Elders of Zion' is believed by so many people that it can become the text of a whole political movement, the task of the historian is no longer to discover a forgery. Certainly it is not to invent explanations which dismiss the chief political and historical fact of the matter: that the forgery is being believed. This fact is more important than the (historically speaking, secondary) circumstance that it is a forgery."
—Hannah Arendt[52]

WHAT IS PROPAGANDA AND WHAT IS ITS RELATIONSHIP TO RHETORIC, PERSUASION, AND EDUCATION?

For ancient philosophers, rhetoric was the art of persuasion. For Aristotle, who wrote the classic how-to manual on the subject, rhetoric was useful to help "things that are true and things that are just" to emerge—so that "we may see clearly what the facts are and, if another man argues unfairly, we on our part may be able to confute him."[53] It involved a "moral purpose," the use of "systematic principles," and "three elements": speaker, subject, and the person addressed. But though Aristotle implied that when the art of rhetoric was used skillfully, truth would inevitably triumph over falsity, he effectively produced an extraordinary guide to how to manipulate others with stealth and cunning.

The art of rhetoric evolved over many centuries as social, political, religious, economic, legal, military, commercial, and technological conditions gave it new shape in different epochs. In particular, the arrival of the printing press in the fifteenth century brought about fundamental changes in how rhetoric was practiced, as the spread of literacy, the growth of reading publics, and an explosion of reading materials such as newspapers and mass-circulation periodicals vastly altered the rhetorical situation. In other words, through print, speaker and audience no longer met face-to-face; what at one time would have been a "crowd" listening to and watching an orator in a public space became a "public" that *read* what the speaker had to say, each member of it digesting the message alone in the privacy of his or her own home. The dawn of radio, telegraph, telephone, cinema—and then later television, and later still, the Internet—further radically complicated the rhetorical situation. By the twentieth century, "the art of persuasion" was infinitely more complex than it had been in fourth century BCE Athens; and this is why, though propaganda had existed in various forms as long as rhetoric had, it now took an entirely new form. It now capitalized on the availability of mass communications and the existence of a mass—yet atomized—public. It also drew on a new body of turn-of-the-century sociological research focusing on managing the behavior of crowds and the harnessing of the "herd instinct." Propaganda was able to manipulate people's thoughts and behavior in whole new ways.

By this point, too, the scholarly understanding of "rhetoric" had enlarged from the limits of the speaker-subject-listener persuasive act to encompass what some have called "the making of meaning." The relationship of humans and language to symbols, the role of motives and identification, and the relationship of discourse to knowledge, power, and ideology became considerations for evaluating the way "meaning" was made. And yet, it has been argued, the issue of persuasion still dominates, even in situations where it appears or purports not to.

Theorists of propaganda have long sought to explain the difference between *propaganda* and *education*—with little success, as education is an essential element of socialization, inducting people into the belief system of their partic-ular society. Education and propaganda both find their venues in a wide swath of sites and institutions both inside and outside the walls of formal schooling.

The French theorist of propaganda, Jacques Ellul, called these modes of enculturation, which are so all-encompassing as to be generally imperceptible, the "propaganda of integration."[54] When most people speak of propaganda, they refer to what he calls "propaganda of agitation"—which would include, for example, the Pope's exhortation to die in a Crusade in the service of Christ, the Nazi spectacle captured in the film *Triumph of the Will*, or George W. Bush's "You're either with us or with the terrorists"—all designed to arouse passions that lead to immediate action. The propaganda of integration, conversely, is so quiet and pervasive it goes unnoticed. It instills an enthusiasm for conformity in individuals through the repetition of customs, rituals, and habits; it stabilizes society by planting ideologies so subtly and permanently in our souls that it effects a "persuasion from within." In the United States, for example, television commercials, "history" explained at national parks and monuments, God on our coins, and the singing of "The Star-Spangled Banner" at sporting events all scramble symbols of faith, consumerism, liberty, community, wholesome fun, and patriotism into one familiar, indivisible mix. What some would call propaganda, or even indoctrination, others would simply call the everyday realities of our lives.

Another theorist of propaganda, Leonard W. Doob, whose influential *Public Opinion and Propaganda* was published in 1948, defined education as *"the imparting of knowledge or skill considered to be scientific or to have survival value in a society at a particular time."* (Italics in original.)[55] Yet he points out that this definition is inherently relativistic, because the concept of "science" is itself relativistic, being simply "knowledge which competent men in a society agree is correct and which is therefore subject to verification."[56] The "'right' kind of education," he says,

> consists of…subscribing to points of view which are considered "good," "just," "beautiful," or "necessary" in the society…. The educator has prestige in our society because it is presumed that he teaches what people want and need to be taught, in order to be socialized according to our standards…. Pick your science or the values you consider important in your society, and then you can decide what education is.[57]

Propaganda is different from education, Doob maintains, insofar as it constitutes

> *the attempt to affect the personalities and to control the behavior of individuals toward ends considered unscientific or of doubtful value in a society at a particular time.…* The dissemination of a viewpoint considered by a group to be "bad," "unjust," "ugly," or "unnecessary" is propaganda in terms of that group's standards. (Italics in original.)[58]

But as we can see, according to Doob's schema, "education" is simply what Ellul calls the "propaganda of integration." This is why it is so easy to point to another society's educational system as "indoctrinating" with "propaganda," while our own educational system seems to reflect reality and common sense. Doob does distinguish, though, between "intentional" and "unintentional" propaganda, and emphasizes that what one usually thinks of as "propaganda" is the intentional sort. Others—one thinks of the bulk of teachers, journalists, clergymen, lawyers—are just ordinary conformists and believers who do not think especially critically about the foundations of their own societal values; they are "seeking to maintain the status quo, and hence [their] efforts are considered praise-worthy and educational."[59]

Philip M. Taylor, too, stresses the definitional importance of "conscious, methodological and planned" *intent*, the "*deliberate* attempt to persuade people to think and behave *in a desired way*...." (Italics in original.)[60] He also comes up with a simple distinction that may serve well in many practical circumstances, though it, too, may crumble upon close scrutiny: perhaps, he says, "propaganda *tells* people *what* to think whereas education *teaches* people *how* to think." (Italics in original.)[61] However, we must remember that different cultures and groups authenticate different *sorts* of thinking, which is why we may end up in the same conundrum as before.

Just as some have struggled to differentiate *propaganda* from *education*, many have sought to distinguish between *propaganda* and *persuasion* or between *propaganda* and *rhetoric,* or even *propaganda* and *information*—again, with great difficulty. As Beth S. Bennett and Sean Patrick O'Rourke have pointed out, Jacques Ellul's exhaustive study of propaganda simply fails to factor the rhetorical tradition into the discussion at all.[62] They further acknowledge that "distinctions between [rhetoric and propaganda] most often are drawn in shades and degrees."[63] Many who attempt to make the distinction inevitably get tangled up in terms that are themselves subjective; for instance, Garth S. Jowett and Victoria O'Donnell define propaganda as "the deliberate and systematic attempt to shape perceptions, manipulate cognitions, and direct behavior to achieve a response that *furthers the desired intent of the propagandist*." (Italics added.)[64]

The problem, though, is that one agent's "manipulation" and "desired intent" is another agent's "reporting" and "truth." Helpfully, Jowett and O'Donnell focus on questioning *the purpose of the process*: it has "an objective that has been established a priori."[65] The speaker's *motive* is to induce the listener to *act* in a particular way as a result of receiving the message. Most theorists of propaganda would add that that *the desired action is one that is for the benefit of the speaker, rather than the listener.* At the same time, most public service announcements—from telling you to wear seatbelts to promoting vaccinations—can be, and often are, seen as "manipulation" and not necessarily representing the best interests of the recipient. Further, Jowett and O'Donnell say, "propaganda…seeks to contain information in a specific area, and…[t]he recipient of the propaganda message is discouraged from asking about anything outside the contained area."[66] They say, too, that propaganda is almost always a form of "activated ideology." But then, one would have to ask, what "education" isn't? What American schools in the Cold War years assigned their students Marx and Lenin for homework so that they could understand in a truly "informed" way what was so purportedly odious about Communism? How many proponents of the monotheistic religions seriously scrutinize the merits of belief in "God" against that of "false idols" to objectively determine which should command the fealty of civilized, enlightened peoples and which their scorn? The exact shape of *propaganda* may be as woolly as the exact shape of *truth* itself.

A BRIEF HISTORY OF WESTERN PROPAGANDA THROUGH WORLD WAR I

The word, if not the practice of, "propaganda" was born in 1622, when Pope Gregory XV established the Sacra Congregegatio de Propaganda Fide (Congregation for the Propagation of the Faith) to counter the Protestant Reformation in Europe and the New World. This work was continued by Pope Urban VIII and others[67] and may explain why the word "propaganda" is used in a neutral, nonpejorative sense to mean "advertising" in predominantly Catholic Latin America today, while it arouses ire in predominantly Protestant countries.

Philip M. Taylor, Randal Marlin, Garth S. Jowett, Victoria O'Donnell, and others trace propaganda—particularly, though not exclusively, war propaganda—back long before it was theorized, to the ancient world, where epic poems and hymns praised rulers in war; palaces, statues, or murals bore homage to the "power and prestige" of the king; war themes were depicted on pottery; and grand public architecture celebrated pharaohs and dynasties.[68]

Jowett and O'Donnell declare Julius Caesar "a master propagandist, equaled only by Napoleon and Hitler in his understanding of meaningful symbols and in his ability to understand instinctively the psychological needs of his audience." This, they say, "induced obedience to the new regime through co-operation and identification rather than subjugation."[69] The portrait of Julius Caesar, while he was still alive, on a Roman coin "reminded the troops of where their interests lay," and other coins "spread...visual images of Rome's triumphs all over the empire."[70]

Later, "Christ and his followers took what were basically traditional messages and put them in a new form"—including the use of parables, human metaphors, and "the choice of twelve disciples...who would carry the message to other groups, who in turn would spread the word through personal contact in a system resembling today's pyramidal marketing schemes."[71] Marlin points out that when Christianity came to the Roman Empire, "The coronation of king or emperor by the Church reinforced the idea of political authority as coming from God."[72] Jowett and O'Donnell remark that "considering that Christ and his followers did not have control over the existing communications media at the time, the ultimate level of adoption of Christianity must be considered one of the great propaganda campaigns of all time."[73] In the Middle Ages, the cross became a recognizable symbol; murals and tapestries proclaimed Christian themes; mass was held before battles, and the chivalric code and songs romanticized fighting; while the pope invoked what we now call "atrocity propaganda" (which came into full flower during World War I) and the idea of holy war to galvanize knights who didn't have a clue what Islam was.[74]

After the growth of European universities in the thirteenth and fourteenth centuries, the invention of the printing press in the mid-fifteenth century (though earlier in China), and the wide availability of cheap paper (rather than parchment), textual persuasion and visual imagery—including the publication of maps—reached vast new audiences.[75] The Renaissance saw the use of military musicians in warfare, as well as uniforms, pageants, and pep talks to rev up the troops.[76] The Reformation exploited the new technology, and as a result, Luther's works were widely read and the pope discovered censorship.[77] The development of copper plate in the seventeenth century engendered the mass distribution of posters and weekly newssheets; the wealthy and powerful were able to hire painters to act as "professional publicists" via their portraits, yet the increasingly literate masses were also becoming empowered to fight back through pamphlets, leaflets, and other shapers of public opinion.[78]

Jacques Ellul asserts that propaganda in its modern form required an ideological setting in which to bloom and found its moment in the post-French Revolution nineteenth century—"a great breeding ground of ideology." "[T]he fundamental ideologies [of our society] are Nationalism, Democracy, and Socialism," he writes, with "democracy" being the core ideology that serves as "a peg, a pretext" supporting the growth of propaganda in such disparate projects as the French Revolution, the US capitalist excesses of the 1920s, and the Soviet Union of the 1940s.[79] During this period, symbols of ideologies proliferated—for instance, the Bastille on the one hand and its storming on the other—while later emerging technologies of photography, electricity, railways, telegraph, cinema, and radio were in turn exploited in the selling of information to massive publics.[80] The nineteenth century also saw the proliferation of national anthems, political cartoons, and propagandist novels such as *Uncle Tom's Cabin* and Charles Dickens's depictions of Victorian social misery.[81] Napoleon, one of history's great propaganda operatives, directed that various texts be added to the school curriculum: Caesar's *Commentaries*, army bulletins, his own official publication, the *Moniteur*, adapted catechisms ("What are the duties of Christians with respect to the princes who govern them, and what are in particular our duties to Napoleon I our Emperor?"). He realized that control of the curriculum, combined with censorship of the press and the arts, could put "a whole nation...successfully...into a kind of intoxication."[82]

BRITISH AND AMERICAN PROPAGANDA INNOVATIONS IN WORLD WAR I

A great leap forward in the use of wartime propaganda appeared via Britain's World War I global communications machinery. The apparatus they pioneered was remarkable in its scale, its level of coordination, its cast of actors, and its effects on allies, enemies, neutral countries, the British citizenry itself, and world leaders such as Woodrow Wilson, Vladimir Lenin, and, later, Adolf Hitler. Unlike other Allied nations, Britain had to motivate its men to enlist in the absence of conscription. The War Propaganda Bureau—known as Wellington House for its site—was inspired by Lloyd George, directed by

C.F.G. Masterman, and operated beginning August 1914 under the auspices of the British Foreign Office. The impetus for its creation was a blitz of German propaganda maligning the Allies, with the intent to influence other countries— especially the United States.

Wellington House ultimately spawned a web of government organizations dealing with propaganda during the war. The manufacturers of commercial products supplemented the government's efforts, devising patriotic tie-ins for their advertisements. For instance, the homesick soldier could combat "depression and longing" by utilizing his "Swan Fountpen," an act that would "bring comfort to you and joy to your mother, wife or sweetheart."[83]

During the First World War, Britain also introduced the widespread propagation of atrocity stories and the use of psychological warfare. Atrocity stories had, of course, been used for a long time—for example, the medieval "blood libel" tales about Jews drinking the blood of Christian children they had killed as a Passover ritual, wartime accusations of the enemy "infecting wells, cattle, and food, not to speak of wounds,"[84] and Benjamin Franklin's employment of fictive "authors" to disseminate fabricated "scalping" stories (savage acts allegedly committed by Native Americans against colonist victims, for the consumption of the British public during the Revolutionary War).[85]

But by the early twentieth century, the spread of mass literacy enabled atrocity propaganda to be deployed on a scale previously unimaginable. By the late twentieth and early twenty-first century, it would be constructed by public relations professionals and performatively promoted. Consider the phenomena of congressional testimony about Kuwaiti babies thrown from incubators by Iraqi soldiers in 1990; "videotaped" footage of asylum seekers off the Australian coast throwing their babies overboard as a ruse to gain entry in 2001; and sensational media saturation of alleged terrorist plots, such as that which boosted the sales of duct tape to protect against the "unthinkable" in the post-9/11 US.

"The aim of British propaganda was to persuade its various audiences that the cause of war against Germany was just, that the Allies were going to win, and that civilization depended on their winning. A key element of this propaganda was a constant harping on the theme of German barbarity," writes Marlin. The "various audiences" included allied, neutral, and enemy populations as well as the troops on the ground and the British home front.

One popular vehicle for mobilizing the emotions of these constituencies was the production of reports that depicted the Germans as brutal, bloodthirsty savages. Among the best-known are the narratives of the sinking of the Lusitania and the murder of nurse Edith Cavell. In the former case, the British-owned, Cunard-operated passenger ship's captain dismissed a clear warning from the Imperial German Embassy, published in American newspapers, that British and Allied ships sailing in a war zone were "liable to destruction."[86] The British government, for its part, lied about the presence of 173 tons of war munitions on board along with the 2,000 people, more than half of whom died. Yet this double dose of negligence was overlooked and depraved German butchery received the full load of condemnation instead. The next day, the *New York Times* culled reactions from various newspapers under the banner, "PRESS CALLS SINKING OF LUSITANIA MURDER: Editorials in New York Newspapers Agree Torpedoing Was Crime Against Civilization."[87]

Five months later, another inflammatory atrocity story broke in the British press: the execution of British nurse Edith Cavell by a German firing squad in occupied Brussels. In addition to nursing the wounded on both sides, her crime had been to help many Allied soldiers escape to neutral Holland. She was commemorated with a statue near Trafalgar Square in London, and Arthur Conan Doyle (who was secretly assisting Wellington House) wrote, "Everybody must feel disgusted at the barbarous actions of the German soldiery in murdering this great and glorious specimen of womanhood."[88] Cavell's martyrdom at the hands of German "barbarians" spiked enlistment in the British army[89] and was used to further rouse American indignation to the point where neutrality would be abandoned.

Nurse Cavell's story was, in fact, a highly publicized case among a litany of "Belgium atrocities" stories that circulated, in Ellul's terminology, as "agitation propaganda." Though Germany was certainly not kind to the people of occupied Belgium, much of its putatively satanic agenda had little basis in fact. In the spring of 1915, the Report of the Committee on Alleged German Outrages was published and became popularly known as the Bryce Report for its chief author. The alleged acts of German soldiers implicated in the report included "decapitating babies, cutting off women's breasts (BR 25-26), publicly raping women in the marketplace (BR 48), bayoneting children and hoisting them in the air (BR 52), cutting off children's hands and ears while forcing parents to watch (BR 47), and nailing a child to a farmhouse door (BR 28)."[90] Nobody appreciated the value of World War I British propaganda more than Adolf Hitler, who in *Mein Kampf* expressed his regret that Germany's propaganda had been so inferior.[91]

One week after the United States finally entered the war on April 6, 1917, President Woodrow Wilson created the Committee on Public Information (CPI), known as the Creel Committee for its leader, George Creel. This propaganda agency was needed to counter widespread wariness about America's involvement in a conflict far away, as well as to stimulate "loyalty" among immigrant groups—Germans, Italians, even the Irish, due to their loathing of the British—whose allegiance was suspect.[92] In addition, pacifists, organized labor, socialists, anarchists, and other radical groups opposed American engagement on the grounds that it simply served the interests of business and political elites; the workers whose lives had been the material of industrial exploitation would now be used, just as cavalierly, for cannon fodder. W.E.B. Du Bois had proposed in 1915 that the war in Europe was really about imperialism, with Africa and others as the spoils.[93] Wilson, who had won reelection in 1916 promising to sustain his policy of neutrality, surprised many by his reversal in the name of "making the world safe for democracy" and embarking upon "a war to end all wars." Some suspected his real motive to be making foreign markets safe for the flow of American goods. J.P. Morgan & Company was already profiting from loans to the Allies and was invested in their victory.[94]

Less than two months after entering the war, Congress passed the Espionage Act, which was broadly used to hunt, raid, convict, imprison, torture—and in some circumstances, deport—those who would "willfully obstruct the recruiting or enlistment service of the US."[95] To ensure mass cooperation with the war effort, repression needed to be supplemented by a seduction of the hearts and minds of the American populace. Thus, the Creel Committee was formed "to sell the war to America."[96]

Swift on the heels of Britain, the United States professionalized and systematized the production of war-bolstering propaganda. As Creel aptly, if immodestly, put it in his post-war reflections, *How We Advertised America*:

> It was in [the] recognition of Public Opinion as a major force that the
> Great War differed most essentially from all previous conflicts.... In all

things, from first to last, without halt or change, it was a plain publicity proposition, a vast enterprise in salesmanship, the world's greatest adventure in advertising.... There was no part of the great war machinery that we did not touch, no medium of appeal that we did not employ....[97]

Under the aegis of the CPI, pamphlets were written by "the country's foremost publicists, scholars, and historians" that "blew as a great wind against the clouds of confusion and misrepresentation."[98] A division devoted to the spoken word "coordinated the entire speaking activities of a nation."[99] A bureau known as the Four Minute Men "commanded the volunteer services of 75,000 speakers, operating in 5,200 communities, and making a total of 755,190 speeches, every one having the carry of shrapnel";[100] these speakers popped up in carefully planned but seemingly impromptu fashion between the reels in movie theaters, delivering pep talks on patriotism for the home front. War exhibits were featured at state fairs and expositions. In the Division of Pictorial Publicity, "the great artists of America" "rallied to the colors" by producing posters, cartoons, banners, billboards, and other visuals.[101] A Division of News controlled the flow of information.[102] Global wireless services transmitted President Wilson's stirring speeches in order to counter foreign perceptions of America as "as a race of dollar-mad materialists, a land of cruel monopolists."[103] A Division of Women's War Work flooded the women's pages with suggestions about how women could help.[104] A Division of Films, partly inspired by *Birth of a Nation*'s demonstrated propaganda effects,[105] collaborated with Hollywood to capitalize upon this powerful nascent medium. By the Second World War, all key leaders—Churchill, Roosevelt, Stalin, Mussolini, and Hitler—were enthusiasts of cinema as a tool of propaganda, and accordingly established government agencies to produce these materials.[106]

Returning to our earlier discussion of the problem of defining propaganda, we can recall that (1) the purpose of propaganda is to get the receiver of a message to act in such a way as the generator of the message wants them to act, and (2) it is difficult to distinguish this process from what we call "education" or "persuasion." Clearly, as we have seen, Zionists did not invent propaganda, nor did they use it in altogether unique ways. Some early Zionists did, indeed, make use of propaganda techniques that were suitable to their purposes at the time.

For instance, in an 1895 letter, Theodor Herzl, widely considered the "founding father" of political Zionism, wrote to the exceedingly wealthy Baron Maurice von Hirsch, whose patronage he hoped to secure: "I have already drawn up...the entire plan." He enumerates some of his logistical requirements, followed by:

> And before all that, a tremendous propaganda...pictures, songs...a flag.... With a flag you lead men...for a flag, men live and die. In fact it is the only thing for which they are ready to die in masses, if you train them for it...Believe me, the politics of an entire people—especially a people scattered all over the earth—can be manipulated only through imponderables that float in thin air.[107]

The word "propaganda" was certainly used more loosely then. Still, coincidentally or not, Herzl's appeal was written within a year of sociologist Gustave Le Bon's *The Crowd,* which influenced later public relations professionals such as Edward Bernays and provided a theoretical basis for arousing their own preferred brand of irrational behavior in the masses.

In 1919 the prolific Jewish writer and journalist Nahum Sokolow, who had successfully engaged the sympathies and support of Christian Zionists in England through appeals to Old Testament beliefs—a stratagem that reached its apotheosis in the Balfour Declaration of 1917—wrote his monumental *History of Zionism, 1600–1918.* In it, he launched a much broader appeal to the Christians of England, arguing that the Bible was as intrinsically English as it was Jewish and thus furnished common moral ground. "History shows that the Zionist idea and the continual renewal of efforts in this direction have been a tradition with the English people for centuries," he wrote. "Zionists, therefore, hope that English Christians will be worthy heirs and successors to the Earl of Shaftesbury, George Eliot, and many others...."[108] Utilizing Aristotle's notion of *ethos,* or manifesting himself as a character who will be credible and trustworthy to his audience, he made an elaborate case illustrating that they had long shared common cause:

> When King James I (1566–1625) in 1604 sanctioned a new translation of the Bible, he let loose moral and spiritual forces which transformed

English life and thought.... Cromwell's life was shaped by the influence of the Bible.... Cromwell's examples were Joshua (2406–2516 a.m.), Gideon (fl. 2676 a.m.) and Samuel (ob. 2882 a.m.). Hebrew warriors and prophets were his ideals.[109]

On the one hand, then, Zionists adapted some of their persuasive techniques from established precedents; yet in order to understand Zionists' specific use of propaganda we need to consider the various actors whose compliance was required in order to activate their vision. How could what was initially a small group of Eastern European Jewish thinkers and activists convince the Jews of the world to agree that they were all one "people" undergoing one shared threat with one shared path to salvation—as well as a shared imperative to seek it? How could they convince the rest of the world to include them respectfully in the family of nations? And how could they convince all involved—including themselves—that their project of liberation was a benign and noble one to which they were entitled, producing no casualties or collateral damage?

WHAT IS ZIONISM AND WHY HAS IT NEEDED PROPAGANDA?

Like virtually every ideology that undergirds a movement, Zionism has not historically expressed itself as one unified vision. It began as an idea in response to particular circumstances and morphed into an array of alloyed, competing ideas. It is often described in public discourse as a response to millennia of Jewish oppression culminating in the Holocaust, a need for a "safe place" for Jews the world over in their "historic homeland." There have indeed been many Zionists who have espoused elements of this picture, but it is important to understand:

- Zionism was conceived in the nineteenth century, decades before the rise of Nazism.
- The notion of "eternal antisemitism"—that the persecution of Jews has been a consistent phenomenon from the late Roman Empire to the present—has been called fallacious by some scholars.
- Zionism sought to rescue Jews not only or even primarily from antisemitism, but from assimilation after Western and Central European Jews came to enjoy new civic freedoms in the wake of Napoleon's conquests.
- Zionism was largely the localized brainchild of Central and Eastern

European Jews and did not draw on the perspectives or lived experiences of Jews internationally.

- Many Jews rejected and opposed political Zionism, even in Eastern Europe.

- In Zionism's initial years, Palestine was only one imagined site of refuge: Uganda, Argentina, Cyprus, South Africa, the USSR—even Arkansas and Oregon[110] were considered, as well.

- The notion of Palestine as a "historic homeland" for a "Jewish people" that currently exists depends upon belief in the biblical narrative as a historical record as well as a belief in a genetic, religious, or cultural cohesiveness among contemporary "Jews" that in fact has been invalidated on many fronts.

- There were others already living in Palestine for whom it was also a "historic homeland." Zionism followed the template of settler colonialism, already established in North America, Australia, and New Zealand (and attempted, though ultimately repelled, in South Africa and Algeria). This was a phenomenon in which Europeans who envisioned themselves as "civilized" and often as victims of their own societies of origin took possession of lands they called "empty"—or at least, in which only people they categorized as "savage" and "backward" resided. The intention in these instances was to create a new society from which the natives would be eliminated, rather than assimilated or exploited for labor.

- As with settler colonial undertakings elsewhere, there was resistance to Zionism as soon as the indigenous people of Palestine realized that overwhelming Jewish dominance and the transfer of Palestinians to other locales were integral to Zionist aims. Though the Zionists publicly maintained that the modernization and development they brought from the West would benefit all in the region, there were clues to the contrary too flagrant to be ignored. Palestinian resistance was expressed—and, in turn, repressed—politically, economically, culturally, and militarily. From early on, propaganda was an integral component of this repression.

THE ROOTS OF ZIONISM IN NINETEENTH-CENTURY EUROPEAN NATIONALISMS AND JEWISH EXPERIENCE

In Western Europe, the French Revolution emancipated the Jews in the sense that religious belief or affiliation became disentangled from the notion of citizenship. The new secularism was grounded in a binary notion that civic equality was the province of the public or political realm, while religion was a matter of the private. One could have both, as long as the boundaries were strictly honored. Equal citizenship was granted to Jews in France's National Assembly of 1791,[111] and by the late nineteenth century this view congealed in what became a constitutional principle of state secularism called *laïcité*.[112] The Jews, who had previously been seen as a tribal people and thus an obstacle to the Enlightenment ideal of universalism, now became, in the words of Maurice Samuels, the Enlightenment's "poster children"[113]—symbols of the transformative power of state-sanctioned reason, fairness, and equity.

Napoleon spread the new freedoms across the lands he conquered. As the ideas of the Enlightenment, embodied in the French Rights of Man and the US Constitution, spread to Holland, England, and later to Germany, Switzerland, Belgium, Italy, Scandinavia, and Austria-Hungary, many Jews in these countries chose to identify as equal and highly patriotic citizens of the civil state, their religion a separate, personal matter. It was the first time this had really been an option, and it involved, along with acquiring the privileges being part of the larger community provided, trading in their own laws, customs, and identity—a truly "radical break with the entire past of Jewry"[114]—which many were quite willing to do. They rejected as antisemitic any insinuation that the Jews constituted a "nation" amongst themselves;[115] they identified as wholly and simply French or German, loyal to the state. They became active parts of the bourgeoisie as they entered the universities, professions, and broader cultural milieus in vast new numbers. Intermarriage proliferated.

Meanwhile, spurred by the thought of the German-Jewish philosopher Moses Mendelssohn (1729–1786), the *haskala,* or "Jewish Enlightenment," emerged as a modernizing movement from within that pushed Jewish education beyond the bounds of traditional yeshiva scholarship into broader cultural and intellectual spheres. Viewing Judaism "more as an impressive fossil than a living faith,"[116] the *maskilim* (the term for the *haskala*'s practitioners) acted as a solvent upon many Jews' bonds with religious orthodoxy and thus ignited the wrath of the rabbinate.[117] Later, Reform Judaism in Germany, which did away with much that was traditional in the Jewish religion—and, many felt, took on features of Christianity—came into being, while some Jews actually went all the way and got baptized.[118]

In Eastern Europe, things were quite different. According to the Israeli historian Shlomo Sand:

> At the end of the nineteenth century, about 80 per cent of the world's Jews and their secular descendants, that is, more than seven million individuals, lived in the Russian empire, Austro-Hungarian Galicia, and Romania.... As distinct from other Jewish communities across the world, the Jewish population of Eastern Europe had preserved ways of life and culture that were completely different from their non-Jewish neighbors.[119]

The historian David Biale describes life there:

> The Pale of Settlement, created by the Russian state in several steps after the partitions of Poland, prevented most Jews from living in the main Russian cities, thus precluding the kind of rapid acculturation that occurred farther to the West when Jews moved in the first half of the nineteenth century to Berlin, Vienna, Prague, and Budapest.... Russian society lacked a strong, emerging middle class, so the Jews did not find a social base for assimilation as they did in Germany, Austria, Hungary, France, Italy, and England. The Russian state failed to emancipate the Jews.... [T]he Jews of the Russian Empire remained subjects, but not full citizens, until the 1917 Revolution.... Whereas in Western and Central Europe it became increasingly possible for Jews to identify themselves as, for example, "Germans of the Mosaic faith," such a purely religious identity was all but impossible for the Russian Jews: they were seen by others, and largely viewed themselves, as a distinct and separate national group within a multinational empire."[120]

The restrictions on Jews living in the Pale of Settlement included a ban on landownership; barriers to Jews' practice in professions such as medicine and law; Russian government control of Jewish educational, rabbinical, and self-governmental institutions; and quotas for Jewish students in secondary and higher educational institutions—all of which contributed to endemic poverty.[121] There was also, notoriously, in historian Benny Morris's words

> a brutal system of twenty-five-year military conscription, which occasionally entailed the virtual kidnapping of their children at the age of twelve, or even sometimes at eight or nine, and their attempted conversion to Christianity by the authorities in special preparatory military schools.... Indeed, an official Russian government commission in 1888 defined the Jews' condition as one of "repression and disenfranchisement, discrimination and persecution."[122]

After Russian Czar Alexander II was assassinated in 1881, a series of pogroms—massacres of Jewish communities involving killing, maiming, and the destruction of homes and businesses—exploded. The attackers operated under the protection of authorities and police and the approval of much of the populace[123]—a phenomenon that would find an echo in twenty-first-century attacks by Israeli settlers on Palestinian residents of the West Bank. Near the end of the nineteenth century, millions left for America and, to a lesser extent, other western (or westernized) countries.[124] When Theodor Herzl met with the British colonial secretary, Joseph Chamberlain, in 1902 to enlist his aid in creating a Jewish colony in what was then Ottoman-ruled Palestine, he had the man's ear in part because the British public was eager to stop the influx of poor Eastern European Jews to England and the cheap labor that that portended.[125]

While the violence unleashed against Jews in Russia, along with Judeophobia elsewhere in Eastern Europe, is often credited as the crucial catalyst toward early Zionist movement-building, there were also other significant factors at play. Most important among these were the ideal of romantic nationalism that took root in much of Eastern Europe and the fear among some Jews that assimilation (as was occurring in Western Europe) might spell doom for Jewish "peoplehood."

Romantic nationalism, as opposed to what is often called "civic nationalism" (derived from the ideals of the Enlightenment and the French and American revolutions), emphasized a sense of cohesion based not on the logic of legal citizenship but rather on *volkishness*—an ethnically based, "blood and soil," mystical connectedness deriving from unconscious memories of a common origin and a common history. It presumed an "organic" connection to others who shared one's language, customs, religion, folklore, traditions—that is, one's spirit or essence—and held that this feeling of union formed the natural basis for a modern state. Some of the key influencers on adherents of this notion were the German philosophers Johann Gottfried Herder (1744–1803) and Johann Gottlieb Fichte (1762–1814), as well as Giuseppe Mazzini (1805–1872), the Italian nationalist revolutionary leader whose *Risorgimento* movement envisaged unifying Italians in a utopian republic whose capital would be the "'third' Rome, successor to ancient and papal Rome."[126] The racial aspects of their theories and some of the contradictions inherent in their adoption have come in for much criticism; Fichte, for example, was a curious inspiration for Zionism, affirming that Jews could not be trusted as loyal citizens of the states they lived in. "How shall we defend ourselves against them?" he asked. "I see no alternative but to conquer their promised land for them and to dispatch them all there."[127]

This concept of competing eastern-western European manifestations of nationalism famously draws on the work of Hans Kohn (1891–1972), the Jewish, Prague-born political theorist who proposed and developed it over many years. Kohn was from a bilingual Czech-German family, lived for several years in Palestine, and spent the remainder of his life in the United States as an academic.[128] Kohn was, for a time, a Zionist, writing in his memoirs, "In my youth, in the atmosphere of Prague, with its pervasive mood of nationalist stirrings and historical romanticism, I myself succumbed to the fascination of such attitudes." He later repudiated Zionism after its repressive response to the Arab uprising of 1929 in Palestine, observing wryly, "Zionist nationalism went the way of most Central and Eastern European nationalism." [129]

Kohn described nationalism as "first and foremost a state of mind, an act of consciousness"[130] that manifested itself differently in different contexts:

> Where the third estate became powerful in the eighteenth century, as in Great Britain, in France, and in the United States, nationalism found its expression predominantly, but never exclusively, in political and economic changes. Where, on the other hand, the third estate was still weak and only in a budding stage in the eighteenth and at the beginning

of the nineteenth century, as in Germany, Italy, and among the Slavonic peoples, nationalism found its expression predominantly in the cultural field. It was there at the beginning not so much the nation-state as the *Volksgeist* and its manifestations in literature and folk-lore, in the mother tongue and in history, which became the center of the attention of nationalism.[131]

Further theorists of nationalism both built on this division and questioned the tidiness of what came to be known as the "Kohn dichotomy," or "the ethnic-civic dichotomy."[132] Among the most salient criticisms were that his rigid taxonomies overlooked the political heterogeneity of particular cultures and regions;[133] that his idealization of Western democracies ignored their less "rational" facets such as slavery and subsequent forms of racial repression, immigration restrictions, and the genocide of Native Americans;[134] and that "shoe-horning people into ethnic boxes distorts and oversimplifies people's real sense of affiliation," which is often multiple.[135] (Today that last objection might be articulated via the concept of "intersectionality.") Nonetheless, John Coakley persuasively argues that "while attempts to equate it crudely with two geopolitical zones in Europe are misguided, the dichotomy itself is not without value in drawing attention to ideal types of collective identity that may in turn shed light on patterns of nationalism in particular states."[136] The distinction between these two "ideal types" remains highly relevant in the twenty-first century, where Israel's oft-aired claims to be "the only democracy in the Middle East" and to be "the state of the Jewish people" (worldwide) rather than of its citizens (20 percent of whom are not Jewish) are highlighted as an inherent contradiction by Palestinian and "post-Zionist" thinkers (and a good many others).

The dominant strand of Zionism until 1977 affirmed a strong attachment to socialist ideals; at the same time, seldom were heard declarations of fealty to "liberty, equality, fraternity." In the 1930s, when Palestine was administered by the British under a mandate from the League of Nations, proposals for self-governing legislative bodies were refused by the Zionists on demographic grounds: Jews were clearly the minority and until immigration rendered them a majority, democratic representative government would only work against them.[137] The Jewish Telegraphic Agency announced in its "Latest Cable Dispatches" of December 23, 1935 that the proposal by British High Commissioner Sir

Arthur Grenfell Wauchope for "the establishment of a legislative council for Palestine.... has stirred all Palestine to the depths. Jewish leaders of all groups throughout the world have long waged an energetic battle against the proposed semi-democratic assembly, charging that Palestine Jewry will be fixed permanently as a minority under such a legislative set-up."[138] In 1922, then-Colonial Secretary Winston Churchill had also rejected the idea of majority rule in Palestine, claiming that it would violate the Balfour Declaration's "pledge made by the British Government to the Jewish people."[139]

Arthur Balfour himself concurred: "Zionism, be it right or wrong, good or bad, is rooted in age-long tradition, in present needs, in future hopes, of far profounder import than the desires and prejudices of the 700,000 Arabs who now inhabit that ancient land."[140] As the legal scholar Victor Kattan has pointed out, this was not surprising; Britain "had an established tradition of supporting minority rule in its colonies," from Ireland to Southern Rhodesia and South Africa. In 1953, five years after the commencement of Israeli statehood, a top adviser on Arab affairs to Prime Minister David Ben-Gurion opposed allowing Arab communities to democratically elect their own local councils; the stated grounds were that such elections would "only augment family feuds" and the councils themselves were "bound to lead to bloodshed. In the Arab community, one must choose a 'middle road' of not-too-much democracy."[141]

Even in the twenty-first century, the fallacy of the "Jewish democratic state" (insofar as "democratic" carries the *civic* inference of equality among citizens and majority rule) is built into the frequently voiced Israeli worry about the "Arab demographic threat." The number of Palestinians under Israeli control compared to the number of Jewish Israelis would soon quash Jewish majority rule if all were enfranchised and granted full rights of citizenship. Thus, the idea of one multicultural, democratic, secular state with rights guaranteed to all its minorities is considered heresy, and those who propose it are often accused of promoting "the destruction of Israel." Israel's "Nation-State Law" of 2018 cemented that position further; among other highly contentious pronouncements, it proclaimed that "the exercise of the right to national self-determination in the State of Israel is unique to the Jewish People."[142]

The Israeli political scientist Zeev Sternhell has argued that the Zionist version of socialism was itself "a mobilizing myth, perhaps a convenient alibi"[143] and that a more apt descriptor would be *nationalist socialism* (the suffix being an important distinction from the *national socialism* of the Nazi variety). "The uniqueness of European nationalist socialism... in relation to all other types of socialism," in Sternhell's analysis,

> lay in one essential point: its acceptance of the principle of the nation's primacy and its subjection of the values of socialism to the service of the nation. In this way, socialism lost its universal significance and became an essential tool in the process of building the nation-state. Thus, the universal values of socialism were subordinated to the particularistic values of nationalism.[144]

Furthermore, he writes, "When nationalism is used for state-building, it is generally incompatible with liberal democratic values."[145] Emerging principally from Jews of the Russian empire, "'[o]rganic nationalism' is far more relevant to [Zionism's] history than the revolutionary socialist movement" or the ideals of civic nationalism.[146]

A PANOPLY OF LIBERATORY THESES

As Eastern European Jews strove to address their predicament, their theorizing pointed them in a variety of mutually incompatible directions. Some chose the path toward political Zionism, similar to other romantic national movements except for the problem that Jews did not already possess a common language and territory; this plotline culminated in the invention of modern Hebrew and the creation of the State of Israel. Some slightly dissident Zionist thinkers, known as the "Territorialists," felt that a suitable location for the project could be anywhere—Uganda, Argentina, Cyprus—though in the end, none of these would have the winning cachet of the "return" to the "historic homeland" of Palestine. Still others considered themselves "cultural" rather than "nationalist" or "political" Zionists, most notably the Ukrainian-born Jewish essayist Ahad Ha'am (1856–1927). These intellectuals felt that Palestine could provide a haven for oppressed diasporic Jews and serve as a world spiritual and cultural center for Judaism, but that the creation of a modern, geopolitical "nation" was a grave mistake—not least because the land was already inhabited. Working through the organization they founded in Palestine, Brit Shalom, they—among them the Viennese-born philosopher Martin Buber (1878–1965) and the American rabbi and first chancellor of the Hebrew University in Jerusalem Judah Magnes (1877–1948)—envisioned a binational state with parity of power between Jews and Arabs. (As history has shown, they lost the programmatic battle.)

Some conceptions of Jewish liberation found their realization in the secular revolutionary socialist Bund, a workers' party that fought antisemitism along with Zionism and class oppression. The Bundists were proud Yiddishists who believed that Judeophobia should be addressed within a broad context of social democratic change, where it actually appeared, rather than in isolated tribal separatism.

Some avenues of emancipatory thought would lead to a deepening commitment to Marxism and alliance with the Russian proletariat (as was the case with Leon Trotsky).

In a little-known alternate universe, the Jewish Autonomous Region of Birobidzhan was founded in the 1930s near the Soviet Union's border with China, and tens of thousands of Jews moved there—though it did not end well. "Why conjure up utopias of inaccessible places, restored languages, of Jews creating their own military? All the Jews really need, according to this thinking, is to be left alone, with their language and their culture in the confines of their own home," writes Masha Gessen of the plan's original logic in her captivating account of this experiment, *Where The Jews Aren't.*[147]

Another anomalous project, the Alliance Israélite Universelle, had been initiated in 1860, at least in theory as a philanthropic gesture of solidarity with Jews worldwide. In great measure it served as a *mission civilisatrice* extended by the Jews of France to Jews in North Africa and the Middle East, "uplifting" them with education in French language and culture along with Hebrew and Jewish history. Initially promoted as a Jewish vehicle of universalist French revolutionary values, it drew mixed reviews from both the Jewish press and observers of colonialism; it ultimately came to support Zionism.[148]

A true one-off was a rather kooky (and failed) plan hatched by the American Jew Mordecai Manual Noah (1785–1851), who between 1818 and 1825 sought to establish a "city of refuge" for Jews on tiny Grand Island near Niagara Falls, which he would call Ararat.[149]

The Orthodox clung to religion and tradition—which mandated waiting for a miracle in which the Messiah would reopen the gates of Zion—rather than acquiesce to a nation-based politics that represented a radical break with everything they believed in.

Meanwhile, huge numbers emigrated to North America, as well as Western European countries and other Western colonial outposts such as Australia and South Africa.

In short, even if the Zionists managed to build it in Palestine, a huge psychosocial apparatus would be needed to induce the multitudes to come.

CHAPTER 3:
"BALANCE" AND THE MANUFACTURE OF DOUBT

"Doubt is our product since it is the best means of competing with the 'body of fact' that exists in the minds of the general public."
—from a 1969 memo written by an executive at Brown & Williamson Tobacco Corp., which later became part of R.J. Reynolds.[150]

BALANCING ACTS

The aphorism encapsulated in the epigraph to this book has become widely known as Okrent's Law. Daniel Okrent was the first public editor of the *New York Times*, and his remark, "The pursuit of balance can create imbalance, because sometimes something is true," was made in reference to a 2004 editorial decision to use the word "genocide" in describing what happened to Armenians at the hands of Turkey in 1915. Previously, the *Times* house style had barred the word in that it suggested something conclusive about a putatively still-contested event; Turkey maintained that there had been atrocities committed on "both sides" and that the use of the word "genocide" thus betrayed anti-Turkish bias. Bill Keller, who had recently become the paper's executive editor, was persuaded to allow the use of the incendiary word. He explained, "I don't feel I'm particularly qualified to judge exactly what a precise functional definition of genocide is, but it seemed a no-brainer that killing a million people because they were Armenians fits the definition." [151]

Beyond ongoing attempts to declassify the Armenian genocide as such because Turkey continues to say it was not one, there have been massive debates about the status of "truth" more generally in a postmodern world. While some critics of postmodernism claim that that school of thought denies the existence of *any* sort of truth, nihilistically eviscerating all historical and cultural realities, it would be more accurate to consider the French philosopher Michel Foucault's notion that there are "regimes of truth" embedded in systems of power.[152] Social change, for him, involves blatantly denuding and then inspecting the structures that produce and sustain those "truths" in order to reveal how and why some forms of "truth" are privileged in what passes for common wisdom and others submerged. In some ways, Foucault's formulation is a more philosophically intricate incarnation of the adage that history is written by the victors, or the anthropologist Franz Boas's contention that social mores are relative to particular cultures, rather than being absolute and universal. Boas's work, carried forward by disciples including Margaret Mead, Ruth Benedict, and Zora Neale Hurston, emphasized that the most critical differences between peoples were not how they wove their baskets or made their canoes—taxonomies traditionally employed by museums to portray remote societies for Western minds—but rather how they formulated their notions of what was "truly" ethical, sacred, taboo, and desirable. Things could be "true," but understanding the meaning of that "truth" required an understanding of its context. [153]

Journalist and scholar Eric Alterman once compared the rigor with which academics and journalists explore the truth-claims of their sources:

> Academics…test their truths with relevant counterarguments and footnoted references that can be examined by those with opposing views.…[O]n the other hand,…. If no evidence is available for an argument a journalist wishes to include in a story, then up pop weasel words such as "it seems" or "some claim" to enable inclusion of the argument, no matter how shaky its foundation in reality. What's more, too many journalists believe that their job description does not require them to adjudicate between competing claims of truth.[154]

The imperative to provide "both sides" of an argument, the credibility of each notwithstanding, was codified in a formal regulation when the US Federal Communications Commission (FCC) created the Fairness Doctrine in 1949. Officially applying only to broadcasters, the term was taken up by print journalists as well; the "both sides" mantra continued to be held as axiomatic in "objective" reporting even after the regulation was officially abolished in the 1980s. Exploiting this beguiling yet specious notion of fairness enabled tobacco, pesticide, fossil fuel, pharmaceutical, and other industries to sustain the illusion of equally plausible credibility as they countered scientific evidence that their products were deleterious to the health of living beings and the planet.[155]

The doctrine of objectivity and the cognitive stalemate at which two "sides" must inevitably dead-end—because people are helpless (or don't have the time or inclination) to effectively assess competing claims—has been applied to ideological, social, and political realities, as well. Whether someone was really sexually harassed; whether a white police officer is really an innocent victim of his sincere belief that he was about to be murdered by a black man when he fired fatal shots at an unarmed individual; whether a "genocide" was really committed—in disputes such as these, where what "really happened" is preemptively deemed unfathomable within a "fair" and "objective" view, the presumption of truth may simply default to the claims of the powerful.

The cultural critic Ellen Willis satirized this problem in a "Glossary for the Eighties," written on the eve of that decade:

> DOGMA: a political belief one is unreasonably committed to, such as the notion that freedom is good and slavery is bad.

> BIAS: predilection for a particular dogma. For example, the feminist bias is that women are equal to men and the male chauvinist bias is that women are inferior. The unbiased view is that the truth lies somewhere in between.[156]

Similarly, in a 2015 radio interview with Terry Gross on NPR's *Fresh Air*, writer, activist, and feminist organizer Gloria Steinem remarked wryly that when she was younger and writing for mainstream media magazines, "the attitude was.... well, if we publish an article saying women are equal, then, in order to be objective, we'll have to publish one saying they're not...."[157]

This notion that "balance" must be applied to any fair argument has long been weaponized as a tactic to neutralize the spread of information about Palestinian rights and liberation. Consider:

- In 2006, the elite private school Fieldston in the Riverdale neighborhood of the Bronx was scheduled to host two Palestinian speakers. The school's principal said that they would be conveying a viewpoint that "few of us, students or faculty, are familiar with or can claim to understand." Yet after a number of parents objected, the event was canceled—as a school spokeswoman said, "because it really wasn't a balanced presentation." [158]

- After Israel's 2006 incursion into Lebanon, the then-public editor of the *New York Times*, Byron Calame, wrote a piece addressing readers' complaints about "imbalance" in the paper's photo coverage. Calame pointed out, "Nearly 1,150 Lebanese died, most of them civilians. That is more than seven times as many as the roughly 150 Israelis, mostly soldiers, who died, according to The Times's latest estimates." Despite this disproportionality in casualties, Susan Chira, the paper's foreign editor, said, "We made an enormous effort to be as balanced as possible [about the photographic coverage], given the facts.... We looked hard to make sure it wasn't dominated by one side." Michele McNally, the assistant managing editor for photography, said, "If we had a Lebanese child on the front the day before, I would try to avoid it again [the next day]." Calame reflected that extra photographs of Israeli soldiers that were not really newsworthy or informative were included to "compensate" for the lack of relevant ones in order "to make the coverage 'balanced.' If that was the case, it represented phony fairness to the parties in the conflict and a disservice to readers." [159]

- In 2013, Harvard law professor and long-time Israel advocate Alan Dershowitz—with others—attempted to derail a scheduled panel on Boycott, Divestment, and Sanctions at Brooklyn College hosted by the political science department. Dershowitz called the event "pure propaganda and one-sided political advocacy," and charged that the panel represented an attempt by the department to "deny equal freedoms to those who disagree with its extremist politics." "Freedom of speech, and academic freedom require equal access to both sides of a controversy," he asserted. The college and the department did not succumb to pressure and the event was appreciatively received by a capacity crowd.[160]

- A 2014 Modern Language Association panel on the academic boycott of Israel came under fire from Hillel International and the Israel on Campus Coalition, which claimed that it was not "a balanced and open discussion" because their point of view was not represented. In an *Inside Higher Ed* article about the panel, Scott Jaschik reported, "Rosemary G. Feal, executive director of the MLA, said that when the program committee reviews proposals for sessions that go beyond a disciplinary topic the goal is not balance. The committee 'often accepts sessions that present a particular viewpoint. In fact, proposals often argue that a particular perspective is important.'" The article also cites David C. Lloyd, an English professor, who said in an email that "for several decades, I have been in post-colonial and Irish studies, and have been involved in various social movements, from Central American solidarity work to South Africa divestment in the 1980s, the East Timor action network, and of course, various Irish-related public events. In none of these contexts has the question of balance arisen. No one ever asked us to host a representative of the Indonesian point of view when we hosted Benedict Anderson on East Timor at Berkeley; no one has ever asked us whether the British point of view on the Irish Famine or on Northern Ireland should be represented on our academic panels, no matter how critical of Britain's colonial legacy we might have been…. [O]nly in the context of Palestine does such a question arise."[161]

- After pressure from pro-Israel groups to cancel a scheduled 2019 event at the University of Massachusetts, Amherst called "Criminalizing Dissent: The Attack on BDS and American Democracy," Chancellor Kumble Subbaswamy allowed the event to proceed on First Amendment and academic freedom grounds; nonetheless, he condemned the event as "one-dimensional" and "polarizing." In a statement to the campus community he said that in the Israeli-Palestinian conflict, "the suffering…exists on all sides," and that it was "troubling" that an event taking place on their campus—though sponsored by a private foundation that leased the space—would be one "where only one perspective is shared…." Faculty, students, and local activists responded that his response was unacceptable. An "Open Faculty Letter to Chancellor Subbaswamy" expressed "disappointment and dismay" that the chancellor's refusal to cancel the event fell "far short of the robust defense of academic freedom, and the integrity of the campus community, that we expect of our chancellor." In a separate rebuke, the Western Massachusetts chapter of Jewish Voice for Peace had this to say in a local newspaper: "For stark comparison, we note that Benny Morris, known Islamophobe who has openly argued in favor of ethnic cleansing of Palestinians and Arab citizens of Israel, recently spoke at UMass, at an event sponsored by four UMass departments. Chancellor Subbaswamy made no such ideological condemnation of that event, nor did he clarify that Mr. Morris' widely criticized viewpoints are not shared by the university...."[162]

Yet the underside of these avowed commitments to "balance"—that is, the actual thinness of those avowals—often surfaces in "authoritative" news sources' coverage of Israel. "Objectivity has become a creed without credence" asserted journalist Barnabe F. Geisweiller in a 2010 *Truthout* op-ed excoriating the *New York Times* for its hypocritical inconsistency in applying that creed to its reporting on Israel/Palestine. He pointed out that the *Times* higher-ups seemed to have no issue with one of their principal correspondents (and later Jerusalem bureau chief), Ethan Bronner, concurrently being the father of a soldier serving in the Israeli Defense Forces—hardly an "objective" observer. Taghreed El-Khodary, a Palestinian journalist who covered Gaza for the *Times* during the 2000s, resigned her position when she found out about Bronner's son. Besides her colleague's conflict of interest jeopardizing her own credibility in the eyes of her sources, she said, "Being a Palestinian journalist, even if you work for Reuters or AP or the *New York Times*, Israel will never give you access to the West Bank or to Israel." Furthermore, "The issue is even if you write a feature, if you write anything: you need the Israeli narrative in the story. You need to balance...."[163]

In short, calls for balance are often—well, unbalanced. When I wrote an earlier draft of this chapter, I added, "And needless to say, on some topics—say, the Holocaust—presenting 'balancing' viewpoints is generally considered out of the question, despite Holocaust deniers' complaints that their 'side' of the issue is not given fair play." But then came 2021, when Texas Governor Greg Abbott signed into law Texas House Bill 3979, which mandated that the public schools teach "opposing viewpoints" on all issues, "without giving deference to any one perspective"—even about the Holocaust.[164]

During the Cold War years there seemed to be no imperative to present pro-Communist views to balance out those representing "American" interests. And I can't forget a student of mine who described, in 1992, the pro and con viewpoints on gay rights he was subjected to in a university class: "I just love hearing a 'lively discussion' of whether or not I should exist."

One other common appeal to the "balance" formula has materialized in the phrase often used by Israel supporters, "It's not fair to single Israel out!" Its prima facie logic—like that of "Israel has a right to defend itself!"—could not be denied by persons of good will. Yet the assertion relies on patently false premises. *Has* Israel really been "singled out" for censure while the equally nefarious deeds of others have been ignored? (Analogously, most people of reason and compassion will agree that *everyone* has a right to defend themselves—but the legal and moral question is, is what is being described actually self-defense, or is it a canny plea to avoid the consequences of committing a crime?)

The usual rejoinders to the "singled out" claim, which essentially implies, "Unfairly imbalanced!", focus on the fact that criticisms of Israel target the way it is *already* willingly "singled out" by its defenders. Most frequent is citing its "special relationship" with the United States, manifested in billions upon billions of foreign aid unrivaled by any other recipient, diplomatic cover via dependable vetoes of UN Security Council resolutions censuring Israel, and allowance of US tax-deductible contributions to "charitable organizations" that support Israel's illegal settlements, turning ordinary US citizens into unwitting subsidizers of the settlement project. Other examples of the US's "singling out" Israel: the no-questions-asked posture vis-à-vis Israel's nuclear weapons program, while certain other countries are vilified and sanctioned for entertaining such aspirations; the ardent protestations of US politicians, Democrats and Republicans alike—heard from the Clintons and Gore to Obama and Kerry and Biden, from George W. Bush to John McCain to Trump and Pence, to scores of members of Congress—that there is "no daylight" between the US and Israel; the United States defunding of international organizations (e.g., UNESCO) that allow Palestine membership and withdrawing from international organizations (e.g., the United Nations Human Rights Council) for allegedly "singling out" Israel for ill-treatment; quietly forgiving and forgetting when Israel attacked the American Navy vessel *U.S.S. Liberty* in 1967, killing and wounding scores of crew members. Many have pointed out, as well, that Israel singles *itself* out as the only nation on earth claiming title to its territory as a special gift from God, who has "chosen" their "people" above all others. In short, this very common response to the claim that Israel is being singled out for its deeds rests on the undeniable truth that Israel has *already* been singled out for special treatment, and for that reason merits special scrutiny.

But the "imbalance" claim implicit in the "singled out" argument also willfully ignores vast portions of history. Countries the US has sanctioned for misbehavior include Iraq, Iran, North Korea, Libya, Syria, Sudan, Cuba, Nicaragua, and Venezuela, causing millions of civilian deaths due to starvation and lack of medical supplies. Countries with whose inhabitants US activists have mobilized in solidarity because the US government has *supported* their regimes' human rights violations include South Vietnam, El Salvador, Guatemala, Egypt, South Africa, and Saudi Arabia. Rather than "singling out" Israel for boycott, US activists have previously targeted South Africa's apartheid system; Montgomery, Alabama's segregated bus system; California grape- and lettuce-growers' labor abuses; the Nestle company's deceptive marketing of infant formula as "better than breast milk" to mothers in poor countries, causing millions of infant deaths; SeaWorld's treatment of orcas, made infamous by the documentary *Blackfish*; even the unrestrained consumerism of Black Friday via the "Buy Nothing Day" movement. There have been boycotts of anti-LGBT businesses such as Chick-fil-A, Hobby Lobby, and Cracker Barrel—and the state of North Carolina in the wake of its 2016 "bathroom bill." In the late 1980s and early 1990s, tourists, performers, sports groups, and conventions boycotted Arizona to penalize it for refusing to observe the birthday of Martin Luther King Jr. as a holiday. Environmentalists have targeted fossil fuel companies such as BP and Shell, as well as Coca-Cola (for its proliferation of plastic) and Kellogg (when its cereals were found to contain GMOs and glyphosate). Nike was boycotted for its use of sweatshops and child labor. In 2020, professional athletes were inspired by the Black Lives Matter movement to boycott their own sporting events in protest of police shootings of Black people. Facebook has been boycotted by advertisers for its laxity regarding posts that incite racial hate and violence. Starbucks and Whole Foods have been avoided for not allowing their employees to wear BLM apparel and for union-busting. Companies with financial ties to Donald Trump—Goya Foods, Bank of America, CVS pharmacies—have been shunned by consumers. Looking back to the early decades of the twentieth century, we may recall that major Jewish organizations established boycotts of German goods when Hitler came to power; the Anti-Defamation League spearheaded a boycott of Ford products in the 1920s after Henry Ford published a series of incendiary antisemitic articles in the newspaper he owned, the *Dearborn Independent*; and Jewish women boycotted kosher butchers on the Lower East Side in 1902 in a revolt against spiking prices. (Their tactics escalated to vandalizing butcher shops and storming synagogues to recruit allies to their cause.)[165]

Thus, rather than being "singled out" by the BDS movement, Israel is in abundant company; innumerable states and businesses have similarly found themselves assailed by grassroots campaigns when injustices were not effectively addressed via legal or governmental measures.

Furthermore, in recent years, much scholarship critical of Israel, rather than "singling it out" as a unique phenomenon, has pointedly regarded it within the global phenomenon of settler colonialism alongside North America, Australia, and New Zealand. As Lorenzo Veracini has cogently summarized the concept, settler colonialism is of the variety that says "you, go away" rather than "you, work for me."[166] Patrick Wolfe has further clarified that settler colonialism's primary aim is to access territory: "Territoriality is settler colonialism's specific, irreducible element." It "destroys [an indigenous society] to replace [it with another society that wants the land for itself]."[167] Concurrently, the history and struggle of the Palestinians have been increasingly viewed within a transnational indigenous studies framework. Scholars who have applied these lenses include Steven Salaita, Nadia Abu El-Haj, John Collins, Patrick Wolfe, David Lloyd, Robert Warrior, Gershon Shafir, Lana Tatour, Brenna Bhandar, and Rafeef Ziadah.[168]

Viewing Israel/Palestine through the lens of settler colonialism and/or of indigeneity clearly removes it from the realm of absolute exceptionalism. While acknowledging that *every* struggle over national sovereignty bears some unique traits, locating Israel within the settler colonial paradigm gives Zionism a context—not an admirable one, to be sure, but one that does not caricature Israel as a personified entity with a big nose and a skullcap. And in fact, that is as it should be. Israel could never have come to exist as a nation-state if the ideologies, policies, practices, and will-to-dominate of Europeans, already rehearsed on other shores, had not enabled, bolstered, permeated, and sustained it.

CRITICAL CONTEXTS: BEYOND UNREASONABLE DOUBT

Naomi Oreskes and Erik M. Conway describe the long-term impact of the 1949 Fairness Doctrine on news reporting—and ultimately on public policy—near the outset of their landmark 2010 exposé, *Merchants of Doubt: How a Handful of Scientists Obscured the Truth on Issues from Tobacco Smoke to Global Warming.* Their thesis is that insistence on presenting both sides of an issue—"rather than giving *accurate* weight to both sides"—is a tactic that keeps conclusions forever misleadingly in abeyance. The "doubt" engendered by the inconclusively resolved competing claims allows noxious but profitable practices to continue unregulated. Orestes and Conway portray a cast of characters (scientists, businessmen, journalists) who launched what they call the "tobacco strategy": establishing doubt in the public mind regarding the veracity of scientific claims about a product by presenting "both sides"—even if one side is fiscally sponsored by industries that produce and profit from the product and the other side represents expert consensus arrived at via peer-reviewed scientific methodology. Pioneering this strategy from the 1950s through the 1970s by provoking a supposed debate over whether or not smoking caused cancer (it was known by then that it did), spinmeisters applied it again and again to critical health and environmental issues such as acid rain, the ozone hole, pesticides, secondhand smoke, and global warming. In each case, they manufactured doubt (and sustained profits while fending off government regulation of known dangers) by creating the illusion that "the jury was still out" on so-called debates that had in reality been settled.[169]

The notion that balance and giving equal weight to both sides is the fair and sensible thing to do has also been used to make fabrications outside of the scientific realm seem plausible. Denial of the Holocaust and of the Armenian genocide, for instance, depend, for their persistent influence, on the liberal pluralist notion that all sides must be given a fair and open-minded hearing, and that as long as opposing viewpoints continue to assert themselves, the "truth" may ultimately be too difficult to ferret out. Until and into the #MeToo era, "he said/she said" contending narratives of sexual harassment or assault were believed to render the truth essentially unknowable—thus letting off the hook accused men who were "innocent until proven guilty." (Unless, of course, the accused was Black and the alleged victim white—from the Scottsboro Boys to the Central Park Five, with countless lynchings in between.) Defense attorneys for police officers who have killed Black men or women have had a historically easy time implanting, in the minds of white jurors, "reasonable doubt" that a police officer would do such a thing intentionally or in depraved recklessness rather than in (real or perceived) self-defense. Across the board, inculcating and buttressing the notion of *doubt* in people's minds when massive evidence has actually been garnered to dispel it forestalls action that could prevent further catastrophes. This takes us back to the epigraph that opened this chapter. Oreskes and Conway write:

> "Doubt is our product," ran the infamous memo written by one tobacco industry executive in 1969, "since it is the best means of competing with the 'body of fact' that exists in the minds of the general public." "No proof" became a mantra that they would use again in the 1990s when attention turned to secondhand smoke. It also became the mantra of nearly every campaign in the last quarter of the century to fight facts.[170]

One approach was heralding the superior wisdom of studies that were actually conducted by consultants funded by the tobacco industry, while masking the fact that these were *not* the ones that appeared in peer-reviewed journals. Another approach was to raise the specter of other possible suspects; after all, diet, air pollution, genetics, and "sick building syndrome" (as-yet-unidentified toxins sickening workers in an office) could just as easily as secondhand smoke be sources of lung cancer in nonsmokers.

There were also the putative "political agendas" of government agencies: the EPA was depicted as part of a cabal determined to squash individual liberties, their attack on secondhand smoke a harbinger of larger crackdowns on lifestyle choices. Constraining smoking in the workplace was said to be a form of employment discrimination. It was claimed that government regulations were promulgated by extremists peddling "junk science" (which could be exposed by the dissemination of "sound science" produced by industry operatives). In a move that presaged a leading strategy of Israel's public relations industry in years to come, it was claimed that new laws unfairly "singled out" secondhand tobacco smoke as the latest way to suppress our freedom.[171] Tobacco industry operatives successfully identified reporters in print and broadcast journalism who were susceptible to the "balance" argument and helped to popularize the notion that the EPA was "controlled by environmental terrorists."[172]

The "tobacco strategy" and the crusade against government regulation were unwrapped and repackaged once again for the global warming debate that commanded public interest in the decades around the turn of the twenty-first century. An influential economist averred, despite the findings of climate scientists, that "the impact of carbon dioxide needed to be assessed together with 'other climate-changing activities,' such as dust, land use changes, and natural variability. It was wrong to *single out* CO2 for special consideration." (Italics added.)[173] The notions proffered by global warming "skeptics" were taken seriously by governmental leaders who weighed regulatory needs and determined budget allocations for research. The mass media, in turn, stayed true to the imperative to offer "balance" in the place of critical inquiry and evidence, writing of "scientific controversies" surrounding the ongoing "debate."[174]

Oreskes and Conway's conclusion: Doubt works. And it works largely because the illusion of inconclusiveness mitigates the sense that our pleasures—smoking, taking gasoline-powered road trips, spraying convenient aerosol products, beautifying our lawns—are harmful and must be given up. "Uncertainty favors the status quo," they say,[175] and usually that means sustaining the interests of the wealthy and the powerful, bound by formidable ties.

Merchants of Doubt focuses mainly on the fabrication of doubt regarding harm caused to people and other living things by industry—and the government agencies that enable them. Whether the alleged culprit is a pollutant on a vast scale or a toxic household consumer product, there is the sense, in these cases, that there is a tangible, empirical foundation for the elusive truth—whatever it may be. But other, far more nebulous sorts of "truths" are often at stake. Because the "truths" of Zionist public relations are so often to be found in this realm, it is worthwhile to examine a few of the other contexts in which they appear.

For example, racial bias in law enforcement and the judicial system has been well documented at least as far back as the nineteenth century, but the brutal beating of Rodney King in Los Angeles in 1991 by white LAPD officers marked a turning point in that such crimes began to be documented on videotape.

Nonetheless, acquittals of the officers involved—with the verdicts slightly modified by the US Department of Justice after riots broke out in protest—established that the sowing of doubt about how people might *interpret* what they *thought they saw* had found its place in the pantheon of legal persuasion.

By the summer of 2014, there was a resurgence of media coverage and public indignation about police brutality against people of color. In July, an unarmed African American man in New York, Eric Garner, died in a chokehold by white police officer Daniel Pantaleo. The death was ruled a homicide by the city's medical examiner, who cited the chokehold[176] as the main causal factor. But there was no indictment of Pantaleo. His defense effectively created doubt about the cause of death, claiming that it could be due to a preexisting lung or heart condition, and fellow officers on the scene later testified that they had believed Garner's unresponsiveness was only a case of "playing possum" to avoid arrest.[177] And though the use of a chokehold violates NYPD rules, it was years before departmental disciplinary action was taken and Pantaleo lost his job.

That August, an unarmed African American teenager in Ferguson, Missouri, Michael Brown, was fatally shot by white police officer Darren Wilson and again, a grand jury did not bring an indictment. Wilson claimed he shot in self-defense, but a number of protocols were violated on the scene that obscured the evidence. First, the medical examiner did not take measurements from the crime scene—saying simply that "it was evident what happened"—and did not take photographs because, he said, his camera battery had died. Then Wilson drove himself, alone, back to the police precinct, where he washed his hands of blood and placed his gun in an evidence bag with no one else present (no one photographed the bloodied hands or gun, either), and the police officers who questioned Wilson after the shooting didn't record the interviews.[178]

Yet even with this wanton disregard for crucial evidence (the absence of which nonetheless seemed, paradoxically, to underwrite the presumption of Wilson's innocence), a grand jury failed to indict Wilson. This was, as always, made easier by the inherently vague meaning of "reasonable doubt," which may be interpreted broadly. Yali Corea-Levy, a defense lawyer in San Francisco, aptly argues that "the *feeling* of certainty is what gives reasonable doubt its seal of approval." Jury members are often predisposed to believe law enforcement officers over civilians or bear racial, gender, or other biases. Crucially, Corea-Levy asks: "How...often is the feeling of being correct, actually correct?"[179]

One may ask the same question about the feeling of doubt, which can jettison a potentially just resolution of a matter into the functionally exculpating limbo of uncertainty.

In the fraction of instances in which such cases do go to trial, convictions of police are rare. Even when video evidence or witness testimony indicates that an officer was not under threat at the time of a shooting, white jurors can often be made to believe that an officer "perceived" there to be a "significant threat" or "danger" when confronted by a Black man.[180] "Legally, what most matters in these shootings is whether police officers *reasonably believed* that their or others' lives were in danger, not whether the shooting victim *actually posed a threat*" (italics added), wrote political reporter German Lopez on *Vox*.[181]

Another scenario in which doubt about whom to "believe" plays a fundamental part is one we have seen much of in the #MeToo era: did sexual assault or harassment actually occur, as one party claims, or was it a fabrication or a mere delusion, as the other party asserts?

The template "he said/she said" case in the public eye was that of Clarence Thomas during his Supreme Court confirmation hearings in 1991, where the candidacy of Thomas was put in jeopardy by an accusation of sexual harassment by his former coworker, Anita Hill. This scenario was reprised in the Brett Kavanaugh/Christine Blasey Ford truth contest of 2018 (though in this case, the alleged crime was rape). Both nominees were ultimately confirmed. In both cases there was a curtailment of the investigative process due to putative time constraints or other invented or unnamed obstacles, leaving critical witnesses and evidence unexamined. Thus, in both cases, the absolute truth was presented as terminally undiscoverable, the "doubt" swinging to the nominee's benefit (even though, as many watchers pointed out, "innocent until proven guilty" is the standard for criminal trials, not Supreme Court confirmations). The *doubt* raised about each woman's testimony, though in vastly different social, political, and public opinion climates, was deemed ample to dismiss her claims as reasonable obstacles to the nominee's approval. In other words, the *doubt* manufactured about each woman's credibility eclipsed any *doubt* there might be about each nominee's ability to decide crucial aspects of the lives of hundreds of millions of US citizens.

Clearly, then, a critical component of manufacturing doubt involves meticulously avoiding clarity, which is often done by withholding crucial information or encumbering a full, impartial investigation. The desired result for manu-facturers of doubt is that the selected "facts" made available stand in for the whole, that the answer be further unprovable, and that the actions leading to the inquiry may therefore continue unabated.

ATTACKING THE MESSENGER

As was the case in the Thomas/Hill and Kavanaugh/Blasey Ford hearings, many of Israel's accounts of its own doings are crafted as grist for the struggle over credibility in the face of incommensurable narratives. A notable document on which Israel felt, rightly, that the struggle for its credibility or "legitimacy" hinged was what became known as The Goldstone Report (GR)—officially, the Report of the United Nations Fact-Finding Mission on the Gaza Conflict, commissioned by the UN Human Rights Council in the wake of the violence in Gaza from December 27, 2008 through January 18, 2009. An investigation into war crimes and human rights violations committed during what Israel called Operation Cast Lead (OCL), the study was fraught from the start. From Israel's standpoint, anything emanating from the UN Human Rights Council—whose (periodic but historically toothless) resolutions condemning Israel's human rights breaches are routinely dismissed as "anti-Israel" reflexes—came intrinsi-cally permeated by antisemitic bias and could not be taken in good faith. On the other hand, Israel had dodged potential confrontations with international justice tribunals thus far, and many expected that, despite harsh criticism from human rights organizations on Israel's role in OCL, the Gaza war would ulti-mately constitute yet another station in its march of impunity.

The perception of bias was reduced, for many, by the appointment of four highly respected and experienced members to the mission with international standing in human rights and war crimes law. At its head was Richard Goldstone, a Jewish former South African jurist who had prosecuted war criminals in the former Yugoslavia and Rwanda. He had also rendered liberal decisions against apartheid in South Africa and investigated apartheid-era crimes during the tran-sition to democracy. He had a stellar reputation for fairness. His appointment gave Israel a glimmer of hope for a moderate assessment of its alleged OCL atrocities because he was a self-proclaimed Zionist, deeply connected in many Zionist channels.

Yet even after he insisted on extending his fact-finding mandate to include Hamas, Israel refused to cooperate in the investigation, denying him access to key Israeli witnesses, vital information, and entry into Israel as well as into Gaza via Israel. As Naomi Klein succinctly put it, "Israel's strategy was transparent enough: It would force Goldstone to produce a one-sided report, which it would then enthusiastically dismiss for being one-sided."[182]

When the GR came out, rife with detailed findings about Israel's war crimes during OCL and, to the lesser extent available, those of Palestinian governmental and militant resistance groups, Israel's supporters were incensed and deemed Goldstone a traitor, ostracizing him from long-standing communities and networks. It turned out that this exemplary jurist couldn't take the heat. In April of 2011, nineteen months after the GR had been released, Goldstone published an op-ed in the *Washington Post*, which some jubilantly called a "retraction" or a case in which "false accusations are taken back" (that last was Netanyahu)[183] and others saw as a vague, hollow capitulation without legal or edifying significance.[184]

His article famously began:

> We know a lot more today about what happened in the Gaza war of 2008–09 than we did when I chaired the fact-finding mission appointed by the U.N. Human Rights Council that produced what has come to be known as the Goldstone Report. If I had known then what I know now, the Goldstone Report would have been a different document.[185]

Intriguing, but he neglects to explain what he learned that changes the picture for him. Instead, he merely changes his mind. Now, magically, he feels that Israel *has* suitably investigated the charges against it; the GR's "allegations of intentionality by Israel" *don't* hold water; civilians were *not* "intentionally targeted as a matter of policy"; outside observers should *not* "second-guess, with the benefit of hindsight, commanders making difficult battlefield decisions"; and unfortunately, the whole experience had *not* begun "a new era of evenhandedness at the UN Human Rights Council, whose history of bias against Israel cannot be doubted." In the GR, the process of obtaining and evaluating evidence—and of dealing with obstacles to obtaining evidence—had been meticulously detailed. In his op-ed, Goldstone sounded very much like the New Historian Benny

Morris, who couldn't retract the voluminous archival evidence he'd provided of Nakba atrocities but *could,* under intense social pressure, change his *evaluation* of the damning data so that he realized all the devastation and the duplicity had been, actually, necessary—understandable steps, albeit with some regrettable collateral damage, toward a laudable goal. Goldstone, too, had had a change of heart—unlike in Morris's case, purportedly based on new empirical evidence, but that evidence, if it did exist, was not revealed. Neither did he mention that, as only one of four investigators and the only one to have had this epiphany, he had no authority to renege on the report's conclusions. (Nor, of course, does an op-ed have the authority to negate an official United Nations inquiry.)

The other three members of the fact-finding mission responded with a pointed article in the *Guardian.* "[We] find it necessary to dispel any impression that subsequent developments have rendered any part of the mission's report unsubstantiated, erroneous or inaccurate," they wrote. "[N]othing of substance has appeared that would in any way change the context, findings or conclusions of that report."[186] Human rights groups, as well as a follow-up committee of independent experts appointed by the UN Human Rights Council to monitor Israeli and Palestinian subsequent investigations into the allegations raised in the report, also raised red flags about Israel's transparency, timeliness, and good faith involving its own post-report inquiries. In other words, they reaffirmed the skepticism about Israel's willingness to legitimately investigate itself evinced in the Goldstone Report.[187]

Nonetheless, predictable critics such as Alan Dershowitz denounced the report's methodology and credibility, insisting that Israel's unilateral account of itself was the more reliable one even as Israel had exempted itself—as it routinely does—from external inquiry under the claim that any such inquiry would be "biased." In Dershowitz's lengthy rejoinder to the GR, he points to secondary sources such as newspaper accounts that he insists are "hard" and "incontrovertible" evidence that disprove eyewitness testimony. He uses such means to cast doubt—when not openly brandishing willful malice and ridicule—on the GR's findings (such as that Israeli soldiers, rather than Hamas, used Gazan civilians as human shields—one of the conclusions at which he takes particular umbrage). On the other hand, his own counter-facts are rendered with the sort of unalloyed conviction, despite the absence of any verifiable data to support them, that makes masses trust demagogues. He makes steely pronouncements such as, "The evidence is overwhelming, indisputable, and widely accepted by people of good will" that Hamas uses women and children as human shields, fires rockets near schools and mosques, and other nefarious things; and he concludes, "Hamas deliberately does all these for the very purpose of provoking Israel into taking military actions that will result in the deaths of Palestinian civilians so that Hamas can then complain to the media and to human rights and governmental organizations. No reasonable person could dispute this reality."[188]

Despite compelling affirmation of GR's work from human rights workers and organizations internationally and in Israel and Palestine, one would have to be an avid follower of humanitarian and war crimes law to sift through the confusion that Goldstone had sown and Israel supporters eagerly reaped. It could easily appear, given the conflicting versions from "experts," that the jury was still out on what had *really* happened in Gaza—and that the lengthy probe involving scores of witness accounts and marked in large part by Israel's stone-walling strategies *might* actually have had an unsavory agenda of its own.

And why not? Israel had repeatedly dodged international scrutiny in the past, coasting by on feigned investigations of itself to ward off external reviews and sustain faithful public opinion. Of countless examples, here's one to illustrate from Palestinian American political analyst Yousef Munayyer: In April 1996, in Kana, southern Lebanon, during fighting between the IDF and Hezbollah that Israel called Operation Grapes of Wrath, Israel shelled 800 Lebanese civilians seeking refuge in a UN compound as their villages were bombarded by the IDF. Most were women, children, and the elderly. The onslaught killed 106 and injured another 106.[189] Veteran Middle East journalist Robert Fisk, arriving the same day, wrote, "It was a massacre. Not since Sabra and Chatila have I seen the innocent slaughtered like this."[190] Major-General Franklin Van Kappen, Military Adviser to UN Secretary-General Boutros Boutros-Ghali, was tasked with conducting a subsequent fact-finding mission. Some of his findings, based on eyewitness and videotaped evidence, were flatly denied by Israel, and some of the questions he posed to high-ranking officers remained unanswered. Van Kappen concluded, "While the possibility cannot be ruled out completely, it is unlikely that the shelling of the United Nations compound was the result [as Israel maintained] of gross technical and/or procedural errors."[191] Israel's response was that it "categorically rejects the findings of the UN report concerning the incident at Kana," calling it "inaccurate and one sided." It averred that it had "thoroughly investigated this tragic incident" itself and that it "profoundly regrets the loss of human life at Kana...." But it laid the blame for casualties on Hezbollah.[192] Munayyer, for his part, sums up that "no one was prosecuted in connection with the massacre."

A case rare in that it drew international attention and outrage—because this time the victim was Palestinian American as well as enormously venerated in the Arab world—was that of long term Al Jazeera journalist Shireen Abu Akleh, fatally shot by IDF troops near the entrance to Jenin refugee camp, in the West Bank, on May 11, 2022. She and her colleagues were covering an Israeli raid into the camp and, as experienced journalists in the region, they had taken extensive safety precautions. Like her companions, Abu Akleh was wearing a protective helmet and vest clearly marked "Press." According to Shatha Hanaysha, another Palestinian reporter who was with her, "We stood in front of the Israeli military vehicles for about five to ten minutes before we made moves to ensure they saw us. And this is a habit of ours as journalists, we move as a group and we stand in front of them so they know we are journalists, and then we start moving."[193] Hanaysha also reported that when they arrived on the scene, all was quiet: "There is no clashes, no boys who throw stones and we start laughing together, joking...."[194] And then a series of shots rang out, killing Abu Akleh and wounding fellow journalist Ali Samudi in the shoulder. The Israeli human rights group B'tselem wrote in its report:

> These investigations [*CNN, The New York Times, The Washington Post, AP*, and others], as well as B'Tselem's, determined that all the findings indicate the shots that killed Shireen Abu Akleh were fired by the Israeli military from a spot where military vehicles were standing, about 200 meters away. The investigations uncovered no records of an armed Palestinian located between the journalists and the military vehicles. All the documentation of armed Palestinians' whereabouts during the incident puts them either at sites without a direct line of fire to the group of journalists or at a distance that does not match audio analysis of the footage.[195]

Other forensic evidence cited by CNN in its own intensive investigation included a number of videos; numerous eyewitness accounts; expert audio analysis that found the bullet came from a location, according to the IDF, where an Israeli sniper had been located; and the analysis of a firearms expert who concluded that the number of shots, and the closely configured shot marks on the tree where Abu Akleh had been standing, "indicate Shireen was intentionally targeted with aimed shots and not the victim of random or stray fire."[196]

Yet the IDF, from the outset, kept doubt aloft, remaining steadfast that it was "not possible to unequivocally determine the source of the gunfire which hit Ms. Abu Akleh." It couldn't be ruled out, in the words of the final report, that she "was hit by bullets fired by armed Palestinian gunmen toward the direction of the area in which she was present in," though at that point—the story had changed several times—they acknowledged a "high possibility" that she was "accidentally hit by IDF gunfire that was fired toward suspects identified as armed Palestinian gunmen, during an exchange of fire in which life-risking, widespread and indiscriminate shots were fired toward IDF soldiers."

Later, to cover all bases, the IDF affirmed that its internal investigation, conducted by "a dedicated task force" composed of "IDF commanders and additional relevant personnel," had proved that, *even if* an errant IDF bullet had felled her, it was not "intentional."[197] A US State Department report agreed that there could be no "definitive conclusion"—this was based mainly on an examination of the damaged bullet that had killed Abu Akleh—and called it a case of "tragic circumstances" rather than an "intentional" murder.[198] Though high-level figures in the Biden administration, including Biden himself, called at first for an independent open investigation—Abu Akleh was, after all, an American citizen killed by a foreign actor—they let the matter slide. The FBI was reputed to follow up, but as of this writing (February 2025), there is no evidence that they have. Democratic Senator Chris Van Hollen of Maryland pursued the matter persistently, unearthing a report by the US security coordinator for Israel and the Palestinian Authority that he intimates contains revealing information, but he's faced an uphill and so far unsuccessful battle to get it declassified. So, as happens repeatedly in these matters: case apparently closed.

The Committee to Protect Journalists noted, in a report published a year after Abu Akleh's killing, that hers "was not an isolated event. Since 2001, CPJ has documented at least twenty journalist killings by the IDF. The vast majority—18—were Palestinian...." They found, furthermore, "a pattern of

Israeli response that appears designed to evade responsibility" in which "[t]he result is always the same—no one is held responsible."[199]

Finally, to illustrate just how deftly US officials enable the resistance to clarification, here is this 2021 exchange between Matt Lee, an Associated Press journalist, and State Department spokesperson Ned Price. The subject had been US rejection of efforts to have Israeli war and humanitarian crimes investigated by the International Criminal Court (ICC):

Matt Lee: Where should the Palestinians go to get accountability for what they claim to be, uh, problems, to Israeli courts? Where, where do they go?

Ned Price: Matt? Look, we, uh, of course, um, the United States is always going to stand up for uh human rights. Uh, we're always going to stand up.

Matt Lee: Where do they go? Where do they go? Where? Where?

Ned Price: Uh Matt? That is why I think you, that is why you have heard. Continue to endorse and to call for a two-state solution to this long-running conflict.

Matt Lee: Should they go to the Israeli courts? Where do they go?

Ned Price: A two-state solution, because it protects Israel's identity as a Jewish and democratic state, but also, uh, because it will give the Palestinians a viable state of their own, where they go their legitimate, uh,

Matt Lee: Where do they go? Where do they go? Where do they go? Where do they go?

Ned Price: —aspirations for dignity and self-determination.[200]

WAS THERE AN ARMENIAN GENOCIDE? WAS THERE A PALESTINIAN NAKBA?

One phenomenon that may be particularly helpful for understanding the manufacture of doubt in the Zionist sphere is the alleged dispute about the Armenian genocide at the hands of the Young Turks during the final years of the Ottoman Empire, 1915–17. The deaths, variously estimated at up to nearly one and a half million due to massacres and executions as well as starvation and exposure on forced marches, have been well documented by witness and survivors' accounts, historians using Ottoman archives, missionaries, and trial testimony. The catastrophe was covered by the *New York Times* as it unfolded. In the face of Turkish objections to the "Armenian narrative" of what had transpired, the International Association of Genocide Scholars wrote firmly in 2005 that the "overwhelming opinion of scholars who study genocide—hundreds of independent scholars, who have no affiliations with governments, and whose work spans many countries and nationalities and the course of decades—is consistent": in April 1915, "under cover of World War I, the Young Turk government...began a systematic genocide of its Armenian citizens...." [201]

Yet for over a century, the Turkish government has employed a series of denial strategies. First it insisted that the alleged atrocities had not occurred.[202] Then they accused the Armenians of being "disloyal and rebellious, a threat to security and the war effort" against Russia, the Ottoman Empire's longtime foe—a "fifth column" that needed to be "temporarily relocate[d]."[203] As the twentieth century proceeded, Turkey, in step with PR tactics of the times, adopted an "It's only fair to consider both sides" argument. As Stanley Cohen puts it, "the massive historical record of the massacres now becomes a series of 'allegations,' 'feelings,' 'claims,' or 'rumours.'"[204] Marc A. Mamigonian locates the Turkish government's approach squarely in the genealogical descent line of the Tobacco Strategy: a "manufactured controversy," in which the truth is presented as contested, controversial, and open to debate, wherein suppressing either of the "two sides" is tantamount to a freedom of speech violation. "In this new reality," Mamigonian writes, "there can never be a consensus and there will always be a debate over basic facts and interpretations."[205] A pivotal dimension of this strategy was to contest whether the Turkish-Armenian case fit the definition of the term "genocide."

In 2005, a group of Turkish Americans and others filed a federal lawsuit against the Massachusetts Department of Education because of its use of the term "Armenian genocide" without the inclusion of "opposing viewpoints" in its school curriculum. As reported by the *Boston Globe*, a high school history teacher who was a plaintiff in the suit said, "If they are sending out guides, they should be helpful, thorough, and *balanced*, where *balance* is required. Why is the state declaring there is no controversy when there is?" (Italics added.)[206]

In 2006, the Public Broadcasting Service (PBS) planned to accompany its broadcast of a documentary called *The Armenian Genocide* with a "debate" on whether or not the events constituted "genocide." The plan to air the debate was vigorously contested by the Armenian National Committee of America, a lobbying group, and set off a dispute over whether including the debate was appropriate. PBS ultimately left it to its 348 affiliates to each decide whether to show the film, the debate, both, or none, and various scenarios were enacted by PBS stations across the country.[207]

In 2007, the Turkish Coalition of America (TCA) nonprofit was formed to "educate the general public." Mamigonian writes that this was done "with $30 million from Turkish-American businessman Yalcin Ayasli, [who] has made the 'academic controversy' project a major focus, funding publications that attempt to undermine the historicity of the Armenian Genocide, supporting a major project at the University of Utah (the Turkish Studies Project), and repeating the existence of a scholarly debate."[208]

In addition to these methods of influencing public opinion, Turkey hired PR firms, formed lobby groups and think tanks, and established "educational" public culture sites. Least subtly of all, in 2005 Turkey introduced Article 301 of its penal code, which criminalizes those who "denigrate Turkishness." Among those prosecuted under this law have been journalists, publishers, professors, human rights workers, and writers, including Turkey's Nobel Prize-winning novelist-memoirist Orhan Pamuk.[209] Meanwhile, Turkish government-run or government-linked websites professing to "correct" or "fact check" Armenian claims about what happened continue to flourish on the Web.[210]

This faux controversy finds an echo in a critical aspect of Israel's own historiography: the question of why Palestinian civilians left their homes during the 1948 war. The "competing claims" framework is manifest in Walter Laqueur's summing-up of the climate of spring 1948 in his well-known *A History of Zionism*:

As the armed struggle became more bitter, the Jews were fighting with their backs to the wall, whereas the Arabs could take refuge in neighboring countries. By the end of April, about 15,000 Arabs had left Palestine. What impelled them to do so has been debated ever since. The Arabs claim that the Jews, by massacres and threats of massacre, forced them out and that this was part of a systematic policy. The Jews asserted that the Palestinian Arabs followed the call of their leaders, believing they would soon return in the wake of victorious Arab armies.[211]

For many years after the war, Zionist spokespeople claimed that in radio broadcasts, the Arab Higher Committee had ordered Palestinian civilians to flee the country, both to avoid the devastation that the Zionist troops were sure to wreak on them and to make room for the Arab armies to invade. The Israeli New Historian Simha Flapan wrote that this claim—"found in all official Zionist history and propaganda and all Israeli information publications"—was intended to bolster the idea that "Israel was not responsible for the exodus and in fact did everything in its power to stop it."[212] Absolving itself of this responsibility has been germane to Israel's refusal ever since to accept the return of the refugees.

The eminent Palestinian historian Walid Khalidi wrote in 1959, "I can find no significant trace of this allegation in Zionist sources in 1948, although one would expect it to be made then."[213] He had searched the press releases of the Arab League, minutes of Arab League General Assembly meetings, and various archives, and everywhere found the same thing: "There is no mention of an order." His now-classic essay, "Why Did the Palestinians Leave?", which details his rigorous quest, was reprinted in 2005 in the *Journal of Palestine Studies*. By that time, the Israeli "New Historians" had produced a body of work based on archival evidence that validated what had long been dismissed as "Arab propaganda." That Benny Morris, Simha Flapan, Avi Shlaim, Tom Segev, and Ilan Pappe,[214] all Jewish Israeli writers, were deemed sufficiently credible to alter the discussion for Israelis and their international supporters, while the exacting research of Khalidi (and others) had been ignored is another part of the story. But for now, let us concentrate on the way that Khalidi pursued the matter.

"What is the explanation?" he asks of the strange absence of Zionist references to these orders at the time they were allegedly issued. "It was only in 1949," he finds, "when the Zionists realized that the problem of the Arab refugees was touching the conscience of the civilized world, that they decided to counter the damaging influence it was having on their cause." In other words, it was an after-the-fact crisis-management PR operation. Khalidi discovers

> two mimeographed pamphlets which appeared in 1949 under the auspices of the Israel Information Center, New York, in which the evacuation order first makes an elaborate appearance.... [One of them] was incorporated in a memorandum submitted by nineteen prominent Americans, including the poet Macleish and Niebuhr the theologian, to the United Nations.[215]

And so it took off from there. Khalidi provides evidence from newspapers of the time that, conversely, the Palestinian leadership had urged the people "to be patient and to bear up and hold their ground," while a leaflet dropped from the air signed "Haganah Commander in Galilee" urged them to escape "in order to be safe. This is going to be a cruel war with no mercy or compassion."[216]

Khalidi's pursuit of substantiation takes him to the British Museum in London, where he reviews Arab and Zionist wartime radio transmissions that the BBC had recorded and filed. He finds that both Arab and Zionist radio announcements from 1948 contradict what the Zionists claimed after the war. The real cause of the Palestinian exodus, he concludes, was "a mixture of psychological and terroristic warfare. The evidence for the latter from the Zionist sources themselves...is overwhelming...."[217] For example, on March 14, Haganah radio announced: "We will answer killing with killing, destruction with destruction. We regret having to undertake reprisal raids in which innocent people may have to pay the price for the crimes of others, but we have warned you." Haganah broadcasts and loudspeaker vans urged Arab civilians to "get out of this blood bath...If you stay you invite disaster." Furthermore, it was "expected," relayed the Free Hebrew Station on March 27, "that such diseases [as smallpox, cholera, typhus] will break out heavily in April and May among Arabs in urban agglomerations...."[218] Benny Morris notes that in April, the Haganah general staff's Psychological Warfare Department produced material for these repeated announcements.[219] His detailed published research—and that of others, notably Erskine Childers[220]—has revealed the extent to which not only threats, but actual massacres and destruction of villages, drove people out and instilled terror in neighboring villages, producing panicked flight with the belief that they would be able to return once the fighting ended.

The vital undertaking involved in "proving the truth" was finding the primary sources. The opening of many archives in the 1980s made this possible for the first time, and key documents—letters, speeches, minutes of meetings, military plans—are extensively quoted in the work of historians writing from that time onward. By examining them, it is possible to distinguish between what was publicly proclaimed and what was discussed behind closed doors.

Before then—and in many cases, even now—the contention that there are "two competing narratives," each worthy of serious consideration, was kept alive via secondary accounts, often appearing in the sort of popular media that don't make use of precise source citation. When I was growing up and being told about Israel's history, much of it came in the form of lore—stories, aphorisms, and creeds that circulated and recirculated within families and communities. "Israel just wants peace!" my mother said many times in my younger years, the cadence of her voice lamenting the fact that, due to hostile, unreasonable neighbors, this objective was so elusive. She truly believed this. She was not trying to foist propaganda on me. She was merely initiating me into the web of axiomatic cultural beliefs that flowed from synagogue and Hebrew school to dinner tables to summer camps to gatherings with friends. The problem, I know in retrospect, is that this wisdom existed in the absence of any formal inquiry or carefully honed criteria about what constitutes "proof." Book group discussions of *Exodus,* James Michener's *The Source,* and autobiographies of Golda Meir and Moshe Dayan were the closest they came to exploring information. They were like most regular people in the Queens of my youth for whom critical analysis was simply not a feature of everyday life.

Others, though, have harnessed deliberate methods to keep doubt alive. Some have simply repeated the original Zionist claims, occasionally tempered by an awareness of the challenges they now face. On the Anti-Defamation League's web page devoted to "Palestinian Refugees," UNRWA comes in for much blame: it is they who have condemned Palestinians to an endless purgatory of refugee camps by obstinately failing to distinguish between "refugees," "displaced persons," and "expired permit Palestinians."[221]

Some sources insist that, to be fair, we must "demonstrate that suffering, expulsion, loss of property, and loss of life, is not the monopoly of *one side.*" (Italics added.) That's what Ben-Dror Yemini wrote in a 2009 piece called "What About the Jewish Nakba?" published by the Begin-Sadat Center for Strategic Studies, a think tank affiliated with Bar-Ilan University in Ramat-Gan, Israel. "The Jewish Nakba was worse than the Palestinian Nakba," Yemini affirms. "The critical difference is that the Jews did not turn that suffering into a founding ethos, but concentrated on rebuilding their lives." Yemini says of the Deir Yassin massacre, "There is no need to hide what occurred (even though the issue of the massacre *is in dispute*).... It was an immoral act, but we must note that it was preceded by a series of murderous terrorist attacks against the civilian population." (Italics added.)[222] In *Haaretz* on February 10, 2022, Avi Shilon critiques the newly released film *Tantura,* assuring us that his comments come at a time when there is "a greater openness about the war" and that "the Nakba is no longer a taboo subject that must be denied or played down." Yet his title suggests an affinity with Yemini: "It's time to stop keeping score: *Both sides* committed massacres in 1948." (Italics added.) The war started out as a "civil war," he says. "A civil war is exactly what the name implies: civilians killing civilians, indiscriminately, from *both sides.*" (Italics added.)[223] In the *Washington Post,* Glenn Kessler published "The dueling histories in the debate over 'historic Palestine'" in 2021. Starting out by recounting some hot water the *New York Times* got itself into over an illustration of the "shrinking map of Palestine," Kessler explains, "We often hesitate to delve into the Israeli-Palestinian dispute, as there are *two competing narratives.* History can be open to interpretation and not always easily fact-checked." (Italics added.) The solution, for him, is to "try to summarize *the two versions* ... for readers who want to hear *both sides of the story.*" (Italics added.) This he duly does—without further comment or analysis.[224]

Another method of discrediting their experience of 1948 is to present Palestinians as sore losers who derive some fetishistic pleasure from endlessly nursing their narcissistic wound—and then comparing them with more evolved models. In a 2014 *Haaretz* piece called "The Nakba—perpetuating a lie," former Likud Knesset and cabinet member Moshe Arens argues that the

Nakba is "a catastrophe that the Arabs brought upon themselves" and ridicules the commemoration of Nakba Day:

> Germans and Japanese, nations that were devastated by war initiated by their leaders, well understand that they themselves are the guilty ones, not only for the crimes they committed against those they considered to be their enemies, but also for the tragedies that they themselves suffered as a result. Victory in Europe Day, May 8, is not commemorated in Germany as the day of the German catastrophe, and Victory in Japan Day, August 15, is not commemorated in Japan as the day of the Japanese catastrophe. The Palestinians can take a lesson here.[225]

Yet another discrediting approach has been a definitional one. Just as Turkish discourse challenges the appropriateness of the word "genocide," Zionists and their supporters have challenged the appropriateness of the word "refugee." When President Trump defunded UNRWA in 2018, he justified it in large measure by casting into doubt later generations of Palestinians' claim to that status. Anne Irfan explains, "According to the Trump administration, the majority of Palestinians were not 'real' refugees because they had been born in exile." The Biden administration, she notes, has not categorically rejected that rhetoric.[226]

And in what may be the most patently duplicitous move of all, documents key to revealing the truth of 1948 have been removed from archives and locked in vaults by Malmab, "the Defense Ministry's secretive security department... whose activities and budget are classified." According to *Haaretz* writer Hagar Shezaf, "An investigative report by *Haaretz* found that Malmab has concealed testimony from IDF generals about the killing of civilians and the demolition of villages, as well as documentation of the expulsion of Bedouin during the first decade of statehood." Some of the documents had already been published by historians. Archive directors who objected to this removal were sometimes threatened. Shezaf writes:

> Yehiel Horev, who headed Malmab for two decades, until 2007, acknowledged to Haaretz that he launched the project, which is still ongoing. He maintains that it makes sense to conceal the events of 1948, because

uncovering them could generate unrest among the country's Arab population. Asked what the point is of removing documents that have already been published, he explained that *the objective is to undermine the credibility of studies about the history of the refugee problem. In Horev's view, an allegation made by a researcher that's backed up by an original document is not the same as an allegation that cannot be proved."* (Italics added.)[227]

Ilan Pappe wrote in the *Electronic Intifada,*

> Those of us working with Nakba documents...were already aware of the removal of these documents. For many years, for instance, historians were unable to revisit "the village files," which formed an important proof in my argument that the 1948 war was an act of ethnic cleansing.... Why are these files being hidden? In 2016, the journalist Lisa Goldman assumed that the reason was that the works of the "New Historians" embarrassed the government and undermined Israel's international standing.[228]

WHATABOUTISM

Even when we are certain that a party has been grievously wronged at the hands of another, there are still ways our moral compass can be blown off course. Here's an argument, seemingly mired in the notion of fairness, by Justin McCarthy, the historian and adamant defender of the "It wasn't genocide" position in Turkey:

> In America, the Armenian nationalists lobby a Congress which refuses to even consider an apology for slavery to demand an apology from Turks for something the Turks did not do.... In France, the Armenia nationalists lobby a Parliament which will not address the horrors perpetrated by the French in Algeria, which they know well took place, to declare there were horrors in Turkey, about which they know almost nothing. [229]

Double standards? Yes, actually. Persuasive? Well, sort of. McCarthy's reasoning here calls to mind the 1961 American film *Judgment at Nuremberg,* a fictionalized and condensed version of the Nuremberg trials following the Second World War. Former Nazis and those complicit with them are tried for "crimes against humanity" and after much philosophical dialogue are sentenced to life in prison. Along the way, though, an argument is raised that, compelling as it seems, mysteriously vanishes into the ether. The Germans were not the only ones doing horrific things, the lawyer for the defense reminds us. The atomic bombs dropped on Hiroshima and Nagasaki, the US government-sanctioned practice of eugenics, the American industrialists who profited by doing business with Hitler—those who perpetrated these destructive acts were not on the side of the angels, either. Moving from there, if one is to talk about genocide, it's certainly irrational to gloss over that of the indigenous peoples of the Americas—though this is routinely done in US culture and discourse.

There is a moral logic to this sort of argument, essentially destabilizing the criticism of one entity by framing it within the moral lapses of others. And it is tricky because it is not altogether devoid of legitimacy. Those who stand their ground and refuse to recognize hypocrisy even when confronted with cognitive dissonance have, I would say, a problem. On the flip side, many people who condemn human rights violations of Palestinians (or African Americans or Tibetans or queers or prisoners) are careful to also denounce human rights violations elsewhere, even when they're not at that moment boycotting everyone who transgresses. The problem arises when it is used simply as a tactic to dismantle criticism at all and thus forestall any sort of action, as is often the case, rather than expanding the immediate case's conceptual reach for the long haul.

Using this tactic as a preemptive gimmick has been called "whataboutism" —a concept updated for current times by John Oliver, host of *Last Week Tonight*. Explaining that this technique was an old Soviet propaganda tool energetically revived by the Trump administration, he illustrates with an analogy:

> A defense attorney could not stand up in court and say, 'Maybe my client did murder those people, but I ask you this: What about Jeffrey Dahmer? What about Al Capone? What about the guy from *The Silence of the Lambs*? .... The problem with what whataboutism is that it doesn't actually solve a problem or win an argument. The point is just to muddy the waters....'

He draws from all this a useful aphorism: "Even if you believe that Democrats are guilty of a double standard, the solution is not to have no standard whatsoever."[230]

"Whataboutism" is often used as a form of the "Don't single out Israel" argument: "UN rights inquiries are always focused on Israel—but what about repressive regimes like China, Cuba, Iran, and Venezuela?" "They criticize the condition of Palestinian refugee camps—but what about the housing those Arabs lived in before 1948?" "Yes, we bombed Gaza—but what about the rockets and the tunnels? What about the innocent children of Sderot?" If the question "What about...?" were sincerely lobbed as an overture for critical discussion, things could get interesting. The problem is that, on the contrary, it usually functions as a conversational filibuster.

CHAPTER 4:
"THE PICTURES IN OUR HEADS" AND THE MANUFACTURE OF DENIAL

"When it comes to the plight of the Palestinians, denial is the default setting of the pro-Israel propaganda machine....Justification—no matter how preposterous or morally bankrupt—is the back-up plan when denial can no longer be maintained."[231] —Sharif Nashashibi, journalist

"The Nakba denial is found in the geography and the history taught in schools, on the maps of the country and in the signs marking places on its surface. All of them ignore, almost completely, the event which made possible the establishment of the Jewish State .... [T]he Nakba represents for the Zionist subject an event that cannot possibly have occurred and—at the same time—had to occur."[232]
—Eitan Bronstein, Israeli educator and activist

"There were no such thing as Palestinians."[233]
—Golda Meir, Israeli prime minister, 1969

"Arab spokesmen regularly complain about what they call 'the Israeli occupation' of the Judea-Samara-Gaza territories. But the truth is that there is no such 'Israeli occupation.'"[234]
—Morton A. Klein, national president, Zionist Organization of America, 2002

"There is no blockade of Gaza."[235]
—Benjamin Netanyahu, Israeli prime minister, 2015

79

THE MANY FACES OF DENIAL

Denial can take a wide range of forms, from the literal and intentional lie (Bill Clinton in 1998: "I did not have sexual relations with that woman!") to wishful self-delusion (a spiritual healer will perform a miraculous cure for a terminally ill patient) to mulishly warding off disaster ("Fascism can't happen here"). Eyewitnesses to a crime may sincerely have conflicting accounts of what happened (the "Rashomon effect"). Denial may be used to exculpate oneself from responsibility ("How could I know the coach was sexually abusing the athletes for all those years?"), and it may be used to keep reality reassuringly seamless, as in not noticing the anomaly in a "What's wrong with this picture?" setup, or in accepting that a country is a democracy despite the disenfranchisement of sizeable chunks of its population.

Many literal denials have been woven into elaborately organized cover-ups. "I can say categorically that [presidential counsel John Dean's] investigation indicates that no one in the White House staff, no one in this administration, presently employed, was involved in this very bizarre incident," President Richard Nixon averred on August 28, 1972, in the early hours of the Watergate scandal.[236] "The blue wall of silence" is a well-known term referring to police officers' code of loyalty, in which they may withhold information about the misconduct of their colleagues to the point of falsifying documents to protect them—even when an innocent person is killed.

Denial may take the form of a speech act—a locution that makes something legally or socially binding simply by stating it, such as the act of "pronouncing" someone married or dead or guilty. A speech act denial may serve a utilitarian purpose, as when declaring land long inhabited by indigenous people "empty" and thus fair game for colonization (Australia's terra nullius, the US's "Manifest Destiny," Zionism's "land without a people"). Another example of this would be "designating" a political party (e.g., Hamas) or a charity (e.g., the Holy Land Foundation of Richardson, Texas) as a "terrorist" entity (rather than, say, a freedom-fighting or humanitarian entity). In 2006, for instance, the *New York Times* reported, "Since December 2001, the Treasury Department has designated Holy Land and five other Muslim charities in the United States as terrorist supporters, seizing millions of dollars in assets and halting their activities."[237] And in 1969, Israeli Prime Minister Golda Meir infamously asserted in an interview with Frank Giles of the *Sunday Times*, "There were no such thing as Palestinians. When was there an independent Palestinian people with a Palestinian state?... It was not as though there was a Palestinian people in Palestine considering itself as a Palestinian people and we came and threw them out and took their country from them. They did not exist."[238] When asked in a *New York Times* interview three years later whether she still adhered to this view, she did not retract her statement but recrafted it: "I said there never was a Palestinian nation."[239] In either event, there was a rhetorical erasure of Palestinians as a group with a history and an identity, thus implicitly absolving Israel from the crimes of removing or oppressing them. Say the magic words, and they will disappear.

Sometimes simply instilling *the possibility of doubt* can itself create the necessary context for denial, as we have seen in the previous chapter. One journalist even identified a term, the "non-denial denial," which he calls "an art that takes many forms in official Washington":

> The basic idea is that when you or your organization are accused of doing something that you did in fact do, you respond with what sounds like a denial, but really isn't. You issue a very narrowly crafted denial involving a lot of hair-splitting, while avoiding the central claim. Or you dismiss the accusation as unworthy of response. Or you deny something else: You raise a straw man accusation and deny that; or—possibly best yet—you take advantage of a poorly worded question.... And if the accusation against you is ever irrefutably proven, then you point out that you never really denied it....[240]

The most salient example of Israel's non-denial denial must certainly be its longstanding policy of flagrant ambiguity or "opacity" regarding its nuclear weapons facility in the Negev city of Dimona. Conceived by David Ben-Gurion, who avidly formulated Israel's nuclear weapons project—at first in total secrecy even from his own citizenry and cabinet—Israel has ever since adhered to

> a code of conduct that is fundamentally different from that of all other nuclear weapons states. Israel neither affirms nor denies its possession of nuclear weapons; indeed, the government refuses to say anything factual about Israel's nuclear activities, and Israeli citizens are encouraged, both

by law and by custom, to follow suit. And so they do, primarily through government censorship and self-censorship by the media. This policy is known as nuclear opacity, or, in Hebrew, *amimut.*[241]

As Avner Cohen conveys in detail in his book *Israel and the Bomb*, Israel's nuclear capability was, for the United States, alternately a matter of concern, complicity, and (willingly or not) being hoodwinked. When Israel's nuclear project began in the mid-1950s, President Dwight D. Eisenhower was inclined to "look the other way"[242] as Israel variously insisted that the facility was a "textile plant," a "metallurgical research laboratory,"[243] a "large agricultural experimental station,"[244] or an atomic facility "'dedicated exclusively' to the needs of industry, agriculture, medicine, and science."[245] The program did meet with some (ineffectual) resistance under the subsequent administration due to John F. Kennedy's concern about nuclear proliferation. Offering a quid pro quo—the US would supply Israel with conventional weapons, including tanks and fighter aircraft, in exchange for absolute assurances that Israel was not developing nuclear weapons—and pressing for inspections of Dimona by US scientists to confirm that its aims were, as Israel professed, purely peaceful, Kennedy found himself stymied by the subterfuges blocking his inquiry and his deal.

As leadership in Israel passed from Ben-Gurion to Levi Eshkol and in the United States from Kennedy to Johnson, Israel continually dodged the specifics of the inspection agreement. First, Israel chose to control the descriptive terminology to make it appear as if the two countries were engaging in a peer-based research exchange, insisting on nomenclature such as "scientific visits" rather than "inspections" and "invited guests" of Israel rather than "inspectors."[246] In addition, Cohen writes:

> The Israelis managed to limit the visits to Dimona to one day, run by a single team of no more than three AEC scientists. They insisted on always conducting the visit on Saturdays (the Jewish Sabbath) or other national holidays, when almost all the Dimona employees were gone and it was easier to control the visit. The team was also closely escorted by Israeli hosts. The team asked to bring its own measuring instruments (such as radiation measuring instruments), but the Israelis denied their request. It

was also not permitted to collect samples of any kind for later analysis. In addition, none of the team members spoke Hebrew.[247]

Yet perhaps the most frustrating of Israel's stonewalling tactics—its most protracted non-denial denial—was its repeated pledge that it would not be the first state to "introduce" nuclear weapons into the Middle East, while sidestepping all requests to define what that meant. Israeli negotiators seemed to have finally met their match when Assistant Secretary of Defense for International Security Affairs Paul Warnke went toe to toe with Yizhak Rabin, then Israel's ambassador to the US, over several days in November 1968, at the Pentagon. Warnke's aim was to produce a memorandum of understanding that would definitively link pending sales of F-4 Phantom jets to Israel's long-deferred signing of the Treaty on the Non-proliferation of Nuclear Weapons, known as the non-proliferation treaty or NPT—which would represent a categorical renunciation of its nuclear ambitions.

As Avner Cohen tells it, Warnke said outright that he "could not find in the record any understanding of what Israel means by the provision: 'Israel will not be the first to introduce nuclear weapons into the area.'" Could Rabin clarify? Rabin replied, "It means what we have said, namely, that we would not be the first to introduce nuclear weapons." Warnke tried to be more specific: what exactly did "introduce" mean? Rabin charged back, "What is your definition of nuclear weapons?" Warnke responded that "if there are components available that could be assembled to make a nuclear weapon—although part A may be in one room and part B may be in another room—then that is a nuclear weapon." As for "introduction," he remained firm: "That is your term and you will have to define it." Rabin posited that a weapon—conventional or nuclear—that has not been tested does not count as a weapon, and that public acknowledgment of the fact was also inherent to the definition. Warnke attempted to explicitly recap: "In your view, an unadvertised, untested nuclear device is not a nuclear weapon" and Rabin said, "Yes, that is correct." Cohen reports, "Warnke remarked that he differed on this, for he would interpret mere physical presence as constituting in itself an introduction" and he "concluded the session by acknowledging the two countries' different interpretation of the definition of introduction.... At the end of the negotiations Warnke was clear about one thing: Israel already had the bomb. Rabin's refusal to accept his physical possession definition of 'introduction' said it all."

Israel did not sign the NPT. The sales of the Phantom jets—and much, much more—went through anyway.[248] Less than a year later, then-President Richard Nixon, who didn't mind nuclear proliferation among friends, had a secret meeting on the subject with then-Prime Minister Golda Meir at the White House. Exactly what they said remains unknown. Years later, Meir wrote, "I could not quote him then, and I will not quote him now," and Nixon told Larry King on CNN that he was sure Israel had the bomb, though he declined to say *how* he knew.[249] "And with that, the decade-long US effort to curb Israel's nuclear program ended," write Avner Cohen and William Burr. "That enterprise was replaced by highest-level understandings that have governed Israel's nuclear conduct ever since."

One notable postscript: in February 2009, the ever-intrepid journalist Helen Thomas, senior member of the White House press corps, mischievously asked Barack Obama at his first press conference whether he knew of any country in the Middle East that had nuclear weapons. Obama's response: "With respect to nuclear weapons, you know, I don't want to speculate. What I know is this: that if we see a nuclear arms race in a region as volatile as the Middle East, everybody will be in danger. And one of my goals is to prevent nuclear proliferation generally. I think that it's important for the United States, in concert with Russia, to lead the way on this."[250]

A consummate non-denial denial, to be sure.

SEMANTIC MAGIC: DENIAL TECHNIQUES FOR EDUCATED PEOPLE

Certain manifestations of denial—from the claim that humans and dinosaurs coexisted on the earth 6,000 years ago to the belief among many Americans that Saddam Hussein was involved in the 9/11 attacks (and that Iraqis were among the hijackers)—leave many rationalists scratching their heads and asking, "How can people believe these things?" Often such evidence-absent thinking is attributed to people of lower IQs and watchers of Fox News.

Yet we know that highly educated scientific "experts" have placed their faith in notions such as mutually assured destruction (MAD)—the theory that the widespread annihilation of humans is a sound military strategy and national security plan. Carol Cohn, a scholar of gender and global security issues, decided to investigate how this was so. She summed up her late-1980s field research in an article called "Sex and Death and the Rational World of Defense Intellectuals." It described her year-long experience as a visiting scholar at a university's center on defense technology and arms control. Her goal for the year, she said, was "to gain a better understanding of how sane men of goodwill could think and act in ways that lead to what appear to be extremely irrational and immoral results."[251]

Throughout the course of the essay, Cohn, who acts as a covert "participant observer" among the male theorists of mass destruction, notes the euphemisms and abstractions that make palatable the unthinkable. The incineration of cities, she finds, is a matter of launching "countervalue attacks." "The "cookie cutter" is the name for a mode of nuclear attack. "The shopping list" is the president's annual memo enumerating weaponry needs. The bombs dropped on Hiroshima and Nagasaki go by the nicknames Little Boy and Fat Man. The elite staff refers to itself as "the nuclear priesthood." Submarine-launched cruise missiles are (derived from their acronym) "slick'ems." On a field trip to a navy base, her cohort excitedly climbs deep inside the bowels of a nuclear submarine and is invited to "pat the missile" that is housed there. Cohn is nonplussed: *Pat the missile?....* Patting is an assertion of intimacy, sexual possession, affectionate domination....It is also what one does to babies, small children, the pet dog. The creatures one pats are small, cute, harmless—not terrifyingly destructive. Pat it, and its lethality disappears."[252]

Yet in time Cohn catches herself ineluctably drawn into the discourse and thinking in its terms. As with the Newspeak of Orwell's *1984,* the parameters of her own reasoning alter and constrict. After a period of immersion, she finds that "talking about nuclear weapons is fun.... The longer I stayed, the more conversations I participated in, the less I was frightened of nuclear war."[253] She sees how easy it is, as Hannah Arendt might put it, to join in the banality of nuclear annihilation, because the imagery "that domesticates, that humanizes insentient weapons, may also serve, paradoxically, to make it all right to ignore sentient human beings."[254] She initially wants to understand what can make people engage in such work because "[t]he current nuclear situation is so dangerous and irrational that one is tempted to explain it by positing either insanity or evil in our decision makers."[255] But many of these men appear to be very nice people; some even consider themselves liberals. Nonetheless, Cohn finds, they manage, through cognitive dissonance, to immerse themselves in a workplace language and culture that "make it possible…to plan mass incinerations of millions of human beings for a living."[256]

Similar locutions obtain in Israeli military discourse. "Focused prevention"—as in, "the Palestinian terrorist was eliminated during a focused prevention operation"—is a term that is used, according to the *Los Angeles Times,* when "Israeli soldiers track and kill a Palestinian militant…." The term "suicide bombers" has been rejected by some Israeli officials in favor of "homicide bombers" to accentuate the plight of the victims and remove all possible hints of "martyrdom" from the bombers.[257] "Most Israelis believed their own propaganda that they were conducting an *enlightened occupation"* (italics added) for the first two decades after 1967, and so were confounded when the First Intifada broke out in 1987, writes Haim Bresheeth-Zabner.[258] A credo called the Dahiya Doctrine, formulated during Israel's Second Lebanon War in 2006, rationalizes the use of "disproportionate force" against villages that would fire upon Israel by renaming them. In the words of OC Northern Command Major General Gadi Eisenkot, they are "not civilian villages, they are military bases."[259] And Bresheeth-Zabner cogently describes

> the presentation of IDF soldiers on Israeli media as "our children," "boys," "our boys," and "our sons" by commentators and politicians alike. This follows years of such characterization of Israeli soldiers in Israeli cinema.…These films presented the Israeli soldier as young, inexperienced, deeply troubled, confused, sensitive, or even poetic.…Israelis know that most of the dead in the attacks on Gaza are children, among them many babies. To describe those who killed them as mere boys and children is to separate them from those other children, the ones without names, the ones one does not recognize. While Palestinian male children are described as young men when they die, Israeli soldiers remain boys when they kill. This infantilization of the soldier is also an infantilization of the public arena, of the debate, of the language itself. It is an Orwellian act of betraying truth and reality.[260]

Pat the missile. Hug the soldier-boy.

The architect and critical theorist Eyal Weizman has chronicled the ways that the IDF has instrumentalized ideas of postmodern intellectuals such as Gilles Deleuze and Felix Guattari to create new paradigms for warfare. Among them is a tactic known as "walking through walls." Sounding every bit as magical as Jesus walking on water, it is a strategy for outwitting the enemy by eschewing all the usual conduits of physical passage—e.g., roads, doorways, windows—in favor of more innovative modes of ingress and egress. Here is what Weizman has to say about it:

> If you still believe, as the IDF would like you to, that moving through walls is a relatively gentle form of warfare, the following description of the sequence of events might change your mind. To begin with, soldiers assemble behind the wall and then, using explosives, drills or hammers, they break a hole large enough to pass through. Stun grenades are then sometimes thrown, or a few random shots fired into what is usually a private living-room occupied by unsuspecting civilians. When the soldiers have passed through the wall, the occupants are locked inside one of the rooms, where they are made to remain—sometimes for several days—until the operation is concluded, often without water, toilet, food or medicine. Civilians in Palestine, as in Iraq, have experienced the un-expected penetration of war into the private domain of the home as the most profound form of trauma and humiliation."[261]

This sort of linguistic sleight of hand is frequently adopted uncritically by mainstream Western media on behalf of Israel. A 2021 report called "Media reporting on Palestine 2021" by the Centre for Media Monitoring (CfMM) in the UK found a persistent practice of grammatically masking agency by using "passive sentence structures which remove the actor from the narrative," as in, "Hundreds wounded in Jerusalem clashes." This headline, the report stressed, "fails to clarify that the hundreds who were 'wounded' were Palestinians, or that they were 'wounded' by the Israeli police"; in a single stroke it conjures the false impression of symmetrical warfare and slickly averts identifying who did the wounding and who suffered the effects. The report found numerous compa-rable instances, such as "a Palestinian who 'dies from wounds in border unrest' and an 'exchange of fire on Gaza border' which kills a Palestinian." The report noted that major news agencies—Agence France-Presse, Reuters, Associated Press—were most often responsible for neutralizing the facts in this way.[262]

There are interlacing and mutually reinforcing stratagems of denial at work in all these accounts. Stanley Cohen, who in his influential work *States of Denial: Knowing About Atrocities and Suffering* cataloged many, would no doubt say that the ploy of using warm and cuddly *euphemisms* to describe deadly interventions is among the most obvious. Certainly the formation of an *organized* and *collective denial* that is systemic and embraced by peers and superiors is an essential element, enabled by and enabling a *consensual reality*: "blind spots, shared illusions and zones of tacitly denied information."[263] Equally important in this constellation is what Cohen calls *interpretive denial*, by which he means phenomena such as gleaning from a Donald Trump stump speech that he stands with the working class, or that the first Gulf War was about defending Kuwaiti democracy, or that attacks on gay and abortion rights "defend the family," or that "guns don't kill people, people kill people," or even that riches will come to you if you simply send a chain letter to ten more people.

Other varieties of interpretive denial intentionally provoked by controlled linguistic formations are addressed in a post-9/11 anthology called *Collateral Language: A User's Guide to America's New War*.[264] Focusing on the Orwellian rhetoric characterizing the Bush administration's response to the attacks, each contributor takes on one of the key terms that, as long as it flies under the radar of critical analysis, can be used to successfully manipulate the public's perceptions and emotions. Words such as "terrorism," "civilization," "freedom," and "fundamentalism" are explored and denuded of the interpretive gloss that the mass media breathlessly and routinely bestowed upon them. In an essay examining the word "targets," for instance, political scientist Philip T. Neisser, in the manner of Carol Cohn, parses the euphemistic and abstract uses of the term that keep the citizenry comfortable with brutal attacks. While most people will approve of a bombing raid that "successfully" hits its "military target"—implying that civilians are not affected and we have committed no war crimes—Neisser reminds us that "targets considered 'military' might be gas pipelines, water treatment plants, bridges, and the like, all things that civilians may depend on for their very lives."[265]

SPEECH ACTS: DESIGNATIONS, DEFINITIONS, AND INFORMATION VACUUMS

In another chapter of *Collateral Language*, philosopher Laura Rediehs analyzes the term "evil," which, like the term "terrorist," begets a raft of ramifications that cannot be gainsaid when arbitrarily assigned to a group or individual.

When viewed within the schema of what Rediehs calls the *individual theory*, "evil is an irrational force that inheres in people."[266] This approach, she argues, denies the complexity of the subject, rendering it a matter of faith and obliterating the possibility of analyzing or responding to it effectively. However, if one views the notion of evil within what she calls the *structural theory*, "the word 'evil' should properly only be applied to specific actions or events.... [T]he people who brought forth evil are thought to have done so either because they mistakenly thought they were doing something good, or because they mistakenly felt justified in inflicting harm."[267] This perspective yields insight that can lead to more productive outcomes than, say, engaging in endless reprisals.

Rediehs's individual theory was the prevailing vehicle through which governmental and mass media deployed the term "evil" in regard to the "fanatics" who executed the 9/11 strikes: they were crazed, preternaturally vile beings who "hated our freedoms" and took ghoulish pleasure in destroying them. This notion of evil, in all its radical simplicity, leaves no viable way of responding other than to simply annihilate the evildoers from the earth. This can, of course, be a useful way of framing the situation when you *want* a public to acquiesce in the annihilation of certain people from the earth. For instance, when the United States and European Union "designated" Hamas a "terrorist organization," the latter's ostensibly wicked acts—suicide bombings, rocket attacks—could only be condemned as the work of depraved, hateful people, despite the fact that Israel, the United States, and many other state actors have perpetrated far more destructive measures against civilians. It was the *group itself*, not simply its specific actions, that received wholesale condemnation, so whatever Hamas did or didn't do henceforth, the taint of irremediable evil would remain with them and continue to justify retribution.

In October 2021, the Israeli Defense Ministry took a more audacious step by issuing a military order designating six Palestinian civil society groups as terrorist organizations, raising an outcry of indignation around the world. "Terrorist" is a term that, when wielded, has the additional advantage of implicating any who would hesitate to condemn the entity to which it is attached. The only way to deflate its potency is to venture to define it, which government leaders and news media scrupulously refrain from doing so as not to reveal the company of their own deeds in its sullied ambit.

Yet UN High Commissioner for Human Rights Michelle Bachelet did this when her office issued an online statement declaring the specified groups "some of the most reputable human rights and humanitarian groups in the occupied Palestinian territory…[who] for decades have worked closely with the UN." More importantly, Bachelet went on to say, "Claiming rights before a UN or other international body is not an act of terrorism, advocating for the rights of women in the occupied Palestinian territory is not terrorism, and providing legal aid to detained Palestinians is not terrorism."[268]

Human Rights Watch underscored the severity of the charge, explaining in a release that, by virtue of a 2016 Israeli statute, the designation "effectively outlaws the activities of these civil society groups, it authorizes Israeli authorities to close their offices, seize their assets and arrest and jail their staff members, and it prohibits funding or even publicly expressing support for their activities." In a joint statement with Amnesty International, the group called the move "an attack by the Israeli government on the international human rights movement" and added, "For decades, Israeli authorities have systematically sought to muzzle human rights monitoring and punish those who criticize its repressive rule over Palestinians."[269]

Strong, persuasive, and necessary statements. Yet we also have here an issue of audience. Who reads UN human rights press releases? Who reads Human Rights Watch and Amnesty International reports? Which news media incorporate their findings in their coverage? Most people learn of the events written about in these documents, if at all, filtered through their news outlet of choice. For many, that is a cable network and/or their local newspaper, and for both, human rights reports almost always fall outside of their circumscribed sphere of reportage.

A good example of the problem: after Amnesty International issued a damning and detailed report called "Israel's Apartheid Against Palestinians" in February 2022, weeks went by and the *New York Times* did not give it a single mention, virtually orchestrating its nonexistence for many *Times* readers. James North, writing in *Mondoweiss,* pointed out that "the best way the *Times* could counter Amnesty was to pretend the apartheid finding had never happened." He noted that the foreign bureaus of most regional US newspapers have closed in recent decades, television news' coverage of foreign stories "is laughably inadequate or nonexistent," and National Public Radio "included precisely one report about Israel's apartheid on its website. Its announcers have said not a word on air." As "*The Times* sets the agenda, at least inside the US," for most people living in the United States, Amnesty's report effectively never happened.[270] It is very hard to convince people that something exists if they have never heard of it.

By contrast, people who are already affiliated with advocacy organizations are likely to learn of events falling outside the scope of their usual news-following via house organs—historically disseminated in the form of mailed newsletters, nowadays on the Internet. Thus, the Zionist Organization of America was able to introduce its readers to the story of the six demonized human rights groups as if only their allegedly overdue, apt, and welcome designation, and not its widespread condemnation, was the breaking news:

> For years, the brutal, Arab-Marxist-Leninist terror organization, Popular Front for the Liberation of Palestine (PFLP), has been operating a network of front-groups that pose as "human rights" non-governmental organizations (NGOs), but in reality aid and abet the PLFP's goal of destroying Israel. These NGOs obtain and funnel to the PFLP millions of dollars of foreign funding, using forged documents and fictitious humanitarian projects; provide critical support for PFLP terror activities; and are led by and employ numerous PFLP terror operatives.[271]

The UN report headed by Bachelet clearly stated, "There is no evidence presented to support these accusations, no information on the type of alleged 'PFLP terror activity,' nor has any public process been conducted to establish the allegations."[272] Yet that critique, too, doesn't have a chance of raising doubts for people who have no idea that it has been made. The pile-up of allegedly malevolent elements that compose these human rights organizations in ZOA's account, each one intended to be read as an a priori "evil" in itself, leaves little doubt that eradicating the groups themselves will bring relief to the good people of the world. In a society where the flow of information is so fragmented, one can't call out something as a lie or propaganda in a realm that that simply obliterates all traces of such challenges. The establishment of information vacuums is a crucial form of denial.

WALTER LIPPMANN AND "THE PICTURES IN OUR HEADS"

One common form of denial involves stage-managing news reporting so that incriminating images of disturbing realities are replaced with pacifying, socially acceptable substitutes. The Pulitzer Prize-winning journalist Walter Lippmann explored in his 1922 book, *Public Opinion,* the ways that people construe realities that are beyond their immediate experience. People then, as now, lacked direct access to the realms in which news was made, observed, or concocted—because, after all, no person can be everywhere at once (even in the age of the Internet, where eyewitness reports and on-site video footage come with their own interventions). Lippmann was concerned that too many accepted ignorance as a comfortable life choice, voting and acting as if they actually knew something when they didn't. He had earlier been a sharp critic of censorship in the Creel Committee, and, more broadly, of unaccountability in news reporting. His 1920 *Liberty and the News* had posed pointed questions about the meaning of democracy when a voting public is systematically ill-informed and dependent on the impressions left by news media, which could be deliberately manipulative or even simply touched by the distorting vagaries of subjectivity.[273] Lippmann held that people grasped reality via the "pictures in their heads,"[274] derived from the media, of the events they could not know firsthand—which, in a complex world, amounted to almost everything. Therefore, participation in important social decision-making was made not by fully cognizant actors but rather by the equivalent of Plato's cave men, content to perceive shadows of shadows as truth.

Our beliefs, then, are constructed from "fictions and symbols," or "mental images" of events derived from other sources. "By fictions I do not mean lies," writes Lippmann. He simply means that we inevitably rely on the second- or thirdhand representations we form of reality. These representations govern our actions, and for Lippmann, propaganda is simply "the effort to alter the picture to which men respond, to substitute one social pattern for another."[275]

Propaganda is also successful insofar as it draws upon what Lippmann calls the "stereotypes" we form of events based on our "stock of images": "We do not so much see this man and that sunset; rather we notice that the thing is man or sunset, and then see chiefly what our mind is already full of on those subjects." Lippmann understands that "[t]here is economy in this. For the attempt to see all things freshly and in detail, rather than as types and generalities, is exhausting...." Nonetheless, this "repertory of stereotypes" is a treasure trove easily dipped into by those who would manipulate us for their own purposes, and it is based on these that "public opinion" is formed.[276]

Knowing that their jobs depend on varying degrees of self-censorship, journalists often inform only from the vantage point they encounter as, say, an "embedded" reporter in a military squadron. At other times, realities are effaced *despite* journalists' attempts to portray what governments don't want their publics to see. Those governments may block reporters' access to spheres of action, manipulate the vehicles of transmission that would convey their stories, brazenly demolish their offices and equipment, arrest or deport them, or, most crudely, kill them. The Israeli government has used all of these methods, almost invariably citing "security" concerns as a rationale for denying the world media (as well as Israeli and Palestinian media) permission to enter the scenes of atrocities. Thus, if those media are to report on an event at all, they are reliant upon the narratives about it delivered by authorized Israeli spokespeople.

SEE NO EVIL

The year 2009 began amid Operation Cast Lead, at that time one of Israel's harshest military offensives in Gaza. In its annual World Press Freedom Index for that year, Reporters Without Borders, an international nonprofit, nongovernmental organization, noted that Israel had taken a "nosedive" in its rankings, falling below Kuwait, the United Arab Emirates, and Lebanon. The main reasons cited were arrests, convictions, and deportations of journalists (both foreign and Palestinian), as well as Israel's ongoing military censorship and the destruction of buildings housing Palestinian news media. Significantly, "foreign and Israeli media were denied access to the Gaza Strip throughout the offensive," they wrote.[277] Unfortunately, the ultimate consumers of the news were largely unaware of this, as the secondhand nature of the reportage became buried in quotations about what happened "according to" carefully trained official sources who, with their impressive job titles, seemed authoritative.

While firsthand eyewitness reportage was blocked, Israel got its message out via the newly formed National Information Directorate, a governmental body designed to rectify the bad *hasbara* that had dimmed world opinion of Israel as it slaughtered civilians and devasted infrastructure in the 2006 Lebanon war. "One of the challenges of Israel's media offensive has been to counter the disturbing images of Gaza in the conflict," wrote Rachel Shabi in *The Guardian* at the time. She quotes Aviv Shir-On, foreign ministry deputy director-general for public affairs: "In the war of the pictures we lose, so you need to correct, explain or balance it in other ways."[278] To plant the correct "pictures" in heads around the globe, the directorate, wrote Shabi, "tightly coordinated key messages and worked on so many levels—mainstream media as well as diplomatic channels, friendship leagues, YouTube, Twitter and the blogosphere—that the effect was epidemic. It got world media repeating the Israeli government's core messages practically verbatim."[279]

Also in *The Guardian,* Chris McGreal, one of those prohibited from entering the war zone "on the pretext of security," wrote, "An Israeli official told me they were delighted at a BBC TV correspondent, broadcasting from Ashkelon in a flak jacket, reinforcing the impression that the Israeli city is a war zone when there is more chance of being hit by a car than a rocket."[280] In the *Jerusalem Post,* Haviv Rettig Gur reported Shir-on citing the results of one eight-hour period of tracking international television stations. Out of 335 combined minutes of Gaza coverage, "58 minutes were given to Israeli representatives, while only 19 were given to Palestinian ones." "Israeli *hasbara* is fulfilling its missions," Shir-on brightly concluded.[281]

The Israeli Foreign Press Association, representing over 400 members of major global print and electronic news organizations, petitioned the Israeli High Court to allow media access to Gaza as well as to what Israeli called a "closed military zone" inside Israel along the Gaza border. "The claim that this is being done 'for our protection' is patently ridiculous," the FPA said in a statement,[282] and called the entry ban "an unprecedented restriction of press freedom."[283] Human Rights Watch concurred, pointing out that they too were barred from entry, and that the exclusion of journalists and human rights workers from conflict areas eliminates "an essential check on human rights abuses and laws-of-war violations."[284] The High Court ruled that some journalists should be allowed in, and the government agreed to admit eight journalists into Gaza "every time it opens the border at the Erez crossing, but so far the crossing has remained closed to entry," HRW asserted.[285]

The journalist Peter Lagerquist, who was among the photojournalists and TV crews consigned to glean what little they could from the Israeli side of the border, later reflected upon an online *New York Times* piece on the situation in Gaza that ran on January 25, 2009, called "Photographer's Journal: A War's Many Angles." As he describes it:

> The feature comprised two sets of images taken from either side of the border, accompanied by the photographers' audio testimony. The Israeli collage is marked by its somber sense of interiority, showing soldiers praying in quiet dignity, mourning falling comrades, taking a break.... Not a single one is shooting, loading a gun, or cleaning a tank barrel. Plumes of smoke across the border are pictured only distantly, one of them from some elevation, unfurling elegiacally from a remote, empty beach. It is as if some other army were in the process of killing fourteen hundred people."[286]

The veteran journalist Robert Fisk wrote in the *Independent* at the time, "Back in 1980, the Soviet Union threw every Western journalist out of Afghanistan.... That the Israelis should use an old Soviet tactic to blind the world's vision of war may not be surprising."[287]

Meanwhile, the Anti-Defamation League did its part by issuing "key talking points" for use in op-eds and other media abroad. Among those points are many whose veracity, for some, will feel ratified by memories of mainstream news coverage at the time, though this is a tautological sort of confirmation: the talking points disseminated by the ADL and the New Information Directorate, rather than the firsthand observations of international journalists, were of course the sources behind the reports to begin with. These points came to pass for common knowledge. Among them were these artfully packaged truisms:

- "Israel's military action in Gaza is in response to the nearly constant barrage of rockets and missiles launched by Hamas and other terrorist organizations in Gaza. Israel is fulfilling its duty and responsibility to protect the people of Israel who have been terrorized by the ongoing assault by Hamas."

- "Israel is taking maximum precautions to avoid harming civilians in Gaza.... The targets include Hamas command centers, training camps, rocket manufacturing facilities, storage warehouses and tunnels used to smuggle arms. According to the Israel Defense Forces spokesman, and confirmed in numerous media reports, 'the vast majority of the casualties are terror operatives....'"
- "Hamas "cynically and deliberately puts ordinary Palestinians in harm's way by establishing its terrorist infrastructure...within densely populated areas, in the midst of homes, schools, mosques and hospitals. Hamas is an Islamic extremist terrorist organization that calls for the eradication of the State of Israel."[288]

These methods of "putting pictures in our heads" were hardly unique to the 2009 siege of Gaza. In its 2021 report, Reporters Without Borders still assessed Israel as a "toxic environment" for journalism:

> Smear campaigns have been waged against media outlets and journalists by politicians with the help of their party and supporters, exposing the targets to harassment and anonymous messages and forcing them to seek personal protection....Because of self-censorship, there is little or no coverage of the reality of life in the Palestinian territories. Foreign free-lancers often have difficulties in obtaining or renewing accreditation. The Israeli Defense Forces often violate the rights of Palestinian journalists, especially when they are covering demonstrations or clashes in the West Bank or Gaza Strip.[289]

In a May 19, 2021 news bulletin, Reporters Without Borders wrote specifically about the impact of denying access to foreign media. The IDF had just begun another round of air strikes on Gaza:

> By obstructing coverage, the ban is preventing international public opinion from being properly informed about what is happening on the ground in the Gaza Strip and is fueling suspicion that the Israeli authorities want to cover up the impact of their airstrikes.... [I]t is the counterpart of the targeted destruction of some 20 Palestinian, regional

and international media outlets in the Gaza Strip, which RSF has already condemned....[290]

Cutting off access to journalists and humanitarian workers during a military campaign has repeatedly allowed Israel to shape its "narrative"—as many refer to it—without interference from objective observers. As a result, even conscientious third-party reports must often resort to an "Israelis said, Palestinians said" sort of recounting, in which evidence-deficient "balance" must substitute for actual data. A 2002 Amnesty International report made the point that the lack of access *was* a centrally significant finding via its title, "Shielded from scrutiny: IDF violations in Jenin and Nablus," which covered Israel's brutal Operation Defensive Shield during the Second Intifada. AI reported that Israeli officials "declared areas 'closed military areas,' barring access to the outside world."[291] Furthermore, "Throughout the period 4-15 April, the IDF denied access to Jenin refugee camp to all, including medical doctors and nurses, ambulances, humanitarian relief services, human rights organizations, and journalists."[292] Israel refused to submit to any sort of outside inquiry:

> A United Nations (UN) visiting mission ordered by the UN Commission on Human Rights on 5 April 2002 and headed by Mary Robinson, UN High Commissioner for Human Rights was not allowed to enter Israel and disbanded; even a high level Fact-Finding mission agreed between Foreign Minister Shimon Peres and UN Secretary-General Kofi Annan and welcomed by unanimous vote of the UN Security Council was not allowed to enter Israel and disbanded after weeks of negotiations.[293]

In addition to blocking outside media observers' view of savage attacks, Israel targets those (mostly locals who are trapped inside Gaza or the West Bank by Israeli travel bans for the long term but linked professionally to foreign or Palestinian media outlets[294]) who do manage to capture evidence on-site. Just a few examples:

- On July 2, 2014, the International Federation of Journalists (IFJ) and the Palestinian Journalists Syndicate (PJS) condemned "a brutal attack by Israeli forces on a Palestinian TV crew in Shufat Refugee Camp, near Jerusalem...." in which "the Israeli soldiers fired gas canisters, stun grenades and rubber coated bullets towards them." IFJ President Jim Boumela commented, "Media freedom is being undermined, basic human rights are being blatantly ignored and Palestinian journalists are being injured and killed for no other reason than they are doing their jobs and reporting the truth."[295]

- On April 5, 2018, Yasser Murtaja, a 30-year-old Gazan news photographer wearing a vest that clearly identified him as press, was fatally shot by Israeli army snipers at Gaza's border with Israel as he covered the Great March of Return. The IDF announced it would investigate the incident, but, according to the *Los Angeles Times,* a year later there had been no probe—only accusations, without any evidence, from the Netanyahu government that Murtaja was "100% a Hamas officer.... There is not a scintilla of doubt." Murtaja was the cofounder of Ain Media, a company that had received a grant from the United States Agency for International Development (USAID) to set up a graphics department after having "navigated stringent U.S. government vetting requirements."[296]

- Israeli forces have repeatedly targeted news agencies and their infrastructure directly. They generally claim to be doing it for "security" measures, aiming at "terrorists" or those "linked to Hamas"[297]—though evidence of such is seldom, if ever, furnished, and the claim is widely considered an alibi for cordoning off credible reporting on Gaza from the world. For instance, in January 2002, Israeli forces destroyed the television and radio building of the Palestinian Authority in Ramallah.[298] In May 2019 they destroyed the building that housed the bureau of the Turkish state news agency Anadolu, demolishing all the bureau's equipment and material.[299] In May 2021, an Israeli air strike leveled the eleven-story al-Jalaa tower in Gaza City, in which the offices of major international media organizations, including the Associated Press, Al Jazeera, and Middle East Eye, were located—just "narrowly avoid[ing] a terrible loss of life," according to the AP.[300] Gary Pruitt, president and CEO of the AP, said that the Israeli military had "long known the location of our bureau and knew journalists were there."[301] Dr. Mostefa Souag, acting director general of Al Jazeera Media Network, said, "The aim of this heinous crime is to silence the media and to hide the untold carnage and suffering of the people of Gaza."[302] *The Intercept* pointed out that, in fact, "more than 20 Gazan media outlets [were] razed by Israeli airstrikes" in that week alone. "All the reporting currently coming out of the territory is being done by Gazan journalists."[303] And "the more the international press relies on them, the larger the targets on their backs become."[304]

THE PICTURES ON OUR SCREENS

As social media evolved into a prime conduit of information-sharing, Israel naturally trained its image- and perception-molding apparatus on the Internet. Like underdogs everywhere, Palestinians had seized upon the newfound ability to bypass formal media and governmental channels to get their message out to the world. Social media has, of course, been touted as a democratizing and field-leveling force for those previously without the power to reach crucial and far-flung audiences. Yet the Internet also exposes the architects and circulators of ideas to vast new levels of surveillance and control.

Tactics to foil the promise of "digital Palestine" have emerged in multiple arenas. Israel has at its disposal sophisticated tracking technologies, a capability that has led to imprisonment of Palestinians in the Occupied Territories for online speech, while its global reach is underwritten by a vast network of Israel advocacy organizations and the complicity of technology companies.

According to a December 2021 article in *Foreign Policy* by Emerson T. Brooking and Eliza Campbell, "As Palestinians found their digital voice through the mid-2000s,....[t]he Israeli Defense Forces (IDF) invested heavily in its online influence capabilities, recruiting bloggers and graphic designers and establishing a strong presence on Facebook, Twitter and YouTube." In addition, "Israeli college students organized *hasbara* rooms" to counter negative portrayals of Israel in international media; "fake Facebook accounts" were created by the Israeli security forces, identifying and leading to the arrest of over 300 "for Facebook activity they claimed demonstrated 'incitement to violence and terrorism'; and in 2016 Israel redefined "incitement" to "include any demonstration of 'solidarity' with terrorism or terrorist organizations" (which, of course, Israel may capriciously "designate" as such).[305] According to a 2015 report by the advocacy organization Palestine Legal and the Center for Constitutional

Rights, titled "The Palestine Exception to Free Speech," in January 2015, "the Reut Institute [a Zionist think tank] reportedly held a 'hackathon,' in which Israeli officials and a number of other Israeli advocacy groups participated, aimed at exploring ways to gather intelligence on and target individuals involved in Palestine solidarity work."[306]

In 2017, *Haaretz* reported that the Israeli government had acquired a software system that allowed it to "monitor social media in general and specific users in particular" as well as to be able to "plant ideas in conversations in social networks and forums through an automated or semiautomated mechanism." Oded Yaron, the article's author, mused, "The real question is what the government is doing with the system." "Swaying an existing debate" was one potential use he considered; another was homing in on individual supporters of the boycott, divestment, and sanctions movement.[307]

Brooking and Campbell note, "According to figures compiled by 7amleh [The Arab Center for Social Media Advancement, pronounced "Hamla" in Arabic], a Palestinian digital rights organization, roughly 2,000 Palestinians have been arrested by Israeli security officials for social media posts since 2017." The article's authors point out that Palestinians "cannot know if a Facebook 'like' directed at any number of Palestinian political bodies may be construed as support for terrorism or when a new group may be declared a terrorist entity."[308]

Human Rights Watch found that Facebook had "wrongfully removed and suppressed" posts revealing human rights abuses in Israel/Palestine. In May 2021, the group wrote that "[u]sers and digital rights organizations...reported hundreds of deleted posts, suspended or restricted accounts, disabled groups, reduced visibility, lower engagement with content, and blocked hashtags." Significantly, HRW points out that "Facebook relies on the list of organizations that the US has designated as a 'foreign terrorist organization,' among other lists."[309] HRW wrote to Facebook in June 2021 to inquire further, but reported that, "the company did not answer any of the specific questions from Human Rights Watch or meaningfully address any of the issues raised."[310]

In May 2021, a meeting took place on Zoom between Israeli Defense Minister Benny Gantz and TikTok and Facebook executives "regarding anti-Israel content that has been uploaded or published on their platforms," according to *The Jerusalem Post*. Gantz "called on the executives to remove content which can possibly incite violence or spread misinformation."[311] Israel National News, a media outlet that describes itself as a "network identifying with religious Zionism," added that in that meeting Gantz further asserted that "we expect your assistance" and that the executives "expressed commitment to act quickly and effectively."[312] The *Post* concluded with the observation—with which Walter Lippmann would certainly agree—that "activists across the spectrum have recognized the power these images have to shape the narrative on the ground." The following week, Al Jazeera revealed that "online posts expressing solidarity with Palestinians attacked by Israeli police at Al-Aqsa Mosque in Jerusalem were...deleted or blocked, users reported."[313]

It is not unusual for technology companies to readily accede to Israel's wishes. Brooking and Campbell describe an Israeli Cyber Unit instituted in 2015 "that has issued tens of thousands of content removal requests to Facebook, Twitter, and YouTube, mostly alleging violent incitement or support for terrorism." Though these are, in fact "requests" and not legally binding, "social media companies have complied with the Cyber Unit's requests roughly 90 percent of the time." The Cyber Unit is an extra-governmental entity, backed by the Israeli state but not subject to its constitutional laws and oversight, so that it can "target the speech of any internet user—that of an Israeli citizen, a Palestinian resident, or a neutral third party anywhere in the world—and launch a suppression campaign that remains effectively invisible to the outside observers." Brooking and Campbell conclude, "The Israeli government has established a remarkably effective series of systems to suppress Palestinian speech. Technology companies, seeking to reduce legal and political risk, have done the rest."[314]

On May 30, 2010, a civilian fleet known as the Gaza Freedom Flotilla attempted to break the Israeli blockade of the Strip and bring in humanitarian supplies. It was intercepted in international waters by Israeli commandos who raided the Turkish ship *Mavi Marmara*, killing ten activists and injuring many more. The tech-savvy activists and journalists on board the boats live streamed their journey to viewers around the world.[315] However, after boarding the ship, detaining the passengers (who were cut off for many days from contact with the outside world), and confiscating their media footage, the IDF handed the booty over to its public relations department. There the videos were edited, captioned, and uploaded to YouTube to support Israel's claim that the commandos had been the victims, rather than the aggressors, of the affair, and had been acting in self-defense.[316] Diana Allen and Curtis Brown write in "The *Mavi Marmara* at the Frontlines of Web 2.0":

> Pro-Palestinian bloggers and commentators—as well as the journalists and activists who had been aboard the *Mavi Marmara,* once they were released from Israeli detention days later—scoffed at this PR strategy, pointing out the evidentiary gaps and the fact that the vast preponderance of video and photographic evidence remained suppressed. Meanwhile, photos and footage successfully smuggled off the ship (in one instance, in a documentary filmmaker's underwear) began appearing online, dramatically contradicting the Israeli narrative.[317]

Israel's online crisis management machinery was fairly well-oiled by then. At the time of Operation Cast Lead—a little more than a year prior to the *Mavi Marmara* raid—Israel had launched its own YouTube channel and an "Internet Warfare Team," whose

> paid members would pose as ordinary web surfers and post pro-Israel commentary and talking points on Twitter, Facebook and in the blogsphere. Other recruits uploaded thousands of "positive" pictures of Israel (desalination plants, solar panel farms, female IDF soldiers in bikinis, etc.) so that Google searches would be less likely to turn up images of occupation and devastation. In 2007, Hasbara Fellowships (cosponsored by the Foreign Ministry) began organizing "a team of Wikipedians to make sure Israel is presented fairly and accurately," and in 2010 the YESHA Council (representing the settler movement) joined in, offering courses in how to edit Wikipedia from a pro-Israel point of view.[318]

Sadly, Israel's formidable reach far exceeded that of the activists. Despite trenchant follow-up questions to the IDF posed by journalists seeking evidence of Israel's claims, "the spokesperson's office had to admit there was no evidence."[319] Allen and Brown reference Malcolm Gladwell's observation that Web 2.0 "makes it easier for activists to express themselves, and harder for that expression to have any impact."[320]

Other manifestations of the "digital occupation" abound and reveal the tech industry's willingness to hew to Israel's "requests." Google did, on the one hand, finally allow that Palestine existed, making it discoverable on its search engine and giving it a homepage soon after the UN General Assembly conferred "non-member observer state" status upon it, similar to that of the Vatican, in November 2012. Palestinian comedian Maysoon Zayid quipped in the *Daily Beast,* "If Google said that Palestine exists, it must be true. They do make the maps and everyone knows if you find it on Google it is an undeniable fact."[321]

However, Palestine—state or not—remains conspicuously absent on Google Maps. "When searching for 'Palestine' on Google Maps," Nayeli Lomeli wrote in *USA Today,* "the map zooms in on the Israel-Palestine region, and both the Gaza Strip and West Bank territories are labeled and separated by dotted lines. But there is no label for Palestine."[322] Tom Suarez had previously written in *Mondoweiss* about "Google's attempt to *de-exist* Palestine" and described its "blocking cartographic information from Palestinians as a tool of ethnic control." Comparing this action to the practice in Orwell's *1984* of sending pesky old truths down the Memory Hole, Suarez wrote, "Google Maps has turned Palestinian towns and cities into ghosts. They appear... yet according to the technology Goliath they do not exist as places one can actually *get* to." He finds, specifically,

> If you want to go between West Bank towns, even major cities such as Jericho, Bethlehem, or Hebron, Google will reply *Sorry, we could not calculate these driving directions from....* But if West Bank settlers want to visit other West Bank settlements, Google is at their service.[323]

"Cartographic thuggery," he calls it, and points out, by contrast,

> When HarperCollins produced a (printed) book for the Middle East market with a map which did not label Israel, the uproar was palpable; the publisher was accused of antisemitism and of wishing to "wipe Israel off the map," understanding the phrase's connotation far beyond the cartographic. The books were pulped.

Introducing a report called "Mapping Segregation: Google Maps and the Human Rights of Palestinians," the group 7amleh noted that "Google holds immense power as the largest source of digital geographic data in the world, to shape and legitimize certain interpretations of the physical world and the politics that underpin it." This, the group aptly maintains, "helps form public opinion that serves the interests of the Israeli government...." Another point raised by 7ameleh is that some Bedouin villages in the Naqab that Israeli authorities do not "recognize" may date back to the seventh century (another speech act denial) yet do not appear on Google Maps. They are marked, instead, according to their tribe or clan names rather than their village names and "are only visible when zooming in very closely but otherwise appear to be non-existent"—in contrast to Israeli villages, which are legible even when zoomed-out. The report mentions, too, that Google's directions within the West Bank steer users to time-consuming routes that pass through Israel rather than more direct routes within the West Bank. "Google Maps is unable to calculate routes within Palestinian rural communities, or to and from Gaza, displaying the message 'Sorry, we could not calculate driving/walking directions from x to y.'" 7amleh adds that Google Maps "automatically calculates routes specifically for Israeli ID holders"—those whose license plates signal that they are entitled to use expedient 'bypass roads' from which Palestinians are banned—while omitting to mark checkpoints at which Palestinian travelers are routinely delayed and frequently harassed.

Other examples of the "digital occupation" proliferate. In May 2021, just after a ceasefire had been actuated in Gaza between Israel and Hamas, seven journalists—and many other Palestinians—got only the message, "Your phone is banned from using WhatsApp. Contact support for help" when they tried to use the service owned by Facebook. (The company did not reply when contacted.) Reporters Without Borders commented, "This is not the first time that Palestinian journalists have been stripped of access to WhatsApp at a time when many news events are taking place and following developments as they happen is crucial," citing previous, similar blockage of WhatsApp service for employees of the BBC and the Turkish news agency Anadolu during Israeli sorties in the region.[324]

Also in May 2021, the electronic payment app Venmo hindered transactions whose recipient's name included the words "Palestine Relief Fund." One user said he was trying to donate money to the Palestinian Children's Relief Fund, an organization designed to help sick and injured children get medical care. His payment was delayed while Venmo did an inquiry into the purpose of the funds. A spokesperson for Venmo wrote in an email that the problem "was OFAC related and we're looking into it." OFAC is the US Treasury's Office of Foreign Assets Control, which "keeps track of countries and individuals under U.S. sanctions." Venmo is owned by PayPal, which has continually refused requests to provide service for Palestinians in Gaza and the West Bank—though it operates in Israel and over 200 other countries. 7amleh has pointed out that this puts Palestinians trying to interact with the global market at an unfair disadvantage.[325]

Other social media suppression strategies that Palestinian groups have reported being subjected to include "shadow banning"—"the practice of restricting social media content that is not noticeable to the user"; "striking"—an escalating series of "disciplinary actions" used by Instagram and Facebook;[326] "language discrimination," in which YouTube users who post Arabic-language videos (including those with Arabic titles or subtitles) are flagged for higher levels of surveillance; "locative discrimination," referring to the fact that "YouTube's surveillance AI machines are designed and operationalized for a higher level of scrutiny of content emerging from the West Bank and Gaza....";[327] "hash matching," in which "a fingerprint of an image is compared with a database of known harmful images"; and "keyword filtering," in which "words that indicate potentially harmful content are used to flag particular content."[328] One West Bank YouTube user conducted an experiment to test his perception of "locative discrimination": "I sent the same video which was deleted from my YouTube account to my friend's YouTube account in Europe [...] and YouTube was fine with the video published in a European country."[329]

There are at least two notorious instances in which "the pictures in our heads" hijacked the pictures on our screens, as if to wryly illustrate Walter Lippman's argument in *Public Opinion* that we "see" what we have *already* been persuaded to see.

In the summer of 2014, Israel killed 2,251 Palestinians, including 1,462 civilians and 551 children (while 73 Israelis died, 67 of them soldiers) during Operation Protective Edge in Gaza.[330] Yet for mainstream media watchers in the United States, what was overwhelmingly encountered was not the carnage in Gaza, but rather the refrain tweeted by the IDF and echoed by countless news anchors and editors that "barrages of rockets are being fired nonstop from Gaza into southern Israel."[331] It wasn't surprising, then, that ABC World News anchor Diane Sawyer, upon seeing pictures of destruction and desolation, instinctively narrated, "We take you overseas now to the rockets raining down on Israel…And here an Israeli family trying to salvage what they can, one woman standing speechless among the ruins."

The pathos was moving, but Peter Hart of Fairness and Accuracy in Reporting (FAIR) had to break the news to ABC World News that they had misidentified the people in the photographs, who were actually Gazans stunned by Israeli missile attacks. "'Running in terror as sirens wail' is how ABC correspondent Alex Marquardt began the segment right after Sawyer's introduction," writes Hart, who observed that at that point there had been little damage and no reported deaths in Israel. Nonetheless, the item of chief interest to US media was Israeli fear of what *could* happen, rather than Gazans living in the tragic aftermath of a real onslaught. Yousef Munayyer of the Palestine Center and Rania Khalek writing in the *Electronic Intifada* had also revealed the error, but their message was unlikely to reach the viewers of corporate news.[332]

Then, in February 2022, as the world's attention and sympathies were focused on the Russian invasion of Ukraine, a photograph taken in the Gaza Strip in May, 2021, by Agence France-Presse photographer Mahmud Hamsimage in the wake of Israeli air strikes was mistaken for something else. "WORLD WAR THREE: Russia has just attacked Ukraine," proclaimed the caption of a February 24 Facebook post; other Facebook postings similarly mislabeled it, reported *USA Today*.[333]

Many Palestinians and their supporters have remarked upon the startling disjuncture between what the media showed us of the wreckage and bloodbath in Ukraine and the dearth of circulation of equivalent images from Gaza. Their rightful charges of "hypocrisy" are more pertinent to the corporate news outlets than to their audiences, who cannot know what they are not seeing and are largely unaware of the existence of independent news media, which could fill in the gaps. Yet the enormous disparity in US public opinion about Ukraine and about Palestine—spurring (or not) boycotts, widespread support for sanctions, foreign aid, fundraisers, charges of "war crimes," calls for justice to be meted out by the International Criminal Court, public declarations of solidarity with the victims from institutions and groups—has everything to do with the media's propagandistic choices to reveal or to conceal atrocities.

American viewers have made it clear that they are ready to commiserate with people whose lives are in ruins, but that response can only come if, first, they are exposed to representations of the ruinous reality, and second, if the brutality is not justified as serving a greater good. While ordinary Ukrainians have been mobilized to fight back against the Russian onslaught, the American mass media does not call them "militants" or "terrorists" (as opposed to "civilians"), questions are not raised about the notion that they are honorably "defending themselves," and there is no sneering about the "martyrdom" of those who have fallen. Thus, when Americans view homes reduced to rubble and innocent people attempting to hide when there is no means of escape, the "pictures in their heads" say "Ukraine" even when the reality is otherwise and the stirrings in their hearts say, "Something must be done to stop this."

CHAPTER 5:
JEWISH NATIONALISM AND THE MANUFACTURE OF CONSENT

"Zionism is one of the greatest public relations success stories of the twentieth century."—Avi Shlaim, Israeli "New Historian"[334]

ENGINEERING PUBLIC OPINION, MANUFACTURING CONSENT

The notion that uniform public attitudes not only *could* but *should* be "scientifically" constructed was formally broached by Edward Bernays, the creator of the field of public relations. An employee of the World War I-era Committee on Public Information (discussed in Chapter 2), Bernays emerged deeply impressed by the group's achievements—not least of which was persuading people to support activities that undermined their own interests and averted basic rationality. As the media critic Mark Crispin Miller has put it, "Here was an extraordinary state accomplishment: mass enthusiasm at the prospect of a global brawl that otherwise would mystify those very masses, and that shattered most of those who actually took part in it."[335]

Bernays realized that what was possible in wartime could be possible, as well, in a host of other spheres and could bolster a wide variety of interests. Bernays's presentation of the project was in the how-to genre. The "technicians" who "engineered consent" among an unwitting public would use tactics similar to those of civil engineers constructing a bridge: research, plan, calculate resources (money, manpower, etc.), and craft a detailed "blueprint" of step-by-step action.[336] Though, as we have seen, propaganda had existed in some form for millennia, Bernays recognized that state-of-the-art tactics could be refined by so-called experts via a new professional field of public relations. This "new propaganda," as Bernays—who happened to be Sigmund Freud's American nephew—also called it, was consciously aimed at its audience's unconscious feelings—that is, at precisely that which is most *irrational* in human beings. Thus it stood as the antithesis of appeals to reason—and a remarkable invention to be peddled to business and political leaders concerned about the rising egalitarian apparatuses of the masses. "The conscious and intelligent manipulation of the organized habits and opinions of the masses is an important element in demo-cratic society," is how he unequivocally opened his 1928 treatise, *Propaganda.* "Those who manipulate this unseen mechanism of society constitute an invisible government which is the true ruling power of our country."[337] He was inexpli-cably confident that the guileful means of this "invisible government" would be put in the service of upright ends—for the masses' own good. Public relations would subsequently be used not only to market products for corporations, but also to sell attitudes and beliefs: political perspectives, economic policies, social conformity, bigotry, patriotism, the corporate ethos, the need for military interventions, perceptions of other countries and cultures, complacency about a rapidly deteriorating environment—and much more.

Even earlier, Walter Lippmann had coined the term "the manufacture of consent."[338] However, in contradistinction to Bernays, Lippmann's analysis was wary and descriptive rather than exultant and prescriptive—a warning rather than a manifesto. Years later, his catchphrase was taken up and made popular by Noam Chomsky and Edward Herman in their 1988 book, *Manufacturing Consent: The Political Economy of the Mass Media.*[339] Just as Lippmann and Bernays had probed the role of the mass media of their own times in construct-ing prevalent attitudes, Chomsky and Herman focused on the consolidation of corporate-owned media in that pre-Internet, virulently anticommunist moment, and those media conglomerates' "symbiotic" interplay with government, "experts," and other business entities to achieve mutually satisfying ends. What the authors called the *real* social role of media in a democracy was the produc-tion of policies that, à la Bernays, protected the interests of the state's business, political, and social elites. Journalists working in that realm knew that the key to professional success lay in internalizing and reproducing the essential mantras that rationalized these interests and rendering them as commonsensical in mass discourse. Similarly, alternative beliefs and discourses had to be fenced outside the margins of civilized discussion and consigned to the realm of the unthinkable. Revelations about nefarious deeds of the US and its allies were to be routinely suppressed, while identical deeds of its enemies would reap scathing exposés.

Feats of manufacturing consent were required to advance the building of nationalist movements that emerged in the nineteenth and twentieth centuries. Much of the writing that launched the Zionist movement contended that all Jews were really part of one "people" or "nation" that differed from other nations principally in their lack of territorial contiguity and a common language. It was their deficient national self-perception, these writers maintained, that kept the flame of eternal antisemitism alive. Inversely, their salvation lay in recognizing and acting upon their latent nationhood, which would make them intelligible as equals to the other nations of the world, commanding their sympathy and respect.

DISAVOWING TWO THOUSAND YEARS OF JEWISH HISTORY

As we have seen, romantic nationalism is predicated on the idea of a modern people sharing continuity with an ancient, common past. Asserting such a connection has constituted one of the main justifications for Jews' claim to the land of Palestine and to their attendant cohesive future. The Jewish "people" may have scattered all over the world, the argument goes, but their experience was exilic, inauthentic, and debased. A central tenet of Zionist philosophy dating from its early days is that of "the negation of the diaspora," also known as "the negation of exile." Zionist historiography leapfrogged over approximately two millennia of Jewish history that unfurled in dispersed geographic and cultural (and inevitably, genetic) circumstances to imagine an unbroken trajectory of the Jewish "people" from the ancient kingdoms of David and Solomon to the "return" to their collective "historic homeland." The ancient time when Jews had last reigned as a "nation" would be welded to the modern nation-state.

This return is described, in Zionist parlance, as "the ingathering of the exiles," accompanied by a sharp repudiation of not only the conditions but the character of diaspora Jews—or at least, those who resided in Europe, since others only appeared in the Zionist imagination as an afterthought. "The Yid" or "the Diaspora Jew" was the reviled, abject Other, or Not-Me, of the emergent Zionist

New Jew, curiously like European antisemitic stereotypes and standing in counterpoint to the New Jew's strapping, dominant, goyish alpha male persona. Here are the words of Vladimir Jabotinsky (1880–1940), an anti-socialist admirer of Mussolini and blunt hardliner, the nemesis of David Ben-Gurion and his comrades, yet another extremely influential leader in Zionist movement-building: "[B]ecause the Yid is ugly, sickly, and lacks decorum, we shall endow the ideal image of the Hebrew with masculine beauty.... The Yid is despised by all and, therefore, the Hebrew ought to charm all. The Yid has accepted submission and, therefore, the Hebrew ought to learn how to command."[340]

From the ostensible other end of the Zionist political spectrum, Ben-Gurion himself referred to the diaspora Jew as "our miserable stepbrother";[341] insisted that exilic life was simply a "miserable, poor, wretched, dubious experience, and it shouldn't be a source of pride;"[342] and declared that there had been no "Jewish history" outside of Palestine. That is, nothing of any significance had happened to the Jews between the Bar Kokhba revolt against the Romans near the beginning of the first millennium CE and the onset of the Zionist "return" in the late nineteenth century.[343]

To make this idea convincing, the Yiddish language itself had to be consigned to the dustbin of history. American rabbi Eli Kavon recounts an incident from the early days of Israeli statehood—that is, not long after the Holocaust—when Ben-Gurion dramatically exited a government-hosted reception for Rozka Korczak, a survivor of the Vilna ghetto and partisan organizer. His complaint: she had delivered her story in Yiddish and, he said, "the language grates on my ears." Kavon points out that Ben-Gurion and every other Israeli leader at that reception spoke Yiddish as a mother tongue yet were committed to silencing that "vibrant and vital language that sustained a civilization for over a millennium."[344]

As Israeli legal scholar Amnon Rubinstein summed it up, "The Hebrew, the new super-Jew, represents everything that has traditionally been associated with the Gentiles, the goyim, the other side.... The Jew would become a 'goy.'"[345] Interestingly, Jews from Arab, Asian, or African countries were absent from this formula; they were not imagined during Zionism's formative years as potentially returning "exiles." They entered this category only much later, when the need for more immigrants to counter Israel's "demographic problem" necessitated thinking outside the European box.

SETTLER COLONISTS CLAIMING INDIGENEITY AND DIVINE RIGHT

Discarding these two thousand years of diverse Jewish experience, along with re-inventing the ancient, prayer-centric language of Hebrew as a modern "Jewish" vernacular, was crucial to embracing the romantic notion of unbroken continuity as a "people." This formulation also conferred upon Jews immigrating from Europe the status of "indigenous" people "reclaiming" their old home, while all those who had arrived over the course of the last two millennia could be depicted as interlopers or "settlers." By this logic, Islam, arriving in the seventh century CE, could be viewed as a hostile, invading dogma, taking over while the legitimate homeowners were away. Lorenzo Veracini, one of the foremost theorists of settler colonial studies, points out, "Indigeneity is always a crucial ideological battle in the politics of representation in settler-colonial contexts":

> ... [A]ll settlers claim in some ways to be or having become "indigenous," or to be "returning." French rule in North Africa was meant to be a "return" to one of the cradles of Western Christianity; the *ventimilia* ("twenty-thousand") peasant colonizers that the Italian fascists sent to Libya were "returning" to Italy's "fourth shore" and to imperial destiny; many Minnesota settlers believed indigenous peoples had exterminated the Vikings who had arrived there first; and even when settler priority cannot be argued, as in Australia and New Zealand, settlers have recurrently fantasized (albeit in very different ways) about indigenous peoples descending from displaced "Aryan tribes" in a way that makes the settlers' ancestors related to those who are indigenous to the land.[346]

One way for settlers to become "effective and convincing indigenizers," Veracini says, "is to craft appropriate foundational stories."[347] David Day, who has delineated how "supplanting societies" around the world create moral justification for their colonial projects, describes several that foreshadow the Zionists in their insistence on a link to legendary societies that far predated them, bolstering their associations with empire-builders and the divine. These provide crucial contexts in which to understand Zionist mythmaking.

For example, Constantinople, which Day says was long "the New York of the Mediterranean world"—also known as Byzantium in its Greek and Roman eras and as Istanbul under Ottoman administration—like Palestine, "was successively conquered and occupied by several different societies, with each in its turn creating a foundation story." The Greeks, he says, "were supposedly guided to the spot by the oracle at Delphi." Constantine, the emperor who famously converted to Christianity and ruled in the fourth century CE, was said to have chosen the site "after being distracted from an alternative settlement by 'a symbolic flight of two eagles.'" When Muslims, led by Mehmet II, conquered the city in 1453, churches became mosques, and the existing symbolic artifacts were replaced with Islamic iconography. "Within fifty years of its conquest by Mehmet, the city of Constantinople, which had no Muslim past, was invested with one," writes Day.[348]

Similarly, when the Spanish dominated the Incas of Peru in the sixteenth century, they disparaged the Inca's own foundation stories as "'fables and extravagances,' portraying the Incas as recent arrivals" and superseding Inca legends with Eurocentric accounts. The Spanish presence in the Americas was portrayed as a defense of the papacy in Rome, the Spanish monarchy having been instituted, it was said, by the Messiah. The combined forces of the Spanish king and the pope entitled them to possess the New World just "as Moses justly took possession of the Holy Land."[349]

In what became the United States, various British colonies each had their own foundation story in keeping with their own ideology, though they later coalesced around the Pilgrim narrative. Despite the fact that the "commercially driven" Jamestown had been established by the Virginia Company thirteen years prior to the arrival of the Mayflower, it was "the more idealistic and religiously driven story of the Pilgrims" that gained broad acceptance because, Day says, it "invested the United States with a supposedly God-given right to its existence and, perhaps more importantly, its right to expand across the continent."[350]

This is all to say that Zionists had many precedents when they crafted their own foundation story as a divine mandate and conceived themselves as picking up where venerable ancient forebears had left off.

BACK TO THE BIBLE

Although the founding generations of Zionists were overwhelmingly secular—as we have seen, their "negation of the diaspora" involved rejecting and ridiculing an entire culture of pale, enervated Talmud scholars studying and praying in dim shtetl rooms—they found their fitting foundational story in the Bible.

Orthodox Jews had over the ages been said to long and pray for a return to Zion, and ended each Passover celebration with the optimistic words, "Next year in Jerusalem." However, that return was not intended to transpire until after the advent of the Messiah; crucially, it was to be enabled by a divine act, not set into motion by human politics. For Jews to take it upon themselves to re-enter the Promised Land without having been granted that honor from above was blasphemous, an extreme violation of their special covenant and the values intrinsic to the Torah. Thus, Zionism ignited the wrath of the Haredim, or ultra-Orthodox Jews. There were long-standing communities of such deeply religious Jews in Palestine itself—among them descendants of the Jews of ancient times—but they looked with resentment upon the newcomers who they saw as overrunning the place with an irreverent conception of Jewishness.

The influential movers and shakers of the Second Aliyah (the wave of Jewish immigration from Eastern Europe roughly between 1904 and 1914) who shaped many of the enduring educational, cultural, and policy-making institutions of the pre-state society and later of Israel, and of which David Ben-Gurion was a part, saw themselves as staunchly secular socialists. Nonetheless, as Israeli historian Anita Shapira has reported, "There was a Bible in almost every worker's room. The Bible was regarded as the storehouse for the memory of Eretz Yisrael as a homeland. It...was used as a *vade mecum* to the geography, flora and fauna of Palestine."[351] In testimony before the British Peel Commission, which investigated the causes of turmoil in Palestine 1936–37, Ben-Gurion asserted that "the mandate is not our Bible; rather, it is the Bible that is our mandate."[352] Chaim Weizmann told the United Nations Committee on Palestine in 1947, as plans for partition were being deliberated, "God made a promise: Palestine to the Jews."[353] Israel's "declaration of independence," produced during the 1948 war, says that "the Land of Israel was the birthplace of the Jewish people. Here their spiritual, religious and national identity was formed. Here they...created a culture of national and universal significance. Here they wrote and gave the Bible to the world."[354]

Ben-Gurion (in parallel with his right-wing rival Vladimir Jabotinsky) repeatedly cited the biblical precedent, and in particular the Book of Joshua, as a blueprint for the Jews' "reclamation" of the land and its military methods, arguing that "the Jewish 'return' to Palestine is actually a 'repeat' of Joshua's conquest of ancient Palestine."[355] He was "instrumental in making the study of the Book of Joshua a major component of the school curriculum in Israel";[356] he introduced a Bible Youth Quiz to take place during annual Independence Day festivities as well as in the diaspora;[357] he hosted a long-term Bible study group at his home; he proclaimed at a 1951 conference, "Not a single biblical commentator, Jewish or Gentile, medieval or contemporary, would have been able to interpret the Book of Joshua in the way the Israel Defense Forces did this past year,"[358] and, according to Anita Shapira, "He saw Joshua, more than Moses, as the true 'father of the people.'"[359] He wrote in a 1929 document he called "Postulates for the Formulation of a Constitutional Regime in Eretz Israel" that "the right of the Hebrew nation is not conditional upon external agreement and does not depend on the will of others." Rather, it "emanates from the unspoken connection of the Hebrew nation with its historic homeland, from the right of the Jewish people to independence and national revival...."[360] Years later, he told the Israeli parliament that the real reason for Israel's invasion in the 1956 Sinai war was "the restoration of the kingdom of David and Solomon."[361]

The theological scholar Michael Prior has declared all this problematic on both human rights and validating grounds: "While there is nothing like a scholarly consensus in the array of recent studies on Israel's origins, there is virtual unanimity that the model of tribal conquest as narrated in Joshua 1–12 is untenable.... Leaving aside the witness of the Bible, we have no evidence that there was a Hebrew conquest."[362] Thomas L. Thompson, who has written extensively about archaeological, geographical, and textual indicators of the area's history, has stated clearly, "Biblical archaeology's assertion of an invasion of nomads from the desert—whether of Amorites or of Aramaeans, whether of patriarchs or Joshua's army—finds no historical support whatsoever."[363]

Ben-Gurion was far from alone in his lay instrumentalization of the Bible. Addressing an audience at the Versailles Peace Conference after World War I, the "deeply secular" Zionist Menachem Ussishkin said:

> In the name of the largest Jewish community, the Jews of Russia, I stand here before you…in order to put forward the historic demand of the Jewish people: for our return to our own borders; for the restoration to the Jews of the land that was promised to them four thousand years ago by the Power Above.…That country was forcibly taken from the Jewish people 1800 years ago by the Romans.…And now I…come…to you who serve both politically and culturally as the heirs to the Romans and make my demand to [you]: Restore that historic robbery to us.[364]

Forging that connection was not restricted to the Second Aliyah cohort. The Israeli military and political leader Moshe Dayan, born onto the first kibbutz in 1915 and forevermore touting its secular ideology, nonetheless connected his deep "love of homeland" to his deep "long[ing] for the Israel of antiquity, the Israel of the 'timeless verses' and the 'biblical names.'"[365] As he detailed in his book *Living with the Bible,* he sought through amateur archaeology, antiquity collections, and frequent sojourns across the land "to bring to life the strata of the past which now lay beneath the desolate ruins and archaeological mounds— the Israel of our patriarchs, our judges, our kings, our prophets."[366] The book's jacket blurb reminds us that Dayan was born "in the Land of the Book" and explains that, from this distinctively situated vantage point, he is able to "depict the great figures of the Bible as they must have been in real life.…Thus, there is, for example, a fascinating account of the battle between David and Goliath, told with the special insight that only Moshe Dayan could provide."

Post-Zionist Israeli expat and historian Ilan Pappe, in his article "The Bible in the Service of Zionism," lampoons this cynical appropriation of the Bible by inserting the wittily oxymoronic (though unattributed) epigraph, "We do not believe in God, but he nonetheless promised us Palestine."[367] In a similar vein, the Israeli-born, self-exiled anti-Zionist scholar Moshe Machover wrote that "while [Zionism's] ego was secular, its id has always been religious" and observed, "The spurious 'right to self-determination of the Jewish people' is a marketing jingle."[368] Indeed, this "marketing jingle" raised eyebrows when Danny Danon, Israel's ambassador to the United Nations, wielded it—along with a physical Bible—at the UN Security Council in April 2019 as "proof" of Israel's claim to all of Palestine. "This is our deed to our land," he proclaimed as he read aloud from Genesis about God's "everlasting covenant" with Abraham.[369]

The "jingle" is also presented seriously as history in Israel's educational system. According to a professor at Haifa University, "Most Israelis today, as a result of Israeli education, regard the Bible as a source of reliable historical information of a secular, political kind.... Abraham, Isaac and Jacob are treated as historical figures.... The historicization of the Bible is a national enterprise in Israel, carried out by hundreds of scholars at all universities...."[370]

Scholars such as Nur Masalha have noted that the "continuity argument" was marketed not only for Israeli and Jewish diasporic consumption but for the Western Christian world at large. The "title deed to the land" concept was, he says, "deeply rooted in the post-Reformation Protestant doctrine that Jewish restoration to Palestine would lead to the fulfillment of biblical prophecies and the second coming of Christ" and was "a way of justifying their colonial project in European Christian eyes."[371] Others have drawn attention to the ways that the Christian investment in the biblical paradigm had fueled prior colonial ventures. Steven Salaita, in particular, has drawn parallels between the paradigm's Zionist and North American implementations. The Bible, he argues, has afforded both societies a way out of adhering to their professed Enlightenment democratic values: "Ethnic cleansing is not an appropriate human activity unless a deity sanctions such an act."[372]

The mirroring of these two colonial pasts, both commissioning the same ideological authorization, continues into the present. Salaita points out that the Israeli historian Benny Morris has rationalized the expulsion of the Palestinians with what Morris clearly felt to be a very persuasive analogy: "Even the great American democracy could not have been created without the annihilation of the Indians."[373] Similarly, in 2013 Knesset member Miri Regev shrugged off the accusation that she wanted to transfer an entire population (the Palestinian Bedouin of the Naqab Desert): "Yes, as the Americans did to the Indians."[374]

Religious studies scholar Keith W. Whitelam, who has written expansively on the ancient history of the area, objects to the "dehistoricizing" of the region's past through its reduction to the biblical narrative. He argues that by looking at it through this narrow lens, we eclipse the experiences of the many other peoples for whom it has also been a "homeland." This tendency can be traced to the flow of visitors from Europe and the United States to Palestine in the nineteenth century, many of whom were biblical scholars, explorers, and archaeologists who came for the purpose of confirming their own civilization's beliefs and unearthing its "roots." As a result, he says, "many earlier periods of its history from Neolithic times to the Late Bronze Age are divested of meaning as they become described as the 'prehistory' to a concern with the Iron Age and the emergence of ancient Israel or the period of David."[375]

Whitelam's point was further driven home by Edward Said, when the eminent scholar was asked, at a lecture, what must have been a familiar question: whether the Zionists had any claim to the land of Israel. Said replied:

> Of course! But I would not say that the Jewish claim—or the Zionist claim—is the *only* claim or the *main* claim. I say that it is *a* claim among many others. Certainly, the Arabs have a much greater claim, because they have had a longer history of inhabitance, of actual residence in Palestine, than the Jews did. If you look at the history of Palestine, there's been some quite interesting work done by biblical archaeologists; you'll see that the period of actual Israelite, as it was called in the Old Testament, dominance in Palestine amounts to about 200–250 years. But there were Moabites, there were Jebusites, there were Canaanites, there were Philistines—there were many other people in Palestine at the time and before and after. And to isolate one of them, and to say *that's* the real owner of the land—I mean, that is fundamentalism....[376]

Michael Prior places the biblical narrative in the "myth of origin" genre, stories which he says one encounters "in virtually every society," and which have been deployed "in the service of particular ideologies."[377] The ubiquity of such stories raises, for Shlomo Sand, the "What if everyone did it?" slippery slope question:

> [I]t always seemed to me that a sincere attempt to organize the world as it was organized hundreds or thousands of years ago would mean the injection of violent, deceptive insanity into the overall system of international relations. Would anyone today consider encouraging an Arab demand to settle in the Iberian Peninsula to establish a Muslim state there simply because their ancestors were expelled from the region during the Reconquista? Why should the descendants of the Puritans, who were forced to leave England centuries ago, not attempt to return

en masse to the land of their forefathers in order to establish the heavenly kingdom? .... In this spirit, we can easily imagine a march of folly initiated by the assertion and recognition of countless "ancient rights," sending us back into the depths of history and sowing general chaos.[378]

LOOKING BACKWARD: INVENTING JEWISH NATIONALITY AND PEOPLEHOOD

The notion of "peoplehood"—as in, "the Jewish people"—and rendering it axiomatic that there *is*, indeed, such a thing has always been germane to Zionism's advocacy of itself. But not all "the people" identified as part of that construct, and so their consent had to be cultivated.

In the Hebrew Bible, relates Michael Stanislawki, there were three different terms used to express the concept of Jewish peoplehood or nationality: *am, goy,* and *leom*.[379] None of these words referred to political sovereignty. *Goy,* as many know, came to signify "gentile" and ultimately became a pejorative term for non-Jews. *Am yisrael* was the one most frequently used in the Bible, and, Stanislawski says, became the front-runner over the centuries. It finally came into rough equivalence with the nineteenth-century, nationalism-infused "people" and later, the twentieth-century term *ethnos* (or *ethnie*), coined by the scholar of nationalism Anthony D. Smith.[380] *Ethnos,* according to Shlomo Sand, best reflects the way Zionists regard the Jews historically, and *am* (people) is now used interchangeably with *leom* (nation)—which became popular with the rise of nationalism in Europe during the nineteenth century.[381]

According to Balashon, an American-Israeli blogger who calls himself the "Hebrew Language Detective," *am* in modern Hebrew "is not limited to citizens of a particular nation-state."[382] This is of marked significance in present-day Israel, where the concept of "Israeli nationality" does not officially exist (though some citizens of Israel, both Jewish and Arab, have unsuccessfully petitioned to apply it to themselves). In the years after political statehood, says Bernard Avishai, Ben-Gurion "began advancing the idea that the 'Jewish nation,' *leom Yehudi*—or *leom ivri,* the 'Hebrew nation,' as it was then often called—was more or less identical to the historic, elect persecuted 'people of Israel,' *am yisrael,* living in Torah culture and by covenantal law. In effect, Ben-Gurion confused the holy people, *am,* with the modern Hebrew nation, *leom,* as if the latter were not a secular Zionist effort to supersede the former." Over the decades that followed, "the state apparatus did recognize Jewish nationality, *leom yehudi,* as a distinct legal designation, first to effect the Law of Return, but also to distinguish Jews from Arabs (and, in rare cases, other nationalities) on identity cards."[383] Sand notes that "in modern Israeli Hebrew, the word *am* does not have a direct association with the word 'people' in a pluralistic sense, such as we find in various European languages; rather it implies an indivisible unity."[384]

For early Zionists, the concept of *nation* did not necessarily signify political statehood; most basically, it connoted the romantic vision of a group that cohered in its essence and, inevitably, its fortunes. Stressing the common essence among a dispersed "people" was a necessary first step toward fortifying bonds of solidarity that would dignify and preserve the group's existence. For many, though not all, this involved establishing a common territory, though not necessarily in Palestine. In any case, realizing the solution of inhabiting a common land depended on first shoring up the proposition that the Jews constituted a people.

The imperative for Jews to recognize their common peoplehood found expression in mid- and late-nineteenth-century Zionist writing. The vision finally reached its political apotheosis in the United Nations' recognition of Israel as a politically sovereign state in 1948, and once again in 2018, when the Knesset passed a Basic Law officially declaring Israel the "nation-state of the Jewish people."[385] The Nation-State Law stirred international controversy, as it codified Israel's longstanding de facto policy of refusing to designate itself as the state of its citizens, approximately one-fifth of whom are not Jewish. This event was the latest in a long history of reclassifying Jewishness, which over time had morphed from a *religion* to a *nation* to a *race* to a *people*—though these developments were recursive rather than linear, replete with slippages that did not always distinguish the concepts from one another and led to arguments that continue to this day about the definition of "Jewishness." In any case, the Nation-State Law served as a latter-day ratification of Israel's genealogy in the romantic rather than civic tradition.

The thinking of the earliest Zionist writers did not make a deep or indelible impression on their fellow-Jews, and their work was, in the word of rabbi-scholar Arthur Hertzberg, "stillborn" in the mid-nineteenth century.[386] For many at that time, assimilation and Reform Judaism were more propitious contenders for ending the problem of Jewish outsiderness. Yehudah Alkalai (1798–1878) and Zvi Hirsch Kalischer (1795–1874) were rabbis who boldly tweaked the age-old Jewish messianic vision of a return to Zion as a miraculous, rather than humanly crafted, event by suggesting that humans could nudge it along. "The Redemption," wrote Alkalai in 1843, "will begin with efforts by the Jews themselves—they must organize and unite, choose leaders, and leave the lands of exile."[387] Kalischer agreed: "[T]he beginning of the Redemption will come through natural causes by human effort and by the will of the governments to gather the scattered of Israel into the Holy Land."[388] To Orthodox Jews, this view contravened God's chosen method of deliverance and thus amounted to heresy, and to the reformed and the assimilated it was of little interest. Though some among the assimilated came to realize that legal citizenship did not necessarily produce the hoped-for cultural citizenship, and some of them did ultimately turn to Zionism as a way to have their modernity and their Jewishness, too, for many, Alkalai and Kalischer were too rabbinic, while for the rabbinate, their break with religious tradition was too iconoclastic.

More in step with what would come some decades later was Moses Hess, a German-born, socialist, assimilated Jew and student of philosophy who had collaborated in publishing ventures with Marx and Engels (they later fell out over ideology and methodology: Hess's socialism was deemed insufficiently "scientific"). Hess's 1862 treatise, *Rome and Jerusalem,* was written from the standpoint of a repentant assimilationist ("After twenty years of estrangement I have returned to my people"[389]) who was now convinced that the problem of the Jews lay in their denial of their "nationality." Their identification as members of sovereign European nations was "false," "dishonorable," "treasonous," and a shameful "deception": "These modern Jews hide in vain behind their geographical and philosophical alibis."[390] In Hess's formulation, the Jewish race, not the Jewish religion, was the true object of antisemites' revulsion: "[T]hey hate the peculiar faith of the Jews less than their peculiar noses."[391] Civic emancipation offered only a pipe dream of inclusion as long as Jews still did not garner respect from their ostensible compatriots. Nonetheless, the real "threatening danger to Judaism" came from Reformed Jews who had debased the religion and who, with their "newly-invented ceremonies and empty eloquence, have sucked the marrow out of Judaism," turning it into "a second Christianity cut after a rationalist pattern."[392]

Hess was influenced by romantic nationalist thinkers and leaders such as Herder and Mazzini. He appealed to "the primal power of Jewish nationalism" to "reawaken" the people from their "slumbers." It was essential to reignite "the creative genius of the people, out of which Jewish life and teaching arose" yet which had "deserted Israel when its children began to feel ashamed of their nationality."[393] "National independence" on "a common, native soil," manifested in "the founding of Jewish colonies in the land of their ancestors," would liberate Jews and lead them to be "recognized in international law as a member of the family of civilized nations." Hess acknowledged that most of the world's Jews would not emigrate there, but believed that "no Jew, whether Orthodox or not, can refrain from cooperating with the rest in the task of elevating all Jewry." As with later Zionist discourse from the nineteenth through to the twenty-first century, a colossal act of persuasion was needed to realize this vision and enlist the support of those Jews who might opt to "refrain from cooperating." "There has been a central unity among the Jews at all times, even among those who were scattered to the very confines of the earth," Hess asserted.[394] Though a meticulous rhetorical and empirical exegesis might flag this as a questionable premise upon which to base a monumental proposal, it is one that has remained remarkably resolute and retained its mobilizing power for more than a century and a half.

While latter-day Zionist theorists such as Leo Pinsker and, pivotally, Theodor Herzl are presumed to not have read these early treatises before they made their own cases for Jewish national identity and asylum, it is highly unlikely that it was mere coincidence that their own work in some ways echoed them. Herzl wrote with surprise in his diary, upon reading Hess, "Everything we tried is already there in this book."[395] The reason, I propose, is that the historical writing of Heinrich Graetz (1817–1891) and Simon Dubnow (1860–1941) constituted important way stations along the trail of breadcrumbs from the mid-nineteenth-century theorists of Jewish peoplehood to late-nineteenth-century full-blown Zionism. Their places in the trajectory of Zionist thought should not be overlooked.

Hess and Graetz knew and influenced each other, and ideas from *Rome and Jerusalem* made their way into Graetz's subsequent, highly successful *History of the Jews from the Oldest Times to the Present,* a work in many volumes published between 1853 and 1876.[396] Sand calls Graetz's multipart history "the first work that strove, with consistency and feeling, to invent the Jewish people—the term 'people' signifying to some extent the modern term 'nation'":

> Although he was never a complete Zionist, Graetz formed the national mold for the writing of Jewish history. He succeeded in creating, with great virtuosity, a unified narrative that minimized problematic multiplicity and created an unbroken history, branching but always singular. Likewise, his basic periodization—bridging chasms of time, and erasing gaps and breaches in space—would serve future Zionist historians, even when they renovated and reshaped it. Henceforth, for many people, Judaism would no longer be a rich and diverse religious civilization . . . and became an ancient people or race that was uprooted from its homeland in Canaan. . . . The popular Christian myth about the wandering Jew . . . had acquired a historian who began to translate it into a pre-national Jewish narrative.[397]

Graetz pioneered the use of the Old Testament as literal, practical, secular Jewish history. Its instrumentalization was especially beneficial because it enjoyed a credible and revered status even by Judeophobes. Sand writes that Graetz's work "remained a presence in national Jewish history throughout the twentieth century" and that "there is no question of its significance and centrality":

> [T]he early nationalist intellectuals in the Russian empire embraced it enthusiastically. . . . Later the first Zionist settlers in Palestine used his work as their road map through the long past. In today's Israel there are schools and streets named after Graetz, and no general historical work about the Jews omits mention of him.[398]

"The first Zionist settlers" included groups such as Hibbat Zion ("Lovers of Zion") and Bilu (a name derived from a biblically based acronym), both nationalist, agriculturalist groups founded in 1881–82 by Russian Jews and catalyzed by the pogroms.[399] Importantly, they preceded the publication of Herzl's landmark *The Jewish State* in 1896 and the First Zionist Congress in Basel in 1897.

Additionally, other writers had begun to coax their fellow Jews to think of themselves as, and act like, a national entity in the 1870s and the 1880s. The writer Peretz Smolenskin (1842–1885) championed the idea of Jewish nationalism in the mid-1870s: "Is the name Israel based on religion, law, observance, or custom? This name exists because of national sentiment…. We have been a people from our beginnings until today. We have never ceased being a people…."[400] Moshe Leib Lilienblum (1843–1910), having traversed the Talmudic and secular spheres of Jewish life, returned, like Hess, to the fold in the 1880s with a vigor fueled by new certainty that in nationalism lay the Jews' only "salvation": "Are the Jews to be a living people or not? In face of this question all the others pale into insignificance."[401] In the fashion of Graetz, he reminisced about a life in which he had "always" felt this way: "All my life I had grieved over the decline of Jewish nationality and the thought that Jewry's existence as a nation was doomed."[402] His enthusiasm allowed him to leap over obstacles to national reintegration such as the paucity of available funds, the interests of the linguistically and culturally diverse communities of Jews in Africa and Asia (who rarely garnered a mention in early Zionist imaginings) in an era before mass global communication, the lure of North America as a site of emigration, and the chilliness of Jews committed to other paths of liberation.

Like Smolenskin and other Zionist writers, Lilienblum seems oblivious to a basic slippage—that is, between the assertion that Jews *self-evidently are and always have been* a united "nation," and the fact that he is *beseeching* Jews to *change* their thinking so that they *will see themselves as, and act like, a nation,* thereby finding geopolitical redemption. The orthodox, the liberals, the Maskilim, the Hasidim, the "freethinkers," all other "renegades trying to lead us away from our fatherland"—each, in Lilienblum's view, must forgo their divisive pet peeves and let their "special questions…take second place to the general question." They must "unite and join forces" with "the over-all trend toward nationalism"—an exhortation which seems curiously at odds with his allegation that, already, "Jews the world over…recognize beyond doubt the need for this sacred task."[403] For Smolenskin, the blame for the fatal disunity of the Jews, which he considers itself the agent of ascendant antisemitism, falls to the assimilated "uncircumcised of heart."[404] The chief culprits among these are devotees of "the *Haskalah* of Berlin…the vicious and corrupt doctrine …[whose] aim was…to cast off Judaism and replace with 'enlightenment.'" Their modus operandi, he declares, is 'Imitate the gentiles!'"[405]

In any case, there clearly was something in the *Volkish*, always-having-been, organically connected, nation-centric zeitgeist that touched many minds in that putative gulf of time between Hess and those who triggered an operational fin-de-siècle movement. Yet for them and others to this day, the new rearview vision of eternal continuity and oneness of the Jewish People had to be hotly defended. Graetz angrily rejected the work of earlier modern historians of the Jewish past—such as Isaak Markus Jost (1793–1860), whose *A History of the Israelites from the Time of the Maccabees to Our Time* appeared in 1820—which held that only a common belief in monotheism, rather than a unified "peoplehood," had connected very disparate communities over time. He attacked as "anti-Jewish" the classical scholar Theodor Mommsen (1817–1903) and the biblical scholar Julius Wellhausen (1844-1918) for their critical readings of the Bible suggesting that the Pentateuch was composed by multiple authors at various dates, and that Judaism had developed in stages rather than existing in one unremitting sweep since the deliverance of the law by Moses.[406] Sand observes wryly that "a nationalist history…does not tolerate lacunae or perverse aberrations"[407] and notes that "almost all the Jewish-nationalist historians would follow [Graetz's] example."[408] Shimoni points out that while "most of the contemporary Jewish intelligentsia…either ignored or ridiculed Hess," Graetz stood out as one who welcomed *Rome and Jerusalem* as "the first unmistakably nationalist exposition of secular character by a Jew, calling for return to Jewish independence in Zion."[409]

Sand calls Graetz "The first protonationalist Jewish historian" and he names Simon Dubnow as "Graetz's successor"—though a significant difference was that Dubnow "was a product of the Yiddish-speaking population of Eastern Europe rather than an academic historian in a prestigious scholarly center in Berlin or Paris."[410] As we have seen, the Jews in the Russian Empire had not undergone the modernizing and assimilating experiences of their brethren in the West. They faced intense discrimination and extremely circumscribed lives, and the societies that surrounded them (Russian, Ukrainian, Polish) were swelling with exclusionary nationalist feelings of their own.[411]

Like Graetz, Dubnow thought the notion of a wholesale Jewish move to Palestine was impractical on several fronts, not least of which was lack of buy-in from those whose presence would be requested. Plus, such a state might embolden the antisemites of Europe to retort to complaining diasporic Jews, "If you don't like it here, why don't you go away and live in your own state?"[412]

Dubnow regarded the Jews as "a living national body"—the "totality of autono-mous Jewish communities" who, "[b]ecause of their common origin, together…constituted a single nation, rather than a scattering of religious communities, as Jost and his colleagues had thought." He also considered his work "scientific" in the sense that—contrary to some who had preceded him—he employed professional historical tools such as evidence and source citations, and, to maintain credibility as a rationalist, he worked his way around the "miraculous" events of the Bible, treating them, when they had to be acknowledged, simply as metaphors. "Dubnow's narrative strategy would be adopted by all the Zionist historians who followed him," writes Sand, "namely, that the Bible is indeed full of imaginary tales, but its historical core is trustworthy…."[413]

Though Dubnow did not believe that Jews should regroup in Palestine, he was akin to the other Zionists in his opposition to assimilation. His was a "diaspora nationalism," a belief in the endurance and vitality of multiple au-tonomous Jewish communities, fueled by their own institutions and people, yet spiritually connected as a "nation." He viewed Europe as the legitimate "homeland" of millions of Jews and declined to attend the 1897 First Zionist Conference in Basel, but the ontological notion of ineffable, transhistorical "peoplehood" that he advanced remained intrinsic to Zionism. His ten-volume *World History of the Jewish People* did not appear until the 1920s, well after the Zionist project was underway, but he published in Russian-Jewish periodicals for many years prior to Herzl's *The Jewish State*.[414]

JEWISH NATIONALISM IN AN AGE OF POGROMS

The focus of the discussion shifted from the romance of historic nationhood to high anxiety and a "What is to be done?" urgency with the onset of the Russian pogroms in 1881. Hertzberg calls this year "a great turning point, as important as 1789,"[415] and Leo Pinsker (1821–1891) epitomized the *volte-face* from an assimilationist to a nationalist prescription for Jewry's deliverance that many Russian Jewish intellectuals experienced at that convulsive moment. For him, as delineated in his 1882 tract "Auto-Emancipation: An Appeal to His People by a Russian Jew," Jewish nationalism was a desperately formulated plan B after hopes for Russia's liberalization and genuine acceptance by other European nations crumbled. As he saw it, Jews formed "a distinctive element which cannot be assimilated, which cannot be readily digested by any nation."[416] The principal reason they would never be respected by the peoples of other nations was their lack of territorial and linguistic nationhood; the Jewish people "has no rallying point, no center of gravity, no government of its own, no accredited representatives. It is everywhere a guest, and nowhere *at home.*" Because of this, "The nations *never* have to deal with a Jewish *nation* but always with mere *Jews.*" (Italics in original.)[417]

Pinsker viewed Jews as too eager to please in countries hospitable to assimilation. They were not only willing to sacrifice their own national character for the chimera of inclusion in the host country but were also in denial about how little they were getting in return. They were in denial, too, about how unsustainable this delicate balance was. Most crucially for Pinsker, they were in denial about how much it all even mattered. Like a sick patient who refuses food and drink, not realizing that his lack of hunger and thirst is itself an alarming symptom, these Jews had to be *convinced* that here was a problem and a solution. "We must *prove,*" he wrote, "that the misfortunes of the Jews are due, above all, to their lack of *desire* for national independence; and that this *desire* must be *aroused* and *maintained* in them." (Italics added.)[418]

Central to Pinsker's argument was his dissection and diagnosis of antisemitism—or, to use his more apt term, Judeophobia. The Jewish people had, he wrote, retained a sense of spiritual interconnectedness—and thus sort of spiritual "nationhood"—but, incongruous and unrecognizable within the constellation of nations, it appeared only as a "ghostlike apparition." A people "without unity or organization, without land or other bond of union," the Jews were essentially "no longer alive, and yet moving about among the living"—an "eerie form scarcely paralleled in history" that "could not fail to make a strange and peculiar impression upon the imagination of the nations."[419] This ghostly presence was understandably creepy to those who beheld "this dead and yet living nation."[420]

In addition to his core "ghost" metaphor, Pinsker offered others, all comparably scary: in varying circumstances over time and place, Jews, he contended, had manifested the embodied symbolism of aliens, vagrants, beggars, exploiters, millionaires, men without a country, and hated rivals for all classes. It was the responsibility of Jews, he maintained, to reverse this perennial state of affairs by becoming "a nation like the others." Such an undertaking was "calculated to attract the sympathy of the people to whom we are rightly or wrongly obnoxious." Only by removing the "*surplus* of the Jews who live as proletarians in the various countries and are a burden to the native citizens" would they "rise in the opinion of the peoples." (Italics in original.)[421]

Pinsker, like Dubnow, was adamant that the Holy Land should *not* be the destination. "[W]e must above all, not dream of restoring ancient Judea," he wrote. The new Jewish homeland would be part of modernity, not an attempt to reconnect with "the place where our political life was once violently interrupted and destroyed."[422] What was needed was a substantive and "inalienable" sanctuary for the persecuted and previously nationless, "*one single refuge*" that would be contiguous and finally unite the dispersed Jewish people. (Italics in original.) Only then would the mass Jewish "self-emancipation" project become intelligible to the other nations, who would finally welcome the new nation as an equal.[423] The concept was of an en masse, and thus fortified, assimilation into the global configuration of states rather than the insinuation of individuals into precarious host societies. It was necessary, he said, to bring this about with the support of the other governments. He did not indicate any other stakeholders, such as those already inhabiting potential territories for the move, who might need to be consulted or considered.

Seven decades later, the German Jewish refugee and political philosopher Hannah Arendt would controversially argue in *The Origins of Totalitarianism* that the concept of antisemitism as eternal and unremitting was a myth, a claim as fantastical as "the corresponding antisemitic notion of a Jewish secret society that has ruled, or aspired to rule, the world since antiquity."[424] According to Arendt, the notion of immutable antisemitism was "a curious desperate misinterpretation" of history, born from "Jews concerned with the survival of their people" who had "hit on the consoling idea that antisemitism, after all, might be an excellent means for keeping the people together...."[425] To be sure, there were lacunae in this purportedly perpetual suffering that could be located if one cared to. For instance, the Jews had enjoyed what is often called a golden age, in eighth to twelfth-century Spain, under Islamic rule. And Yale historian of Jewish and religious studies Ivan G. Marcus has written of a "Jewish-Christian symbiosis" in the early culture of Ashkenaz between approximately 950 to 1300. The now-infamous blood libel— accusations that Jews ritually murdered Christians and ingested their blood—were the rare horrifying exception rather than the norm, and this, says Marcus, "is one reason Jews or Christians or both chose to remember them."[426]

And it has certainly been said that another golden age awaited Jews in twentieth century America. From New York to Hollywood, from science and economics to music and literature, the prominence of Jews in myriad fields and spheres has been taken as evidence of a mind-boggling success story. In the United States, it is true, appalling anti-Jewish events occurred, from Henry Ford's production of antisemitic literature to the mass shooting at a Pittsburgh synagogue in 2018. But violent animus has certainly also been directed at Irish, Italian, Asian, Latinx, and African American communities, in the context of which Jewish persecution stands as a far less singular phenomenon.

But for Pinsker and those he influenced, amid what then appeared as intractable violence toward Jews, reinventing the Jewish nation had the appeal of an escape route from persistent terror rather than simply a reclamation of an ancient identity. With nationalism now a remedy rather than a telos in itself, "Auto-Emancipation" constituted a new dimension of Zionist thought. The pamphlet attracted the predictable pique of the orthodox and the universalists, and like its predecessors, it failed to engage a wide, devoted mass of followers. It was to be another fourteen years before Theodor Herzl would publish *The Jewish State* and one more again before he would begin convening the Zionist Congresses that mobilized a movement. Yet ultimately, Graetz and Dubnow—as well as polemicists such as Smolenkin and Lilienblum— were links in a chain that connected Moses Hess to Leo Pinsker and Theodor Herzl, even if the chain itself was invisible to the latter writers, accounting for the uncanny sense of déjà vu that Herzl noted in his diary upon reading Hess.

The time for transfiguring the notion of a perpetual, unabating history of Jewish persecution into an argument for Jewish national reunification was—for its proponents—now right. First, though, there was a need for a leader and a movement that could activate the consent of the assorted nationals.

THE CROWD, THE PUBLIC, THE HERD, AND THE LEADER

As mentioned at the outset of this chapter, Edward Bernays's concepts of propaganda and public relations drew heavily on the theories of his uncle,

Sigmund Freud—in particular, Freud's depiction of the power and suscep-tibilities of unconscious desires. Freud and Bernays each, in turn, built on ideas of turn-of-the-twentieth-century social psychologists who had analyzed the mentality and behaviors of crowds. Freud devotes the first chapter of his 1921 book on mass psychology to a discussion of Gustave Le Bon's *The Crowd,* published in 1895. Recapping Le Bon's thesis, Freud writes: "[G]roups have never thirsted after truth. They demand illusions, and cannot do without them. They constantly give what is unreal precedence over what is real; they are almost as strongly influenced by what is untrue as by what is true."[427]

According to Le Bon, individuals—counterintuitively, even those of high intelligence—are swept into a "collective mind" when in a crowd—and "in crowds it is stupidity and not mother-wit that is accumulated."[428] In a state resembling one of hypnosis, the individual becomes "a barbarian—that is, a creature acting by instinct" who is more easily moved to violence "by the absence of all sense of responsibility."[429] In this drunken sort of state, the crowd's inability to think critically permits it to engage in what George Orwell, half a century later, was to call doublethink—accepting two contradictory ideas simultaneously, without any awareness of a contradiction. "Logical minds," Le Bon says, are always astonished at "the utter powerlessness of reasoning when it has to fight against sentiment."[430]

Another French sociologist, Gabriel Tarde, found Le Bon's argument in-sufficient and expanded it. In a 1901 essay called "The Public and the Crowd," he asserted that crowd "contagion" only existed among people in close physical proximity. When people congregated in the town square, the marketplace, the carnival, the church, the sporting arena, one would witness crowd behavior. But the rise of printing in the sixteenth century, followed by other new technologies of communication and transportation such as the railroad, the telegraph, and the telephone, had produced the era of "publics" in which interpersonal connection in physical absentia was possible. A "public," unlike a "crowd," was composed of people "all sitting in their own homes scattered over a vast territory, reading the same newspaper"; their bond lay in "their awareness of sharing at the same time an idea or a wish with a great number of other men."[431]

Whether in crowds or in publics, herd-like behavior is instinctive in humans, according to British neurosurgeon and social psychologist Wilfred Trotter, writing in 1916; it is a biological given that must be recognized and used effectively by leaders. Like other gregarious animals, he asserted, humans rely on the herd instinct for survival, and its use is reinforced by natural selection in both aggressive and protective ways: "The wolf which does not follow the impulses of the herd will be starved; the sheep which does not respond to the flock will be eaten."[432] For humans, the herd instinct manifests in conformity. Being in a state of synchronicity with the herd gives the human a sense of power, security, and connection.

Several years later, in *Group Psychology and the Analysis of the Ego,* Freud was to mildly praise Trotter's book as "thoughtful" and "deservedly famous"— though he faulted Trotter for ignoring the role of the leader in a herd, a subject Freud takes up at length and which is germane to his own analysis. And while relying a great deal on Le Bon, Freud also criticizes him for simply *describing* crowd behavior without questioning the psychological forces that motivate it. For Freud, the leader is a primal father figure who represents the ego ideal of the group members—that is, the notion of perfection that the ego strives to attain, derived from the internalization of the parents' values. He agrees with Le Bon that there is a "hypnotic" effect taking place in the crowd, but faults him for failing to ask who the hypnotist *is*. The hypnotist, in Freud's view, is the leader.[433]

Freud emphasized that understanding group dynamics also required recognizing the role played by the libido—not to be understood narrowly in just the sexual sense, but as the energy that is related to affective ties generally. "Libidinal ties are what characterize a group," he says;[434] "love relationships (or, to use a more neutral expression, emotional ties)...constitute the essence of the group mind."[435] To be in love is to be in a state of hypnosis, and "the hypnotic relation" as we usually understand it, says Freud, is simply "a group formation with two members."[436] He emphasizes that group formation is not simply *like* hypnosis; it *is* a hypnotic condition. In this state, group members experience *identification* with one another in their egos, while submitting to the same *object* (the leader) as the repository of their ego ideal. This, he says, explains why groups behave like neurotics or children: they are guided strictly by psychological, not objective or rational, reality. Rational ideas that threaten the libidinal ties won't have a chance.

"LEGEND HAS IT...."

It could be said, then, that the formation of national group consciousness requires the building of libidinal ties among a dispersed and, regarding many accompanying characteristics at least, heterogeneous multitude of people. As we have seen, the early theorists of Zionism, culminating in Pinsker, posited that the solution to antisemitism lay in the ability and will of Jews to recognize that they shared a "nationality" or "peoplehood." For them, this "true" affinity lay latent and pitifully underutilized in their consciousness and had to be awakened. But for far-flung Jewish "groups" and "publics" to cohere around a national identity, they would, according to Freud, need a leader who would orchestrate the requisite "hypnotic" work. For Zionism, that leader appeared in the form of Theodor Herzl.

Herzl—whose residence in nineteenth-century Vienna happened to coincide with that of Freud, his neighbor—was in most ways a highly unlikely candidate for the job of "founder of modern political Zionism." He was a cosmopolitan, a dandy, an aesthete, a journalist, a novelist and a playwright; he agonized over his uphill struggle to get his literary work recognized and despondently nursed his narcissistic wounds when it was rejected. He was an assimilated Jew who knew nothing of the religion, of the Hebrew language, of the Jewish traditions, of the efforts of the Zionist writers and the European Jewish immigrants to Palestine who went before him, or of the plight of the suffering Jewish masses in the Russian territories who would later greet him as the Messiah. Those present at a planning meeting for the First Zionist Congress found Herzl "the most un-Jewish Jew they had ever met. He mesmerized them more by his style than by his thoughts."[437]

He never outgrew his infantile attachment to his parents, was a member of an antisemitic German nationalist fraternity, a pedophile, a harshly contemptuous husband who in large measure financed his movement work by depleting his reviled and apolitical wife's dowry, and a begetter of tragically dysfunctional offspring. In his writing, he lampooned materialistic Jewish stockbrokers and fatuous bourgeois Jewish pretensions. His "good" female characters were "blond, sunny, and blue-eyed."[438] According to Jacques Kornberg, "Herzl's Jewish contempt ran deep.... Physical revulsion overtook him" upon seeing the visages of congregants in a synagogue. Quoting from Herzl's diaries, Kornberg recounts Herzl's impressions of their "...bold, misshapen noses;

furtive and cunning eyes." Even after his conversion to Zionism, Herzl would, says Kornberg, "employ terms such as 'Jewish vermin,' *Mauschel,* against his Jewish detractors."[439] In short, Herzl would not have fared well as a Jewish icon in twenty-first- century "cancel culture."

But in his own time and for long after, he was lionized as a savior of the Jews. One of his biographers, Alex Bein, writes, "He felt himself to be both leader and father, the manager of every aspect of the Jewish problem. And the masses of Eastern European Jewry in Galicia, Roumania and Russia saw him in the same light."[440] Bein also called him "a monumental figure" who was "an all-human exemplar...towering above all and leading the way for all."[441] The American Zionist Louis Lipsky described him in an introduction to *The Jewish State* as "the hero of a great and lasting legend. The pamphlet is one of the chapters in the story of his struggle to achieve in eight years what his people had not been able to achieve in two thousand years."[442]

How and why did this transformation occur? A cynical answer, which may nonetheless be an apt one (alongside others), is Israeli political scientist Shlomo Avineri's contention that rehabilitating a deeply bruised ego might have been involved: Zionism "would turn [Herzl] from the mediocre writer and play-wright that he acknowledged himself to be into a leader of a political movement who conferred with Europe's most powerful men."[443] The traditional answer, however, is that based in Paris during the course of his career as a journalist for the Viennese newspaper *Neue Freie Presse,* Herzl came face to face with the antisemitic fallout of the Dreyfus Affair in 1895.

Albert Dreyfus was a Jewish officer in the French military who was accused of treason in 1894; he maintained his innocence throughout his trial and prison term and was exonerated years later. He was defended by Emile Zola in "J'Accuse!"—a famous fulmination against the antisemitic manifestations of the case. On the other side, Dreyfus was denounced by those gentiles who felt he embodied the ruse of assimilation, in which a "dual loyalty" to both France and a Jewish "nationality" lurked stealthily beneath a veneer of pure French patriotism, defying the integrity of *laïcité,* France's cherished notion of secular citizenship. An important ingredient of the story's moral, for many sources—including current ones such as the website of the National Library of Israel—was the claim that Herzl heard "a mob yelling 'Death to the Jews!'" and thus "became convinced of the need for a Jewish state."[444]

In short, it has often been repeated that, shocked and horrified at such vicious eruptions of anti-Jewish sentiment in an enlightened liberal democracy where Jews believed themselves to be comfortably assimilated, the lightbulb of Zionism flared in Herzl's head and recalibrated his life's course. This myth was generated by Herzl himself, as he constructed it retrospectively four years later.

The parable of Herzl's conversion was adopted by many others, including Herzl's biographers. Bein bluntly insists—without explaining why—that the backward-looking account is the one that matters. "We need Herzl's formulation of the situation as set down in 1899," he writes, "in order to put his impressions of January 1895 in the proper light."[445] Herzl's 1899 professed perspective, as conveyed by Bein, gives Zionism a clear raison d'être that burst forth in an apocalyptic instant:

> In that fateful moment, when he heard the howling of the mob outside the gates of the *Ecole Militaire,* the realization flashed upon Herzl that Jew-hatred was deep-rooted in the heart of the people.... [T]he ghastly spectacle of that winter morning must have shaken him to the depths of his being. It was as if the ground had been cut away from under his feet. In this sense Herzl could say later that the Dreyfus affair had made him a Zionist.[446]

Elon, likewise, tells us that Herzl was present in the courtroom at the time the conviction was announced and that these thoughts ran through his head:

> In Herzl's eyes the scene was symbolic in a wider sense: the degraded man symbolized the Jew in modern society, conforming to its ways, speaking its language, thinking its thoughts, sewing its insignia onto his shoulders only to have them violently torn off on a gray winter morning to the ominous sound of drums. Dreyfus represented a stronghold, for which European Jews had fought, and were still fighting, but "which—let us not delude ourselves—is a lost one."[447]

In fact, in his 1972 *A History of Zionism,* Walter Laqueur sums up in a sentence what virtually all accounts until fairly recently claimed: "Herzl had become a Zionist as a result of the Dreyfus Affair...."[448] Some people had to learn the lesson the hard way, but the truth—that assimilation for Jews in European society was merely a chimera—now seemed proven.

Avineri, however, asserts that "there is in fact no evidence" for this piece of "common wisdom"—"not in Herzl's voluminous diaries nor in the many articles he sent from Paris to his newspaper in Vienna."[449] He cites Herzl's reportage on the case for the *Neue Freie Presse* at the time, in which Herzl asserts that the mob shouted, "Death to the traitor!" Avineri pointedly observes, "It's telling that in the Hebrew translation of the article that appears in nearly all the history textbooks used in Israeli schools and in most other Hebrew-language books about Herzl, the mob chants 'Death to the Jews!' But that is not what Herzl wrote...."[450]

The British historian Henry J. Cohn had, in fact, made this case as far back as 1970 in the scholarly journal *Jewish Social Studies*. He pointed out that *The Jewish State,* written in 1895 and published in 1896, "did not mention the Dreyfus case and described antisemitism in France as no more than a social irritant." Herzl's complete diaries had been finally published in 1960 and enabled scholars such as Cohn to parse the entries in full. Cohn found that in the years that followed the Dreyfus case, Dreyfus was mentioned only eleven times over 1,630 pages. "Seven of these," he adds, "are merely passing allusions...."[451] "The diaries at this time," he writes, "while not mentioning Dreyfus, are more pre-occupied with antisemitism in Vienna and Austria than in all other European countries put together."[452]

Cohn's argument concerning the real trigger for Herzl's Zionist awakening presages that which Avineri began giving voice to almost three decades later: that it was the sharp rise of populist antisemitism in Austria, bolstered by startling wins in electoral politics there, that prodded him to action. "It was the Vienna of the 1890s that...saw the emergence of a populist-nationalist movement, the Christian Social Party, led by Dr. Karl Lueger, whose xenophobic and anti-Semitic politics catapulted him...to the post of mayor" that was the actual catalyst for Herzl's conversion.[453]

The construction of the Dreyfus-as-stimulus myth drew on Herzl's public relations savvy and that of his followers. It worked well. Cohn comments, "With very few exceptions, almost any recent book or article which alludes to Herzl's conversion to Zionism, whether it is about Jewish, French, or Austrian history, and whether written by a Jew or a non-Jew, ascribes a leading role to the Dreyfus

Affair. All are agreed on its paramount influence...."[454] Though Cohn's "recent" was circa 1970, the apocryphal version of events is still being promulgated over two decades into the twenty-first century.

Why was the parable important enough to promulgate? We have seen that competing solutions to the problem of antisemitism had been advanced. By the time Herzl offered the retrospective explanation for his epiphany, the Zionist movement and its supporting principle that there *was* no other viable response to antisemitism had taken root. By then, assimilationists who didn't buy into the program had to be either converted or dismissed, and for about a century, Herzl's dramatic "realization" proved to be a powerful publicizing refrain.

THE MASTER HYPNOTIST

Herzl had concocted several dubious schemes for liberating the Jews both before and, later on, supplementing the one he hit on with traction. One involved mass conversion to Christianity. Another entailed bribing and cajoling the Turkish sultan: Herzl promised to relieve Turkey's crippling national debt—with funds he didn't actually have—in exchange for the gifting of Ottoman Palestine to the Jews. At another point he "devised a fantastic plan," spawned from his predilections for theater, swashbuckling, and grandiosity:

> He envisioned a scenario of flamboyant heroes and sensational effects. Karl Lueger, Prince Alois Liechtenstein, and Georg von Schonerer were the great leaders of Austrian anti-semitism. He, Herzl, would challenge one or all three to a duel. It would be by pistols, and fought to the death.... The idea was to create a stir and so catch the conscience of the world.... Herzl thought his plan out carefully, to the last dramatic detail. A magnificent *coup de theatre,* he hoped, would compel men to serious thought. Before the duel he would write a letter fully explaining his motives. If Lueger should shoot him, 'The letter would tell the world that I fell victim to this most unjust movement. Thus my death might at least improve the minds and hearts of men.'".... But if he shot Lueger, or Shonerer, or Prince Liechtenstein, he would turn his prosecution in court into a show trial against anti-Semitism. He would deliver a magnificent address.... Then he would present the court with

a detailed analysis of the Jewish tragedy.... It would impress world opinion.... The Jews of Austria would undoubtedly now offer to elect him to parliament....[455]

If this was his most spectacular stratagem, perhaps the most ignominious was his personal appeal to Russia's notorious antisemitic figure, Interior Minister Vyacheslav von Plehve, in the wake of the Kishinev pogrom of 1903. The latter ploy was uncannily (and, to many of Herzl's contemporaries, unsettlingly) rational. Herzl proposed that the Zionist leader and the despot in St. Petersburg could find common interest in getting the Jews out of Russia and into Palestine. (Most of them, at the time, preferred to immigrate to North America.) Herzl warned von Plehve that the Russian Jews were indeed revolutionaries at heart and would be grievously active in that endeavor if not ousted in time. If the czar were to intercede on the Zionists' behalf in Constantinople, Herzl would put in a good word to the Jewish financiers in Western investment banks who controlled the credit and loans that Russia wanted but were being withheld due to Russia's unfortunate international reputation for butchering Jews. He would assure the world press who would be reporting on his speeches at the upcoming Sixth Zionist Congress that Russia's approach to the Jewish problem was a "humanitarian" one; there would be no need to mention the pogroms, except to assure his constituents that rumors of further massacres were simply an "abominable falsehood." He championed Jewish emigration from Russia—rather than equality and justice within it—as the righteous solution (even though some within the Zionist movement favored the latter). Such bonhomie was established at the meeting that von Plehve reminisced to his new acquaintance that some of his best boyhood friends had been Jews.[456]

When Herzl's fantasies did turn to the creation of a Jewish state, they were lavishly inspired by Wagnerian opera, replete with grand theatrical spaces, men in full tails, and expensively dressed women.[457] He wrote detailed plans for the state's formation in his diary—with no mention of Palestine's present inhabitants. As his biographer Amos Elon put it,

> He laid down plans for an aristocratic constitution fashioned after that of medieval Venice.... He outlined... plans for mass entertainment ("as soon as possible—German and international theater, circuses, café-concerts,

a Champs Elysees, a new Louvre)..... also construct something like the
Palais Royal or the Venice Piazza San Marco."

Herzl added, "A lot of toasts will be drunk to me."[458]

In addition to soliciting the support of world leaders, Herzl pitched his
project to wealthy Jews who might finance it. In the sixty-eight-page "Speech
to the Rothschilds"—the text of which served as a basis for parts of *The Jewish
State,* the pamphlet that made him famous and led to Zionism's crystallization
as a movement—Herzl tried to scare his would-be benefactors into compliance.
They were rich, but they were Jews, he reminded them, and because of this their
wealth would ultimately endanger rather than shelter them, whether expropriation were to come from revolutionaries or antisemitic tyrants. But not to panic.
"I bring you the salvation," he promised them, like a television pitchman who,
having alerted viewers to their offensive hygiene, brandishes a product to spare
them further mortification. To confidantes, he proclaimed, "I have solved the
Jewish problem!"[459]

He tried—unsuccessfully—to persuade the liberal Jewish editors of the
newspaper he wrote for to publish a special edition with the front-page headline,
"The Solution to the Jewish Question, by Theodor Herzl," assuring them, "The
very moment my idea is publicized, the entire Jewish question is solved honestly."
In his diary, he wrote, "I shall be counted among the greatest benefactors of
mankind" and "I shall be the Parnell of the Jews." In his felicitous imagination,
writes Elon, "The momentous transition would come with exquisite ease. Herzl
foresaw no cultural, political, economic, military, or absorption difficulties; it
was all a problem of proper stage direction."[460]

Again, this is not the way the story is usually told. It is true that *The Jewish
State,* published in 1896, was a surprising breakthrough for Herzl. In it, he
outlined his plan for, as he put it in his opening line, "the restoration of the
Jewish State," based on the principle "We are a people—one people."[461] But
despite the patrician ideals that we know, from his diaries, were fundamentally
enmeshed in his vision, his book's biggest fans were not the Jewish bourgeoisie
and liberal intelligentsia of Central and Western Europe, where he was widely
derided.[462] Nor were they found among British Jewry; in England, the notion
of the return to Zion drew more enthusiasm from upper-class Protestants
than from Jews. Rather, the book appealed most to the distressed masses of

Eastern Europe (czarist Russia, Galicia, Romania, Bulgaria)[463]—and to some antisemites.

Even as Russian censorship kept the text itself from reaching those in the shtetls of the East, Herzl's burnished reputation spread there and sparked immediate ardor. According to Elon, the ten-year-old David Ben-Gurion of Plonsk, Poland, "later recalled a rumor spreading suddenly that 'the Messiah had arrived—a tall, handsome man, a learned man of Vienna....'"[464] Speaking in London before a crowd of Jewish immigrants from the East, Herzl was compared to Moses and called "the new Columbus."[465] At a stopover in Sofia, Bulgaria, he was met by an adulating throng; people kissed his hand and one man exclaimed, "You are holier than the Torah!"[466]

Herzl was, at the same time, quite ignorant of these people's lives. Elon tells us that he "was astonished to discover...that Russians were 'Europeans.'"[467] After the Russian Zionist Menachem Ussishkin came to call on him, Ussishkin declared, "He does not know the first thing about Jews. Therefore he believes there are only external obstacles to Zionism, no internal ones."[468]

Nonetheless, *The Jewish State* was translated from its original German into other languages and increased its circulation. Herzl continued to vigorously promote his program and, with those who had been inspired by his message, to organize a movement. He published a weekly newspaper plugging the Zionist project, the Vienna-based *Die Welt*. An international Zionist congress took place—the first of many—in Basel, Switzerland, in 1897 to establish formal institutions and governing bodies for the movement. The World Zionist Organization was founded there, with Herzl elected as its president. Though he was, as we have seen and many have noted, an improbable instrument for its initiation, there is little question that his organizational acumen, theatrical capabilities, public relations smarts, and sheer tenacity—along with his ability to compartmentalize or flout pertinent facts about Palestine and its inhabitants—made him a brilliant choice of a leader.

Akin to Freud deeming the role of a leader as that of a master hypnotist, the rhetorician Kenneth Burke described the persuasive speaker as a sort of magician, creating states of identification among people and ideas that transcended divisions and thus fortified social cohesion.[469] The rhetor, through what Burke called "dramatistic" means, used language as "symbolic action" to effect results, often in ways that were not discernible as persuasion itself.[470]

To the performance-loving Herzl, the art of producing such effects came naturally. Avineri notes,

> On several occasions [in his diaries] Herzl mentions the need for symbolic language and the power of symbols in politics. When coming up with the idea of building a permanent hall for Zionist Congresses in Basel, he says to his friend, the architect Oscar Marmorek, "With nations one must speak in a childish language: a house, a flag, a song are the symbols of communication."…. [M]ore than anyone else then active on behalf of the Jews, he understood the power of mass communication in the matters of the weak and downtrodden.[471]

Avineri also points out that, following Herzl's oft-quoted, self-congratulatory diary entry of August 1897, "[A]t Basel I have founded the Jewish state"—which Avineri names as a key artifact in the "Zionist pantheon"—are several lines that are "almost unknown":

> The foundation of a state lies in the will of a people for a state…. At Basel…I created this abstraction which, as such, is invisible to the vast majority of people—and with minimal means. I gradually worked the people into the mood for a state and made them feel that they were its National Assembly.[472]

This image, crafted by Herzl, was taken up by others. Avineri observes that, indeed, the "painting by Menachem Okin of the opening of the congress, melodramatic and stylized in the way it pictures Herzl in front of the delegates, clearly suggests an Assemblée Nationale, a Reichstag—the rebirth of a nation."[473]

Avineri cites other "symbolic actions" Herzl performed to woo observant Jews on the occasion of the First Zionist Congress. He forced himself, albeit with complaints, to eat "the unpalatable kosher food" and he took the unprecedented move of attending synagogue on the sabbath before the congress opened.[474] Meanwhile, other suggestive iconography was created, such as the token shekel, whose purchase certified its owner as an official member of the Zionist organization. Avineri explains that the shekel "evok[ed] memories of the contributions made by Jews all over the Roman Empire to the coffers of the Temple in Jerusalem during the Second Commonwealth."[475] Alex Bein and others have noted Herzl's sartorial requirement for attendees at the First Zionist Congress: a frock coat and white tie, signifying, in grand European style, the dignity and stateliness of the occasion.[476]

Herzl was also convinced that a national body needed to be branded by a flag: "With a flag one can lead men wherever one wants to, even to the Promised Land," he had written to the Jewish philanthropist Baron Maurice de Hirsch in an 1895 fundraising pitch.[477] Herzl's close colleague David Wolffsohn saved the day by adapting old symbols for the occasion: a blue and white motif ("the color of our prayer shawls") with a star of David fixed prominently at the center.[478] Draped across the entrance to the meeting hall, the banner welcomed delegates to the Basel conference with reassuringly commingled allusions to religion and the continuity of history. Alex Bein observes that "the majority of the delegates actually took it for granted that this was the old Jewish flag."[479]

Like other acolytes, the Russian Zionist writer Ben Ami did his own part to promote the desired impression. This was his description of Herzl presiding over the packed room:

> Before us rose a marvelous and exalted figure, kingly in bearing and stature, with deep eyes in which could be read quiet majesty and unuttered sorrow.... [I]t is a royal scion of the House of David, risen from among the dead, clothed in legend and fantasy and beauty. Everyone sat breathless, as if in the presence of a miracle. And in truth, was it not a miracle which we beheld?[480]

CHAPTER 6:
"WE BOUGHT IT": ERSATZ NARRATIVES AND THE MANUFACTURE OF OWNERSHIP

"From the earliest phases of its modern evolution until it culminated in the creation of Israel, Zionism appealed to a European audience for whom the classification of overseas territories and natives into various uneven classes was canonical and 'natural.'" —Edward Said[481]

"In a way, the world-view of the Party imposed itself most successfully on people incapable of understanding it. They could be made to accept the most flagrant violations of reality, because they never fully grasped the enormity of what was demanded of them...." —George Orwell[482]

"Anyone who believes you can't change history has never tried to write his memoirs." —David Ben-Gurion[483]

There are, of course, many perspectives from which one can tell a story, and the story of colonial land acquisition has, as many have come to realize, generally been told from the perspective of the conquerors. As a child in what was known as "Hebrew school"—an after-school program that imparted Jewish history, customs, and beliefs and introduced us to the Hebrew language—I was taught modern Jewish history unequivocally from the perspective of the Zionists. A virtually identical story was conveyed years later in a credit-free course about Israel taught by a university rabbi. Not knowing of any alternative resources, I had sought this out in a vain effort to uncover the factual realities undergirding the heated and contradictory claims vying for my attention in the late 1970s.

Though later events that transpired in Palestine have drawn more public attention, one feature of the narrative that particularly struck me was the claim that the Jews had "purchased" land from "the Arabs" in the years surrounding the turn of the twentieth century. "Land purchase was the underpinning of Zionism," Benny Morris has written.[484] The claims, I found out later, were not exaggerated; my instructors reported that about 6 percent of the land had been acquired in that way, and most sources agree on this point. So, what was the problem? Where was the "conflict"? Why would anyone find fault with a "sale," which implied two willing transactors having reached mutually agreeable terms? A deal's a deal.

THE POLITICS OF DEFINITION AND CATEGORIZATION

Neither slave auctions nor the traffic in Elgin Marbles sprang to my mind to temper this certainty, though such associations would have been useful. The politics of definition are crucially significant when it comes to adjudicating legal, medical, and scientific matters. What, exactly, is a "sale," and why should it matter? Lest this seem obvious, consider: What, exactly, is a "person"? The answer has much to do with designating abortion as "murder" and thus illegal— or not. The politics of categorization are closely related.[485] The category of mental disorder a psychotherapist designates for a client can determine whether the patient will be reimbursed by insurance, be held responsible for a crime, or receive compensatory damages in a personal injury lawsuit. At various points and sites in history, homosexuality was considered a "crime," a "sin," or a "sickness," subject to the juridical, religious, or curative sanctions each demanded. Even that most sacrosanct domain of ordering, the Dewey Decimal System, came up for serious reshuffling as more librarians became aware of Melvil Dewey's racist, sexist, and antisemitic past and the ways that his own assessments structured the ways libraries organize knowledge."[486]

Similarly, when it came to land acquisition in Palestine—as elsewhere in the colonized world—crucial points at issue were the definitions and ensuing classifications of "ownership" and "property" themselves. When colonial powers staked claims in other regions, notions like *terra nullius* and the "Doctrine of Discovery" allowed monarchs and explorers to declare that lands were "empty" and ripe for appropriation if there weren't Christians with deeds and boundary markers living off them; thereby they rationalized and mobilized their own claims of European-style title. It is, then, important to closely examine the paradigms that entitled the parties in these transactions and to consider whether an enabling cultural imperialism, drenched in its own solipsistic conceptual economy of definitions and classifications, determined an outcome that, interpreted according to other paradigms, could easily be seen as not exactly a "fair deal."

PROPERTY OWNERSHIP AND THE POLITICS OF CLASSIFICATION UNDER OTTOMAN RULE

The area that came to be known as Palestine existed under the rule of various near and distant conquerors for millennia. From 1517 to 1917 it was a part of the far-flung, multicontinental Ottoman Empire, whose administrative center was in Constantinople. "Palestine" or the "Holy Land" was never a designated administrative unit under the Ottoman government; what were recognized were the province (*vilayet*) of Greater Syria[487] and the *sanjaks,* or districts, of Jerusalem, Nablus, and Acre.[488]

There was, indeed, a short break from Ottoman rule when Egypt occupied Palestine from 1831 to 1840, an interval that concluded with a Palestinian revolt against aggressive taxation and conscription.[489] And Nur Masalha has made a persuasive case that, unnoticed by most historians (who have based their accounts largely on the lives and perspectives of the urban notables rather than the much more numerous peasantry), a de facto "statehood" existed in Palestine in the eighteenth century under the leadership of Dhaher al-'Umar al-Zaydani (1689–1775). Powered by the *fellahin* (peasant farmers), a strong military, the new political economy created by Palestine's entrance into the international market, and al-'Umar's skillful governance, it was what Masalha calls "the closest Palestine got to a modern independent state," "sovereign in substance and reality, while nominally still part of the Ottoman Empire," by which it was "formally recognized ... as an autonomous Emirate.[490] But by the latter part of the nineteenth century, even as Palestine was being eyed and visited with increasingly fervent interest by foreign religious leaders, pilgrims, biblical scholars, archaeologists, governmental figures, and merchants, it was, according to Lester I. Vogel, "relegated to near-inconsequential status within the Turkish realm" and "governed by means of a disjunctive mélange of bureaucracies."[491]

Traditionally, land in the Ottoman territories was classified within two categories. *Mülk* land, roughly equivalent to Western notions of privately owned property, represented a tiny proportion of the Empire's agricultural production. *Miri* land, on the other hand, was owned by the state and cultivated by small farmers with permission of the sultan, providing tax revenues for the government and security, via the fruits of their labors, for the farmers. Up to 90 percent of land in the empire was classified this way.[492] *Miri* lands were taxed at a much higher rate than *mulk* lands were, so landholders sometimes sought the latter designation, either through legal or extralegal means.[493]

Up to the years surrounding the turn of the twentieth century, *miri* land in much of the Levant was farmed under the *musha'a* ("commons") system, wherein *fellahin*, who comprised most of the population,[494] shared stewardship of a common piece of land and cooperatively organized its use. According to Noura Alkhalili:

> The land was held in common by all members of a village or community rather than divided into individual parcels of land belonging to certain members of the community. *Musaa'* lands could not become private property.... The practice of *musaa'* is mainly characterized by periodic redistribution—typically every one, two or five years—of agricultural plots based on criteria related to various qualities of the land such as soil type and terrain, among peasant cultivators with claims to the land.... This guaranteed accessibility to the more fertile and arable lands for all within a community.... [The plot's] boundaries were verbal, defined by natural landmarks, while the land redistribution process was based on direct negotiations.[495]

During the Industrial Revolution, Palestinian cotton and wheat began to be exported to Europe and became integral to the burgeoning European capitalist economies.[496] At the same time, shipments of European products were imported to Palestine, which was itself connected via overland trade routes to the markets of Syria and Egypt.[497] "Palestinian agriculture began bowing to powerful external market forces. Local agriculture was now locked on marketing, which meant that subsistence crops gave way to cash crops," writes Ilan Pappe.[498] Production for the international market in the eighteenth century also "brought about a new relationship between (larger) cities and towns, and the hundreds of villages where most people lived and worked."[499] This was significant especially because elite urban notable families (*a'ayan*), who acted as local officials and had long functioned as intermediaries between the *fellahin* and the central government in Constantinople, now became invested with greater powers as tax collectors and landowners. The *a'ayan* were "loyal Ottomanists" who early on opposed Arab and Palestinian nationalisms, though they would later embrace them.[500]

The Ottomans were eager to become legible to European powers as agents of modernity to fend off predatory foreign powers' interest in their territories as well as to consolidate taxation and streamline conscription. Their efforts toward this end included enacting, as part of their nineteenth-century *Tanzimat* reforms, a land code in 1858 that formally abolished these collective land rights (though in reality, many Palestinian lands still operated according to *mushaa'* custom for several more decades).[501] The noose tightened as other laws followed, notably one in 1867 that allowed foreigners to purchase land, providing a crucial opening for Russian Zionists to acquire territory that would later be deemed exclusively Jewish.[502]

Under the new Ottoman laws, only individuals could register land titles, and later, after World War I, the occupying British instituted land courts that sustained and more forcefully implemented these laws.[503] What ensued was both defensive and opportunistic scrambling of the realities and legalities of landholding. George Bisharat explains:

> The Palestinian peasantry, ever distrustful of state authority… attempted to avoid full taxation by understating the size of their lands, by disavowing claim to the lands, or by simply evading the land registrars of the Ottoman government. To escape conscription, groups of villagers would vest title of village lands in the hands of a few village leaders or would register them in the name of a fictitious or long-deceased individual. As a result, discrepancies between official titles and the realities of occupancy widened. Local notables, now with legally enforceable rights in land, actually gained in power, transforming themselves into landlords and their co-villagers into tenants.[504]

There was also a shift in power among the populace from the rural sheiks, who had traditionally adjudicated conflicts, to the urban elite Palestinian families. According to Pappe:

> [T]he a'ayan of Palestine adapted easily to the new [Ottoman] policies.... The notables learned how to join and gain control of the new organizations the Ottomans introduced, such as municipalities and regional councils, and they continued their mediating role, this time as officially paid clerks of the empire.... Before the reforms, these urban notables would not have been able to climb beyond the lower rungs of the bureaucratic ladder; by the end of Ottoman rule, they held ever higher positions in Jerusalem and Beirut, and even in Istanbul. Thus "the politics of notables" prevailed. The reformers, after all, needed the urban notables to help them implement their reforms, and the population needed them as a protective shield against excessive conscription and tax abuses.... The new ruling elite, consisting primarily of large land owners and agricultural producers, discovered that the most attractive way to increase their capital was through land speculation.[505]

"Prosperous urban merchants from Beirut, Damascus, Haifa and Jaffa were quick to realize the opportunities" now available to them, writes Rashid Khalidi. "In the succeeding decades, many of them managed to acquire title to large areas of these fertile lands."[506] Daniel Bitton stresses that many of the holdings were "essentially acquired...by deceit from peasants who still believed themselves to be the usufruct "owners" of the land, as had been the case for hundreds of years."[507] Furthermore, writes Bitton, "Zionist leaders were well aware of the effects of their purchases. The contracts between Zionist buyers and Arab vendors normally specified that the Arab vendors were responsible for obtaining eviction orders, which were then executed by Ottoman, and later British, forces."[508] Rashid Khalidi, using pre-World War I land-sale figures and newspaper accounts, reports that between 1878 and 1907, 58 percent of land acquired by Zionists was purchased from non-Palestinian absentee landlords, while 36 percent came from Palestinian absentee landlords and six percent from local landlords and *fellahin*. The category "non-Palestinian absentee landlords," he says, includes "foreigners, foreign diplomats, Beirut merchants, as well as

Turkish government officials. This and the second group sold 94 percent of the land that changed hands before 1914 for which we have detailed figures."[509]

Parsing the polemic *The Case for Israel* by the fervidly Zionist lawyer Alan Dershowitz, Bitton finds Dershowitz emphasizing—just as my mentors did—that the early Zionists "lawfully and openly bought land…from absentee landlords."[510] Dershowitz comes back to this, reiterating that the land was "fairly purchased,"[511] "primarily from absentee landlords and real estate speculators."[512]

This is all true—just as it is not a lie that at one time in the United States white enslavers lawfully and openly bought people and others lawfully and openly bought real estate that had not been willingly "sold" to them by Native nations. Deportations to Auschwitz were lawful, as well. Lawfulness and transparency are some of the conventional red herrings mobilized in apologetics about land sales to Zionists under late Ottoman rule and later under the British Mandate.

Some of the things that are *not* true in Dershowitz's account: that "much of [the land purchased] was thought to be nonarable"; that the purchases "displaced very few local fellahin"; that violent Arab resistance to Jewish immigration to Palestine was "religiously inspired"; and that "some on each side see their claim as based on God's mandate."[513]

MAKING THE "NONARABLE" LAND BLOOM

Regarding the putatively "nonarable" land: this was an oft-repeated theme, frequently supplemented by observations about how desolate and barren the country had been before the Jews arrived to save it. For instance, Haim Gerber describes a lecture David Ben-Gurion gave in 1944 called "The Burden of Wilderness." Though Ben-Gurion had, at this point, lived in Palestine for many decades, he still, Gerber says, fostered

> the perception of the country as a wilderness apart from the Jewish contribution to its development. Describing a virtual trip in the country from Jerusalem to the north via the Jordan valley and to the south via the same route, he was able to conclude that most of the country was a wilderness. The eighteen or so Palestinian towns and 800 Palestinian villages did not exist for him.[514]

In the lecture, Gerber tells us, all those who had lived there over the ages except for the Jews were likewise erased; the non-Jewish powers who had ruled the land over many centuries were referred to as "foreign occupiers" and "step-children." This, of course, included the Arabs who lived there in the nineteenth and twentieth centuries.

In a standard effort to "prove" that Zionists arrived from Europe to find a land that had grown barren during their 2,000-year-old absence, Alan Dershowitz quotes from Mark Twain's novel *The Innocents Abroad,* a satirical account of an expedition of Americans to Europe and the Middle East in 1867. Zionists have made much of Twain's disparagement of what he found in the Holy Land, citing it as eyewitness testimony to its purportedly neglected, backward state, desperately in need of redemption by modern people with the know-how, equipment, and passion to restore it to its historic glory. In the passage Dershowitz furnishes, Twain finds himself in the Galilee, his eyes taking in "two or three small clusters of Bedouin tents, but not a single permanent habitation" as he laments "these unpeopled deserts, these rusty mounds of barrenness."[515]

In truth, that is just the tip of the iceberg of Twain's scorn. While marveling that he is "standing on ground that was once actually pressed by the feet of the Saviour," he notes the contrast of that exalted fact with "the usual assemblage of squalid humanity" he sees around him, the women and children "remind[ing him] much of Indians," watching him and his companions "with that vile, uncomplaining impoliteness which is so truly Indian, and which makes a white man so nervous and uncomfortable and savage that he wants to exterminate the whole tribe." He is disgusted to observe that just as with "the noble red man," these people "were infested with vermin, and the dirt had caked on them till it amounted to bark."[516] "[B]y nature they are a thankless and impassive race," he ruminates, and for him it is indeed nothing short of miraculous that "Christ knew how to preach to these simple, superstitious, disease-tortured creatures."[517] And on it goes.

As noted, Zionists usually cite Twain's observations as evidence that, even if Palestine wasn't really a land without a people, it was a land without people whose custodial reliability rendered their existence worthy of respect and preservation. The critical rejoinder to this has usually been that Twain viewed the Levant through the Western, Orientalist, colonialist gaze of others of his time and place. This may very well be the case, but equally significant is the fact that these lines appear amid over four hundred pages in which he lampoons virtually everyone and everything—including Jews. Visiting Gibraltar, he encounters representatives of many cultures including "Jews from all around, in gabardine, skullcap, and slippers, just as they are in pictures and theatres, and just as they were three thousand years ago, no doubt."[518] Strolling in the markets of Tangier he remarks, "The Jewish money-changers have their dens close at hand, and all day long are counting bronze coins and transferring them from one bushel basket to another."[519]

No one escapes his jeers. He is "full of veneration for the wisdom that leads [Moorish women] to cover up such atrocious ugliness."[520] The women of Paris are "like nearly all the Frenchwomen I ever saw—homely."[521] In Italy, he mocks the art of the great masters: "Wherever you find a Raphael, a Rubens, a Michelangelo, a Carracci, or a da Vinci (and we see them every day), you find artists copying them, and the copies are always the handsomest."[522] He is equally mocking of his fellow travelers. At the Sea of Galilee, some of them haggle so tenaciously over the price of a coveted boat ride that the boatmen find it not worth their trouble and depart without them. "[T]hey sailed serenely away and paid no further heed to pilgrims who had dreamed all their lives of someday skimming over the sacred waters of Galilee and listening to its hallowed story in the whisperings of its waves, and had journeyed countless leagues to do it, and—and then concluded that the fare was too high."[523]

In short, Twain's derogatory remarks about Palestine in the mid-nineteenth century have been cherry-picked by defenders of the "barren land" view from a volume laden with derogation of every imaginable sort. And while it is beyond the scope of this discussion to survey the literary devices employed by Twain in this work, it is very hard to come away from the memoir believing that Twain's commentary has been earnest rather than ironic. For this reason, it is worth questioning why his travelogue is so frequently summoned to authenticate the claim of Zionists that they arrived to create something from virtually nothing, for the good of all.

It did take considerable sleight of hand to sustain the myth of empty and nonarable land once people had seen the productive market economy of Palestine for themselves and gleaned some awareness of its role in global enterprise. As discussed earlier, Palestinian crops were imported to Europe from the eighteenth century onward; Masalha describes the way they satisfied "the insatiable [British] demand for cotton for its mills" and "helped save the growing population of France from famine" in the eighteenth and nineteenth centuries.[524] Besides that, sesame from the districts of Haifa and Jaffa was famed for its high quality as far back as the sixteenth century,[525] wheat exported from Jaffa was considered ideal for Italy's macaroni industry,[526] and barley from Gaza, known for its "superb quality," was "in great demand by the breweries of England, Scotland, and Germany."[527]

The Lebanese historian Marwan R. Buheiry contended in 1981:

> The economic importance of Palestine has traditionally been underes-timated, generally for myth-construction purposes: a dominant theme, taken for granted by the Western world, is the Zionist claim that the region was a desert which bloomed with the arrival of the first wave of Jewish colons-pioneers late in the nineteenth century. In fact, Palestine has always been an important producer of key agricultural commodities and was experiencing a significant expansion of agriculture and allied manufactures at least two generations before the arrival of the first colons from East Europe....[528]

The German researcher of Middle Eastern history and political science Alexander Scholch wrote that "the literary *topos* of the economically stagnat-ing, unproductive, and neglected Palestine before 1882 (that is, before the beginnings of foreign colonization on a significant scale) is to be confronted with reality."[529] One key part of the reality that he identifies is the Jaffa orange, whose mass export, he said, began after the Crimean War of 1853–1856, in which the Ottoman Empire was part of the coalition that defeated Russia; in the two and a half decades that followed, "Palestine experienced a remarkable economic upswing" and the value of the exports of Jaffa skyrocketed.[530] "In 1873," he wrote, "there were already 420 orange groves in the vicinity of Jaffa, yielding 33.3 million oranges annually".[531] The *fellahin* benefitted to some extent, but the biggest winners were "merchants, middlemen, big landowners and tax-farmers—all those who invested capital in trade and agriculture.... The upward movement and the growing prosperity of Palestine were undeniable facts to every attentive observer."[532]

A British Foreign Office report of 1893 on "Irrigation and Orange Growing at Jaffa" noted that

> Jaffa oranges, thanks to their excellent flavour, have of late years acquired a world-wide reputation, and…enormous quantities of it are now exported to Europe, America, and even to India….Owing principally to the trade in oranges, Jaffa now ranks next after Beyrout in importance among Syrian coast towns….[533]

Another report, written in 1886 by Henry Gilman, then the American Consul in Jerusalem, even "outlined the reasons why orange growers in Florida would find it advantageous to adopt Palestinian techniques of grafting directly onto lemon trees."[534]

We can see, then, that the Jaffa orange was not only a widely consumed product but also an internationally renowned and coveted "brand" long before corporate "branding" of products grew ubiquitous. Its appropriation as a Zionist metonym and logo has been especially painful, to say nothing of galling, for Palestinian refugees who recall its scent and taste as acutely evocative reminders of their lost homeland. The Near Eastern language and literature scholar Carol Bardenstein has called the Jaffa orange one of the "three most hyper-saturated and contested symbols mobilized"—along with trees and the prickly-pear cactus—"in Palestinian and Israeli discourses of indigenousness and 'rootedness.'"[535] "The Jaffa Orange," she writes, "once exported in the region as a product of Arab labor, ultimately came to be identified as the quintessential Israeli agricultural export and fruit of Hebrew labor in extensive markets abroad."[536] Historian Mark LeVine has also written of how "citriculture evolved into one of the 'sacred symbols' of the Zionist experience in Palestine, inextricably tied to the Labor Zionist mythos…."[537]

Perhaps nowhere have the symbolic meaning and manifold representations of the Jaffa orange been plumbed more intensively and creatively than in Eyal Sivan's 2009 documentary *Jaffa, The Orange's Clockwork*. In the film, Ismail Abou Shahadeh, who is identified as a "Palestinian orchard mechanic," tells the viewer that to this day, "Israel still exports oranges with 'Jaffa Oranges' written on the crates, even though none grow in Jaffa now."[538] We are shown footage of old propaganda films, travel advertising, and Orientalist paintings that illustrate the land's purported tragic abandonment by Arabs and stunning revival at the hands of Jews. In one black-and-white film, we see grainy images of Arabs in a barren desert; the voiceover in English proclaims, "This is the land which God promised to Abraham. Once, while the Jews lived in this land, it was the center of a great civilization. When the Jews were driven out, the land gradually declined. Primitive life returned."[539] Shortly after, we see young "sabra" (Palestine-born Jewish) workers marching in shorts with work implements slung over their shoulders, singing, "As the sun blazes on the mountain and the valleys' dew still glistens, we love you, our homeland, in joy, in song, and in labor."[540] As images of camels in the desert melt into those of smiling Zionists aloft on ladders picking fruit, we are told, "The Promised Land wasn't offered on a platter. They had to return the soil's fertility to times of flowing milk and honey."[541]

The Palestinian historian Elias Sanbar, who can be seen watching all this wryly on a screen beside his desk, comments, "Here, we've moved into the Western. It's done. We've crossed the Atlantic. These are tales of the New World."[542] Watching another clip in which Jewish women are dressed up in "Arab" regalia, dancing to Arabic music with bowls perched on their heads and a banner with Hebrew lettering behind them, Sanbar exclaims, "Orientalism at its best! There's a point where there arises the idea of donning the skin of those to be replaced," adding about one of the figures, "She seems closer to a Cecil B. DeMille character than a real Bedouin."[543] Not coincidentally, this image calls to mind American children "playing Indian" in what they imagine is Native American garb while acting out their stereotypes of whoops and rituals.

In another interview, the Israeli historian Amnon Raz-Krakotzkin is seen viewing the images on his own screen. He remarks that the scenes of happy, healthy young Zionist "pioneers" picking oranges, so energized by laboring in the orchards that they burst into folk dances during breaks, are appropriations of Soviet propaganda imagery. "They're not in the Orient but in Russia," he says;[544] they are not only exploiting socialist iconography but also performative-ly retaining an aura of their own immutably European character.

In other clips we meet the Israeli art historian Rona Sela. Leafing through early Holy Land photographs, she explains:

> In the twenties propaganda departments were formed within Zionist
> institutions to market the Zionist idea, to orchestrate a highly disciplined

system of images. The orange was part of it. When the Image Unit started…one of those in charge said, "I'm going to build a Zionist archive for generations.… They utterly controlled photography, instructing what and how to photograph. If photos didn't fit the lexicon, photographers would have to take another one. Or the Unit wouldn't buy. So, photographers learned what to take.…Here we came and liberated the land, we made the oranges, we made the desert bloom. Thus, the orange turned into a key symbol of the Zionist idea.[545]

ON THE "TRANSMISSION BELT": "A LAND WITHOUT A PEOPLE FOR A PEOPLE WITHOUT A LAND"

As for Dershowitz's claim that few *fellahin* were displaced by land purchases: he goes on to repeat one of the classic canards of Zionist public relations—that the Palestine of that time was "vastly underpopulated." This is a claim that dovetails with the claim that the land was "barren" when the Zionists "reclaimed" it around the turn of the twentieth century and has often been summed up in the well-known Zionist slogan, "A land without a people for a people without a land." The quote is of debatable provenance yet was unquestionably taken up by Zionists and entered the lexicon of many Jews who, in my own experience, recirculated it even while at a great remove from (and lacking interest in) the primary source whence it sprang. The slogan is often attributed to the early British Zionist Israel Zangwill, a writer and a great proponent of forcibly expelling Arabs from Palestine to make way for the Jewish state; he is sometimes said to have "formulated" it[546] and at other times to have "popularized" it.[547] In any case, according to historian Anita Shapira, the slogan "was common among Zionists at the end of the nineteenth, and beginning of the twentieth, century. It contained a legitimation of the Jewish claim to the land and did away with any sense of uneasiness that a competitor to this claim might appear." It also, she adds, "tended to avoid the existence of the problem entirely or at most to accord it a miniscule importance."[548]

Much later, when the origins and aims of Zionism came to be more widely inspected and criticized, there was backpedaling regarding the ownership and use of the saying. That the phrase had become counter-productive as a rationale for Zionist colonization by the turn of the millennium was made evident by Adam M. Garfinkle in a 1991 article called "On the Origin, Meaning, Use and Abuse of a Phrase," in which he alleged, "Anti-Zionist polemicists take Zangwill's authorship at face value when they have used the phrase in their efforts to discredit Zionism as an insensitive, racist and exclusivist movement."[549] In 2008, Diana Muir published "A Land Without a People for a People Without a Land" in the *Middle East Quarterly*; the article remains on the Jewish Virtual Library website. In it, Muir asserts, "In the minds of many of Zionism's detractors, the 'land without a people' formulation has become a defining element of Zionism's original sin."[550] Yet Muir and Garfinkle take different approaches to undermining the ways the phrase has been implemented to hoist Zionist ideology on its own petard.

Muir argues that "the phrase was coined and propagated by nineteenth-century Christian writers" including the British politician and reformer Lord Shaftesbury in 1853. She traces its evolution as it appeared in various incarnations and presents quotations to support her assertion that "[b]y the late nineteenth century, the phrase was in common use in both Great Britain and the United States among Christians interested in returning a Jewish population to Palestine" and "Christian use of the phrase continued into the first decades of the twentieth century." According to Muir, Zangwill was the first Jewish Zionist to use the phrase, in 1901, but she also contends that it is *not* "true, as many anti-Zionists still assert, that early Zionists widely employed the phrase." She proffers several other slogans that she says were in much wider use at the time, including one that she claims was the "official Zionist mantra": "The aim of Zionism is to create for the Jewish people a home in Palestine secured by public law." (She does not cite a source or an organizational affiliation for this "official" representation of the movement's aims.)

She also presents the results of a survey she conducted of seven major American newspapers. In them, the phrase "Jewish national home" gets mentioned over 3,000 times through 1948, she says, and "no other Zionist phrase or slogan comes close," with the "land without a people" refrain scoring only four, all before 1906. Yet Muir's failure to find it in the pages of mainstream American newspapers such as *The New York Times* and *The Boston Globe* in the early twentieth century does not mean that it was not in circulation in Jewish Zionist-affiliated communities. Once influencers or thought leaders (as they are now called) such as Zangwill and Weizmann issue such statements, numerous oral and written vehicles for their further dissemination are usually engendered.

While it is beyond the scope of the present work to trawl through the pre-internet archives of various Zionist organizations, I can personally vouch for having heard the statement reiterated at my Hebrew school and at my Zionist summer camp in the Catskills in the 1960s, as well as among fellow ulpan-goers on a kibbutz in the Jezreel Valley in the 1970s. Tellingly, liberal Zionist Leonard Fein in a "Speech to Hadassah on Arab Israelis and the Zionist Enterprise," in the year 2000, at one point remarked ruefully, "It would have been easier, ever so much easier, if we had been, as some thought we were, a people without a land for a land without a people," clearly assuming an audience long familiar with the catchphrase and identifying as part of that "we."[551] Even Israel's Ministry of Foreign Affairs webpage on "Herzl and Zionism" allows that though "most" knew that the land was populated, "some spoke naively of 'a land without a people for a people without a land.'"[552]

Muir's principal strategy seems to be two-pronged: (1) to prove that the slogan "A land without a people for a people without a land" (or some version of it) was coined and used widely by Christian Zionists prior to Zangwill's usage of it; and (2) to insist that Zionists have barely used the phrase at all. The first seems unproblematic and at the same time does nothing to undercut criticism of the slogan. The sources she cites are persuasive and consistent with much that we know about Christian interest in the Holy Land in the nineteenth century. The Palestinian writer Ghada Karmi, for instance, dates the inception of Christian Zionism to the Reformation in the sixteenth century, when the Old Testament was revived as a text of interest and, as a result, the return of the Jews to Palestine began to be viewed as a precondition for the well-being of all via the Second Coming of Christ (which would climax in the "Rapture"). It was influential among British politicians, from Lord Shaftsbury to Arthur Balfour (whose 1917 "Declaration" was one of the most pivotal moments in the promotion of Zionist colonization) and beyond (even, Karmi suggests, to Winston Churchill and Tony Blair). Such a literal reading of the Old Testament and belief in its imminent ramifications was brought by the Puritans to America and spawned numerous denominations and movements, which in turn informed the thought of politicians here.[553] This biblical prophecy has been said to influence, among others, Woodrow Wilson, in his support for the Balfour Declaration.[554]

However, Muir's second line of argument—that Jewish Zionists have not used the slogan very much—is questionable on two counts. Introducing her topic, she acknowledges that the phrase is "one of the most oft-cited phrases in the literature of Zionism." Yet she only proceeds to demonstrate what she alleges is *its misuse by anti-Zionists* (along with its legacy in Christian Zionist thought); she eschews examples of its Jewish use in the "literature of Zionism" throughout the ages since its conception without mentioning which Jewish periodicals and organizational archives she consulted to reach the conclusion that its appearance there was negligible or nil. She emphasizes that the notion that "early Zionists widely employed the phrase" is a falsehood promulgated by "many anti-Zionists" but simply omits evidence that runs counter to her claim.

Evidence that it *was* employed by prominent early Zionists exists. For instance, Nur Masalha quotes one of the most important of the early Zionist leaders, Chaim Weizmann, speaking in front of the French Zionist Federation in Paris in 1914:

> In its initial stage, Zionism was conceived by its pioneers as a movement wholly depending on mechanical factors: there is a country which happens to be called Palestine, a country without a people, and, on the other hand, there exists the Jewish people, and it has no country. What else is necessary, then, than to fit the gem into the ring, to unite this people with this country?[555]

Masalha clarifies: "Neither Zangwill nor Weizmann intended these demographic assessments in a literal fashion. They did not mean that there were no people in Palestine, but that there were no people worth considering within the framework of the notions of racist European supremacy that then held sway." To illustrate, he quotes Weizmann's dismissive reply to a question by Arthur Ruppin about the Arab people who already lived there: "The British told us that there are some hundred thousand niggers [Hebrew: *kushim,* negroes] and for those there is no value."[556] He also tells us that "Zangwill himself spelled out the actual meaning of his slogan with admirable clarity in 1920":

> If Lord Shaftesbury was literally inexact in describing Palestine as a country without a people, he was essentially correct, for there is no Arab

people living in intimate fusion with the country, utilizing its resources and stamping it with a characteristic impress: there is at best an Arab encampment.[557]

Muir concurs, albeit in very different terms, with Masalha's elucidation that the phrase actually meant that "there were no people worth considering within the framework of the notions of racist European supremacy that then held sway." In what constitutes an aside in Muir's piece—though the idea takes a much more central role in Garfinkle's—she reflects,

> What may be odd, viewed from the Arab perspective, is the lens through which Westerners look at the land. In Western eyes, the eastern Mediterranean is permanently overlaid with the outline of a territory called "the Holy Land" or "the Land of Israel." Because Westerners equate lands with peoples, even post-Christian Westerners expect to find a people identified and coterminous with the Holy Land.

She asserts that Muslims, on the other hand, "neither perceived Palestine as a distinct country, nor Palestinians as a people." Once again, as with the culturally determined notions of "property" and "ownership," the rectitude of appropriation is sustained by an assumption of the superiority of interpretations and taxonomies framed by Western subjectivity.

Garfinkle, unlike Muir, does not underplay the expression's usage in Jewish Zionist circles. He acknowledges from the outset of his article that the famous phrase is "ubiquitous" and that "even those with a casual interest in Zionism and the Arab-Israeli conflict have invariably heard some version of it."[558] Rather, he changes the subject. He goes to great lengths to argue that many have misapprehended the slogan's authorship, often attributing it erroneously to Herzl or, as Muir argues, neglecting its life in Christian Zionism prior to Zangwill's writing it down in 1901.

Again, I would say that once these factual points about its origin are brought to our attention, we may all agree upon them. But the rest is a straw man argument that does nothing to mitigate the illogic of Garfinkle's accusation that "[a]nti-Zionist polemicists take Zangwill's authorship at face value when they have used the phrase in their efforts to discredit Zionism as an insensitive, racist and exclusivist movement."[559] No one, to my knowledge, has said that *Zangwill's specific alleged authorship* is the problem; the problem has been the perpetual echoing of the myth itself. Whoever invented the phrase—and whoever regurgitated it—certainly *was* insensitive, racist, and just plain wrong. But *who* it was is not what's at issue. If one attributed the observation that "brevity is the soul of wit" to Oscar Wilde rather than Shakespeare, the point would remain pithy regardless of the benighted speaker's error. Conversely, the fact that the "land without a people" mantra originated in Christian, rather than Jewish, Zionist thought doesn't make its adaptation to suit Jewish Zionist colonial ends any less pernicious.

In any case, Garfinkle seems to mangle his own point when he goes off on a tangent about John Lawson Stoddard, the multimillionaire, non-Jewish lecturer/entertainer from Brookline, Massachusetts, whom he calls the "second inventor" of the saying after Shaftesbury. "Not only was Stoddard generally popular," writes Garfinkle; "he also received hundreds of letters about his pro-to-Zionist sentiments from Jews." He then reprints an 1892 letter to Stoddard from Jacob H. Schiff, in which the prominent Jewish businessman and philanthropist expresses "appreciation of the tribute you have rendered to our race."[560] Garfinkle also speculates that "Schiff might very well have been part of the transmission belt that conveyed Stoddard's invention to European Zionists."[561]

Garfinkle's other tactic is a familiar one to anyone who has heard Palestinian rights dismissed on the grounds that until the advent of Zionism, Palestinians didn't identify as a "nation" or a "people," as Western hegemonic discourse had carved out these categories and associated them with entitlement to statehood. "Most believed that the land was desolate because there was not in Palestine 'a people' in the then current European sense of a group wedded to a particular land whose members defined themselves as composing a separate nation," he writes.[562] Israel's critics, he says, have intentionally omitted the "a" before "people"; "the absence of the indirect article 'a' before the word 'people' substantially changes the meaning of the phrase from the political to the demographic and literal." He charges, "All of this reflects a high degree of either ignorance or willfulness, and astonishing sloppiness, on the part of many."[563] Among the guilty he cites are those who were dismayed by Golda Meir's 1969 comment that upon her arrival in Palestine in 1921, she found that "[t]here was no such thing as Palestinians.... They did not exist."[564]

"There was no premeditated early Zionist claim of natiocide against the idea of a Palestinian people," he insists; "there did not need to be one for there was no such people."[565] On the one hand, he dodges even the "literal" interpretation problem by saying, "Most nineteenth century Zionists were ignorant about conditions in Palestine and oblivious to the Arabs who lived there." They were "so preoccupied with escaping a European predicament" that they failed to perceive what lay ahead at their intended destination. On the other hand, he acknowledges that "many other Zionists" were "acutely aware of the Arab issue," including leading figures such as David Ben-Gurion and Max Nordau, who "chastised [Herzl] in 1897 for saying that Palestine was 'virtually empty.'"[566] He also mentions Ahad Ha'am's famous 1891 "Truth from the Land of Israel Speech,"[567] which, like Yizhak Epstein's "Hidden Question"[568] (to be discussed soon), bluntly depicted the reality on the ground for Zionists who had yet to arrive. Yet according to Shlomo Sand, although Ha'am was a respected author and well-known in Jewish communities at that time, "his pained protest aroused no serious discussion within the emerging nationalist camp…. [A]fter all, such a discussion would have neutralized the drive of the movement and damaged the moral foundation for much of its claim."[569]

So: were they "literally" oblivious or were they not? Muir says (contra Sand) it was "unlikely" that Zionists believed Palestine to be "literally empty" after Ha'am's speech "sparked debate over conditions in Palestine," and other Zionists have scoffed at the suggestion that anyone ever believed the saying verbatim at all. Garfinkle seems to be claiming both but goes a step further to cover all bases, concluding that "what happened in Palestine between Jew and Arab was less a sin than a collision of cultures and intellectual epochs."[570] Regarding the "cultures": as with the "clash of civilizations" thesis made infamous by the political scientist Samuel Huntington, Garfinkle suggests here that an ontological stalemate was inevitable. As for the "intellectual epochs": the Jews, he feels, were understandably distracted by what was going on in Europe, and could not be expected to notice, under the circumstances, that the eras of European romantic nationalism and colonial voraciousness were on their last legs—and that Palestine already had people in it.

Whichever way defenders of the alleged Zionist slogan would like to have it, there is now ample published evidence culled from archives that Zionist leaders envisioned the need to whisk the indigenous Arab people of Palestine elsewhere from the beginning. These wishes were manifested increasingly through and beyond the Nakba of 1948. And while more liberal-leaning Zionists tend to attribute the most extreme policies and prescriptions solely to Vladimir Jabotinsky and the far-right parties and organizations he spawned—casting them as the "bad cops" to the socialist labor parties' "good cops"—Masalha argues otherwise:

> It should not be imagined that the concept of transfer was held only by maximalists or extremists within the Zionist movement. On the contrary, it was embraced by almost all shades of opinion, from the Revisionist right to the Labor left. Virtually every member of the Zionist pantheon of founding fathers and important leaders supported it and advocated it in one form or another....[571]

Israel Shahak agrees: "The real difference between the mainstream and those who may be called extremists, it seems, is simply the addition of pragmatism—the knowledge of how politics operate—and not the ultimate aim of a Palestine completely without Palestinians or completely Jewish."[572]

Examples abound. Benny Morris quotes the noted Zionist writer and historian Joseph Klausner: "Our whole hope is that in the fullness of time we will be the masters of the country." And there's this: "In 1908 Moshe Smilansky wrote that Zionism must strive for a Jewish majority and those who opposed this goal were committing a 'national sin.'" Smilansky publicly spurned Epstein's "Hidden Question" advice, countering, "The Zionists should indeed get to know the Arabs, not in order to help them develop but to know better how to fend them off."[573] The Zionist Nahman Syrkin wrote that "Palestine...must be evacuated for the Jews."[574] Zangwill wrote in 1919 that the Palestinians "should be gradually transplanted" to Arab countries; and in 1920, he "advocated an 'Arab exodus' that would be based on 'race redistribution.'"[575] Chaim Weizmann saw the Palestinians as "rocks of Judea...obstacles that had to be cleared off a difficult path."[576]

At a conference in Zurich in 1937, transfer became Mapai party policy, "planned and supported by most of the highest-ranking leaders and opposed on moral grounds by none."[577] Drawing on the subsequent version of the conference's proceedings, which were edited and published by David Ben-Gurion,

Shahak reveals Ben-Gurion's linguistic acrobatics as he advocates transfer while claiming that he's not. In appreciation of the Peel Commission's first reference to the idea, Ben-Gurion said:

> The Commission does not suggest dispossessing the Arabs; it advocates their transfer and settlement in the Arab states. It seems to me unnecessary to explain the fundamental and deep difference between expulsion and transfer. Until now, we also, have achieved our settlements by way of transfer of population from place to place...only in a few places of our colonization were we not forced to transfer the earlier residents.[578]

Similarly, Eliezer Kaplan, who was to become Israel's first minister of finance, offered, "The matter here is not one of expulsion, but of organized transfer of a few Arabs from a given territory to an Arab state, i.e. to the vicinity of their own people."[579] And Berl Katznelson, labor leader and close comrade of Ben-Gurion's, stated, "My conscience is clear on this point absolutely. A remote neighbor is better than a close enemy. They will not lose from being transferred and we shall certainly not lose from it."[580] Golda Meir concurred: "I would agree that if the Arabs leave the country my conscience would be absolutely clear."[581]

The resolve did not dissipate with time. In 1941, afforestation planner and Jewish National Fund leader Joseph Weitz wrote in his diary:

> Except perhaps for Bethlehem, Nazareth and Old Jerusalem we must not leave a single village, not a single tribe....And only with such a transfer will the country be able to absorb millions of our brothers, and the Jewish question will be solved once and for all. There is no other way out.[582]

But they also knew that subtlety and subterfuge would be necessary, as was reflected in their own private statements about keeping these plans under wraps. For example, the historian Benny Morris quotes from Herzl's diary of June 12, 1895:

> "We must expropriate gently...We shall try to spirit the penniless population across the border by procuring employment for it in the transit countries, while denying any employment in our country....Both the

process of expropriation and the removal of the poor must be carried out discretely and circumspectly."[583]

Morris also quotes Eliezer Ben-Yehuda, the mastermind behind resurrecting the ancient sacred language of Hebrew as a modern vernacular for the Zionist enterprise, writing with a comrade to someone back in Vilna, "We have made it a rule not to say too much, except to those...we trust....The goal is to revive our nation on its land... *if only we succeed in increasing our numbers here until we are the majority.*" (Emphasis in original.) At that point, they were sure, they could "easily take away the country [from the Arabs] if only we do it through stratagems...."[584]

FRIENDS WITH BENEFITS

To that end, in their public statements Zionists presented their program as something that, rather than imposing exclusion and displacement, would be of great benefit to the Arabs of the region. Haim Gerber, the Middle Eastern studies scholar who taught at the Hebrew University in Jerusalem, wrote in 2008 about the rhetoric enlisted for this attempt at conciliatory persuasion:

> In Palestine the theory was developed that the Zionist project, while it did not come into the world to help the Palestinian masses, was nevertheless to their pure benefit. That they did not seem to agree was simply because they had been brainwashed by their greedy, selfish, and wicked elite of effendis, who maliciously convinced them to lash out at the Jews. The explanation was simple: they wanted to keep these masses under their tight control and lucrative exploitation, while the Zionists wanted to free them and make of them independent human beings. Hence, the real interest of the working masses in Palestine was to go with the Zionists, not against them, which meant of course also agreeing to their political program. The problem which no Zionist thinker at the time (and very few Israelis to this day) was willing to face was that this analysis rested on a lie: there was an insoluble tension between Zionist ambitions and the fate of Palestinian workers and peasants.[585]

Shabtai Teveth, David Ben-Gurion's biographer, illustrates Ben-Gurion's convoluted advocacy of this marketing idea:

> From the start [Ben-Gurion] was one of the few Zionists who wished to anchor Zionism's claim to Palestine not only in history and myth, but also in the argument—equally important to him—that Zionism was a movement of peace and justice, a blessing to non-Jews in Palestine and its neighbors as well.... Although he knew that the conflict [with the Palestinians] existed, for tactical reasons he had to deny it.... After the revolution in Russia he began asserting that there was no conflict of interest between Zionism and the Arabs, since labor Zionism's vocation was to expedite the socialist revolution in the East. With the establishment of socialism in the region the conflict would disappear as if it had never been, since it had been created arbitrarily by the exploitative, feudal Arab effendis and clerics, who sought to benefit only themselves, fearing progress and the social and national liberation it would bring.[586]

In 1902, six years after the appearance of his seminal treatise, *The Jewish State,* Theodor Herzl famously publicized the notion that Zionism would furnish an Eden for everyone with his utopian, futuristic novel *Altneuland* ("Old New Land"). In it, he depicted a new society in Palestine that was both a Jewish homeland and an egalitarian, multicultural open society in which European culture, science, technology, and industry found its apotheosis, and all were welcome to partake of it. Near the outset, the protagonist—a young, secular, disaffected café habitué named Dr. Friedrich Loewenberg (a description that, aside from the name, fit Herzl himself)—attends a soiree at the Viennese home of a bourgeois Jewish family, where he finds himself amidst a conversation about encroaching antisemitism. "I feel it coming," says one guest. "We'll all have to wear the yellow badge." Someone else says, "Or emigrate." "I ask you, where to?" asks the first speaker, a lawyer who, we are told, has changed his name from "Veiglstock" to "Walter," though his next line denotes the futility of assimilation: "Are things better anywhere else? Even in free France the anti-Semites have the upper hand." A diffident, elderly rabbi from the provinces among the company mentions the project of Zionism. His description is met with much mirth. "Will there be theaters in Palestine?"

asks one of the guests, petulantly. "If not, I shall not go there."[587]

Not to worry. The land may be old in the sense of being viewed as an inheritance from the Jewish patriarchs, but it is new in terms of it being in the vanguard of colonial modernity—in essence, Europeanness. Voltaire's Pangloss would no doubt be forced to concede that this was "the best of all possible worlds," bearing all the amenities that affluent Europeans could desire and anyone else would be keen to bask in. Time passes, and, at last touring the country with his traveling companion—a "Prussian officer and Christian German nobleman" named Adalbert von Koenighoff[588] who is, for some reason, more generally known as a curmudgeonly English aristocrat named Kingscourt—Friedrich is introduced to the wonders of the New Society. Twenty years earlier, he discovers, Jerusalem "had been a gloomy dilapidated city; now she was risen in splendor, youthful, alert, risen from death to life."[589] At the time of their visit, "the spell of the Sabbath was over the Holy City, now freed from the filth, noise and vile odors that had so often revolted devout pilgrims of all creeds...."[590] They encounter "a large park laid out in the English fashion, fronted by an edifice marked "Health Department of the New Society," which, observes Kingscourt, "is evidently modeled after the Imperial German Health Department."[591] The presidential mansion "reminded them of the palazzi of the Genoese patricians," and in the playgrounds "half-grown youngsters were playing English games": tennis, cricket, and football.[592]

At the villa of their guide, David Littwack—whom we met earlier as a pitiable, impoverished child of the diaspora void but has been transfigured into a confident, successful leading figure in the New Society—the guests enjoy a Passover seder. Afterward, they repair to the drawing room, where their host plays a phonograph recording of a speech by Joseph Levy—the general director of the Department of Industry and venerated polymath—in which the amazing development of the New Society is explained. The appropriateness of the occasion is elucidated by Littwack: "Once more there was an Egypt, and again a happy exodus—under twentieth century conditions, of course, and with modern equipment."[593]

"While the local Zionist groups were selecting their best human material for Palestine," Levy's recorded voice expounds, "English, French, and German firms established branches in Haifa, Jaffa, Jericho, and before the gates of Jerusalem. The natives were astonished at the sudden appearance of Occidental goods in the country, and at first could find no explanation for the marvel." He remarks that in "an amusing letter," one of their colleagues had

> "described the solemn puzzlement of the Orientals. 'Grave camels stood stock still,' he wrote, 'and shook their heads.' But the natives began to buy at once, and word of the new bazaars spread quickly.... The customers streamed in on all sides. Our enterprise, casting its shadow before, brought on a commercial revival."[594]

On another day of their journey, coming upon a neighborhood with "many elegant mansions surrounded by fragrant gardens," the visitors are told that "these were the homes of prominent Moslems." Standing at the gate of one is Reschid Bey, a distinguished Arab citizen of the New Society who has nothing but praise for it. A native of the East who has taken mightily to the infusion of the West, he wears "dark European clothing and a red fez" and has a doctorate in chemistry from a German university. He is hailed by David Littwack in Arabic, but he replies in German—"with a slight northern accent." "Who's the little Muslim?" asks Kingscourt. "'He studied in Berlin,' replied David laughingly. 'His father was among the first to understand the beneficent character of the Jewish immigration, and enriched himself, because he kept pace with our economic progress.'"[595]

Later, joining the entourage, Bey offers testimonials to how life has improved since the advent of the Zionists: "Our profits have grown considerably. Our orange transport has multiplied tenfold since we have had good transportation facilities to connect us with the whole world. Everything here has increased in value since your immigration."[596] When an astonished Kingscourt asks him, "Were not the older inhabitants of Palestine ruined by the Jewish immigration? And didn't they have to leave the country?" Bey sets him straight: "It was a great blessing for all of us." As for those who "had nothing" before, Bey explains that they

> "could only gain. And they did gain: Opportunities to work, means of livelihood, prosperity.... When the swamps were drained, the canals built, and the eucalyptus trees planted to drain, and 'cure' the marshy soil, the natives (who, naturally, were well acclimatized) were the first to be employed, and were paid well for their work.... These people are better

off than at any time in the past. They support themselves decently, their children are healthier and are being taught something. Their religion and ancient customs have in no wise been interfered with. They have become more prosperous—that is all.... The Jews have enriched us.... They dwell among us like brothers. Why should we not love them?"[597]

So, as we can see, while leading Zionists privately shared their intentions to transfer the indigenous population to "other Arab countries" to create an all-Jewish or Jewish-majority state, they concurrently aired public proclamations that that same population would harvest the advantages of Zionist accomplishments. Speaking "out of both sides of their mouths," as the saying goes, their "sides" were precisely aimed at two different audiences to further two different objectives. They surely knew that, once realized, these objectives would catastrophically collide with one another.

THE NOT-SO-HIDDEN ANSWER: IT WAS ABOUT DOMINATION AND DISPLACEMENT, NOT RELIGION

In his disingenuous defense of Zionist land-purchasing practices, Alan Dershowitz also claims that "many, although not all, of the Jewish refugees sought to establish good relations with their Arab neighbors."[598] We have already seen the schism between the public statements to that effect and Zionist leaders' private statements of quite opposite intentions, accompanied by their awareness that discretion regarding the latter was crucial to achieving their aims.

To illustrate his point, Dershowitz ignores the accumulated published evidence of the Zionists' secretively expressed objectives and instead simply lauds the magnanimity of Yitzhak Epstein, a Russian-born Zionist of the First Aliyah who, Dershowitz says, "proposed giving local Arabs access to Jewish hospitals, schools, and libraries."[599] What he does not cite: the reaction, ranging from dismissive to hostile, to "The Hidden Question," a speech Epstein gave at the Seventh Zionist Congress in Basel in 1905 and had published in 1907 as a pamphlet. Epstein was a distinct outlier among his peers, hardly an archetype of their *Weltanschauung*. Adam Shatz, in a prefatory note to the speech in his book *Prophets Outcast*, calls Epstein's address "taboo-breaking" and notes that Epstein "punctured one of the central myths of Zionism: that the Arabs of

Palestine had no national rights which the Zionist movement was bound to respect."[600] Nur Masalha observes, "Reflected in the Zionist establishment's angry response to Epstein's article are two principal features of mainstream Zionist thought: the belief that Jewish acquisition of land took precedence over moral considerations, and the advocacy of a separatist and exclusionist Yishuv (colony) in Palestine."[601]

"The Hidden Question" makes it clear that at the very time that land sales and widespread Zionist movement-building were taking place, denial of what the Palestinian presence might portend—morally, legally, and politically—was in effect. In Epstein's speech, he charges his audience with letting their relations with the Arabs go "completely unnoticed" and points out that the reality of their existence is "barely mentioned in the literature of our movement." (Notably, many have remarked on the absence of any reference to the Arabs' claims in what is considered Theodor Herzl's blueprint for Zionist development, *The Jewish State.*) Epstein calls the Zionist movement "irresponsible" in ignoring this "fundamental issue" and accuses it of "deal[ing] with issues superficially" rather than "delv[ing] into their core." To perpetuate the idea that Palestine is "a land without a people" and to convince oneself that there will be no backlash against Zionist colonization from those it has injured is to put one's head in the sand, he argues. He grants that for the earliest Zionist settlers, who were "not familiar with the country and its inhabitants," this blind spot may not have been "intentional." But by this point in time, that excuse has exhausted its statute of limitations. He declares point-blank:

> The time has come to dispel the misconceptions among the Zionists that land in Palestine lies uncultivated for lack of working hands or laziness of the local residents. There are no deserted fields.... We must not uproot people from land to which they and their forefathers dedicated their best efforts and toil. If there are farmers who water their fields with their sweat, these are the Arabs."

Importantly, Epstein urges his audience to "leave justice and sensitivity aside for the moment" and take a hard look at the blowback that is sure to come from the dispossession that is in the process of occurring. "Will those who are disposed remain silent and accept what is being done to them?" he asks, and answers his own rhetorical question: "In the end, they will wake up and return to us in blows what we have looted from them with our gold!" The Zionists are, essentially, inciting resistance, quite possibly a violent one. He warns, "Let us not tease a sleeping lion! Let us not depend upon the ash that covers the embers: one spark escapes, and soon it will be a conflagration out of control." For all these reasons, concludes Epstein, if the Zionists are to operate in an "enlightened" way, they must both get educated about Arab culture (something they have tragically neglected) and truly share with the indigenous people—as they publicly profess they will—not only the land but their science and technology and the infrastructure they develop.

Epstein's warning was not heeded, though the issue did not go undiscussed. In Zionist community deliberations it was largely reframed as a matter of expediency: how were Zionists to overcome the obstacle the Arabs presented to achieving their vision? In a 2003 article, Middle East historian Abigail Jacobson writes that "[f]ollowing Epstein's essay, the debate regarding the Arab question became a central one in the Hebrew press of Palestine."[602] Focusing on the years 1912 to 1914, she shows that the Ashkenazi workers' papers *ha-Po'el ha-Tza'ir* and *ha-Ahdut,* published by fairly recent, mainly Russian Jewish immigrants to Palestine, were pragmatically concerned with how Jewish control could be achieved in Palestine. In particular, they focused on the "conquest of labor" (or "Hebrew labor"), which entailed the exclusion of the Arab work force from its operations.

The contention that an all-Jewish labor force was a prerequisite for developing a Jewish state would gain momentum over time and reach fever pitch in the 1920s and 1930s, when Histadrut-instigated boycotts, pickets, riots, assaults, and death threats broke out against Palestinian workers and their Jewish employers at citrus groves and urban construction sites. As Steven A. Glazer has pointed out, the claims of the Histadrut (the Jewish worker federation that had tentacles reaching into virtually all aspects of the life in the Yishuv) that hiring Arab workers siphoned off jobs for Jews flew in the face of the reality that Jewish workers demanded higher pay than was being offered at these locations and simply took their labor power elsewhere. Glazer argues that in large measure, the boycotts were performative public relations stunts posing as urgent economic measures. Garnering huge boosts in the form of mass rallies and media coverage, and in one site inciting an enraged crowd to loudly demand "war against the displacers of the Jewish worker,"[603] Glazer says that these measures were really "part of a propaganda exercise." The stated goals "were far less important than the long-term goals of positioning the Histadrut and the Zionist labor parties in the forefront of militant communal nationalism" and "depict[ing] the Histadrut as an aggressive champion of Zionist interests."[604] He notes that, in any case, it is instructive to "compare the Histadrut's rhetoric of the day—which insisted that the Zionist labor union put the highest priority on efforts to achieve Arab-Jewish cooperation"[605]—with what actually happened. This was not hard for observant Palestinians to do. Serving as further evidence of the Zionist movement's ultimate plans and the hypocrisy of its leaders' public pro- testations, the "Hebrew Labor" actions intensified already-inflamed Palestinian sensitivities and contributed to a cumulatively swelling Palestinian nationalism. This, of course, was precisely the result that Yizhak Epstein had foretold.

Walter Laqueur, in *A History of Zionism,* acknowledges that some Zionist reference works of the period simply omit mention of Epstein's speech altogeth- er.[606] Bitton points out that "The Hidden Question" is "rarely cited" and that it was not until 2001 that it was even translated into English.[607]

But back in 1908, in the immediate aftermath of the responses Epstein had provoked, a Zionist movement office led by Arthur Ruppin opened in Jaffa. It worked in affiliation with the central office in Istanbul to promote Jewish labor and new Jewish settlements, activating considerable consternation within the Arab communities and prompting the new autonym "Palestinian," which marked their resistance and indigeneity as distinct from Zionist newcomers.[608] Resentment built as the Zionist immigrants clearly, despite their public denials, sought to establish a separatist Jewish society even while retaining their foreign citizenship, backed by a host of new exclusive institutions and fundraising apparatuses.

To calibrate this discontent and its possible strategic ramifications, Ruppin's office opened a press bureau in 1911 that translated selected articles from the Arabic press suggestive of Arab public opinion about Zionist development. At the same time, it published articles that, according to Jacobson, "attempted to create a more positive attitude to the Zionist movement among the Arabs" by "explain[ing] the nature and goals of the Zionist movement,...emphasiz[ing] the common interests of Arabs and Jews in Palestine, and...not[ing] the advantages that the Jewish population could bring to the country and to the

Arab population."[609] Much like a public relations firm's damage control scheme in response to a crisis, the aim was not to change the actual conditions on the ground, as Epstein had urged, but to respond to the growing anger and suspicion toward the Jewish community with a campaign "to try and change Arab *perception* of them."[610] (Italics added.)

Yet the realities on the ground and their coverage in the Arabic press eclipsed the spin and firmed up the sense that it was simply another insidious manifestation of the problem. According to Rashid Khalidi, it was opposition to land sales to the colonists, especially by absentee landlords, that over time brought the *a'ayan*, the *fellahin*, and broader pan-Arab elements together in common cause.[611] With the Young Turks revolution of 1908 and the ensuing press freedoms throughout the Ottoman Empire under the ruling Committee of Union and Progress (CUP), writes Khalidi, newspapers both in the directly affected areas and as far away as Beirut, Cairo, and Damascus "informed their readers not only of the day-to-day details of the progress of colonization...but also explained to them the aims and extent of the Zionist movement as a whole...."[612] Surveying hundreds of articles culled from twenty-two Arabic newspapers and periodicals between 1908 and 1914, Khalidi finds Zionism "clearly to have been perceived regionally, and not just in Palestine itself, as an ominous and potentially threatening phenomenon."[613] Mazin Qumsiyeh writes of the appearance in 1914 of a circular headlined "General Summons to Palestinians: Beware of Zionist Danger." It was signed by "a Palestinian" and it advised that there was a "Zionist desire to settle in our country and expel us from it."[614]

In the vanguard of the opposition newspapers was *al-Karmil,* whose editor supplemented in-house objections to Zionist settlement with reprints from other Arabic newspapers and translated pieces from the *Encyclopedia Judaica* that afforded "extensive background information on the history, objectives, and significance of the Zionist movement," including reports on the unstinting work of Theodor Herzl.[615] Other newspapers such as *Filastin, al-Mufid,* and *al-Muqtabas* were similarly outspoken in their critiques of land sales to foreigners (including as objects of their condemnation the Arab landowners, both Palestinian and not, who did the selling) and also of the CUP, whose laxity was perceived as passively enabling Zionist immigration and land acquisition.[616] Even pro-Zionist articles that "sought to assure [their Arab audiences] of the benign nature of Zionist intentions," says Khalidi, "seem to have provoked and aroused Arab readers, particularly those in Palestine, who could see with their own eyes what the Zionists were in fact doing," as well as contrast those assurances with "the blunt and disturbing words of Zionist leaders directed to European and Zionist audiences."[617] By degrees, gaslighting becomes perceptible.

Khalidi notes, "In no article among the more than 650 examined for this analysis of the press and Zionism was there a call for armed resistance to the colonizers, although…in a few areas the peasants had already spontaneously engaged in such resistance."[618] But a salient theme running through the articles, he finds, is the fear that, despite Zionists' denials, the ultimate aim of their movement was to establish Jewish political sovereignty by engineering a majority Jewish population, with the Arabs either reduced to a minority or removed altogether.[619] As we have seen, and as has become increasingly obvious ever since, this fear was well-founded.

CHAPTER 7:
THE JEWISH NATIONAL FUND AND THE MANUFACTURE OF ENVIRONMENTAL STEWARDSHIP

"The JNF is Israel's oldest propagandist, promoting Israel as a 'green' and progressive nation since 1901; its parks have long been Israel's most tangible propaganda maneuver."
—Rebecca Manski, American writer and editor[620]

"Ever since its founding, the State of Israel has used tree planting as a means to either cover up the past or pave the way for the future."
—Meron Rapoport, Israeli journalist[621]

"The JNF is not the trustee of the general public in Israel. Its loyalty is given to the Jewish people in the Diaspora and in the state of Israel.... The JNF, in relation to being an owner of land, is not a public body that works for the benefit of all citizens of the state. The loyalty of the JNF is given to the Jewish people and only to them is the JNF obligated. The JNF, as the owner of the JNF land, does not have a duty to practice equality towards all citizens of the state."
— Response of the JNF, dated December 2004, to a petition filed by the independent Palestinian human rights organization and legal center Adalah to the Supreme Court of Israel—HC 9205/04.[622]

AFFORESTATION AND ITS DISCONTENTS

Many of the "stratagems" employed to "take away the country" from the Arabs[623] were enacted under the aegis of the Jewish National Fund (JNF),[624] founded in

1901 and persistently active over the next twelve decades. Today it remains a nongovernmental organization (NGO) with 501(c)(3) charitable status in the United States and classed as a charity in at least twenty-two other countries.[625] Its original mission was, according to the group's website, "to purchase land in Eretz Israel for the Jewish People"[626] (meaning the Jewish people the world over, including but not limited to those who reside in Palestine). The "Jewish people" would retain ownership in perpetuity, according to the 1929 JNF constitution. That is, the citizens of the Israeli state, of which roughly a fifth are non-Jews, have in that status alone no claim on these lands and have no right to live, buy, cultivate, or build on them because these lands are technically not under state control. Via such maneuvers, writes Dan Leon, "the State of Israel as such…could not be accused of expropriating the land."[627]

Under Ottoman law, land that was not cultivated was to be repossessed by the state or its prior owner, and so not only acquisition but immediate development of the land fell under the JNF's purview.[628] Over its 120-year lifespan, JNF has shape-shifted from consumer or appropriator (or as the group put it, "redeemer") of land to creator of agricultural settlements to builder of forests, roads, tourist destinations, parks, "defense" outposts, water resources, schools, and other infrastructure—but always with the objective of creating "facts on the ground" that indelibly restrict future entitlement. The historian Yaara Berger Alaluf maintains that the "roots of the Nakba" are to be found well before 1948 in these early land transactions and the activities that followed. Alaluf, who is also the Coordinator of Community and Education in the Israeli NGO Zochrot, which promotes awareness of the Nakba, quotes from Yosef Weitz's diary from 1940. Weitz wrote there that "land purchasing" alone would not bring about the state; what was also needed was "redemption" (always a keyword for the JNF's undertakings), involving a "Messianic concept" and—he is quite blunt about this—transfer of Palestinian Arabs to "Iraq, Syria, and even Transjordan. For that goal, money will be found—even a lot of money," he wrote. In short, land purchase, fundraising, Messianism, and population transfer are ineluctably bound together in state-creation, which Weitz calls a "final solution…to the Jewish question."[629]

Weitz, the director of the JNF's Lands Department, would go on to spearhead the Transfer Committee, which—conveniently *sort-of with* and *sort-of without* the knowledge and consent of Ben-Gurion—was key to the expropriation of Palestinian Arab land and the expulsion of its inhabitants at the time of the Nakba. The JNF's ambiguous status as a nongovernmental organization that was nonetheless indispensable to the government's work was the critical ingredient of its power. As Uri Davis and Walter Lehn have argued, this was hardly an atypical discursive maneuver:

> Israel's land legislation, as all Israeli legislation with the single exception of the *Law of Return* (1950), is *consciously* calculated to generate...uncertainty....Through deliberate and conscious legal formulations predicated on the manipulation of the meaning of terms such as *person, nation,* etc., the State of Israel has succeeded in presenting to Western intellectual and public opinion its far-reaching apartheid legislation as progressive social democracy....[I]n Zionist usage,... "person" is read as "Jewish person," "public" as "Jewish public," "the people" as "the Jewish people," "nation" as "Jewish nation," and "Israel" as "the people of Israel" (i.e., the community of adherents to Judaism, to be distinguished from the citizens of the state of Israel—and even from the Jewish citizens of the state). (Italics in original.)[630]

Thus, employing this precise imprecision so that it could act as a quasi-front group for state officials, the JNF took over land from which Palestinians had been expelled militarily and bound it in language that rendered its reclamation by the refugees impossible. As Alaluf puts it:

> [T]he land transfer to the JNF enabled the Israeli government, which wanted to remain within the boundaries of international law, to launder the refugees' assets. The transfer of land to the JNF prevented refugees and internally displaced persons from returning to their land or being compensated for it, by distancing the properties both from their original owners and from the fledgling mechanisms of law and order....[631]

Daniel E. Orenstein and Steven P. Hamburg further explain:

> Following the 1937 British Royal (Peel) Commission Plan for the partition of Palestine, [pre-state bureaucracies such as the JNF] redoubled their efforts for increased Jewish rural development, as they realized that

the borders of the emerging Jewish state would be drawn along lines of Jewish settlement....

The expanded partition borders for a Jewish state as proposed in the United Nations Partition Plan in 1947, and in particular the inclusion of the Negev in the Jewish state, were in part a response to new Jewish settlements established in the interim period....The new government and quasi-governmental settlement agencies prioritized settlement in strategically located regions, particularly in border areas and in areas that had originally been allocated to the Arab state by the UN Partition....[to] secure an Israeli claim to the land and preempt efforts of Arab refugees to reclaim the land.[632]

Many, however—including Ben-Gurion—assumed that the JNF would become obsolete after the establishment of the Israeli state in 1948. "Then," says Dan Leon, "came the UN resolution on the refugees [UN General Assembly Resolution 194, which affirmed Palestinian refugees' right of return or compensation for property], arousing the fear of grave international repercussions if the state were to take over Arab land directly. The JNF was used to circumvent the issue and it was given a new mandate, later popularized in the slogan 'Making the desert bloom.'"[633]

The early years are hard to consider in isolation from the JNF's later work because the various components of realizing its abiding vision were structured according to an intentional domino effect. Taking a long-term view, we can see how the JNF's early work both achieved its purpose—its "facts on the ground" came to be regarded, de facto, as ineradicable when it came to justifying territorial prerogatives—yet also backfired, as, in its haste to turn what they deemed "wasteland" into agricultural settlements and produce a European ambiance for their immigrants, they destroyed vital ecosystems and planted forests of non-native trees not suited to the Mediterranean climate. It is, of course, very nice to have a picnic in a shady park on a hot summer day. However, the adage, "The operation was a success, but the patient died" may be apposite here.

The JNF has, since its inception, burnished its image as a highly qualified protector of the land, whether by dint of employing "pioneers" who "drained the swamps" and "greened the desert" or, much later, by framing itself as an actor within the discourse of sustainable development and the global environmental movement. Yoav Galai has argued that, throughout, the term "redemption" remained germane to the JNF's projected image, even as its meaning changed in a "rebranding" project. Originally the JNF's "redemptive" role lay in restoring the "natural" biblical landscape as it was before it was purportedly ruined by reckless interlopers.[634] It also "redeemed" guilt feelings Israelis may have had if JNF forests hadn't covered over the ruins of eighty-six Palestinian villages emptied in 1948, rendering them invisible to the visitor's gaze and thus bolstering the JNF's contention that nothing except wasteland lay beneath. "Redemption is not reflected merely by land deeds or registration, which are open to and understood by few, but by what the eyes can see: a tree or neighborhood, a village or town, a school or university," the JNF's website covering its "Second Decade: 1911–1920" pronounces.[635] Not mentioned in this auto-history is what the eyes *cannot* see and how that, too, shapes historical understanding. Ilan Pappe has popularized the term "memoricide" to describe JNF's intentional disappearing act, augmented by an official "Naming Committee" which overwrote extant Arabic designations of sites with Hebrew nomenclature. "Pine trees were planted not only over bulldozed houses, but also over fields and olive groves," writes Pappe. He quotes the JNF website, which, he says, "proudly proclaims that these forests and parks were built upon 'arid and desert-like areas' . . . ." All in all, says Pappe, "guided only by . . . JNF signs, visitors will never realize that people used to live here."[636]

Some of the most popular destinations the JNF has created are its parks, refreshing weekend sanctuaries in a hot climate. Canada Park, whose construction by the JNF was enabled by tax-deductible contributions from Jewish and Christian Zionists of the country that bears its name, spills silently over the Green Line into the West Bank.[637] The donors are honored by plaques bearing their names at the entrance to the park. Though the fact is concealed by the "historical" narratives the JNF provides, which focus on ancient ruins rather than those of the twentieth century, the greenery sits atop the ruins of three Palestinian villages: Imwas, Yalu, and Beit Nuba. These villages were demolished by the Israeli army during the 1967 war, their unarmed inhabitants (including children, the elderly, and the disabled) expelled and consigned to permanent refugee status if they survived the rough conditions of the evacuation. The JNF's Toronto and Israel offices flatly deny that the park is built on the debris of these villages, despite the clear evidence of physical remains.[638]

Yitzhak Rabin, then army chief of staff and later Israel's "dovish" prime minister, openly acknowledges in the Canadian documentary *Park with No Peace* that he gave the order to destroy the villages. Yet, contradicting eyewitness testimony by Israeli soldiers as well as Palestinian survivors, he denies that there were civilians present to be expelled, insisting instead that the villages were being used as hiding places for Egyptian commandos.[639]

Other JNF parks and forests are similarly named for the countries of donors, such as Italy Park, located on the Alexander River, which the JNF claims it has "rehabilitat[ed] for coexistence."[640] British Park was planted in the 1950s over the ruins of Palestinian villages Ajjur and Zakariyya, which were ethnically cleansed in the Nakba.[641] South Africa Forest covers the former site of the village of Lubya, also destroyed in the Nakba. Interestingly, in 2015 a group of South Africans who donated to create it visited the site and issued a public apology to those who were forcibly removed and their descendants.[642]

The themes of some JNF parks and forests are meant to show Israel's affinity for those who struggle for justice globally. One in honor of Martin Luther King, Jr., was planted in 1976; attendees sang "We Shall Overcome" at its inaugural ceremony.[643] The Coretta Scott King Forest, plugged as "Perpetuating her message of equality and peace,"[644] was "built over the ruins of six destroyed Palestinian villages located in the Safad region."[645] In November 2022, in central Israel, a memorial garden was constructed inside Tel Mond Park to honor South African Jews who fought apartheid while supporting Israel. Speaking at its inaugural ceremony, Ruth Wasserman Land, a South African member of Israel's Knesset, commended "this park, donated by the South African Jewish community, which is known for its staunch support for and loyalty to South Africa on the one hand and its love of Israel on the other." Significant South African critics of Israeli apartheid such as Nelson Mandela and Desmond Tutu were, apparently, not mentioned.[646] The American Independence Park was first developed in 1976—according to the JNF, "the 200th anniversary year of American independence, to celebrate the relationship between the two freedom-loving countries, Israel and the US."[647] The highest dispenser of justice, outshining them all, is likewise honored with greenery: God TV Forest is a tree- and shrub-planting collaboration in the northern Negev between the JNF and the global Christian evangelical network. There, Bedouin communities are consistently uprooted—though they then return and rebuild, ad infinitum—to set the scene for the homecoming of Jesus Christ.[648]

In later years, under domestic and international pressure from a flourishing ecology movement, the JNF remade itself as a new type of "green organization." Now, the group proclaims that its "redemptive" work includes "protecting the environment, caring for Israel's open spaces and natural woodlands, and much more." In addition, says Galai, in its contemporary afforestation schemes—such as those being attempted in the Negev—the JNF has shrewdly partnered with foreign entities, using the cachet of "international cooperation" to shield itself from "here Israel goes again" denunciations for its unpopular practices.[649]

Moreover, says the Israeli public policy scholar Ravit Hananel, up through the 1980s, Israeli national land policy embodied the traditional Zionist-nationalist discourse of the agrarian ideal, wherein agricultural cooperatives' back-to-the-land fervor dovetailed nicely with the vision of preserved arcadian serenity. But by the 1990s, as these cooperatives' earning power dissolved and their members sought new forms of revenue through development of their lands—housing, industry, and commerce—their aspirations collided with the increasingly vocal thrust of environmental/preservationist advocacy. Perusing documents of the Israel Lands Council (a land-policy-administering offshoot of the Israel Lands Administration that works in cooperation with the JNF), Hananel finds, "Throughout the 1990s, despite the substantial increase in environmental awareness in Israel and throughout the world, and contrary to the environmentally sensitive land use policy that was adopted, there was no discourse in the ILC indicating an increase in the importance of environmental considerations." ("Also," she adds, "the protocols examined do not mention the word 'Arabs' nor is there any direct mention of the Arab sector.")[650]

GREENWASHING

Some of what I have just described has been classified as "greenwashing"—originally, a term used by environmentalists to describe corporations' superficial promotion of environmentally-friendly policies to mask the ecologically destructive (though profitable) practices that lie beneath. Now the term has attained broader use, and the JNF, along with manifesting its traditional meaning—for example, creating landscapes that look good but are unsuitable and ultimately harmful to their local habitat—stands accused by many of using ostensibly "earth-friendly" practices to cover up ethnic cleansing. To understand the roots of these practices, it is useful to examine, in greater detail, the JNF's oft-flaunted "draining the swamps" and "greening the desert" projects and how they unfolded.

In its decade-by-decade history of its work, the JNF concludes the "Second Decade: 1911–1920" installment inside the minds of KKL-JNF "pioneers" and their dreams for the future: "Gazing down onto the valleys through their binoculars, staffers could see only festering swamps. But, the Fund's work, they knew, would transform the desolation and stagnant water into broad expanses dotted with the gleam of wheat, the green of trees, and the strips of fields plowed and sowed."[651]

"Draining a swamp" does indeed sound like valorous work until you consider that a "swamp" is also known as a "wetland" and as such has protected status in places where ecologically sensitive law prevails—and for good reason. Wetlands provide crucial habitat for flora and fauna, reduce carbon emissions into the atmosphere, improve water quality, and maintain water levels that can mitigate flood or drought. "Wetlands are among the most productive ecosystems in the world, comparable to rain forests and coral reefs," says the US Environmental Protection Agency on its website.[652] Owners of shopping malls and sports stadiums, developers of sprawling suburban residential tracts, and managers of landfills have, over time, ecologically abused "swamps" and then, as environmental consciousness and pressures grew, attempted to revivify them.

An infamous example of this phenomenon played out in the Galilee region of northern Israel, where zealous Zionists under the auspices of the JNF "drained the swamp" called Hula Lake in the 1950s to adapt it for agricultural development. "Draining the Hula, north of the Sea of Galilee, was a powerfully symbolic national enterprise, celebrated with patriotic fervor much as the space program was in the United States," Joel Greenberg wrote in the *New York Times* in 1993, by which time work was being done to redress the project's unforeseen and insalubrious effects. These latter-day reclamation efforts, he says, reflected "a basic shift of priorities." He reports that at the triumphant time of the "draining," Israeli Agriculture Minister Kadish Luz had announced, "Land had been redeemed from hostile nature, and water that had been a menace to health turned into a blessing." Yet Greenberg also quotes Israeli conservationist Azaria

Alon suggesting that environmentalists who tried to caution against the project at the time were muffled; draining the Hula swamp "was difficult to talk about, because anyone who spoke out was considered anti-Zionist."[653] The zoologist and conservationist Heinrich Mendelssohn, who Alon Tal says is "now considered the father of ecological science in Israel,"[654] recounted to Tal in a 1997 interview his attempt to persuade Weitz, soon after statehood, to retain at least some of the Hula swamp as a nature preserve before draining it for farming:

> "He started screaming at me and banging on the table. 'You want the land for the animals and plants, and if it was up to you, there'd be none left for the Jews. You're an *ocher Yisrael* (an enemy of Israel)' he yelled and then threw me out of his office."[655]

As Daniel E. Orenstein and Steven P. Hamburg aptly put it in a 2008 article for the journal *Land Use Policy*, "These two concerns, political-demographic control and environmental protection, create very different paradigms for how to think about open space policy."[656] Noam Levin et al. wrote in the journal *Landscape and Urban Planning*, also in 2008, that the draining of the Hula lake and swamps "resulted in serious agricultural and ecological problems" and that, more broadly, "the fate of wetlands along the coastal plain of Israel over the past 150 years"—including "a drawdown of the water table" and "a detrimental effect upon natural aquatic habitats"—"has been the result of human impacts."[657] Among the casualties in the Hula Valley were the disappearance of 119 animal species, including the extinction of the Hula painted frog (*Discoglossus nigriventer*), the extinction of numerous freshwater plant species, the rerouting of migratory birds flying between Europe and Africa, and the unanticipated population explosion of the vole (*Microtus socialis*), which rampantly destroyed crops and led many to cease farming there—in turn accelerating soil deterioration.[658] According to Alon Tal, "When the JNF drained the Huleh region, it removed an essential 'nutrient sink' that absorbed much of the nitrogen and phosphorus from the surface runoff into the Kinneret [the Sea of Galilee]. In addition, the rich organic peat, newly exposed and nitrified, was washed down into the reservoir."[659] Greenberg adds these details:

> Dried peat soil from the bottom of the marsh has decomposed, burned

and released pollutants that once were filtered by the swamp, leaving a wasteland unfit for farming.... The dry peat disintegrated, sank and burned in underground fires caused by spontaneous combustion. The fertility of the soil declined sharply.... As farmers stopped cultivating large areas, the land was overrun by mice and weeds, and peat dust whipped up by winds covered the region.[660]

The JNF and its champions laud the organization's restoration work of the 1990s, boasting that they have wooed wildlife back and turned the area into a prime ecotourism and bird-watching destination.[661] Yet others have raised questions about the impact of nature tourism itself on wildlife. In a study published in the journal *Tourism Management*, researchers Noga Collins-Kreiner et al. point out that the people who flock to observe the repatriated birds in the Hula Valley are, in turn, stressors who can cause those very objects of interest to flee, producing "tourist disturbance stimulation" that can have "a detrimental effect on animal fitness and individual survival."[662]

As for its work "greening the desert," the JNF's self-portrayal is once again displayed on its website. This time it appears under the heading, "FORESTRY & GREEN INNOVATIONS: Turning the desert into a vibrant, green oasis." The blurb is a prelude to a fundraising pitch and offer of hands-on volunteer opportunities ("Traveling to Israel? Get your hands dirty and plant some roots of your own. Schedule a trip to our Tree Planting Center....")[663]

The body of the section begins, "Beautiful, isn't it? Since our founding in 1901, we've planted an incredible 250 million trees in Israel. And the results have been transformative and breathtaking. Once a desert-nation, today Israel has blossomed into a garden oasis." In step with contemporary sensibilities, it mentions the need to "grapple" with the new "challenge" of "balancing the phenomenal growth and development Israel has experienced in the last decade with the maintenance of an ecologically sound environment"—which the JNF as "guardian of the land" is uniquely equipped to oversee.

Or is it?

"Almost from the start," writes Ilan Pappe,

the JNF executive opted mainly for conifers instead of the natural flora indigenous to Palestine. In part this was an attempt to make the country look European, although this appears nowhere in any official document as a goal.... The three aims of keeping the country Jewish, European-looking and Green quickly fused into one.[664]

In his 1974 book vindicating and promoting the JNF's tree-planting enterprise, *Forests and Afforestation in Israel*, Joseph Weitz frames his case with the usual Zionist tropes demonstrating the "restoration" by modern Israel of biblical geographies—which, until the Jews were forced into exile, had existed "in a natural state."[665] "When ... the Hebrews took possession of the land of Canaan," he writes, "they found mixed woods of fruit trees and forest trees...."[666] He cites references in the bible as "evidence" for the presence of particular species at that time, and integrates the forests into the lives of biblical figures. Claude Reignier Conder, a researcher for the nineteenth-century Palestine Exploration Fund, conducted a survey of woodland vegetation that Weitz claims "heralded the realization of Job's vision in which the desiccated root puts forth new shoots."[667]

These references appeared to signal that God wanted the ancient Hebrews to do with the land precisely what the modern Hebrews are doing in a miraculous reenactment that fulfills a divine vision. "Now," writes Weitz, "a new era was about to be opened by a different type of man who would stand on nature's side ... by planting and sewing (sic) new forests in the Holy Land."[668] Literary "evidence" and speculation are conflated to putatively establish veracity: "One may draw up an entire inventory of commonly used wooden articles which are mentioned in the Mishna, and since the cutting down of fruit trees was forbidden, these *must have been* fashioned from the wood of forest trees." (Italics added.)[669] Unnamed "written sources and documents that Professor B. Dinur quotes in his 'History of Israel'" are helpful—except when they are not: "Obviously the 'cedars of Lebanon' mentioned here cannot be taken literally, and must refer to pines which grew in the Jerusalem hills."[670]

Weitz quotes Ben-Gurion, speaking in 1949 as the first prime minister of Israel:

> We must plant hundreds of millions of trees.... We must clothe every mountainside with trees, every hill and rocky piece of land which cannot successfully be farmed, the dunes of the coastal plain, the Negev plains east and south of Beersheva.... We must also plant along all our borders

for reasons of security, along every highway, road and track, around buildings and civilian and military installations.... We shall not be fulfilling one of the cardinal obligations of the state—that of conquering the desert—if we confine our efforts solely to the need of the hour.... We are a country... doing its best to repair the damage of centuries, both to our nation and our land.[671]

"Repairing the damage of centuries" ultimately entailed creating new sorts of damage. The trees planted by the JNF in its afforestation campaign were mainly Aleppo pine and cypress—rather than the trees native to the area.[672] Flammable and excessively compromised by a dry climate, further debilitated by frequent droughts brought by climate change, the forests have been home to increasingly recurrent and destructive wildfires in recent decades.[673] Notably, these have included the Mount Carmel Forest Fires of 1989 and 2010 near Haifa through the 2021 and 2022 blazes in the Jerusalem Hills and the Upper Galilee. The nonprofit online watchdog group Global Forest Watch reports that fires "were responsible for 25% of tree cover loss in Israel between 2001 and 2021."[674]

And contrary to Weitz's historical claims, archaeobotanist Nili Liphschitz and geographer Giden Biger, both of whom taught at Tel Aviv University, present evidence from their research to support a very different conclusion: "Aleppo pine (Jerusalem pine in its Hebrew name), in spite of its name, was rare in the native arboreal landscape of Israel during the last 10,000 years. The forest landscape of Israel today is therefore a very new phenomenon without any relation to the past."[675] They explain that the species was first described as *Pinus hierosolumitana*—the "Jerusalem Pine"—in 1755 by one B. Buhamel, and though it received other names over the years, Buhamel's was the one adopted for the 1931 *Analytical Flora of Palestine,* written in Hebrew. Nonetheless, they say that "the Aleppo pine which exists today in Israel resembles the Aleppo pine in central Italy" and may have been the result of seed transfers between that and other countries, namely Israel's neighbors Cyprus, Lebanon, Turkey, and Greece.[676]

An infamous example of afforestation run amok, counter to JNF's assertions, is that of the Yatir Forest, planted in the 1960s by the JNF two hours from Tel Aviv. According to Fred Pearce in an article published at the Yale School of the Environment, Yatir is "the country's largest planted woodland, with 4 million trees spread across 7,400 acres. Dense stands of Aleppo pine gird the hillside, in vivid contrast to the dun-colored Negev desert."[677] Pearce explains:

> KKL-JNF has made wide-ranging claims for the environmental benefits of the Yatir Forest, saying it is holding back the desert, recharging soils with moisture, preventing flood in Be'er Sheva, and fighting climate change by capturing carbon dioxide from the air. But this showcase forestation project also has its share of critics, with some Israeli ecologists saying that, whatever the benefits, the collateral damage has been too great. The trees, the ecologists say, are obliterating grasslands that contain rare endemic species. There is also evidence that the new Israeli desert forests have so far caused more warming than cooling, as the dark mass of the Yatir Forest's trees is absorbing solar radiation, while the lighter colors of the desert once reflected the sun's heat back into space. The Yatir, some experts say, is an example of the ecological damage that can occur when large-scale forestation projects are undertaken in places that have not had forests in recent times.

Semi-arid locales such as this "teem with ground-nesting birds and specially adapted reptiles" that are at grave risk under such abruptly changed ecological circumstances. Pearce quotes Alon Rothschild, director of biodiversity at the Society for the Protection of Nature in Israel (ISPN): "Reptiles need sun. Trees take away the sun and provide branches where [predatory birds] can sit looking for lunch." Rothschild says that in the case of Yatir and other Negev JNF-run desert forestation programs, the JNF "is rarely called to account for damaging [species'] habitats," and "only 4 percent ... have any national protection." Aleppo pines' true natural habitats are wetter; when planted in arid areas such as these they require intense irrigation to facilitate sapling growth and suffer major irreparable losses in droughts. And unfortunately, says Pearce, "Climate models predict declining rainfall in the Negev."

UTILIZING ALL THE AVAILABLE MEANS OF COLLECTION

Yona Kremenetzky, upon being elected as the Jewish National Fund's first chairman in 1901, quickly "began to think of ways to implant the Fund in

Zionist hearts" in order to galvanize donations from the Jewish diaspora but, more importantly, to consolidate global Jewish identification with the project.[678] If, for Aristotle, rhetoric involved utilizing all the available means of persuasion, for the JNF persuasion was intimately bound up with utilizing all the available "means of collection" (a term the organization itself used). Yoram Bar-Gal calls these "means of collection" the "central propaganda symbols" of the JNF.[679] "Commercial propaganda essentially aspires to achieve the same goal we are trying to achieve, and that is to arouse as many people as possible for a known purpose to do something they would not have done without the propaganda," explained an internal JNF document from 1921. "We also wish to cause the large Jewish multitudes to remember the JNF at all times."[680]

The most famous of the "means of collection" was the "Blue Box," a little slotted tin coffer placed in diasporic Jewish homes, synagogues, schools, clubhouses, offices, kindergartens, and other community locations, decorated in blue and white with a map of Eretz Yisrael (though the specific design varied from country to country and over time). Bar-Gal affirms that "the right décor for a Jewish house always included the blue box."[681] This calls to mind Edward Bernays's campaign to establish the trend that fashionable houses must include a music room; with that built into the architectural and interior design plans, homeowners would feel compelled to furnish it with a piano, the product that Bernays was covertly selling all along. Similarly, the Blue Box served to establish a scene in which further actions integral to one's commitment to the "redemption" of Palestine—and, indivisibly, to one's Jewishness—would naturally follow. Bar-Gal notes that the "JNF officials constantly stressed that the conspicuous place of the box in the individual domain was to remind one of one's daily obligation to contribute, just as the Sabbath candlesticks signified the weekly commandment."[682] Bar-Gal notes that by the end of World War II, "an estimated two to three million boxes had been distributed throughout the world...."[683]

The JNF of Canada still describes the Blue Box as "a proud symbol of Jewish identity" and "a vehicle for educating youngsters and involving them in these efforts in order to foster their identification with the Zionist enterprise and the State of Israel."[684] Another JNF website says bluntly that "the box was more than a tool for money collection: from the beginning, it was an important educational tool for the distribution of the Zionist idea and strengthening of the Jewish people's connection with their homeland."[685]

The intended audience of the JNF's Propaganda Department efforts was overwhelmingly the international Jewish sphere rather than the non-Jewish world outside it. The department's purpose, according to Bar-Gal, was to "strengthen national consciousness" and "to win over the person." "*Propagandistim*"—emissaries trained in the latest propaganda techniques—were dispatched to sites in the diaspora to spread the word. Equally well-prepared propaganda workers staffed JNF offices in major world cities, keeping abreast of current propaganda methods including the use of new technologies of recording and mass dissemination of messages: phonographs, radios, photography, cinema. These were used to transmit speeches of Zionist leaders in Polish, Yiddish, and English as well as a range of images to dispersed global networks. The Jewish press mobilized, printing articles and announcements about the JNF in its massive network of periodicals as well as advertisements and posters. By 1920 there were JNF bureaus in over fifty countries and operating in myriad languages; besides an expanded presence in Europe it had "penetrated new areas in North Africa and the Far East, under the auspices of the various colonial powers."[686] In the US, the Union of Hebrew Teachers of New York worked to bring JNF resources into the schools; teachers, principals, and Jewish youth groups became enmeshed in JNF activities, to the point where "the redemption of the land" became institutionalized as part of the Hebrew school curriculum.[687]

The JNF leadership was not shy about using the word "propaganda." Like Edward Bernays and many others before World War II, at which point the word became tainted by its association with Nazism, they freely bandied it about and delighted in the almost magical powers of influence it represented. The Propaganda Department was its own openly designated administrative unit at the JNF's Head Office. Bar-Gal explains, "There was no real separation between the Propaganda staff and Youth Department staff; they worked together throughout the years and produced the propaganda material distributed to adults, young people, and schools."[688] They "saw Eretz Yisrael as a product they had to market to different segments of the population using persuasive techniques common at that time."[689]

The Blue Box typified Jacques Ellul's concept of "integrative propaganda" (see Chapter 1). In a somewhat similar vein, it also illustrated what the British sociologist Michael Billig called "banal nationalism": the cumulative effect of those artifacts that regularly signal what is normal and indubitable about the centrality of the nation to everyday life. As with Ellul's "propaganda of integration," these items are so omnipresent and thus so unremarkable that they are rendered in essence invisible and are simply naturalized; their very familiarity foments unconscious conformity to a culture and its norms. For Billig, a prime example is the national flag in its "unwaved" state—that is, when it sits, passive and unsaluted but always in sight, in front of schools, the post office, and on people's lawns. Paradoxically, for Billig, this is where the flag wields the greatest power, precisely *because* it acts at an unconscious level; it is one of the "reminders of nationhood [that] serve to turn background space into homeland space."[690] Other actuators of banal nationalistic feelings may include phenomena such as patriotic brand names (e.g., American Eagle apparel and Liberty Mutual insurance), mall parking spots reserved for veterans, and a "World Series" that does not extend beyond national borders (and is played out between the American League and the National League).

For children who lived with Blue Boxes prominently situated in their homes and schools and who regularly participated in rituals, festivals, holidays, and competitions that were devised to highlight the box in all aspects of their lives, the Blue Box, says Bar-Gal, created a "cultural experience" and "turn[ed] it into a way of life with clear-cut norms."[691] Songs and plays were written about the box for schools. "JNF corners" constructed in domiciles and schoolrooms contained pictures of Zionist leaders and maps of Eretz Yisrael, the national symbols cumulatively creating an aura of, in Bar-Gal's words, "a sort of little temple of the Zionist movement."[692] The little box itself, he says, became personified, an "anthropomorphic creature" that "had feelings and influenced events"; it "laughed, got angry, felt sad—all according to the various local and national events taking place." In 1924, the Head Office created animated segments for one of its films "in which it was presented as human and appeared as the film's real hero: it spoke, asked for contributions, kissed children, and cried"—the latter, of course, when children forgot to make their regular coin deposits.[693]

As with all propaganda, these depictions evolved as new technologies did. In the twenty-first century, a character named Blue Box Bob—played by a volunteer—visits elementary school students, "connect[ing them] to modern Israel while teaching them the history of our homeland!" Blue Box Bob, of course, has his own Facebook page where you can "like" his posts and send him messages.[694]

During the JNF's first decade, other propaganda methods introduced by Kremenetzky that passed as fundraising operations included the issuance of stamps bearing Zionist images that Jews could affix to organizational documents and personal letters. According to the online stamp and coin collecting site *WOPA+*, thirty million copies of the original "Zion stamp" were printed in eighteen countries and were "a significant way of spreading the Zionist idea around the world."[695] Later, thousands of other images appeared on JNF stamps, commemorating Jewish holidays and history as well as some of the signal achievements claimed by the JNF in regard to the environment.[696] Starting in 1926, some of the stamps were miniatures of JNF-issued "symbolic" maps—that is, those not bound by the rules of "scientific" measurement. These often played loose with the borders of the envisioned future state, portraying the desired "Biblical borders" to openly renounce the official geographies of the British Mandate. Later, their maps similarly challenged those that depicted a partitioned country, which the British Peel Commission recommended in 1936 and was approved by the United Nations in 1947. JNF maps tended to aggrandize JNF land acquisition and minimize private purchases by competing Zionist groups by painting the former in vivid colors, and Arab villages tended to simply vanish from the scene. As Head Office secretary A.M. Epstein wrote in a 1931 memo, "There is no need...to include all the (Arab) villages and hills in the map of the Negev, since the average donor has no idea of their existence." This, of course, reinforced the popular notion of an "unpopulated land" that was ripe for the taking.[697]

These "means of collection" actually constituted a relatively small part of the JNF's income. Even the Blue Box, the most successful of them, brought in only one half a percent of the Jewish capital that came to Eretz Yisrael between 1918 and 1938; private land purchases, as opposed to those that would be nationalized through the JNF, received the bulk of donated funds. Yet the methods were continued because, as Bar-Gal puts it, though "[t]he real, direct contribution of the Blue Box to the 'redemption of our country's land' was miniscule,... its symbolic value was enormous."[698]

As time went on, the interactive activities multiplied. The JNF harnessed the occasion of Tu BiShvat—originally a marker for farmers of trees' rebirth into the new spring cycle—as the "Jewish Earth Day." In its "Jewish National Fund Tu BiShvat in the Schools, 2020/5780 Making the Desert Bloom Facilitators

Guide," the JNF explains that "Tu BiShvat has its roots in the Bible" (inferred because "God created 'seed-bearing plants'" and set Adam to tend them), but "over the years" it has become "JNF's holiday." Events include readings, study sheets, and discussion of the JNF children's book *Our Tree Named Steve*; tree-purchasing competitions for students via "an online tree ordering platform" in which "schools that plant 100 trees or more ($1800+) will receive special recognition listing at American Independence Park in Jerusalem"; a "Yoga Tree Pose Challenge" in which participants post pictures of themselves in that position to Instagram or Facebook with hashtags such as "#PoweredByJNF"; and a "Tu BishBox" program on college campuses, where JNF's Positively Israel Ambassador will put in an appearance.[699]

Lastly, a deep-rooted Zionist ritual that does not fall specifically within the bailiwick of the JNF yet fully bespeaks its "redemption" ethos is that of the *tiyul*—a hike that is believed to build a sense of authentic, intimate contact between the hiker and the land. "*Tiyulim* [plural form] were deemed a crucial means of linking nature to nation, of connecting Jewish history in Eretz Yisrael to a set of Zionist political claims in the present, therein fortifying the latter," writes Rebecca L. Stein. The practice began to acquire prominence and prestige in the 1920s in conjunction with the *Yediat ha-Aretz* ["knowledge of the land"] movement that took a central place within Zionist education, to a large extent via textbooks and classroom discussion but most importantly via what schools now call "experiential learning."[700] It was perceived as a nation-building heuristic with secular, spiritual, and scientific dimensions. In 1943, the first conference seeking to create a mass popular science of *Yediat ha-Aretz* took place, organized by the Jewish Palestine Exploration Society in Jerusalem.[701]

Derived from German and Swiss hiking traditions, the Zionist *tiyulim* were discussed only in the newly revived Hebrew language "using words that brought old ideas of pilgrimage to life" and were seen to traverse land that "was not just any land, but…the mythic Land of Israel…. It was an act that connected Zionist youth with their ancient Jewish forebears and which became burdened with existential, and even salvific, import," says Shay Rabineau.[702] Stein says that despite its roots in European romanticism, it was reconceived as "an organically Zionist practice" that "conferred indigeneity on the hiker by cementing her belonging to both landscape and homeland."[703] Another function of some of the *tiyulim* that has been reported was their use as a cover for reconnaissance missions in which the hikers took photographs, made maps, and recorded copious facts and figures about Palestinian villages for future military use.[704]

THE JNF SHARPENS ITS PERIPHERAL VISION

In 2006, environmental activist Devorah Brous wrote in *Haaretz*:

> [C]onsider the dissonance between two recent events. Just prior to Tu BiShvat, 2,500 dunams of Bedouin fields were destroyed by the Israel Land Authority's (ILA) "Green Patrol." On Tu BiShvat itself, a small group of politicians placed a smattering of saplings in holes dug by the Jewish National Fund (JNF), in the Negev. The candidates, planting for PR purposes, had permits; the Bedouin villagers, engaged in self-subsistence, did not. The Bedouin "broke the law." The Jews "made the desert bloom."[705]

The Negev, which accounts for approximately 60 percent of Israel's land, was where David Ben-Gurion lived out his retirement years on a kibbutz called Sde Boker. In his memoirs he rhapsodized about the desert, seeing it as both a place of spiritual restoration and a place of enormous practical potential for expanding the Zionist project—demographically, industrially, and militarily.[706] "The Negev affords me the pleasure of watching a wasteland develop into the most fruitful portion of Israel by a totally Jewish act of creation," he wrote.[707] In a 1937 letter to his son, he wrote, "Negev land is reserved for Jewish citizens, whenever and wherever they want [...] we must expel Arabs and take their places...in order to guarantee our own right to settle in those places."[708]

Yet not all Zionists shared his enthusiasm for the region. As over time Israel's central Tel Aviv-Haifa-Jerusalem corridor swelled with cosmopolitans and urban tech workers (while "the rest of the country is left largely uninhabited," JNF fallaciously explains),[709] attempts to lure Jews to the Negev largely fell flat. By the twenty-first century, however, it was perceived that there was no place left to expand in the overbuilt, overpopulated center. Chaim Chester, treasurer of the Jewish Agency and the World Zionist Organization, wrote in 2001 that

> new models of rural settlement cannot be based on agriculture. The key to their success must be in hi-tech, tourism, specialized education, and

service industries that can be carried out at some distance from major urban centers…. Today and tomorrow we must find new models that will ensure population growth in the periphery.[710]

Developing a new "frontier" in the Negev—as well as in the Galilee, also considered part of Israel's "periphery" because of its proportionally smaller Jewish population, as well as its location far from the madding crowd—would later create such "new models" in the booming tech hubs of the "start-up nation."

It would also intensively and intentionally Judaize the areas' residents. After 90 percent of the Negev's Bedouins were expelled to Jordan and Egypt's Sinai Peninsula in 1948, 11,000 remained under Israeli military rule—grown to a population of about 300,000 now—and were confined to a small area called the *Siyag*, or "fence." Cut off from the lands they had tended for centuries and forbidden to use nearby designated "state lands" authorized for Jewish Israeli use only, they were unable to continue their traditional work of farming and herding. At the same time, Bedouin residential construction and even whole preexisting villages were classified as "illegal."

After martial law ended in the 1960s, many of the Naqab Bedouin were relocated to Israeli-devised "townships" from whose planning they were excluded, and which similarly circumscribed their activities. As Rebecca Manski writes in a comprehensive article on the JNF's plans to ethnically reconfigure the Negev, the area's reality is far from the arcadian image the JNF projects on its website in its attempt to lure immigrants: "Long treated as a lawless 'dumping ground,' the Naqab hosts dozens of chemical factories, multiple mining operations, Tel Aviv's excess waste, the largest toxic waste facility in the region, and the national principal nuclear facility at Dimona."[711] Tom Pessah adds that it "houses military live-fire training zones as well as incarceration facilities for Palestinian prisoners and African refugees. During the 2014 conflict with Gaza, the Iron Dome anti-missile system was programmed not to protect this 'empty' region."[712] Neither are shelters set up to safeguard "unrecognized" villagers from the much-hyped rockets from Gaza. Furthermore, as Devorah Brous explains,

> Since the seven Bedouin towns built by the Israeli government were planned without business districts, the drug trade and theft represent

viable economic opportunity for Bedouin youth....Although Bedouin citizens in unrecognized villages are denied access to basic municipal services (including water, electricity, sewage and health care) more than half the Bedouin population still prefers the desert's open space rather than relinquish their land claims and livestock for a house with toilets that occasionally flush.[713]

According to housing and land rights worker Joseph Schechla, the categorization of some villages as "unrecognized" first occurred in the Building and Construction Law of 1965, where "district outline plans" were made that excluded rural Arab areas. Moreover, "The land on which they were built was classified in the law as 'agricultural,' a planning category where no residences or other structures are permitted, making any dwelling already there automatically 'illegal'" and prohibiting, as well, "connecting water, electricity, or telephone networks to unlicensed buildings...." These criteria, he says, allowed the residents of these villages to be expelled, now "by administrative, not military means." In 1986, the Markowitz Commission—more formally, the Interministerial Commission Concerning Illegal Construction in the Arab Sector—expanded the use of the term to include "entire villages and neighborhoods of 'recognized' Arab towns where the buildings were 'unlicensed,' thereby giving a name to an extant but previously ambiguous category."[714]

Amnesty International has said that the "non-recognition of Bedouin villages is central to Israeli policies of segregation and urbanization of the Bedouin and to the Israeli denial of Bedouin traditional way of life in the Negev/Naqab."[715] Even so, the Negev Coexistence Forum for Civil Equality (NCFCE) emphasizes that many of the conditions inflicted upon Bedouins in the "unrecognized" villages are operative, contrary to PR, in the "legal" or "recognized" townships as well: "There is no significant difference between the recognized villages and those which remain unrecognized. In most of the recognized villages there are no detailed urban plans, so that the residents cannot obtain building permits, the demolition policy continues, and basic infrastructures of water, electricity, sewage and roads are either non-existent or lacking."[716] And according to the Association for Civil Rights in Israel (ACRI), "All 35 of the villages that have not yet been recognized meet every criterion listed by the Central Bureau of Statistics (CBS) for the definition of a 'township'.... The sole criterion that the unrecognized villages fail to meet is the Interior Minister's official declaration that they are indeed 'townships.'"[717]

Bedouin homes in villages designated as "illegal" and "unrecognized" are in constant danger of being wiped out. Some villages, such as Al Araqib, have been demolished—and rebuilt—repeatedly. According to a June 23, 2022, Israeli Committee Against House Demolitions (ICAHD) report, it had at that date been destroyed and reconstructed over 200 times since 2010; the tally has steadily mounted since then. Writing in early 2022, independent journalist Dalia Hatuga clarified that the state "refus[es] to recognize their traditional land ownership mechanisms, which historically did not rely on physical deeds." Thus, "almost 100,000 Palestinians with Israeli citizenship live in nearly 45 villages in the Naqab, 35 of which are unrecognized."[718] In short, thwarting Bedouin efforts to construct safe, permanent homes and to obtain basic infrastructural services is the flip side of enticing middle-class Jews to move into new housing with suburban amenities, created just for them. While this has been true primarily in the Negev, there are "unrecognized" villages in the Arab Triangle and Galilee, as well; Shira Robinson has noted that "citizen-refugees" from several of them undergo tenacious efforts parallel to those in Araqib to reclaim their land.[719]

Where does the JNF figure in here? As it has done elsewhere in Palestine since its inception in 1901, in the Negev and in the Galilee the JNF's manifest activity continues to be using afforestation as a smokescreen for displacing Palestinians from their lands and replacing them with Jews. The Akevot Institute for Israeli-Palestinian Conflict Research, which is dedicated to facilitating broad access to archival documents that expose facts behind popular myths, describes the minutes of a 1979 Settlement Committee meeting chaired by then-Minister of Agriculture Ariel Sharon. "According to Sharon," they write, "these actions [mass afforestation and the building of Mitzpim (small Jewish settlements)] were designed to Judaize the Galilee and secure 'land reserves for settlement activity of the next 20, 30, or 40 years.'"[720] A similar scenario was envisioned for the Negev.

A series of overlapping projects in the decades spanning the twentieth and twenty-first centuries have promised to "revitalize" the Negev. Still, the upbeat development and environmental talk is frequently interchanged with the discourse of combatting the Bedouin "threat" to Jewish Israeliness. For instance, writes Dalia Hatuga, when the Israel Land Authority (ILA)—an outsized, critical mass of whose governing body is represented by the JNF—announced its intention to plant 40,000 dunams (15 square miles) of non-indigenous trees in the Naqab in 2020, it claimed the purpose was "to conserve open spaces and nature from illegal control" by "trespassers" and "squatters."[721] But the actual "threat" to Israel, argues Mansour Nasasra, citing UN Special Rapporteur on human rights in the Occupied Territories from 2008 to 2014 Richard Falk, was that the Bedouin—like indigenous peoples in colonized lands elsewhere—"represent a competing nationalism within the boundaries of the state." They "challenge two fundamental statist notions—that of territorial sovereignty, and that of a unified 'nationality' juridically administered by government organs."[722] Nasasra notes that special state agencies "were created…to deal with the Bedouin 'problem' and their 'encroachment' on state land…."[723] Regulations implemented during the military rule era (1948–1966) were sustained permanently for "security reasons"—putatively "to protect the safety of the public, to protect the state, to maintain public order, to quell rebellion or riots, and to secure the supply of essential services."[724] "Sometimes," writes Nasasra, "the army would make its customary claim that the land of certain tribes was needed for military use. This became the main justification used when evicting the Bedouin from their native land into the closed zone." Evicted tribes were deceptively promised that they could soon return to their lands, even as many villages were demolished to prevent this.[725]

In the 1950s, Bedouin lands were seized by Israel under the pretense that the Bedouin had supplied no official Ottoman or British documents certifying their land ownership. Yet they had. Reports from the Ottomans and the British asserted that the Bedouin land had continuously been maintained by its owners—a key determinant of title at the time—and a 1952 letter from the military governor of the Negev was produced substantiating that the Bedouin had paid land taxes. A 1952 report by Yosef Weitz further testified to Bedouin ownership of the lands they claimed.[726]

In the 2009 book-length puff piece *Start-Up Nation: The Story of Israel's Economic Miracle,* authors Dan Senor and Saul Singer enthuse that Yatir Forest in the Negev is "the largest" but "perhaps the most improbable of all" JNF's planting projects: "Satellite pictures show the forest sticking out like a visual typo, surrounded by desert and drylands in a place where it should not exist."[727] (Of course, this statement could also draw nods from some whose interpretation left them less impressed.) Begun in 1966 to realize, in JNF's words, Yosef Weitz's dream of "us[ing] trees to roll back the desert" and "halt desertification," Yatir is extoled by JNF for having "significantly affected the quality of the environment" and brought "unanticipated strength in the war on global warming."[728] Corey Balsam notes that the JNF also "boasts of its 'breathtaking desert views.' But, he adds, it "fails to mention…that one of the major goals of planting in Yatir has been to keep the so-called illegal Bedouin construction and grazing at bay."

Quashing Bedouin undertakings is sometimes accomplished in the Naqab by planting barrier rows of trees that separate villagers from their land. Meanwhile, Bedouin are not permitted to plant trees and their crops have been sprayed from helicopters with the toxic herbicide Roundup "until too many were hospitalized with chemical poisoning and the [high court] forbade it."[729] Balsam remarks, in addition, that bucolic visions aside, Weitz "was adamant about the establishment of the forest, which he envisioned as a security zone to protect Israelis from the West Bank, then under Jordanian rule."[730]

As can be seen, different strands of justification—natural beauty, sustainability, security—have been braided together to rationalize the razing of Bedouin villages and their replacement with Jewish cities, towns, and suburbs in the Negev. Over time, varying pitches were made to prospective Jewish residents to convince them to move there. Yet it didn't turn out to be an easy sell.

BLUEPRINT NEGEV

In order to recruit new Jewish inhabitants for life in the Negev, the JNF mounted massive programs with attendant publicity campaigns. "Our goal is to bring 500,000 new residents to the Negev," they wrote of their Blueprint Negev initiative, and then acknowledged with seemingly disarming frankness, "But before that happens, anyone looking to settle amid that arid landscape must first stare down its challenges…."[731] The need for water, sewage, irrigation, energy systems, jobs, and "amenities to support a good quality of life" were among the "challenges" identified. But the JNF would take care of all that—for inbound Jewish residents. To achieve its goal, the JNF asserts, it is "playing a major role in community development across this region, building parks, playgrounds, and youth centers; providing employment and education opportunities; promoting tourism; improving transportation; and building water and agricultural infrastructure. Today, Be'er Sheva and the surrounding communities are blooming in a once barren desert."[732]

The vision embodied in Blueprint Negev goes a long way back, at least to Ariel Sharon's mid-2000s Development Plan of the Negev, which fizzled out. (This project is in tandem with the plan for "developing" the Galilee, Go North, to be discussed in a moment.) In 2006, President Shimon Peres touted the Negev's appeal for Americans "who want to make *aliyah* and live in style." Writes Rebecca Manski, "Soon, he told the Israeli public, there would be a haven for wealthy young Americans in Israel's Negev Desert. There would be homes with air conditioning and other Western amenities, a lavish community center with gym facilities and an Olympic-sized swimming pool." The JNF, writes Manski, assured that there would be "an organic farm, a bed-and-breakfast and an art gallery" as well as "shops, synagogues and a think tank devoted to religious diversity," "eco-tourism," and, in general, "an American sensibility."[733] But for those looking for a pastoral escape from foul late-capitalist civilization as they knew it, there was a completely converse pitch. Manski quotes from a *B'Nai B'rith Magazine* article about JNF's Blueprint Negev: 'In southern Israel, far from the strip malls of Tel Aviv's suburbs, the Negev is the closest thing to the clean slate many of Israel's pre-state pioneers found when they came to the Holy Land."[734]

Two things are particularly striking about JNF's public calls for participation and support. One is their tacit acknowledgment of the necessities, let alone the luxuries, communities require—even while denying them to Bedouin communities. The other is that very rarely does one see the word "Jewish" applied as a modifier for the "people" who are invited to enjoy this new life. Illustrating Davis and Lehn's point about "the manipulation of the meaning of terms," the JNF writes of itself:

> Each project, each program, each partnership, is consistent with our strategic vision—*population growth* in the north and south, connecting *the next generation* to Israel, *infrastructure development*, ecology, *forestation, heritage preservation*, and more—all for *the land and people of Israel*. (Italics added.)[735]

Obviously, if one organization is simultaneously working toward *creating* housing for some and *demolishing* housing for others, *the land and people of*

Israel is nationalist code. It is a dog whistle to the JNF's intended audience, establishing the context wherein terms like "population," "infrastructure," and "heritage" signify exclusively *Jewish* population, infrastructure, and heritage. Why is this distinction not made explicit? It may be helpful to recall the outdated generic pronoun "he"—which sometimes stood for "everyone" and sometimes didn't, the slippage making deniability of the speaker's intended meaning highly convenient. In the case of the JNF, this tricky ambiguity allows for claims such as, "Blueprint Negev aims to improve quality of life for *all residents* of the region...." (Italics added.) [736]

In one case, there is a seemingly compassionate introduction to a press release about JNF's Sderot Indoor Recreation Center: "*Every child* deserves the opportunity to experience the euphoria of exploring a playground...." The reference is to the dangers the Jewish children of Sderot, just outside the Gaza Strip, face from incoming Palestinian rockets. Therefore, they explain, the recreational facility "doubles as a bomb shelter," albeit one with a "state-of-the-art playground, jungle gym, baby jamboree, mini-soccer court, ping pong tables, multiple private celebration rooms"—"everything *children* love and more." (Italics added.)[737]

The superficially heartfelt recognition of what "*every* child deserves" stands in callous contradiction to the well-documented denial of basic services and educational opportunities to Bedouin children. The lack of specifics misleadingly occludes, publicly, the distinction between what is available for *Jews* and for *Bedouins* of the region, allowing Jewish liberals and other JNF donors to rationalize guilt they might feel about participating in a segregationist enterprise.

The JNF goes even further with the smarmy tactic of including in its *Blueprint Negev Strategy* website post a subsection called "Supporting the Bedouin Community." Devorah Brous once warned that "the JNF's engagement in a campaign to fund symbolic projects in partnership with Bedouin, is nothing short of dangerous in the context of the JNF-KKL's political and strategic objectives."[738] Donor beware. Included in this JNF promotion are lines such as, "The needs of the Bedouin community and the changes that must come about are one of the original pillars of *Blueprint Negev*" and "We respect Bedouin culture and our investment is designed to leverage Bedouin values, aspirations, and experience in desert agriculture with sustainability principles and cutting-edge approaches to animal husbandry, renewable energy production, resource recycling, soil enhancement, and arid land stewardship."[739]

An essay by Jesse Benjamin, an Israeli citizen who grew up in North America and elsewhere, prompts serious questions about these claims. As a student intern in the late 1980s at the Negev-based Association for the Support and Defense of Bedouin Rights in Israel, Benjamin visited the Sde Boqer Research Center. There, he says, "all sorts of scientists working on studies of the harsh desert environment" vindicated their unwillingness to share their research with the local Bedouin through comments such as, "They are unwilling to learn" and "They refuse to change from their ancient and destructive ways."

Yet later, doing field work to the south near the remains of an ancient Nabatean city, Benjamin learned of the inventive systems the Nabateans had used to conserve the scanty desert rainfall—reflected in methods the Bedouin are using now. "Bedouin were also using and maintaining the elaborate cistern catchment pools adjacent to wadis, which filled in seconds when the annual or semi-annual flashflood rains came, and then held thousands or even millions of cubic meters of water for years at a time, usually unbeknownst to regional authorities and other passersby," he writes. He found that these techniques and the drought-sensitive shepherding skills that the Bedouins still put into practice were of no interest to the scientists, however. Clearly, accessing a treasure trove of invaluable information about desert agriculture was not worth disrupting what Benjamin says was the "fundamentally racial assumption that all Bedouin use of the land was primitive and therefore destructive, while all Jewish use was modern and therefore beneficial."[740]

Another contradiction to the JNF's claim that their services are "for all residents of the region" does not appear in JNF's advertising but is embedded in Israeli law that undergirds their projects. "Admissions committees" operate in numerous Israeli Jewish communities; their purpose is to vet applicants for land purchase and/or residency there. The committees may reject applicants based on "unsuitability for the local communal life" or for the community's "social-cultural fabric," which essentially preserves the communities' Jewish-only makeup. An Admissions Committee Law to this effect restricts the committees' operations to communities on communal property with up to 400 households, but it is routinely violated with impunity, including by Israeli authorities. In May 2019, a Knesset report found that at least twenty-four communities in the

Negev and Galilee were illegally using this method by applying it to neighborhoods whose population far exceeded the 400-household limit.[741]

The far-right Israeli coalition government that took office in December 2022 has made the admissions rules applicable to a wider range of communities. Signed or pending agreements with various extremist parties in the Likud-based alliance enabled this. For example, Likud agreements with the Religious Zionist Party (RZP) and the Jewish Power Party (JPP) would allow the Admissions Committees to operate in "towns of up to 1,000 households....Based on [criteria such as "social suitability" and "culture"], Palestinian citizens of Israel, as well as other groups (LGBTQ people, Ethiopians, and more) are excluded from living in these communities, built on 'state land.'" The newly renamed position, Minister for Development of the Negev, Galilee and National Resilience, has been allotted to JPP.[742]

Full implementation of the Blueprint Negev initiative languished due to interruptions by wars, budget crises, and insufficient participant buy-in. As Manski points out, that was not a unique situation: "[O]ver Israel's sixty years of existence,...all of its Naqab development schemes failed."[743] A similar fate befell the corresponding Go North project in the Negev. Then, in 2020, another endeavor, strikingly comparable in its demographic vision but recalibrated to focus on Israel's new image as a global technology leader, took hold alongside them: KKL-JNF 2040: Moving to the Land of Tomorrow. (If the name calls to mind Disneyland or a futuristic animated film, that is surely because it is meant to instill the same breathless awe at being on the precipice of a magical new world.)

ISRAEL 2040

More generally known as Israel 2040, the undertaking is familiar in setting of numerical goals (a million "citizens"—though sometimes called "residents" and sometimes "settlers"— projected to move to the Negev, half a million to the Galilee) and its vision ("strengthening Israel's peripheral regions"). But it also has the added, very explicit goal of "expanding the borders of 'Startup Nation' to the Galilee and Negev." It is, they say, "the 21st century version of KKL-JNF's initial mandate to redeem and develop the land," this time by "forg[ing] a connection throughout the country between the land, society and technology."

"The Israel 2040 project," KKL-JNF declares, "will turn the Negev and the Galilee into Israel's new engine of growth over the next two decades."[744]

While there are some who oppose BDS on the mistaken belief that the Israeli spheres of war, culture, education, business, and housing are fragmented and unyoked, with many "innocent" Israelis and companies unfairly being made answerable for the exploits of the army or the government, they may be disabused by this blunt statement on KKL-JNF's website: "Israel 2040 is being carried [sic] in collaboration with friends and partners around the world, the Israeli government, the IDF, Israeli academia, and the local and international business sectors, among others."[745] "Others" includes the infamous (for its hacking, spying, gay-and-cancer-patient-blackmailing) Jewish-only, elite cyber-security agency, Unit 8200.[746]

In 2019, the *Jerusalem Post* reported KKL-JNF world chairman Daniel Atar's declared intention of attracting "Israelis[747] with a strong socioeconomic background" and to make them "full partners in the local hi-tech industry, which will fortify Israel's economic and nationalistic resilience [in] the country's peripheral regions." Atar also explained, "Investment in the Galilee will create an Israeli Silicon Valley.... In the Negev, selected professionals will be incorporated into the development of cyber development zones." All this will be done, he assured, as KKL-JNF remains committed to "preserving the country's natural surroundings and resources" and "continu[ing] our efforts to promote environmental protection and sustainability...."[748]

Dovetailing with, but also considerably expanding upon, *Blueprint Negev's* footprint, *Israel 2040* continues to establish amenities that will not only attract new Jewish inhabitants to the region but also draw world Jewry's attendance for projects that will build a sense of affinity and might very well inspire long-term residency. There is, notably, the World Zionist Village in Be'er Sheva, an "ecosystem—the only one of its kind in the world—for global Jewry of all ages to convene at once or at different times on a single campus with programming, shared space, accommodations, and harnessing the power of positive Israeli/ Jewish conversation." Sporting the first-ever Zionist adult education center, a high school for visiting American and international students, an "innovation center" for "post-graduates interning in Be'er Sheva based high-tech, medical tech and cyber security companies," and proper housing and conveniences for all, the village is meant to "revolutionize Zionist and Jewish education and engagement for the decades ahead."[749] Then there is the Be'er Sheva River Park, inspired by San Antonio's Riverwalk, bolstering the municipality's claim that it is becoming "Israel's 'water city' in the desert" (which comes with "the fastest-rising home prices in the country"). The park also features "Israel's largest man-made lake" and three amphitheaters that can hold a total of 30,000 people, described as "Israel's largest and arguably most impressive entertainment venue."

On the business front, the Lauder Employment Center aims "to offer comprehensive career services, guidance, and resources" to regional students, alumni, and businesses—the latter of which include companies such as Sodastream, Dell, and Intel. Such enterprises, a JNF YouTube video informs us, are "thirsty for young employees" but find that local college graduates lack relevant experience. There the Lauder Center steps in with job training, paid internships, and preparation for careers of the future such as "human-robotic relations."[750] The NetGev Hubs provide "affordable work spaces for local entrepreneurs" and training for jobs in high-tech industries."[751]

Public relations strategies for garnering buy-in include participatory experiences for target audiences. Reminiscent of some of the Blue Box schemes, JNF-USA's "Envision Tomorrow's Israel" was a global competition for structural design of elements of the World Zionist Village. Noting that "London has Big Ben and Hollywood its famed sign," Jeffrey E. Levin, chairperson of JNF-USA's board, explained that the goal of the competition was "to create interest in and brand what we are creating in Be'er Sheva." Joseph Wolfson, first vice president of JNF-USA's National Board and chair of the Be'er Sheva Executive Committee, emphasized the anticipated payoff: "In 10 to 15 years, thousands will have passed through the Village's gates, returning home as ambassadors for Israel, and community leaders."[752] Other hands-on opportunities include membership on the Housing Development Fund Task Force, where donors come on an "annual mission" to explore and support "new needs of emerging pioneering communities throughout Israel's peripheral areas."[753]

Israel 2040 picks up where not only Blueprint Negev but also Go North left off—or faded out. Interestingly, most of the content on JNF's website devoted to promoting these ventures is undated—except, sometimes, for a current copyright notice buried at the end. One would have had to download copy from years past to see how the messages have evolved—or not—over time. This creates a bit of confusion for anyone trying to pay close attention and compare the initiatives. Have Blueprint Negev and Go North abandoned their plans, yielding the field to Israel 2040? Or, unwilling to acknowledge their past flops, have they jointly and quietly morphed into Israel 2040? Their promotional copy gives no sense of closure. Are we trapped in the movie *Groundhog Day,* unsuspectingly reliving experience but in tweaked form based on what happened yesterday?

Israel 2040's plans for the Galilee are no less feverish than its plans for the Negev, but in this case its business logic is intertwined with the sybaritic life rather than merely bound to the pecuniary rewards of the tech sector. In particular, Israel 2040's Galilee aspirations center on creating state-of-the-art culinary and hospitality industries; promotional efforts coyly refer to the Galilee's future brand as Silicon Wadi.[754] The centerpiece of this vision is the Galilee Culinary Institute in the Greater Kiryat Shimona area, which is "home to over 80 different ethnicities"—a "melting pot of culinary traditions." This gastronomic diversity will, they say, help the region become "a global culinary and hospitality center of excellence," a "hub for food businesses, including technology, business management, cooking, restaurants, food and agricultural research and development, hospitality, and hotels."[755] Also key to this will be the Beit Asher Food Innovation and Technology Center, a research site and incubator for food and agricultural start-ups. "The north is the breadbasket of Israel," says Yael Levontin, PR & Communications Manager in Israel, JNF-USA. "We are going to be a leading culinary institute. People are going to come, they're going to do a year, two years, and they're going to get their certificate, and they can go work in any Michelin star restaurant across the world. And it's going to be kosher! Which is really, really cool!"[756]

As with its work in the south, the JNF is seeking "young families" who will help to "bring prosperity" to the area as they obtain it for themselves. To that end, as in the Negev, JNF will create the high "quality-of-life" infrastructure that will make participation in the Galilee's "massive renaissance" attractive—gated upscale housing, medical centers, after-school activities, community services, and the like. The group believes all this will "motivate venture capitalists and entrepreneurs to further invest" in the area," thus transforming the Galilee into a "culinary capital on a global scale."[757]

But Go North was hardly Israel's first effort to Judaize the Galilee. According to Gershon Shafir, "the central Galilee is the only region of Israel in which Palestinian citizens—who make up 75 percent of this region's population—form the majority...." This, he says, has galvanized the "Zionist fear of decolonization"—anxiety that land under state sovereignty might yet "revert to Arab hands unless it was buttressed by Jewish ownership and presence"—and caused the area to be "singled out" for demographic change within the Green Line. (He refers, in fact, to the "codependence" and "ongoing bonds" between Israel's colonial activity in the occupied Palestinian territories and in the Galilee and Negev.)[758] Various "population dispersal" policies (code for moving Jews into peripheral regions while containing or shrinking Arab space there) have been tried over time. As Palestinian American businessman, writer, and editor Sam Bahour has pointed out, "As the parties quibbled over who violated the Oslo Agreement first and most, Israel never stopped strangling the Palestinian towns and villages inside [the Green Line]."[759]

The first stage of Judaizing the Galilee, says Bedouin Israeli-Canadian geographer Ghazi Falah, began with the 1948 war-induced flight of many Palestinians from the area. Soon after, Jewish settlements encircled what remained, effectively fencing off Arab communities from each other. Adding to the "decolonization" worry was the fact that this was a region originally designated as part of the proposed Arab state under the UN Partition Plan of 1947 (whereas it was the Jewish-allotted parts that underwent the most demolition). Falah explains that the state was concerned about "preventing the creation of an Arab 'core area' which could eventually lead to the formation of an independent Palestinian state within Israel." This first period of Judaization of the Galilee, adds Shafir, spiked in 1954 when the Jewish-majority city of Nazareth Ilit (Upper Nazareth) was constructed, followed by the creation of Karmiel in 1962. Both were built on land expropriated from Arab villages but also absorbed some of their residents into the municipalities in new "mixed," yet still segregated, cities with municipally enforced discrimination that Shafir calls an "open secret." The JNF, for its part, commandeered arable and pasture lands for afforestation as Arab towns "urbanized" amid the loss of their agricultural livelihoods.[760]

The second stage of the Judaization of the Galilee included what Shafir calls an "accelerated urban strategy." The towns of Karmiel and Upper Nazareth were expanded and developed, at the expense of Arab communities that were crammed into ever-smaller spaces and further severed from one another. By

1980, the JNF had completed roughly eighty kilometers of new paved roads linking Jewish settlements to each other and to other Jewish communities while further breaking the contiguity of Arab spaces. The situation reached a boiling point on March 30, 1976, when Palestinians amassed in a general strike. Six Palestinian citizens of Israel were killed by Israeli border guard units; the event has been memorialized every year since as Land Day.

This uprising, unprecedented in scope and organization, frightened the Israeli authorities, as can be seen in a document written immediately afterward by Israel Koenig, the Northern District (Galilee) Commissioner of the Ministry of the Interior, and submitted to Prime Minister Rabin. Labeled "Top Secret: Memorandum-Proposal—Handling the Arabs of Israel," the Koenig Report (as it became known) cites various factors that appear to the author to have contributed to Arab nationalization, particularly in the Galilee. It laments the fact that the "Israeli Arab is no longer passive" and warns of dire developments such as "the shouting of slogans of solidarity with the PLO during student demonstrations and on other occasions." These circumstances, writes Koenig, "will endanger our control of that area" as they give "the Arab nationalists a feeling of power and hope.... especially... in an area like northern Israel, where the physical Arab presence in contiguous areas represents a checking obstacle." One suggestion about how to redress the threat was, "Expand and deepen Jewish settlement in areas where the contiguity of the Arab population is prominent, and where they number considerably more than the Jewish population; examine the possibility of diluting existing Arab population concentrations."[761]

This concurrent "deepening" and "dilution" was addressed in part in the third stage of Judaizing the Galilee, which Falah dates to the time after 1982. This period saw the creation of the Misgav Regional Council, which exacerbated Zionist "economic control and domination of the region's natural resources." Arab farmers, now needing permits to engage in their livelihoods, increasingly became a "landless proletariat," dependent as laborers on the Jewish economy in other towns. The Markowitz Report of 1986, which studied "illegal construction in the Arab sector," trapped Galilee Arabs (many of whom were Bedouin), like their counterparts in the Negev, in a vicious circle whereby "nonrecognition" of villages led to the absence of a master plan, which meant that anything they *did* build was labeled "illegal," which often led to demolitions of houses and entire villages.[762]

Shafir places the beginning of the third stage in 1979 with the burgeoning of the *mitzpim* movement. The *mitzpim* were a network of small rural hilltop "lookout settlements," many of which later became *kibbutzim* and *moshavim*.[763] In Shira Robinson's words, this was "a new methodology of settlement" in which, rather than waiting "for a critical mass of Jewish citizens to move to the region," the state "would create a strategic constellation of smaller colonies...that could watch over Palestinian communities from above and undertake expansive regional development plans designed to suffocate them from outside."[764] At the same time, the Ministry of the Interior employed the passive aggressive technique of squelching the development of Arab villages by simply failing to create zoning or master plans for them.[765]

The *mitzpim,* or "hilltop community settlements," in some (albeit subtler) ways reiterated the "Tower and Stockade" operations of the 1930s, when the Great Palestinian Revolt of 1936–39 prompted the ultra-fast-track construction of prefabricated, fortified compounds in remote JNF-acquired spots. These structures created strategic new "facts on the ground" with panoptic surveillance capabilities.[766] In other ways, they foreshadowed JNF's later "community-building" schemes. Rather than appealing to those who longed to reenact the old "pioneer" ethos, the *mitzpim* drew middle-class, educated, professional, liberal families who principally wanted to get away from stressful city life and have a private house with a garden. It was a "quality-of-life," rather than a political, decision to move to these suburban-like communities, though it also, conveniently, served state interests. As Shafir puts it, it was an "upwardly mobile 'lifestyle' colonization" and the result of "spillover settlement practices and justifications" from the Occupied Territories."[767]

The *mitzpim* maintained their homogeneity, or "social purity," then, as their descendants in Israeli communities do now, via admissions committees. But again, this practice was obfuscated so as to reach its target audience efficiently and preserve plausible deniability at the same time. "Technically, they don't say it is for Jews only," says Waleed, an architect from Nazareth, in a 2005 article in which author Isabelle Humphries describes the plan to link Ariel Sharon's unilateral Gaza disengagement with Jewish development of the Galilee and Negev. "But," he continues, "we are excluded. For example, a while back they created a housing project in Nazareth Illit.... But when they saw that large numbers of those who had put their names down were Arabs they canceled it. Next thing it reappeared as a housing project for those who had served in the police or army, which of course is not us. They always find a way around it."[768] Humphries adds,

> While the state and high court system maintain the pretense of keeping opportunities open to all, independent private organizations have no obligation to do so.... The latest development plan for the Galilee and Negev is in full cooperation with the World Zionist Organization (WZO), the Jewish Agency (JA) and the Jewish National Fund (JNF)— non-state actors with an open Zionist and racist agenda.

Shafir notes the irony that community settlement residents are predominantly "liberal" politically, despite some contradictory behaviors. They are Labor and Meretz party voters who embrace collaborative initiatives between their towns and nearby Arab and Bedouin communities, yet, Shafir says, "most of these are educational and cultural initiatives and rarely address discrimination in access to housing, planning, and employment. Thus, they fail to attract many Arab volunteers." In 2000, when a High Court ruling threatened the admissions committees' hold on the settlements' homogeneous composition, some turned to the conservative Likud and Israel Beitenu parties to safeguard the policies legislatively. "From behind the walls of admissions committees," says Shafir, "they can oppose both Arabs as next-door neighbors and anti-Arab racism." At one point, the settlements resisted the mandate for more open admissions policies by simply saying no to any new members at all.[769] In an attitudinal survey of community settlement residents in 1997, Oren Yiftachel and Naomi Carmon found them to be surprisingly sanguine in their beliefs about Jewish-Arab "coexistence," though a large majority said that they wished to preserve the all-Jewish character of their communities in the future and seemed oblivious to the land issues the settlements had created for their Arab neighbors.[770]

In these communities, even the "security" pretexts that have classically underwritten exclusionary Zionist practices have been largely rejected as too flagrantly racist. Shani Shiloh, writing in *Haaretz*, recounted the view of Naama Katz Ben-Sasson, who studied public policy at Hebrew University of Jerusalem. Shiloh summarizes, "Today, discussing territorial threats is frowned upon. The issue still exists, Ben-Sasson says, but it's just gone undercover. What's happened is that people now say: Let's all live together with people just like ourselves, she explains. 'They don't say, let's Judaicize the Galilee, as used to be the case.' That would be politically incorrect." Alongside those issues, Shiloh says, there is the problem that "nobody thought about the environmental impact of building 52 towns on hilltops throughout the region, where each "requires its own 'city center,' its own water and sewage and electricity systems, its own roads."[771]

Apparently, it's occurred to some residents that if Arabs can be barred from membership, there's no reason to stop there. In a *mitzpim* promotional travelogue published in the *Jerusalem Post* in 1993, Aviva Bar-Am visits *Mitzpe Hararit* and writes, "According to resident Esti Cohen it is the only such outpost which accepts singles as well as people of any age. Smokers are not permitted to join, and members must be involved in Transcendental Meditation (TM)." Shafir mentions that "[o]ver three decades, most Jewish applicants, among them singles, single-parent families, the elderly, the disabled, Haredim and immigrants, have been rejected by admission committees while only a handful of Arab families have even applied."[772]

As with earlier efforts to Judaize the "peripheral areas," these plans, while constraining Arab life and bolstering Jewish ventures, failed to attract the influx of Jews to the area that had been hoped for or change the demographic mix. Furthermore, says Falah, the harsh measures "served to unite the region's Palestinians in their resolute determination to remain on their lands."[773] As the JNF builds its new master plan, it is clear that it will differ from the previous ones particularly in its scope—that is, its effort to turn the Galilee into a spot of international prestige, attracting students and entrepreneurs from around the world and helping Israel to make its mark as a twenty-first century "light unto nations"—much as the advent of the "start-up nation" brought Israel unprecedented global, secular cachet. Unlike the World Zionist Village of the Negev, designed as a meeting-ground for Jews the world over, the culinary and hospitality industries of the Galilee are intended to maintain a prominent place for Israel on the map of world culture and finance, very consistently with its branding efforts of recent decades.

One final note: Israel and the JNF are not the only entities in the world to use the discourse of societal or environmental "improvement" as a cover for removing long-term residents whose continued presence threatens the complacency and hegemony of the newly arrived privileged. In many of the world's prominent cities, this has been the story of gentrification—where, not coincidentally, middle-class professionals gambling on neighborhoods that bode to be "up-and-coming" declare themselves "pioneers," as did the early Zionist settlers as well as those who believed themselves to be thrusting toward Manifest Destiny in the American West. Liberal gentrified and "urbanly renewed" residents have usually averred that the whitening brought about by their neighborhood's transformation is a lamentable side-effect of the *real* aims—to modernize, to invest in real estate where prices are still low, but property values are expected to go up, to make an area "safe" or "sustainable"—and not evidence of racial prejudice. But let us not forget that in the mid-1960s, the writer James Baldwin popularized a saying that circulated in Black communities: "urban renewal" really meant "Negro removal." A comparable maneuver has long been, and continues to be, operative in the Negev and the Galilee.

CHAPTER 8:
THE "CAUSAL NEXUS": THE HOLOCAUST AND ISRAEL

"The connection of Israeli power and power practices of the new, Jewish state with the history of total powerlessness and victimhood of the Holocaust had began (sic) to be forged while the war was still raging, and developed in gradual fashion and at various levels. It was not born out of a formal, explicit decision, but was rather part of the continuous effort invested in the political and educational endeavor of nation-building by the dominant cultural and political elites in Israel. This connection had gathered momentum and evolved into a self-evident presence, expounding itself as part of the great narrative of Israeli redemption, until it became the narrative itself."
—Idith Zertal[774]

"The Holocaust and the birth of Israel were separated by only three years. So it's hardly surprising that many find a direct causal or even an organic connection between what is (for everyone) the worst event in post-exilic Jewish history and what is (for a great many) the best. But what exactly is the connection?....
[T]he belief in some sort of connection, or causal nexus, remains widespread.... One frequently alleged connection is the claim that the Holocaust "tragically vindicated" Zionism. Publicly, Zionists made this claim from 1933 on; it was repeated often during the war; it figures in the 1948 Declaration of Independence; it has been repeated endlessly ever since."
—Peter Novick[775]

"The establishment of the State of Israel was, according to President Ezer Weizman, "the will of the victims fully materialized," and according to

Shimon Peres it was "the ultimate response of the Jewish people to the Nazi scheme." Yosef (Tomi) Lapid, a popular and populist right-wing journalist and politician who is himself a Holocaust survivor, wrote in the daily right-leaning Ma'ariv *newspaper that "the Holocaust is the cosmic explosion from which the state of Israel was created."*
—Yosefa Loshitzky[776]

"The great narrative of Israeli redemption," as Idith Zertal puts it, has been, in various forms, the fulcrum of Zionist doctrine since its earliest days in the nineteenth century. But Tomi Lapid's vision of the Holocaust as the big bang that yielded a miraculous new Zionist universe has nonetheless gained widespread traction. It might even be said that the less one knows about the actual evolution of the Zionist project, the snugger the ineluctable link between the nadir and the zenith of Jewish history appears to be.

Theories about the nature of this "causal nexus" (Novick's term) range from the supernatural (divine redemption) to the social psychological (the 1947 United Nations vote to recognize Israel assuaged the world's guilt about having stood by as the Holocaust occurred). In this chapter, I am going to focus on two strategic uses Zionists have made of the Holocaust during, but primarily *after*, the event. They are not mutually exclusive and there is much overlap.

The first way Zionists instrumentalized the Holocaust was simply as an opportunity to shore up the Zionist project, despite the fact that—or perhaps to disguise the fact that—leaders in the Yishuv had flatly rendered the salvation of European Jews a subordinate concern to that of building a Jewish state. The specter of the Holocaust could forever be evoked as a fear tactic to rally the population or to draw backing from the world community in various endeavors or crises. The Holocaust was the best reminder of the real, ever-present threat of antisemitism and the previously unimaginable extremes to which it could be taken, and the best justifier of any steps Israel might take to, in its own formulation, ward off another one.

The second way the Holocaust served Zionist ideology came via schematizing it in a binary relation to Jewish experience in Eretz Yisrael—its antipodal counterpart. We saw in Chapter 5 that a significant aspect of the early Zionist ethos involved scorning, and distinguishing oneself from, the enervated, servile "other" that was the diaspora Jew. What better way to demonstrate the utter abjection and hopelessness of the diaspora Jew, and how this condition could be remedied by a shift in identity from victim to warrior, than to juxtapose the Holocaust experience against the Israeli superhero experience? (This contrast was especially effective after the 1967 war.)

"BUT AS LONG AS HE EXISTS...."

For Zionist leaders in Palestine during the war years, Jewish state-building took precedence over rescuing European Jewry. As early as 1936 Ben-Gurion had declared, "[W]e are interested in seeing Hitler destroyed, but as long as he exists, we are interested in exploiting this fact to build up Palestine."[777] At the May 1938 Mapai convention in Rehovot, Ben-Gurion further developed the view, which he held throughout the war, that the disaster befalling the Jewish people could be used as "political leverage" for the Zionist project. "This dreadful situation," he explained, "where they want to destroy millions of Jews...might bring...world public opinion closer to the Zionist idea."[778] Three years later he more pointedly argued that the US public should be brought to regard Jewish statehood as "the *only* solution to the Jewish question." (Italics added.)[779]

An oft-quoted declaration by Ben-Gurion to the Mapai Central Committee in 1938 puts the case most bluntly and bears repeating—especially in the light of efforts by Zionist entities to foreclose on alternative destinations for European Jewish refugees:

> Were I to know that the rescue of all German Jewish children could be achieved by their transfer to England and of only half their number by transfer to Palestine, I would opt for the latter, because our concern is not only the personal interest of these children, but the historic interest of the Jewish people.[780]

In 1939, the British, governing Palestine under the Mandate, issued a policy paper (known as the White Paper) that stunned the Yishuv. It posited sharp quotas on Jewish immigration to Palestine and a future Palestinian state that would effectively leave the Arab majority with decisive powers. The White Paper, which seemed to efface hopes of partition, was seen by the Zionist leadership as an evil to be fought at all costs. Yet there was this paradox: they had to be aligned with the British to vanquish Hitler even as that same colonial power trampled upon their political aspirations. "We must support the [British] army as though there were no White Paper and fight the White Paper as though there were no war," Ben-Gurion famously told the Mapai Central Committee in September 1939.

By 1942, credible sources brought news of Hitler's extermination plans for European Jewry, which were nonetheless met with considerable denial in the Yishuv. Whether the information was just too enormously horrible to be believed, or rejecting the accounts served other psychological and political needs, much was dismissed as the sort of "atrocity propaganda" the British had manufactured in World War I.[781] Yet Ben-Gurion managed, once again, to seize the opportunity for advertising the Zionist cause, saying in a fiery speech:

> We are the only people in the world whose blood, as a nation, is allowed [to be shed]...for one sin...because the Jews have no state, no army, no independence, and no homeland... [Then addressing the Jews of Europe]: [Y]our tragedy is our tragedy; your blood is our blood.... We shall have no rest until we redeem you both from the Nazi hell and from the debilitating exile and bring you...to the land we are building and redeeming, to our land.[782]

Shabtai Teveth, Ben-Gurion's biographer, remarks, "If there was a line in Ben-Gurion's mind between the beneficial disaster and an all-destroying catastrophe, it must have been a very fine one."[783]

"JUST ONE IMMIGRATION OPTION: PALESTINE"

Once the war ended, Zionist agents of various political affiliations flooded the displaced persons (DP) camps in Europe to recruit what they deemed "good human material" for immigration to Palestine. They sought new soldiers for their paramilitary armies to fight in the anticipated "War of Independence" and to swell the ranks of each of the rival parties beyond the war. Though many DPs expressed a desire to relocate to the US, Canada, Western Europe, South America, and Australia, and some even preferred to return to the countries from which they had so recently escaped trauma, such as Germany and Poland, the

Zionist agents in the camps mobilized all their persuasive and coercive abilities to steer them toward Palestine. Members of the anti-Zionist Jewish Bund pressed for Jewish refugees to be able to immigrate to countries other than Palestine, but they were outnumbered and out-resourced by the Zionists—even though by the late 1940s some western countries had begun to increase their immigration quotas.[784]

The future of Jewish children was especially contested. Yosef Grodzinsky writes:

> Jewish orphans were to be found in many places, having survived thanks to the goodness of Christian families and institutions that hid them throughout the war. Brigade men, directed by the Jewish Agency...were mobilizing to retrieve them, and assemble them in specially designated orphanages, where they were to be cared for, receive Zionist education, and be trained for immigration to Palestine.... The removal of children from adopting families required violence at times. Many families who rescued Jewish children were now treating them as if they were their own.... One of the best-known institutions was the orphanage in the Northern Italian town of Selvino.... Run by soldiers, the House had a strict, tersely worded code [including rules such as]: the sole language to be spoken is Hebrew;...prying into the past is not advised.... [R]esident children were not permitted to go out and search for surviving relatives, for fear that that would lead them to remain in Europe, rather than go to Palestine....[785]

The Central Committee of the Liberated Jews in the American Zone of postwar Germany (known as the Z.K.), which asserted itself as their representative body and thereby claimed authorization to speak for them, thwarted auspicious efforts to transfer Jewish children to France and England. Even when permits were obtained for hundreds of Jewish refugees to enter France, the Z.K. issued a statement that said, "Liberated Jews have just one immigration option: Palestine." Z.K. Chairman Dr. Zalman Grinberg further elaborated by pronouncing a decisive end to "intermediate steps that are not real solutions *en route* from the crematoria and gas chambers. Either the children go to the place they need and have a right to go to—Palestine—or they stay in the camps."

Ben-Gurion vehemently supported this position, asserting that preventing emigration to any place besides Palestine was "good for the Jews."[786]

The Haganah infiltrated the DP camps, sometimes managing to do so by presentingthemselves as refugees, and vigorously recruited Holocaust survivors for paramilitary training. What began as a voluntary event morphed into a facsimile of a compulsory military service apparatus, and those who attempted immigration to the US were branded as "deserters."[787] In the early stages, classic enlistment propaganda was circulated through leaflets and posters bearing nationalistic slogans such as, "Generations have waited, you won, fulfill your duty!" and "Have you done everything you could for your people?"[788] Later, though the recruiters had no legal status to back up their orders, those who refused their "draft" suffered various sorts of sanctions including job loss, apartment eviction, limited food rations—and violence.[789]

As the 1948 war in Palestine approached, the criteria for selecting candidates for immigration tightened to focus on those who would best serve the IDF. Grodzinsky explains that "a ban was put on the weak. Women, children, and the handicapped and elderly who lacked fighting capabilities were thus kept from coming, as they were of no military use. But it was exactly these who needed protection from [postwar] German raids."[790] Furthermore, he maintains, "On grounds of general civic duties it is difficult to find justification to the conscription of non-citizens, who live outside the territory of the coercive government, who had never set foot there, do not speak the local language, and for the most part have no interest in going [to Palestine]."[791]

EXODUS: A PROPAGANDA SPECTACLE IN THREE PARTS

Meanwhile, dramatic spectacles such as the *Exodus* affair, later made even more famous via a novel by Leon Uris and a Hollywood film, were curated to rouse support for easing England's restrictions and quotas on Jews attempting to reach Palestine. The story of Holocaust refugees engaged in a do-or-die effort to break through the British blockade was dramatized for propagandistic purposes in each of its incarnations, from reality to the screen.

The ship, originally called the *President Warfield*, underwent a name-change to the more proto-Zionist *Exodus 1947* while at sea. Choreography involving the competing stances of the British, the Italians, the French, the project organizers of the Mossad and the Yishuv, and the 4,500 refugees on board reached a climax in the port of Haifa, where the passengers were forcibly removed from their ship by the British and placed on "prison ships," remanded to the Europe they had just escaped. The performance had a very targeted audience: the members of the UN Special Committee on Palestine (UNSCOP), who were tasked with adjudicating the future of Palestine and, just then, on-site to perform their investigation. Eventually, they prescribed the end of the British mandate and the partition of the country between Jews and Arabs, which was precisely the Zionists' aim in staging their event.

According to Idith Zertal, messages sent from Mossad headquarters in the Yishuv to the ship in its final approach contained instructions to clearly communicate "descriptions of the suffering of the refugees, with an emphasis on their fierce desire to reach their homeland," along with "a call for UNSCOP to intervene," to "board the ship and record living testimony," and to thus "come see with their own eyes the plight of *Exodus's* passengers."[792] Zertal observes, "As in previous incidents, the Zionist struggle ostensibly fought over the fate of the Jewish refugees was, in fact, aimed higher, directed toward the great, decisive battle for the establishment of a Jewish state.... The Zionists had never intended to actually bring the 4,500 refugees onto the shores of Palestine, and such an effort had no chance of success since the *Exodus* was a show project from its inception." However, says Zertal, they "made intuitive and effective use, as the incident developed, of the 'weapon' they had at their disposal—the survivors themselves...."[793]

The *Exodus* sailed back to France, its official point of departure, but the refugees refused to disembark. They continued to insist upon Palestine as their destination, and the sympathetic French, even under British orders, made it clear that they would not compel them to enter—though they were welcome. A standoff ensued for twenty days, which included a hunger strike and, boosted by Yishuv operatives, international publicity. Once the dramatic peak of the UNSCOP visit had passed, however, Zionist leaders lost interest and acceded to the ship being returned to Hamburg. "In a way," observes Zertal, "sending the refugees to Germany was, for the Zionists, an additional and unexpected—if cruel—propaganda windfall." They "went so far as to obstruct every possibility of saving the refugees the trip."[794] Yet afterward, Ben-Gurion extolled their "epic" drama as "one of the greatest expressions of the Jewish struggle, of Jewish pride, and of the connection with Palestine."[795]

During the 1950s, Israeli leaders realized that in Hollywood lay an extraordinary opportunity for swaying the world to their cause and began to scout about for an appropriate screenplay or producer. Teddy Kollek—later a very long-term mayor of Jerusalem, but then General Director of the Prime Minister's Office; Moshe Pearlman, who founded and headed the Government Press Office and handled the government's information services; the Hasbara Department of the Ministry of Foreign Affairs (MFA); and the Israeli consulates in Los Angeles and New York were all involved in the quest. "At stake," writes Giora Goodman, "was not only the propaganda potential of Hollywood films, but the commercial opportunity of attracting big productions spending much-coveted foreign currency while broadening the country's exposure to the Western tourism market."[796]

Leon Uris was a Jewish American writer who already had to his credit a war novel that had been made into a film. He was recruited by Dore Schary of MGM to write a screenplay about the birth of Israel, and he also signed with Random House for the novel version, which he wrote first.[797] Less knowledgeable than enthusiastic about his subject, Uris had his research intensively shored up by materials, tours, and meetings with key figures supplied by Israeli officials, including Ilan Hartuv of the MFA's Hasbara Department. Goodman notes that in thanking Hartuv for his help in the preface to *Exodus,* Uris said nothing of his MFA connection. And, reported Uris's wife, a senior MFA official "greatly helped Leon in the editing" and noted that the goyish American nurse, Kitty Fremont, who falls in love with Uris's Jewish, Palestine-born protagonist, Ari Ben Canaan, would have "*hasbara* value for us" with the book's non-Jewish American readership.[798] As Amy Kaplan puts it, "Kitty represents the American who discovers in Zionism the mystical qualities of the Holy Land that she heard about in Sunday school…. Kitty speaks the language of the recently invented Judeo-Christian tradition." And she is "magnetically attracted" to Ari, 'who does not act like any Jew I've ever met.'"[799]

The novel was published in 1958. The first half of the book consists of a highly altered version of the real *Exodus's* journey, albeit with plentiful flashbacks to the fictional refugees' prior lives in Europe. The passengers are mostly child concentration camp survivors, rather than adults; the ship is being held in Cyprus and its passengers in a detention camp by the British in violation of their ardent wish to go to Palestine—rather than being returned to Europe; a hunger strike and suicide threats that greatly exceed the original in scope are launched; and finally, in the face of all this determination and worldwide negative PR, the British cave and let them through. "The children who had brought the mighty British Empire to its knees were arriving!.... The *Exodus* had come home!" concludes the omniscient narrator of this long adventure, as the Palestine Philharmonic Orchestra jubilantly plays "Hatikvah," the Zionist (later Israeli) anthem, in Haifa Harbor.[800]

The remainder of the novel covers politics and events leading up to, and beyond, the achievement of Israeli statehood and (as Uris would have it) the clash of national interests with the Arabs. The reality on which the story is based requires some delicate—that is, transposed and misleading—handling of the explosive tensions between the paramilitary groups Haganah (the good guys, who will become the Labor Party that leads Israel until 1977) and Irgun (officially, though in reality hardly exclusively, the "terrorists" who will morph into the Likud of Menachem Begin and Bibi Netanyahu). The Zionists' ire with the British is also somewhat calibrated for geopolitical consumption. (Well, somewhat. As Kevin Mims observes in an article looking back at *Exodus* sixty-five years after its publication, "Even while World War II is raging, many of the novel's Zionists have to be convinced that, between the British and the Nazis, the former are the lesser of the two evils."[801])

In 2012, *Ha'aretz* columnist Bradley Burston wrote, "Uris's life would change forever with the explosive reception to 'Exodus,' which, according to [his biographer Ira B.] Nadel, sold more copies than any other American book beside 'Gone With the Wind' and topped the *New York Times* best-seller list for a full five months."[802] Kevin Mims reports that "by 1975, *Exodus* had sold a total of 5,473,710 copies in all formats (hardback, paperback, book club, etc.) in the US alone.... It was translated into dozens of languages and foreign sales accounted for millions more copies coming into print.... It has never been out of print and remains relatively popular to this day."[803]

Yet the schism between the book's popular and critical reception was huge. Burston explains, "Like its creator, Leon Uris, [the novel] was savaged by critics and academics, and resoundingly ignored by literary prize committees. When the book appeared in 1958, however, it was nearly as common to find a copy of 'Exodus' in American-Jewish households as to find the Bible...."[804] Jenny Singer wrote in the *Forward*, "[T]here has always been a gulf between the way historians and critics read *Exodus*—as a piece of nonsense—and the way readers received it—as transcendent."[805] Amy Kaplan observes, "Fiction supplanted history, as tourists would ask to visit places where events from the novel occurred.... [O]ne visitor...asked to see the Galilee, a place he 'read about in *Exodus*.'"[806]

Some key behind-the-scenes players voiced mixed assessments, as well. When the *Jerusalem Post* writer Ruthie Blum Leibowitz interviewed Ike Aronowicz, who had been the actual captain of the ship *Exodus 1947*, in November 2008, he recounted an interview Uris had done with him in 1956 while preparing to write the book. "I told him he was a very gifted writer, but not a historian, and therefore it shouldn't be he writing the history of the *Exodus*," recalled Aronowicz. "He was very offended. But, of course, I turned out to be right, because afterwards, he wrote a very good novel, but it had nothing to do with reality. *Exodus*, shmexodus."[807] And Ben-Gurion's succinct appraisal has been quoted in numerous articles about the book: "As a literary work, it isn't much. But as a piece of propaganda, it's the greatest thing ever written about Israel."[808]

Many would agree with him. Jenny Singer has observed, "*Exodus* is one of the stranger artifacts of 20th century literature: a 626-page novel that, in fictionalizing many of the historic events surrounding the formation of the state of Israel...ended up shaping not just generations of American perceptions of Israel, but policy, too." She points out its enduring utility for American politicians eager to prove their Israeliphilic bona fides: both Barack Obama and John McCain "wooed Jewish voters with mentions of reading Uris" during the 2008 presidential campaign.[809]

But the novel's contempt for Arabs garnered critical comment, as well. "I view *Exodus* as a piece of vintage propaganda, a document that helped teach America to see Palestinians as subhuman. [My father] sees it as a classic of Jewish literature," writes Singer. Alan Elsner, a J Street member writing in *Jewish Journal*, points out that "the word 'Arab' rarely appears without the adjective 'dirty' or 'stinking' appended."[810]

In 1958, the highly successful, Jewish immigrant film producer Otto Preminger bought out the film rights to *Exodus* from MGM, enlisting United Artists as backer and distributor. However, mounting tensions between Uris and Preminger soon led to Uris's removal as screenwriter, a job that ultimately fell to

Dalton Trumbo. When time came for production to begin, Israel supported it in ways it uniquely could: lending navy destroyers[811] and procuring permission to film in ordinarily inaccessible venues such as courts, government buildings, religious institutions, and the port of Haifa—which, says Goodman, "was practically closed down for a whole day during filming. The police afforded protection during filming in Haifa, Acre, and Jerusalem, blocked off roads, and provided old British police uniforms and prisoner outfits. The Israeli army supplied dozens of trucks, military equipment, and groups of soldiers to act as British military units."[812]

The period of filming was an opportune time to create foreign buzz around the project. Preminger's PR staff invited influential American film critics and journalists to visit during the process, while the MFA Hasbara Department "encouraged visiting journalists to write about the country as well, adding an invitation at its own expense to the European correspondent of the *New Yorker*." The film's actors and crew, potential ambassadors for the cause, were also the recipients of a Zionist charm initiative; they were invited to meet with important officials, including the prime minister, and hosted at events such as a kibbutz Passover seder and the Independence Day parade in Haifa. The objections of those in local Arab villages (at that time living under Israeli military rule), including those voiced in the press and in calls to boycott the production due to the story's depiction of Arabs, also had to be quieted or negotiated. It fell to government and military figures to curry, via special deals, the cooperation of locals, from villagers to mayors—when, for example, a fictional "settlement" with its infrastructure needed to be erected on their land.[813] Some particularly nasty scenes were cut or rewritten, including one at the behest of the mayor of Nazareth, but, says Goodman, "Despite these changes, the film went further than the book in absolving the Jewish side from the moral dilemmas of the 1948 war." For example,

> [W]hen Zionist leader Barak Ben Canaan in the midst of mass Jewish celebrations on the UN vote calls on the Arabs to stay in their homes and not choose 'the weary path of exile,' the film powerfully supported one of the most pronounced Israeli propaganda claims about the creation of the Palestinian refugee problem, the ongoing sore spot of Israeli diplomacy.[814]

Exodus the movie opened in New York in December 1960, and, once again, it was regarded dubiously by critics but produced unambiguous profits at the box office. Along the way, its narrative took on a specious authenticity of its own. "*Exodus*," writes Amy Kaplan, "transformed a historical failure into a fictional success."[815] In its portrayal of the "New Jew" trapped in what some have called a "bad neighborhood," it purports to demonstrate that

> Jews exercise violence with restraint; Arab violence is irrational, excessive, and vengeful.... Unscrupulous Arab leaders ignobly whip up their followers into shrieking frenzies by promising them 'easy victories, loot, and rape.' Throughout the novel Uris transforms political resistance on the part of Arabs into irrational sexual violence.... This recurring theme of sexual violence and vengeance makes it impossible for Ari—or the reader—to imagine Arab opposition to a Jewish state as politically motivated.[816]

It seems apt to conclude this section with Goodman's final observations about the far-reaching influence the "*Exodus* book and film phenomenon" has exerted on readers and viewers. In its "shaping...[of] favorable international perceptions of Israel," it has demonstrated, he contends, "the propaganda value of mass-culture products, often greater than any disseminated propaganda." In particular:

> [T]he central themes of *Exodus* fit in almost perfectly with Israeli international propaganda themes: the constructive nature of Zionist colonization and its welcoming by friendly Arabs; the flow of Holocaust survivors towards solace and an ancient national home in Palestine; the general moderation of the Jewish leadership despite the regrettable and condemned turning of an understandably militant minority to violence; the heroic overcoming of British and Arab opposition to national independence; and yet still the Israeli offering of a progressive hand for peace.[817]

INTERNECINE ZIONIST SLANDERFARE

Another key component of strengthening the Zionist project involved using the Holocaust to cultivate approbative postwar public opinion, not only internationally but also among the contentious domestic Israeli political parties.

While the specter of the Holocaust could be used, on the world stage, to cast Israel's many military exploits and strongman tactics as "self-defense," done in the name of "security," it could also be deployed to burnish or befoul the policies and personalities of one Israeli faction vis-à-vis the others.

For David Ben-Gurion, invoking the Holocaust to illustrate the importance of building Israel into a strong, secure state helped to vindicate his controversial (among both Israeli leaders and populace) decisions to kiss and make up with Germany via seeking reparations money and establishing mutually beneficial diplomatic, economic, and military relations. The advantages for each party were clear: for Israel, enormous amounts of funds and supplies that served to build up the infrastructure and military capabilities of the country (as well as new swimming pools for kibbutzim, new apartments for individual survivors, and fundraising windfalls for organizations such as the World Jewish Congress [WJC] who claimed to represent the "Jewish people as a whole"[818]); for Germany, intent on resurrecting and rebranding itself as a major postwar European power, a benediction for its place in a civilized new world order.

But there were also decided disadvantages for Israel—not material ones but, as many saw it, matters of conscience and moral fiber. Ben-Gurion's mission dramatically broke with broad immediate postwar perspectives, when "boycott [of Germany] was considered a national duty"[819]. Some insisted that in normalizing relations with Germany Ben-Gurion was desecrating the memory of the "six million" and, by association, of Jews worldwide. The opposition was composed of strange bedfellows—from the Communists on the left of the political spectrum to Menachem Begin's Herut party on the right and included moderate newspapers as well as Holocaust survivors. There were even opponents, including Golda Meir, among Ben-Gurion's own Mapai party, which led the governing coalition and was often the object of others' resentment.[820]

Among the survivors, some sharply preferred vengeance to money, as expressed by this former concentration camp prisoner and member of the Vilna ghetto underground: "If you ask me what I want to receive from the German people, I would say, a mother for a mother, a father for a father, a child for a child. My soul would be at rest if I knew that there would be six million German dead to match the six million Jews."[821] Ben-Gurion stressed that he placed the "national interest" above all else, but, comments Segev, "he often identified the country's interests with those of Mapai, and vice versa."[822] (Meanwhile, those in Mapai still bore the stain of their hands-off behavior during the war itself, as their opponents were wont to remind them.)

Menachem Begin, for his part, declared that those in the Knesset who voted to support negotiations with Germany were "treasonous," the negotiations themselves a "holocaust," and the members of Mapai were "Nazis." Herut party posters were mounted bearing the message: "The bones of our martyred parents—to the Mapai-Nazi Blood Market."[823] Ben-Gurion had his own countervailing Holocaust-sourced apothegms, such as "Let not the murderers of our nation also be its heirs" and admonitions that this was a "new" Germany, not the one of yesteryear.[824] The latter contention supported his dogged insistence on uncoupling "Nazis" from "Germans," aimed to finesse his dealings with West Germany both at home and in Europe.

As always with him, appeals to "security" were paramount. Justifying the massive military support obtained from Germany—which included aircraft, tanks, submarines, missiles, and training of Israeli pilots and officers by Germans, in Germany[825]—Ben-Gurion fulminated:

> [I]f anyone concludes that the Holocaust forbids us to negotiate with Germany, I say that person lives in the past and not the present, cares more about his feelings than about the existence of the Jewish people. And if anyone says, "Let us not forget the dead," I say, "Let's concentrate on keeping the Jews living in this country from being slaughtered."....
> If certain things are not done in our time, there is no certainty that our children and our grandchildren will remain alive.[826]

On another occasion he advised ominously, "We do not want the Arab Nazis to come and slaughter us."[827] This was only one of numerous references that would come over the years—from many Zionists—to Arabs as "Nazis," the ultimate scarecrow always looming above Eretz Yisrael. Zertal dubbed it "the Nazification of the enemy." Benjamin Netanyahu called Yasser Arafat "Hitler"; Saddam Hussein was called "little Hitler" at a Tel Aviv gathering of Polish survivors during the Gulf War; and *Ha'aretz* compared Gamal Abdel Nasser to Hitler at the outset of the 1967 war. Most frequently effected to vilify Arabs, the routine was also freely adapted for internecine Zionist battles. In the leadup to the partition of Palestine after World War II, Menachem Begin compared those Zionists who favored the idea to the Judenrat, willing accessories to "a programme of annihilation." During the signing of the Oslo agreement in Washington, DC, a woman settler in Palestine said bitingly of Yitzhak Rabin, "I see an Israeli prime minister who reminds me of Marshal Pétain shaking the hand of the chief Nazi and handing over the Jews of his country." Ben-Gurion once wrote to Israeli writer Haim Guri that "Begin is clearly a Hitler type.... When I first heard Begin speak on the radio, I heard Hitler's voice and words." [828] Meanwhile, the Israeli scholar Nurit Peled-Elhanan has said that in Israeli school textbooks, present-day Palestinians are still conflated with the Nazis of World War II Germany to serve as an ongoing mobilizing trauma.[829]

One figure who made this conflation easy—much to the satisfaction of Zionists who seized upon its far-reaching propaganda value—was Haj Amin al-Husseini, the Grand Mufti of Jerusalem from 1921 to 1937 under the British Mandate. Though initially appointed by and aligned with the British, he came to loathe them in the wake of the Peel Commission's 1937 plan to partition the country, which favored Zionists, and their brutal repression of Palestinian resistance during the Great Arab Revolt of 1936–39. A fierce nationalist, Husseini's infamy grew out of his wartime support for the Axis powers, whom he believed would win the war and then eliminate the Zionist movement in Palestine. Most notoriously, in a 1941 meeting with Hitler, he sought a public declaration of support for Arab national independence in Palestine (or as Tom Segev put it, "a kind of German Balfour declaration for the Arabs"), offering an Arab-driven helping hand in return. Hitler was warm but evasive; however, Husseini put his foot in it further by agreeing to be photographed with Hitler—"which," says Segev, "has haunted the Palestinian cause ever since."[830]

An antisemite, to be sure, Husseini has had additional and spurious culpability melodramatically bestowed upon him by enemies such as Ben-Gurion during the 1960 trial of Adolf Eichmann, where he encouraged the prosecutor to assert "firm links" between the mufti and Eichmann, and by Netanyahu, in a 1993 book and again in a 2015 speech to the World Jewish Congress. Both leaders claimed that it was Husseini, rather than Hitler, who at that meeting initiated the idea of the Final Solution. Not only is there evidence to the contrary—the wheels of extermination were already well in motion when the two leaders met—but Holocaust scholars and Israelis such as Dina Porat, Yad Vashem's chief historian, and Isaac Herzog, the leader of the opposition Labor

Party in 2015, were quick to correct the claim's ahistoricity. Further, they and other critics of Netanyahu's allegations charged that beyond being baseless, those claims essentially let Hitler off the hook. Despite this, Netanyahu persisted, in Zertal's words, in branding "Arafat and his organization...[as] spiritual and political descendants of the Mufti of Jerusalem."[831]

A frequent and plausible explanation for the mufti's support for the Axis powers comes in the form of the aphorism, "The enemy of my enemy is my friend." Husseini pointed out to Hitler at the beginning of their meeting that they had as mutual adversaries "the English, the Jews, and the Communists." Certainly, anyone who has swallowed America's friendships with world dictators and perpetrators of genocide, because they repressed who it was in America's interest to repress, can understand this. (Think Anastasio Somoza of Nicaragua, the Shah of Iran, Ferdinand Marcos in the Philippines, Augusto Pinochet of Chile.) Furthermore, the Stern Gang, the pre-state Zionist militia that employed terrorist tactics against the British as well as the Arabs (and some of their rival Zionists), made similar overtures to the Nazis, rationalizing, "If we are duty bound to fight the foe [the British], we may utilize the aid of the arch enemy [the Nazis], given because he is the foe of our foe."[832]

Rationalized in a more practical vein was the 1933 *Haavera* ("Transfer") Agreement between leaders of the Zionist Labor movement and the German government. In this negotiated exchange, which some believed to be of mutual benefit—though members of Jabotinsky's Revisionist party were tenaciously opposed and the American Zionist movement was intensely split—German Jews were allowed to emigrate to Palestine with some of their assets in return for the cessation of the worldwide Jewish boycott of German goods, the efficacy of which lay in its imposition of a propitious vulnerability on the Nazi regime at a time of severe economic depression. Though not exactly an "alliance" with Germany, as the mufti was proposing, it was certainly a marriage of extreme convenience that many called a pact with the devil. Yet while the Jewish agency concealed its controversial role in the deal until 1935, and the agreement has occupied a discreetly obscure place in the history books, the mufti is still regularly invoked as the Arab Nazi collaborator par excellence. Reminders of his villainous role illustrate that Arab intentions to destroy Jews are contiguous with those of the Nazis and that supporters of Israel must thus remain ever vigilant. Peter Novick observes that in the *Encyclopedia of the Holocaust*,

"The article on the Mufti is more than twice as long as the articles on Goebbels and Göring, longer than the articles on Himmler and Heydrich combined, longer than the article on Eichmann—of all the biographical articles, it is exceeded in length, but only slightly, by the entry for Hitler."[833]

Finally, triggering images of the Holocaust became a useful way to rouse the Israeli public's support for wars and silence dissenters by stirring up their most fearful associations. Israeli historian Gulie Ne'eman Arad uses the term "holocaustal anxiety" to signify the mood first observable during the three-week "waiting period" leading up to the onset of the 1967 Six-Day War. At that time, she says, "the Shoah was summoned to validate demands for 'war now'.... Public rhetoric turned apocalyptic, and a week before fighting broke out the threat was described as if at issue was 'the existence or nonexistence of the Jewish people.'" After the trauma of the surprise attack on Israel in the 1973 "Yom Kippur War," the "angst...evoked [was] nurtured and kept alive" and "a Shoah risk was accepted as a perennial possibility." Shimon Peres, she writes, "defined the Shoah as a 'national lesson' that proved that 'the whole world is against us....'" (This cynical slogan became a popular song.) For Menachem Begin, the Israeli invasion of Lebanon in 1982 was imperative because "the alternative is Treblinka...."[834]

In the twenty-first century, the notion of a "second Holocaust" is frequently invoked to warn of what could happen if Iran is allowed to develop its nuclear capabilities.[835] It is also marshalled, says Arad, to explain "why Israel could not return to its pre-war 1967 borders, which former Prime Minister Yizhak Shamir dubbed the 'Auschwitz border'"; to justify "caution in embarking on the road to peace"; and to clarify "why it must expand its military capabilities...." All these purported causes of Israel's endangerment, she points out, pointedly ignore the fact that its lack of security stems from its ongoing colonialism and occupation.[836]

Famously, the Hamas-led attack on southern Israel on October 7, 2023, has become known as "the deadliest day for the Jewish people since the Holocaust." *The Jerusalem Post* said it repeatedly and called the event "Holocaust 2." *The Times of Israel* said it. President Biden said it. NPR said it. *CNN* said it and went on to quote one of the kibbutz survivors of that day: "They did worse than Nazis. The Nazis had...a little human in them just to gas us."[837] The World Jewish Congress reminded its followers in a fundraising letter to remember

Kristallnacht "at this devastating time."[838] Netanyahu said that Hamas were "the new Nazis" as he called for unity and international support in "this just war against the modern barbarians, the worst monsters on the planet."[839] Meanwhile, any connection drawn between Israel's genocidal war on Gaza and the Holocaust is roundly condemned.

LIONS AND LAMBS

As we saw in Chapter 5, "the negation of diaspora" or "the negation of exile" denoted, for Zionists, the blanket rejection of two thousand years of Jewish experience outside of Palestine as inauthentic and embarrassing. The muscular, assertive New Jew—always a hyper-masculinist construction—would eclipse all that.

With the postwar arrival of the Holocaust survivors in Israel, this dichotomy was exacerbated, as if a prediction had proven to be true. In those years, it was common to derisively refer to Jews who died in the Nazis' gas chambers as having gone "like lambs to the slaughter."[840] That is, they represented the apogee of the spineless, subserviently cringing exilic Jew—a trope that would hereafter be displaced by that of the strapping, brave, and well-armed Jewish warrior who would proudly, no matter the challenge, "fight to the end." Here can be seen the roots of the militarism that came to hold such essential moral and social capital in Israeli culture. The Holocaust scenarios that best symbolized the sort of valor prized by Zionists were those of the ghetto uprisings. The Warsaw Ghetto uprising in particular—in which Zionist residents of the ghetto did play a role, but a very partial one, working in concert with Bundists and others and without support from the Yishuv—was appropriated by the Zionist leadership as an emblem of what the New Jew would, and could, do, with tributes and monuments galore to signal the fact. Grodzinsky observes that a 1956 eighth-grade Israeli textbook creates the impression that it was these uprisings that led to Israel's independence five years later.[841]

The Holocaust refugees who had *not* been part of an armed resistance were seen as the antithesis of the pioneering, visionary, rugged New Israelis. They were, after all, refugees—people who had elected to immigrate only by default because they had been divested of their lives, rather than having made an idealistic choice to pursue *aliyah* ("ascent"—the designated term for making the decision to go to Israel and join the Yishuv).[842] They did not fit in with the dominant Israeli culture and were shunned for their difference—or pressured to assimilate. Many of the child survivors were sent to kibbutzim to bolster the population of those communities, even though many of them wanted to be in the city, where the vast majority of Israelis lived, and to study rather than till the fields. Still recovering from their war experiences, many lacked the stamina needed for farm work; and having lost many of their closest relatives and witnessed the beatings of others, many suffered from a combination of grief and what we would now call post-traumatic stress disorder (PTSD). They were often regarded as mentally ill by the established Israelis, classified in Freudian diagnostic categories as if they were bourgeois neurotics or pathological. There were, at times, certain forms of segregation promoted—separate living quarters or dining halls—because the survivors were too downbeat for the regular kibbutz members and felt compelled to share grim stories that no one wanted to hear.[843]

Idith Zertal makes an interesting psychosocial observation about this state of affairs, drawing upon Freud's 1919 essay "The Uncanny." The feeling of uncanniness, Freud postulates, "belongs to all that is terrible—to all that arouses dread and creeping horror.... the uncanny is that class of the terrifying which leads back to something long known to us, once very familiar." Yet it is the very proximity between that which is *Heimlich* ("familiar and congenial") and that which is *Unheimlich* ("concealed and kept out of sight")—and the fragility of the border between them, threatening to merge the two into one and the same thing—that is so unnerving.[844]

Zertal writes that for Freud, "anxiety of this kind is evoked through an encounter with something that, paradoxically, is experienced as at once foreign and familiar, distant and close, totally estranged and unknown and at the same time strangely recognizable and known." She goes on to say, "My argument is that the encounter between the Zionist Israeli community and the post-Holocaust diaspora represented by the survivors... indeed produced the uncanny effect that Freud claims is created by the return of the repressed, the coming to light of what should remain concealed, the unearthing of the unconscious. It is the return of the diaspora in its role of Zionism's unconscious."[845] The survivors symbolized, after all, the abjection that Zionism was invented to make obsolete yet was now right there serving as a constant reminder of its refusal to disappear.

Zertal points out that when Ben-Zion Dinur, the noted Hebrew University historian who was then serving as Minister of Culture and Education, drafted the "Holocaust and Heroism Remembrance Law—Yad Vashem, 1953," he "made the crucial, exclusive link between Holocaust memory and the State of Israel":

> Dinur mentioned them all: the dead, the destroyed Jewish communities, the heroes, the partisans, and ghetto rebels. Only one category was not mentioned by the minister responsible for the Holocaust commemoration law: the survivors. They, those who had experienced the horrors directly, who were living in Israel in their hundreds of thousands, the most immediate, direct bearers of the unprecedented memory, the prime source, the most valuable asset of Holocaust memory—were discounted in the state where they were picking up the pieces of their shattered lives.... Holocaust commemoration, which the State of Israel instated as law, was a memory without rememberers.[846]

This reluctance to hear about concentration camp experiences held true in US Jewish communities as well as in Israel. Peter Novick writes,

> Survivors were constantly told...that they should turn their faces forward, not backward; that it was in their interest, insofar as possible, to forget the past and proceed to build new lives....American Jews, or Jews in the Yishuv, would have been incredulous at the idea, later a commonplace, that survivors' memories were a "precious legacy" to be preserved. There is, in fact, an eerie symmetry between the messages survivors received in the forties and fifties and those of the eighties and nineties. Earlier, they were told that even if they wanted to speak of the Holocaust, they shouldn't—it was bad for them. Later they were told that even if they didn't want to speak of it, they must—it was good for them. In both cases, others knew what was best.[847]

In any case, for many in the Yishuv, this "lesson" of the Holocaust was clear: all that had transpired in Hitler's Europe was a perfect illustration of what can happen in the absence of a Jewish state. Had Israel existed in the 1930s and 1940s, they insisted, it would have presented a valiant defense against the

Nazis. The survivors themselves were not so sure, aware that the Zionists' single-minded focus on state-building during the war years had taken precedence over rescue or support for those trapped in Europe. "'You danced the hora while we were being burned in the crematoriums,' said Yosef Rosensaft, a DP leader at Bergen-Belsen, who settled in America."[848]

The tendency to blame Holocaust victims and survivors for their putative "lambs to the slaughter" deportment pivoted in the 1960s. The most dramatic turning point came in 1961 with the trial of the very high-ranking Nazi and Holocaust planner Adolf Eichmann. A year prior, he had been apprehended by the Mossad, Israel's national intelligence agency, and was brought from hiding in Argentina to Israel to stand trial for his crimes. The jurisdiction of the trial was a matter of controversy. Many, including the Anti-Defamation League, argued that his deeds of totalitarian ruthlessness should be tried in an international venue as a crime against humanity at large.[849] But Ben-Gurion saw the case as a grand opportunity to showcase the power a self-determining Israel could exercise in the pursuit of justice for an otherwise interminably vulnerable Jewish people, and he prevailed in siting the trial in Jerusalem.

His aim for the trial was, as he himself acknowledged, not about gathering evidence to incriminate and punish Eichmann (whose guilt was a foregone conclusion, anyway). Principally he sought to mount a spectacular morality play in which Israel emerged as the defense counsel and redeemer of "The Six Million."[850] "Finally," writes Zertal, "the Holocaust could be faced, looked at, but from a very different specific perspective—from a position of power, sovereignty, and control." For Ben-Gurion it was, she says, "the perfect vehicle for his grand national pedagogy. The total helplessness of European Jewry in World War II could now directly serve as the 'counter metaphor' to the discourse of Israeli omnipotence and also as its ultimate justification."[851] It was necessary, Ben-Gurion said, that "our youth.... should be taught the lesson that Jews are not sheep to be slaughtered but a people who can hit back."[852]

Another aim, for Ben-Gurion, was to entice the Mizrahi Jews of Israel into patriotic common cause when, in fact, the Holocaust had barely been their experience. "The Jewish people" was generally used as a metonym for European Jewry and unthinkingly excluded the Jews of Africa and Asia; likewise, "the Holocaust" was (and still often is) uncritically posited as a universal Jewish phenomenon.[853]

The trial happened to begin as a new election campaign got underway and, predictably, provided much fodder for anti-Arab scaremongering and "defensive" rabble-rousing, such as the Mapai secretary general's declaration, "150 meters from the courtroom there is a border, and behind that border *thousands of Eichmanns* lie in wait, proclaiming explicitly, 'what Eichmann has not completed, we will.'"[854]

In general, says Segev, the case against Eichmann was framed in mystical rather than analytical terms, to the point where the "evidence" often bore very little connection to the acts of the man being tried and, instead, the focus was on "the sufferings of the Jewish people." To this end, the prosecutor, Gideon Hausner, operating with some direction from Ben-Gurion (who was allowed to revise some of the opening remarks), called as witnesses a stream of Holocaust survivors who, for the first time, were directly and publicly questioned about what they had endured. As a result, a mass Israeli audience—both in the over-flowing theater that served as the court and in their homes across the country as they listened to live radio broadcasts—finally heard their testimony. The proceedings had been designed to produce maximum emotional effect: "Hausner instructed the witnesses to recount every horrifying detail of the atrocities they had endured, including acts of sexual abuse," writes Segev. But rather than simply illustrating the hopeless pathos of diaspora existence in need of rescue, an unanticipated message was engendered. The script was flipped: from the ashes of the contempt that had always been directed at these survivors emerged compassion and empathy. In addition, a younger generation, who had come of consciousness at a remove from the war and its immediate aftermath, became interested in the Holocaust and sympathetic to its victims for the first time.[855]

However, there was still the other front—that of the grand lesson the trial was meant to impart about Nazi/Arab evil versus Jewish victimhood and the Jewish people's now-nationalized right to defend itself. The potentially dramatic closure of Eichmann's hanging on May 31, 1962, was somewhat diminished by a new and generally unwelcome interpretation of the story by German American Jewish refugee and political philosopher Hannah Arendt. Her 1963 series of articles about the trial for *The New Yorker* magazine that were ultimately consolidated in a book, *Eichmann in Jerusalem: A Report on the Banality of Evil,* punctured the neat binary that the Zionists had worked so hard to establish. Arendt didn't dispute the premise that Eichmann's deeds were "evil"; she merely redefined *evil,* positing it as something that did not reside innately in certain monstrous people but rather emerged from the actions of quite ordinary people doing quite ordinary, socially sanctioned things they regarded as "good." This phenomenon was apt to materialize, she argued, in the absence of critical thinking. In some ways the concept echoed social psychology's notion of crowd or group behavior as described by Gustave Le Bon, Sigmund Freud, and others (described here in Chapter 5) who posited that an individual's ability to reflect rationally and ethically easily dissolves in a group environment.[856]

One small but widely enraging facet of her discussion involved the *Judenrat,* members of Jewish councils in the ghettoes who cooperated with the Nazis in exchange for what they believed was a reprieve from the general fate of their communities. By raising the idea that, even in those dire circumstances, people could make, and were responsible for, moral choices, she again violated the aims of the lesson plan and infuriated many. Discussion of the *Judenrat* had been largely omitted from the trial.[857]

Arendt was widely vilified—and, I would argue, misunderstood, willfully or otherwise—for her thesis. A contemporaneous review in *The Jewish Spectator* by its editor, Trude Weiss Rosmarin, titled "Self-Hating Jewess Writes Pro-Eichmann Series for the New Yorker" and Michael Musmanno's assertion in the Sunday *New York Times Book Review* that Arendt had "attacked the State of Israel, its laws and institutions" reveal some of the tenor of the attacks.[858] Interestingly, as Segev puts it, while fury about it raged within Israel because "a monster was needed to make sense of the horrible memories of the Holocaust survivors and to justify the politicization of those memories," the book was not translated into Hebrew—"aside," Segev says, "from a few chapters that were printed in *Haaretz.* A book written to prove that Arendt had distorted the truth was, however, translated."[859] In other words, the primary source at the heart of the controversy was not available for Israeli readers to evaluate for themselves until 2000.[860]

MODES OF REMEMBERING

Holocaust scholar James E. Young observes in his book *The Texture of Memory: Holocaust Memorials and Meaning*:

> "Ironically...by linking the state's raison d'être to the Holocaust, the early founders also located the Shoah at the center of national identity: Israel would be a nation condemned to defining itself in opposition to the very event that made it necessary. The question for the early state became: how to negate the Diaspora and put it behind the "new Jews" of Israel, while basing the need for new Jews in the memory of Shoah?"[861]

Enter the Yad Vashem World Holocaust Remembrance Center (popularly known as Yad Vashem) in Jerusalem, a museum, archive, research center, gallery of arts, and scene of commemorations—from a "Remembering Kristallnacht" ceremony to bar/bat mitzvah tours—brimming with monuments, memorials, and tributes. Numerous other Holocaust memorials within Israel and internationally have emerged (and, administrators of Yad Vashem have worried, threatened to steal its thunder and hinder its message that Israel is the sole true representative of the Holocaust martyrs and experience). But this one retains an iconic status and remains a must-see site for visiting dignitaries and millions of other travelers to the Holy Land.[862]

The original Yad Vashem was established in 1953 after years of planning, though exhibitions were not mounted until the 1960s. It grew steadily from there. In 2005, a forty-five-acre, highly elaborate complex was erected in its stead. Amos Goldberg, a senior lecturer in Holocaust Studies at the Hebrew University of Jerusalem, observes that the museum itself, which aims to present "the story of the Shoah from a uniquely Jewish perspective" (Yad Vashem's claim, with which, albeit from a different vantage point, he concurs), is—really, like any museum—"more than a text; it is a performance." Accordingly, "the two days of inauguration ceremonies were among the biggest diplomatic and international events ever to take place in Israel, perhaps second only to Prime Minister Rabin's funeral." At least one visit is mandated for soldiers during their training, and it is a frequent destination for Israeli students.[863]

Although the museum morphed materially over time, a certain underlying theme seems to have endured. Tom Segev, describing a visit to Yad Vashem in his 1991 book, *The Seventh Million,* notes that after guiding one through the miseries of the Holocaust, the tour "concludes with the establishment of the State of Israel." Furthermore, he says, "One of the last photographs in the museum shows Adolf Eichmann in his glass booth. Thus the museum leads the visitor 'from Holocaust to rebirth.'"[864] James E. Young, who refers to Yad Vashem as "Israel's preeminent national shrine," wrote in 1993 that the exhibition he saw concluded with "a walk outside into the blindingly bright light of Jerusalem.... 'That has all come to this,' the museum seems to be saying."[865] And Goldberg, reflecting in 2012 on his visit to the museum's latter-day incarnation, writes:

> The display ends with a beautiful viewers' balcony, constructed as if floating in the air on the verge of the abyss and from which the beautiful scenery of the blooming Judaic hills and villages is seen.... The whole story is now redeemed with this uplifting, beautiful natural and Zionist view and the visitor, after reaching this cathartic point, can sigh with relief—thank goodness this metaphysical drama has a happy ending.[866]

Goldberg's principal critique of the museum is its identification of eternal antisemitism as the *sole* explanation for the Holocaust, isolated from the other complex phenomena that need to be considered when formulating any useful analysis of it. It is a compelling critique especially because, as he acknowledges, this sort of one-lane narrative track can so often be found in Holocaust education elsewhere. The museum's story excludes, he says, the contexts of history, other genocides, other facets of World War II, postwar diasporic communities, non-Jewish victims, and "the burning historical, psychological, social philosophical and ethical questions concerning the perpetrators." (And, for that matter, concerning the bystanders.) "What we get," he says, "is a mythic drama that begins with antisemitism, followed by the huge catastrophe, and redeemed by the Zionist landscape." All this is bookended by the singing of "Hatikvah."[867]

One significant counterpoint to this "redemptive narrative"[868] can be found in the homage paid to the Warsaw Ghetto uprising. In a retroactive introjection of Warsaw Ghetto fighters into Zionist ideology and even history, Zionists sifted out these venerated Holocaust actors from the rest of the diaspora chaff, lionizing them and appropriating their heroism as Zionism's own rather than its raison d'être. In 1976, a Warsaw Ghetto Uprising Monument recognizing them was added to Yad Vashem. In Yad Vashem's description of the monument, it is explained, "It comprises two central elements: the first, a low relief titled: 'The Last Journey,' depicting Jews being passively led to their murder; the second, the dynamic and heroic 'Warsaw Ghetto Uprising' sculpture, representing the heroism of the fighters."[869]

Marek Edelman, a surviving Bundist leader of the Warsaw Ghetto uprising of 1943 who lived out his postwar life as a cardiologist in Poland, rejected what he had been designated to symbolize: the heroic fighter embodying all that was boldly intransigent about Israel. This attitude ultimately earned him dismissal from the Zionist canon of heroes, and *The Ghetto Fights*,[870] his chronicle of the uprising, though published in 1945 and translated into many languages, did not appear in Hebrew or in Israel until 2001. When a delegation of Israeli dignitaries led by Yizhak Rabin went to Warsaw to commemorate the fiftieth anniversary of the uprising in 1993, they vowed to skip the ceremony if Edelman appeared on the program. His visits to Israel were similarly boycotted by the Zionist establishment that could not forgive his unshakeable identification with Bundism, which challenged their own declared ownership of the uprising.[871]

Edelman persistently disputed the canard that armed rebellion was a "braver" act than walking into the gas chambers. Bluntly puncturing the death dichotomy so popular in Israel, he told Hanna Krall, in an extended interview that became the book *Shielding the Flame,*

> You have to understand this once and for all. Those people went quietly and with dignity. It is a horrendous thing, when one is going so quietly to one's death. It is infinitely more difficult than to go out shooting. After all, it is much easier to die firing—for us it was much easier to die than it was for someone who first boarded a train car, then rode the train, then dug a hole, then undressed naked.[872]

Later in the interview he deflated the Zionist balloon of mythic awe surrounding the uprising itself. "Can you even call that an uprising? All it was about, finally, was that we not just let them slaughter us when our turn came. It was only a choice in the manner of dying."[873] He mocked, too, the glorified depiction of the fighters in monuments, such as this one over the graves of two of the fallen:

> [T]here stands a monument: an upright man with a rifle in one hand, a grenade upraised in the other one, he has a cartridge pouch sashed about his waist a bag with maps at his side, and a belt across his chest. None of them had ever looked like this: they didn't have rifles, cartridge pouches, or maps; besides, they were dark and dirty. But in the monument, they look the way they were ideally supposed to.[874]

The "redemptive narrative" can be found as well in another, more experiential telling of the Holocaust story: the reputedly heuristic annual odyssey known as the March of the Living. The MOTL's 2024 website[875] describes it as an "educational program" initiated in 1988 that, all told, has involved over 300,000 participants from fifty countries. A ritual established by the Israeli Ministry of Education, the program's first week takes place in Poland during the holiday *Yom Ha-Shoah* (Holocaust Remembrance Day) and entails immersion in Holocaust culture and events: interactions with survivors; visits to museums, synagogues, and historic sites; discussions; speeches; songs (including "Hatikvah," the Israeli national anthem); most notably, a three-kilometer walk from Auschwitz to Birkenau that recreates the wartime march to the gas chambers (for which current participants are draped in Israeli flags); and finally, a ceremony memorializing the victims held outside the gas chambers and crematoria.[876]

After enduring this nonstop emotional wallop, the students are whisked to Israel, where they visit famous attractions and participate in Israel's Independence Day (*Yom Ha'azmaut*) celebration—which occurs immediately on the heels of a second mournful holiday, *Yom Hazikaron* (Memorial Day for Israel's fallen soldiers). A siren separates the two, indicating an emotional and abrupt public transition from grief to joy. Following all this, according to the MOTL website, is "the International March of the Living Yom Ha'atzmaut celebration with thousands of participants."[877]

The Canadian MOTL's website advises potential participants:

> Your visit to Poland and Israel will be a study in contrasts. In Poland, you will search for traces of a world that is no more. .... In Israel, you

will encounter a country that is striving valiantly to keep the age-old flame of Jewish nationhood alive. The Holocaust is a stark reminder of the anguish of our past—but Israel represents the hope of our future. This experience will show you how important both aspects are to your identity as a young Jewish person.[878]

Writing in *Haaretz* in 2018, Ariana Melamed called the event "among the most powerful forces in shaping the national consensus over the narrative of the Holocaust" and a "mandatory milestone in shaping [teenagers'] identity as Israeli Jews."[879] Among its goals, MOTL lists building Jewish identity, performing *Tikkun Olam* (the Jewish duty to "be a light unto nations" by repairing the world), and, of course, memorializing, remembering, and honoring victims, heroes and other actors from the past. There is emphasis on fighting antisemitism in particular and discrimination in general—on "building a world free of oppression and intolerance, a world of freedom, democracy, for all members of the human family." And there is the goal of helping participants "to understand the importance of the existence of Israel," which, in the spirit of *Meshoah Le'tkumah* ("from destruction to rebirth"), constitutes "the hope and future of the Jewish people."[880]

While many commentators speak of the trip and its impact reverentially, others have found food for irony. Here is Norman Finkelstein's summary of the phenomenon: "In this Zionist-inspired spectacle with a cast of thousands, Jewish youth from around the world converge on the death camps in Poland for first-hand instruction in Gentile wickedness before being flown off to Israel for salvation."[881] According to Tom Segev, Saul Friedlander once called the symbol-laden trip "the union of kitsch and death."[882] Peter Novick calls it "Holocaust-to-redemption theater," a "meticulously orchestrated...pageant in which the Zionist message is driven home."[883] A (serious) highlight of the 2006 MOTL season was a television episode called "Oprah Goes to Auschwitz," which featured the celebrity touring the camp accompanied by Elie Wiesel.[884]

Others have more acutely questioned what is learned through this process. Australian Holocaust and Jewish Studies scholar Avril Alba, who twice served as an educator on the program, questions whether "atrocity education"—which immerses participants in the irrational and inexplicable evil of the past—can furnish the insight needed for bringing about the hoped-for result of a better world. She notes that "the one expression that appears time and again in … student evaluations is 'life changing.' Yet it is difficult to ascertain exactly what students mean by this phrase."[885] She finds "very little … that related specifically to the acquisition of historical knowledge and its effects." Jessica Lang, writing in *Jewish Exponent,* concurs that the marches, "aimed principally at Jewish identity-building through the Holocaust … offer a limited rendering of history, narrow in reach." They "fail the objective of Holocaust remembrance itself through sheer simplification" and by dodging a more "profound wrestling with history and its consequences … "[886]

THE LESSONS

The Israeli journalist and critic Boaz Evron wrote in a 1981 essay, "Two terrible things happened to the Jewish people this century: the Holocaust and the lessons learned from it."[887]

As we have seen in this chapter, Zionism's primary inference was that an armed Jewish state was both essential for preventing an ever-looming second Holocaust and would have mitigated the first one. For Elie Wiesel, the Holocaust survivor, Nobel Peace Prize winner, and humanitarian voice warning against the perils of being a bystander to atrocity, the Holocaust was both unparalleled in history, "a sacred mystery, beyond mundane social analysis"[888] and yet also illuminated the need to speak out and act boldly when we see others in trouble. However, as the *Nation* columnist Alexander Cockburn wrote when Wiesel was selected as a Nobel laureate in 1986, "it is difficult to find examples of Wiesel sending any message on behalf of those victimized by the policies of the United States, and virtually impossible when it comes to victims of Israel."[889]

For Jewish studies scholar Deborah Lipstadt, the primary lesson of the Holocaust is that its history must be affirmed in such a way that all its bases except for antisemitism are beside the point. She is, most of all, dedicated to vanquishing the arguments of deniers, which she has researched and parsed thoroughly. In her memoir, *History on Trial,* Lipstadt chronicles the libel suit brought against her by Holocaust denier David Irving, which she successfully fought with a superb team of legal and scholarly experts in a London courtroom. Yet even as they made their meticulously supported case, Lipstadt worried that the right message eluded the judge and the courtroom. She urged that a more explicit link be drawn between the plaintiff's antisemitism and Holocaust denial, and to not let the topic of antisemitism drop until Irving was questioned about his connections to specific racists such as David Duke. Richard Rampton, the "leading barrister in the field of defamation and libel" who was representing her, refused. "We've made our point. We can risk overdoing it," he counseled wisely.[890]

Lipstadt holds postmodern indeterminacy responsible for making such skepticism seem plausible. In her earlier book, *Denying the Holocaust* (the one containing her discussion of Irving that led to the libel suit), she decries "the moral relativism prevalent on many campuses, and in society at large. The misguided notion that everyone's view is of equal stature has created an atmosphere that allows Holocaust denial to flourish."[891] She does not name the scholars who have said that "everyone's view is of equal stature" or quote supporting passages from their work to illustrate how their theories lead down the slippery slope to Holocaust denial. There are simply right and wrong understandings of history, and Deborah Lipstadt knows what they are.

I will give the last word on the subject to Peter Novick, who is dubious that there *are* valuable "lessons to be learned" from the Holocaust. "The problem with most of these lessons," he says, "is not that they're wrong but that they're empty, and not very useful. It's hard to believe that there are many American adults today—bombarded as they are daily with images of murder in the streets, terrorist bombings, and mass atrocities—who, without the Holocaust to remind them, would remain oblivious to the presence of evil in the world."

CHAPTER 9:
GREAT EXPLANATIONS:
THE ARTS AND CRAFTINESS OF *HASBARA*

"Hasbara has its roots in earlier concepts of propaganda, agitprop, and censorship. Like them, it is communication calculated to influence cognition and behavior by manipulating perceptions of a cause or position with one-sided arguments, prejudicial substance, and emotional appeals.... [I]t seeks to promote selective listening. The purpose is to constrict the demand for information, not its flow.... [I]t focuses on limiting the receptivity of audiences to information."
—Ambassador Chas W. Freeman, Jr (USFS, Ret.)[892]

"[An effective public diplomacy apparatus] must include informal hasbara representatives that operate alongside official ones.... This element was... well internalized by the Israeli apparatus and it has established organizations in various countries throughout the word (sic) whose purpose is to deliver hasbara messages through 'indirect channels' without officially identifying themselves as such (i.e. as a part of the Ministry of Foreign Affairs).... [I]t can be estimated that Israel's informal hasbara apparatus includes hundreds of Israelis and non-Israelis working to advance Israel's hasbara goals in public opinion centers both in the US and throughout the world...."
—Molad: The Center for the Renewal of Israeli Democracy[893]

"The whole world is against us
Don't worry we'll overcome
They don't care about us

Don't worry, we'll manage
The whole world is against us
Don't worry we'll overcome
We too, about them
Don't give (a damn) anymore"
—"Ha'Olam Kulo Negeinu," a popular Israeli song[894]

WHAT IS *HASBARA*?

Discussions of the phenomenon of *hasbara* frequently begin with the assertion that it cannot be accurately translated from the Hebrew into any other language. As the government-owned Israeli Missions Around the World website maintains, "It is not mere propaganda, nor is it an attempt to merely 'explain' Israel's policies and reality, nor is it just a matter of providing information. 'Hasbara' sounds passive and apologetic, yet there is nothing passive about it and Israel has nothing to apologize for. A much better term would probably be 'public diplomacy.'"[895]

Like Israel's nuclear program, *hasbara* is a concept with which Israelis are highly familiar, yet which is shrouded in obfuscation when its power and reach threaten to become compromising: hence the focus on what it is *not*. The above-referenced kinship to *public diplomacy* is one widely accepted understanding of *hasbara,* but it is worth looking at how it has been variously described by others.

Margalit Toledano and David McKie, in a comprehensive book on public relations in Israel, get us started:

> *Hasbara* is a Hebrew noun form of the verb *le'hasbir,* which means "to explain" or "to account for." In *The Lexicon of the State of Israel* (Shatz & Ariel, 1998), the editors relate to Hasbara under the item "Taamula" (Propaganda) and explain it as the government of Israel's attempt to deal with unique internal and external challenges. From this perspective, Hasbara describes a persuasive communication effort.... Its usage comes from a paternalistic attitude towards a population who are assumed to require explanations to be able to understand the place of Israel in the world and the associated meaning of news items and their fit with official

narratives. Hasbara stresses positive messages and unifying issues that help create a national consensus.[896]

In a 2018 article called "Israeli Public Diplomacy Toward the United States: A Network and Narrative Approach," three researchers favor the translations "public diplomacy" and "propaganda," but they go on to explain,

> Hasbara has been alternatively translated as soft propaganda, public relations, government advocacy, and Israeli public diplomacy....Hasbara does not mean accuracy in explanation; rather, it refers to a kind of strategic information warfare for the sake of the nation by defining issues for the media, delegitimizing critics' arguments, and applying the best discourse by using social networks and the intelligentsia to perform the job....[897]

Israeli historian Giora Goodman tells us that "'propaganda,' *ta'amula* in Hebrew, is mostly reserved for what opponents do, but the term was often used by the Zionist movement to portray its own efforts to influence mass audiences."[898] Former Israeli intelligence officer Shay Hershkovitz says that the "common aim of hasbara is to present the world with Israel's point of view and to counteract prejudices and critiques of Israel and the Jewish people."[899]

Jonathan Cummings suggests terms such as "explanation," "clarification," "government advocacy," "public relations [that implies] an information offensive," and "a concept unique to the Zionist movement and the State of Israel," in which "the persuader attempts to influence the persuadee to adopt a change in a given attitude or behavior...."[900] That last, in fact, comes closest to the notion of propaganda proposed by Jowett and O'Donnell that we read about in Chapter 2: "the deliberate and systematic attempt to shape perceptions, manipulate cognitions, and direct behavior to achieve a response that furthers the desired intent of the propagandist."[901] In other words, what is important here is the speaker's *motivation* to produce a particular behavior on the part of the message's recipient that suits, above all, the needs of the speaker.

As we have seen, the term "public diplomacy" comes up often in relation to *hasbara*; yet while *hasbara* is unique to Israel, public diplomacy is a broader, widely known and practiced global phenomenon. It is, then, worth taking a detour to examine what it means and how it operates. "Public diplomacy" and "nation branding" are interrelated, overlapping rhetorical/practical strategies used by many nations, and they may also be understood as subsets of what is called "soft power."

SOFT POWER AND PUBLIC DIPLOMACY: ATTRACTION, NOT COERCION

According to soft power guru James S. Nye, Jr., the term was coined by himself and refers to "the ability to get what you want through attraction rather than coercion or payments. It arises from the attractiveness of a country's culture, political ideals, and policies."[902] Traditional "hard power" involves force, threats, or economic offers that can't be refused. Hard power alone can fail—as we saw the United States, by far the world's strongest military power, fail in Vietnam and, much later, in Afghanistan. "Soft power," on the other hand, is about co-option. The Vatican is sustained, at least now, by soft power—it is not weapons that whisk people to church or cause them to reach into their pockets when the collection plate is passed. Foreign students who attend American universities constitute a source of soft power because of the new, American perspectives they bring back to their home countries. Much American soft power, says Nye (writing in 2004), comes not from government but from civil society: Hollywood, Harvard, Microsoft, and Michael Jordan are four prime examples.[903]

According to Jan Melissen, a political scholar in the Netherlands, while traditional diplomacy "is about relationships between the representatives of states, or other international actors," public diplomacy "targets the general public in foreign societies and more specific non-official groups, organizations, and individuals."[904] Nicholas J. Cull, a prominent scholar on the subject, dates its popular emergence to the United States Information Agency's need for a "benign" alternative to the word "propaganda" in the 1960s.[905]

The purpose of public diplomacy is to circumvent (or supplement) the strictures of traditional diplomacy and instead directly influence public opinion in other countries via various agents of civil society. Fulbright scholarships, touring national ballet companies, regional cookbooks, fine wines, film festivals, the Peace Corps, YouTube videos, and international athletic events have all been vehicles through which countries have sent "messages" about themselves to foreign audiences. Nye points out that Norway, despite its small size and lack of an international language, has internationally identified itself as a broker of peace via its public diplomacy niche in conflict mediation.[906] (Think "the Oslo Accords.")

NATION BRANDING

"Nation branding" is one form of soft power, a derivative of the corporate marketing practice of assigning "identities" or "personalities" to consumer products. The aim of nation branding is usually to boost tourism, foreign investment (which can include even the very personal choice of purchasing a vacation home abroad), trade, and similar matters in which a nation competes with a host of others. However, it can also be used to promote a sense of the nation's legitimacy vis-à-vis transnational corporations, NGOs, and foreign governments—who may, for example, impose trade or travel restrictions due to perceived nefarious practices, particularly if members of a nation's citizenry have raised an objection.[907] In any case, tropes and images articulate the distinctive attractive qualities of a nation for the world. Self-defined "nation branding specialist" and inventor of the annual survey Nation Brands Index (NBI) Simon Anholt pointed out that the hugely popular 1980s outback comedy *Crocodile Dundee* did much to brand Australia as a place of wit and good times.[908]

Branding expert Wally Olins says, "Major consumer brands from Prada in Italy to Coca-Cola in the United States to Guinness in Ireland don't just sell the product, they sell the nation they come from." As we saw in Chapter 8, *Exodus*—the cumulative power of the event, the novel, and the film—sold much of the world on Israel. Sometimes, though, this doesn't take: Samsung has conferred no special prestige upon Korea, nor would Helena Rubinstein cosmetics benefit from a "made in Poland" tag. If a brand is truly to embody a country in a way that "sells" the nation on the coattails of the product, then large-scale, highly conscious coordination of national symbols, practices, and policies is vital.[909]

This last feat may be particularly difficult for some countries to achieve. One sort of obstacle may be the need to overcome the long-held, politically motivated demonization of certain states, such as that implanted via mass anti-Communist propaganda campaigns during the Cold War. A marketing study found that American attitudes toward their long-maligned neighbor Cuba could be softened by tourism advertising. Conducted on the cusp of the 2014 "Cuban thaw," in which relations between the two countries were normalized for approximately two years, the study demonstrated that viewers were moved by a commercial that began, "Perfect weather. Pristine waters. Spectacular scenery. Soaring architecture. Exotic wildlife. Exuberant nightlife. And a distinctive procession of vintage automobiles. This is not just another island getaway. This is Cuba."[910]

This sort of rebranding has, of course, great relevance for Israel, which was long guided by the philosophy of The Israel Project (TIP), a US-based PR organization. TIP utilized what Bernays called "the old propaganda": countering the increasing "delegitimization" of Israel via conventional talking points, such as, "These are the myths presented to you, here are the facts"; "Israel wants peace, not war"; "Israel is the only democracy in the Middle East"; "Israel's enemies deny its right to exist"; etc. "The overall strategy of communicating Israel's image has been to emphasize how we are right and they are wrong," explained Foreign Ministry media officer Ido Aharoni.[911] But rapid changes in electronic media reportage—including, of course, social media—provided enough contrapuntal evidence to unsettle those messages. In addition, in 2005 the Palestinian-led international BDS movement was born to nonviolently "work...to end international support for Israel's oppression of Palestinians and pressure Israel to comply with international law."[912] To steer the sinking ship that was world opinion of Israel back toward safety, what was needed—at least *in addition* to the old approach—was Bernays's "new" approach: that of masking the real persuasive intention behind a mesmerizing and apparently unrelated cover story.

That same year, directors of "Israel's most powerful ministries"—the Foreign Ministry, the Prime Minister's Office, and the Finance Ministry—met to discuss the results of "specialized research conducted by American marketing executives" and PR experts who constituted the Brand Israel group. Their investigation revealed that "Israel will win supporters only if it is seen as relevant and modern rather than only a place of fighting and religion." Israel's promotion efforts veered to the counsel of ISRAEL 21c, a PR organization based in California's Silicon Valley, started in 2001, that focuses on upbeat "lifestyle" issues rather than simply "crisis management."[913] Israel would now project an image grounded in, for example, its contributions to health and technology. "Christopher Reeve: Israel is at center of world research on paralysis" ran a website headline under its "Innovation" banner. They were quoting the popular cinematic portrayer of Superman who had become a quadriplegic—and a celebrated advocate for issues related to spinal cord injuries—after being injured in a horse-jumping accident.[914] Meanwhile, Israel's "economic miracle" netted it a reputation as the Start-Up Nation—an unanticipated magnet for venture capital, entrepreneurs, and corporate facilities of global companies such as Intel.[915]

Israel shed its rugged "pioneering" fame of yore and came to incarnate the archetypal "good life": opportunities for adventure and immersion in unblemished nature, along with food, wine, and film festivals both domestically and around the world, all showcasing hip Israeli products. One might even try enjoying a Rosh Hashana apple dipped in honey while skydiving onto one of Israel's Mediterranean beaches!—or so suggested an ISRAEL 21c-produced video, along with other ideas for extraordinarily fun ways to celebrate the High Holidays.[916] Israel also peddled its vibrant, humanistic, Western-style liberal democracy via its advocacy of "ethical" practices such as animal rights and veganism, with IDF "vegan soldiers" clad in leather-free boots and wool-free berets (a practice its less beguiled observers coined "veganwashing").[917] Perhaps most notably, there was the newly burnished luster of Tel Aviv's gay pride scene—or, as many LGBTQ rights proponents would have it, "pinkwashing": the strategic deployment of putative gay-friendliness to deflect attention from a state's more nefarious practices.[918] A January 2012 *Haaretz* headline, "Tel Aviv Declared World's Best Gay Travel Destination," celebrated a happy outcome of "the Tel Aviv Gay Vibe campaign, organized in coordination with the municipality's Ministry of Tourism."[919]

One strategy suggested to overcome the limits of Israel's *hasbara* and soft power endeavors has been "un-nation branding"—that is, promoting the cities of Tel Aviv and Jerusalem as desirable destinations in themselves while simply leaving the country in which they are housed out of the discussion. The "Two Cities. One Break" campaign, launched in 2016 by the Israeli Ministry of Tourism in collaboration with LAPAM, the government's ad agency and Allenby, its marketing firm, depicts Tel Aviv as a sexy, partying, sporty, beachy hangout spot and Jerusalem as an El Dorado of ancient wonders and archaeological treasures. With the charms of these cities dissociated from the state of

Israel, such topics as the conflict, the occupation, international law, apartheid, and the other usual baggage were meant to simply evanesce. The campaign targeted global audiences and, according to international relations and digital diplomacy scholars Rhys Crilley and Ilan Manor, "has been viewed by the Israeli government as a great success."[920]

HASBARA'S ORIGINS

There are various origin stories for the practice of *hasbara*. Psychological warfare specialist Ron Schleifer, tracing Jewish argument and debate through the ages, sees in Herzl (as do many others) a pioneering *hasbarist* due to his tenacious work to establish the "historical right" of the Jews as a nation to the Land of Israel—and creating the momentum to fulfill it.[921] As we saw in Chapter 5, Herzl's penchant for symbol and spectacle, along with his relaxed relationship to facts, indeed took the Zionist cause beyond the realm of rational argument and into the world of "spin."

"It was Nahum Sokolow," maintains Jonathan Cummings, "who brought the term *hasbara* into the Zionist lexicon.[922] Sokolow was, for a time, an associate of Herzl, and went on to assume various leadership positions in the World Zionist Organization (WZO). According to Cummings, by the 1960s in Israel, *hasbara* as Sokolow had inculcated it "was largely seen as legitimate and necessary," while "propaganda" was its antithesis, carrying unwelcome associations with totalitarian regimes from which many Israelis had recently escaped."[923] However, this distinction seems wishful at best. Sokolow's Zionist activist colleague Yitzhak Grinbaum called him "the Hebrew journalist par excellence," but in the same laudatory sentence said, "His propagandizing talent flowered...."[924] According to Margalit Toledano and David McKie, Sokolow "is considered the father of Israeli journalism." Yet as they clarify just what sort of "journalism" he practiced and preached—not least through "guides" he published for use by Zionist propagandists—it becomes clear that it was not the sort usually associated with the "free flow of information" model of liberal pluralist media:

> [W]hile using the media to promote the Zionist agenda, Sokolow abolished demarcation lines between the roles of politicians, journalists,

and propagandists in the Israeli public sphere.... [He] "defined the role of the Hebrew press as responsible for Zionist education and national unification.... Sokolow represents the official Zionist leadership's expectations that the Hebrew press should foster national responsibility and promote the movement's political goals.... [E]ditors and journalists were keen to be involved and serve the movement. Not surprisingly, strong collaboration evolved between the press and the political system, and their close cooperation continued to influence the Israeli public sphere many years after the establishment of the state.[925]

As one *Maariv* reporter put it, the government control of the media was tantamount to "the Israeli version of *Pravda*."[926]

Of propaganda, Sokolow said, "this is a science and we must study it."[927] Gideon Kouts stresses that Sokolow was adept at influencing audiences by addressing them on their own terms, whether they were orthodox, non-Zionist Jews, or the religious Christians of Britain for whom, according to biblical prophecies, the Jewish return to Zion would presage the return of Jesus Christ. In a letter addressed "To the Select Zionist Executive" on June 29, 1912, Sokolow outlined his ideas for "an active and forceful *hasbara* among Christians."[928] One initiative he undertook himself was authoring a book in English, *History of Zionism, 1600–1918,* aimed specifically at the English. For it, Kouts tells us, he drew on research he had done at the British Museum about "the romantic connection with the idea of the Jews returning to Zion."[929]

In the early days of nation-building, but well in advance of statehood, individual organizations that were key to the Zionist project developed their own *hasbara* apparatuses and through them, according to Cummings, "the political culture of *hasbara* emerged ....[930] As the Ottoman Empire ended and the British Mandate took hold, guided in part by the somewhat ambiguous intentions of the Balfour Declaration, the Jewish agencies began to devise new ways of managing media and messages. Gershon Agronsky, who headed the Palestine Zionist Executive (PZE) press bureau in Jerusalem from 1924, "quickly established an Association of Foreign Press Correspondents in order to develop relations with the international press and to ensure greater understanding of the Zionist movement."[931] The Jewish Agency for Eretz

Yizrael (JA), which handled facets of nation-building such as immigration, land purchase and development, and cultural advancement, was established in 1929 and created a *hasbara* bureau in 1939.[932] As we saw in Chapter 7, the Jewish National Fund's *hasbara* machinery had a wide reach over a long period of time. As Toledano and McKie put it, "Via their involvement in the education system, they persuaded the Zionist public that what was good for the JNF was good for the people."[933]

In 1934, the WZO's *hasbara* department moved from London to Jerusalem and also created a telegraphic news agency, the Palestine Correspondence Agency (or *Palcor*), designed to get its message out to international media.[934] In the spirit of "responsible journalism," where "unity and consensus" were the ideals to manifest in public life and discourse (as opposed to the "individual freedoms" and "neutrality" model of US journalism),[935] cozy relationships developed between the press and the Zionist leadership in the national institutions. With multiple channels of input, an "editors' committee" was formed and, writes Cummings, "with no fear that its independence might be compromised, the editors expressed hopes that the arrangement would be 'an appropriate and desirable tool for influencing public opinion in the spirit of Zionist policy at this time.'"[936]

Throughout the 1940s—both before and after Israel achieved statehood—the Zionist movement opened a plethora of press offices both at home and abroad. According to Goodman, "Efforts by JA officials to forward the Zionist cause by cultivating the foreign press in Palestine and abroad were of particular importance, not only because the JA was the internationally recognized, official mouthpiece of the Zionist movement, but especially because its press work was deemed successful in an era in which important sections of the Western media became highly supportive of Zionist goals."[937] Galvanized by the sophistication of the British Press Information Office (PIO) of the 1930s, the JA launched its own Public Relations Office (PRO), headed by Walter Eytan, a seasoned and proficient Zionist propagandist who arrived in Palestine from Oxford in 1946. When the Haganah (which aired daily *Voice of Israel* radio broadcasts of its own) began its blockade-running operations and armed revolt after the war, says Goodman, "The JA and British authorities engaged in an intensive propaganda battle for the hearts and minds of the dozens of foreign correspondents flocking to Palestine to cover the insurgency and related political events." The British press focused on "Jewish terrorism in Palestine," while, with Jewish victimhood and its redress a winning theme to exploit in the post-Holocaust era, "[t]he JA propaganda continued to concentrate on refugee misery and Zionist settlements."[938]

By early 1947, the bulk of the JA's press and propaganda work had moved to the US, falling under the aegis of the Zionist Organization of America (ZOA) and the American Zionist Emergency Council (AZEC). Offices were opened in Washington and New York, and relationships were cultivated with publishers of leading US newspapers. In one highly "confidential" quid pro quo, the *Nation* and its fundraising arm received a $50,000 grant from the JA in the wake of a favorable article by a *Nation* staff member who had traveled to Palestine. As had been the case earlier in Britain, "Zionist propaganda had its greatest success with the American liberal and left-wing press" while British policy in Palestine was viewed "as part of a discredited imperialist plot: supported in the Middle East by powerful American oil interests."[939]

Nonetheless, there was no shortage of *hasbara* preparation for the UN Special Committee on Palestine (UNSCOP)'s visit of inquiry to Palestine in the summer of 1947, intended to inform their notion of what the region's future might look like. Goodman writes of this time:

> With UNSCOP came a new crowd of American and foreign correspondents from all corners of the world. The British authorities remained decidedly aloof…so as not to give an impression of trying to influence the proceedings, while the Arabs rigidly boycotted the committee's visit. The Zionists had practically an open field for providing positive stories for the large press pack pursuing the committee….[940]

HASBARA IN THE 1948 WAR

Of course, *hasbara* also played a crucial role in that very critical event in Palestine's history—the 1948 war that for Israelis demarcates the onset of sovereign statehood and for Palestinians is known as the Nakba.

As we saw when we looked at Zionist conscription schemes in the DP camps, soldiers sometimes had to be convinced that fighting in a war was both their duty and furthered a cause consistent with their own moral values and personal goals. While we are privy to official justifications for the proceedings of warfare, social history (frequently called "history from below") may reveal other perspectives through slices of the materiality and epistemology of ordinary people's lives. Such insight can furnish an interesting counterpoint to idealized or mythologized notions of life in a particular time and place.

It is for this reason that I find one account of the 1948 war, Shay Hazkani's *Dear Palestine: A Social History of the 1948 War,*[941] so unusual and so valuable. As we consider the different sorts of *hasbara* strategies used by the powerful on those masses whose cooperation is needed to effect the master vision, we must also look at how the foot soldiers of conquest and colonialism are persuaded to carry out acts that are brutal and often lethal, against people of whom they know almost nothing.

The research tools of social historians are mainly primary sources—artifacts found in archives or attics such as letters, diaries, flyers, meeting notes, artistic or cultural works, recordings of broadcasts, advertisements, publications, or even revealing physical objects such as clothing, utensils, or vehicles. In *Dear Palestine,* Hazkani utilizes some of these resources to examine the messages that the average people who came to fight in the 1948 war—both on the side of the Zionist forces and on the side of the Arab Liberation Army (ALA) –were fed by their superiors. What motivated them to embrace or resist propaganda about nationalism, ethnic and religious identity, the demonized Other, masculinity, justice, a desirable outcome of the war, imperialism, the rules of engagement? Hazkani's perusal of instructional materials as well as soldiers' letters offers some clues.

It is interesting to consider some parallels that Hazkani notices in the indoctrination tasks of the "two sides." A striking example involves the need to instill an ideology that will induce a soldier to fight pitilessly in war, yet which must be recast for civilized living when the war is over. For both armies, it was necessary to ignite anger that would explode into immense feats of aggression. For Israel, that belligerence would have to be tamed later to maintain the lore of "the most moral army in the world" guided by "Jewish values" in a "humane" society. For the ALA commanders, the worry was that "the soldiers' anticolonial fervor" might "extend to fighting the Arab regimes that remained client states of the British and French"—in other words, that their righteous fighting spirit could become enlisted in "the overthrow of the corrupt regimes in their own countries."[942]

Meanwhile, leaders on each side drew on religion-based, mytho-historical archetypes to rouse the soldiers' zeal. On one side were "stories of Islamic glory and modern Arab heroism" and a depiction of Zionists as "disciples of the crusaders."[943] On the other were "the trope about the Arabs as the descendants of Amalek and the Seven Nations of Canaan, the archenemies of the Israelites" and the use of the Bible to

> promote the idea that "activism"—a euphemism for militarism—was the only course of action for the Jewish people. Numerous education pamphlets in 1948–49 stressed the bravery of the Jews from biblical times to the present and their mastery of the sword. Willingness to sacrifice oneself—like the defenders of Masada had done when they committed suicide so as not to fall into the hands of Romans—was hailed as one of the critical characteristics of the Jewish soldier.[944]

What had been the Haganah's *hasbara* department became the IDF's "education department" in early 1948. This unit produced a weekly magazine, *Bamahane* ("In the Base Camp") and "pamphlets with lesson plans that could be used to indoctrinate soldiers." They also conducted "hasbara talks." Certain topics were pointedly directed at those suffering qualms about the violent acts they were expected to perform. A pamphlet titled "Morality in Israel's Army" drew on religious precepts to assure the soldiers that in the Torah, God "demands a revenge of extermination without mercy to whoever tries to hurt us for no reason." Hazkani writes, "The education officers then explained that in biblical times Saul exterminated all of Amalek, men and women, youth and elderly, and even sheep and cattle." In a war of conquest, the pamphlet says, "the army is allowed to take spoils including women and children to be slaves and concubines. It is a must to kill the male captives in this sort of war."[945]

Another pamphlet, published on April 5, 1948, was called "Answers to Questions Soldiers Frequently Ask" and began with the question, "Why don't we agree to the return of Arab refugees during the lull [in fighting]?" The answer was, of course: the security risk. "It was also stressed," writes Hazkani, "that the Arab states were not really concerned with the humanitarian aspect of the refugee problem and that it was merely a political maneuver." In *Bamahane* there was further justification:

"We will not be weak at heart from seeing the thousands of refugees sprawling in the streets, bending over their few belongings, with their gloomy faces. They threw stones at us and shot lead at our skulls, ran wild and promised to throw us into the sea. Their fantasy was our downfall, our spilled blood pleasing to their eyes. This is their punishment."[946]

Hazkani makes some intriguing observations. For one, he says, "The volume of pamphlets discussing the Palestinian refugees suggests the issue was one in which soldiers were particularly interested. Again and again, education pamphlets emphasized that the Palestinian exodus was not Israel's fault." We find here the declaration that countless Israeli leaders have made in a variety of circumstances: "We did not have a choice." The "new Israeli narrative"—that the refugees had not been pressured to leave by the Zionists, and that they themselves felt they would be better off resettled in Arab states rather than returning to Palestine—took off from there.[947]

And here is one more striking conclusion that Hazkani came to after perusing the research materials he had gathered:

It is noteworthy that ALA propaganda includes no mention of "extermination," pushing Jews into the sea, or killing the Jewish inhabitants of Palestine in an organized manner, which Israeli propaganda had claimed at the time was the Arab war objective. The claim is used, even to the present day....[948]

HASBARA IN A SOVEREIGN STATE

Since achieving "independence" in 1948, Israel has produced such a cornucopia of *hasbara* outlets—in its various ministries, its media and cultural organizations, its military, its educational system, as well as through its nonprofit and nongovernmental organizations, political parties, worker and youth movements—that even the most devout researcher might have great difficulty keeping track of all of them. The Ministry of Foreign Affairs (MFA), the Ministry of Tourism, the Jewish National Fund, and the Jewish Agency, among many others, have each retained their own official *hasbara* division in addition to the multiple *hasbara* departments housed in the Prime Minister's Office. For example, in 1954 a Hasbara administration under the aegis of the Prime Minister's Office was aimed at influencing domestic audiences. Included under its umbrella were the Israeli Film Service and the Government Publications Service. Subsequently, the units were bounced to the Ministry of Education and Culture, only to then be disentangled from one another and restored to the Prime Minister's Office. Previously, they had also been linked to—and then de-linked from—the IDF's spokesperson's unit and the broadcasting service, which was responsible for *Kol Yisrael* radio, the public "voice of Israel" radio service. As Cummings puts it, "This frequent shifting of responsibility, the multiplicity of agencies, and the lack of central authority over the issue as a whole did not improve Israel's ability to articulate a clear message to international audiences."[949] These shortcomings of Israel's *hasbara* apparatus, among others, have long been the subject of complaints by the nation's citizenry, who see them (many, including myself, would argue: mistakenly) as the cause of Israel's negative image in the world.

David Ben-Gurion sniffed at the idea of *hasbara* ("I'm interested in guns, not stories"[950])—though it could certainly be said that he manufactured not a little bit of it in his own way. However, Moshe Sharett, who succeeded him as prime minister, felt it was a dimension of foreign policy that the government must invest in. His attempts to create a cohesive "government information service" that cultivated press relations, and whose oversight would be shared by various departments, endured a range of bureaucratic reshufflings and other stumbling blocks until it, like similar efforts along those lines over the years, derailed.[951] Among these, for example, were a Ministry of Information from March 1974 to March 1975;[952] a National Information Directorate, formed to remedy the public relations disaster of the 2006 Lebanon War;[953] and a Ministry for Public Diplomacy, which was attached to the Ministry for Diaspora Affairs in 2009.[954] Years later, in 2015, the Ministry of Strategic Affairs and Public Diplomacy was tapped by the Israeli government to coordinate multipronged anti-BDS activities.[955] It was later attached to the Ministry of Foreign Affairs where, according to journalist Alex Kane in 2019, it "finances and leads a campaign of online trolling, legal harassment and intelligence-gathering against BDS activists worldwide...."[956] After October 7, 2023, from a special command center in Tel Aviv, A National Public Diplomacy Directorate in the Prime Minister's office "wag[ed] a global public diplomacy campaign of unprecedented scope in order to foster legitimacy for Israeli policy and efforts on the battlefield."[957] In June, 2024, a *Times of Israel* headline read, "Public Diplomacy Directorate Said Crumbling after Departure of Chief and Most of Staff."[958]

In the fall of 1953, near the beginning of Sharett's term as prime minister, Israel executed the "Qibya massacre." This was one of a series of raids on Palestinian refugee communities just over the border in Jordan by the IDF's special (and notoriously brutal) commando Unit 101, led by Ariel Sharon. Like other such raids, this one was organized as a "reprisal" operation responding to "infiltrators" who entered Israel from Jordan—and who in this case had killed a thirty-two-year-old woman and two of her young children. Israeli historian Avi Shlaim writes, "Sharon's order was to penetrate [the village of] Qibya, blow up houses, and inflict heavy damage on its inhabitants. His success in carrying out this order surpassed all expectations." Observers who appeared on the scene the next morning found that "[t]he village had been reduced to a pile of rubble: forty-five houses had been blown up, and sixty-nine civilians, two-thirds of them women and children, had been killed." Word got out and, despite the Israeli government's best attempts at damage control (which included flagrant lies about the identity of the perpetrators—i.e., that they were not IDF-affiliated but rather random irate vigilantes)—international condemnation, fed by the findings of a UN commission, followed.[959]

According to *Washington Post* blogger Doug Rossinow, desperate efforts to repair Israel's resulting invidious image on the global stage were managed by I.L. "Si" Kenen, the head of the American Zionist Council who founded the American Zionist Committee for Public Affairs in 1953–54 (renamed the American Israel Public Affairs Committee [AIPAC] in 1959)—and "thus launched the modern Israel lobby." The most urgent items on their agenda were "to manage political fallout over Qibya, and to prepare for any future shocks coming out of Israel." According to John J. Mearsheimer and Stephen M. Walt in *The Israel Lobby and U.S. Foreign Policy,* "AIPAC generally followed 'Kenen's Rules' to advance Israel's cause. Rule No. 1 was: 'Get behind legislation; don't step out in front of it (that is, keep a low profile).'"[960] Though mainly known as a lobbying group, AIPAC has played a central role in *hasbara* efforts since its inception.

More than thirteen years later, during the buildup to the June 1967 war, information minister Yisrael Galili was, as Cummings puts it, "caught in a dilemma. On the one hand, it was important that domestic and international audiences should be reassured by Israel's capacity to contain aggressive Egyptian and Syrian postures.... On the other, Israel also needed international support...."[961] This was only one of many times that conflicting *hasbara* exigencies would dog efforts to produce a coherent message. In fact, writes former director of the Israel Government Press Office Meron Medzini,

> Already in the early years of Israel, the heads of the *Hasbara* faced a major problem—how to portray Israel. Should they focus on a nation at war, a country still largely under siege, constantly involved in small border skirmishes with its neighbors. (sic) That would be helpful for the purposes of fund raising. The other option was to depict Israel as a normal nation, involved in a long and difficult process of nation building. Siege mentality would frighten potential immigrants, tourists and foreign investors. Portraying Israel as a nation at peace would not reflect reality.[962]

In the weeks leading up to the war, foreign journalists flooded Israel, and the Government Press Office gladly accommodated them with facilities, access to key personnel, materials, information officers, and fly-ins on military planes to sites of unrest. "Foreign media access was orchestrated with a certain amount of sophistication," writes Cummings. "[A]s one IDF liaison officer recalled at the end of the war: 'One particular problem...was how to organize the foreign journalists' tours so that they would be in the right place at the right time...without thinking that they were being herded like sheep.'"[963] All this assistance and familiarity bred sympathy, and, writes Cummings, "The sense of impending annihilation encouraged the correspondents to write articles supportive of Israel...." Furthermore, they "were much taken with Israel's image of pioneering independence in the face of Arab opposition and with institutions in Israeli society such as the Kibbutz and the IDF. Israel was seen by many as a success story. Public opinion in the West firmly supported Israel in the face of the buildup of Arab aggression."[964] Meanwhile, domestic radio broadcasts served to reassure a frightened citizenry and Arabic-language broadcasts in local dialects were meant to inspire opposition within enemy states.[965]

Once the exhilaration of the quick victory and the initial awe of some foreign onlookers subsided, Israel was left with a new public relations problem: it was now an occupying power, oppressing Palestinians, building settlements, and prevaricating about its intentions regarding the newly acquired, militarily ruled territories. New *hasbara* was needed, says Giora Goodman, "to persuade both elite and mass foreign audiences that the Israeli occupation was for the present a basic security need, not expansionism, and that Israel respected its duties as an occupying force."[966] In the newspaper *Maariv*, an "editorial about the hasbara 'battlefront'…urged the production of 'intelligent' hasbara to ensure 'that the world will not look at us and our deeds through distorting glasses of pity and sympathy for the defeated, who only yesterday wanted to destroy us.'" The Ministry of Foreign Affairs had an immediate *hasbara* budget of two million Israeli lira approved, used to fund "publications and exhibitions in various languages; photographs, newsreels, and documentary films for television; hosting foreign journalists, writers, and politicians; and sending abroad Israeli propagandists, academics, students, artists, and trade unionists, mostly to North America and Western Europe."[967]

Israel's official stance on the Occupied Territories was that it was waiting to exchange them for peace and the regional countries' recognition of its "right to exist." Publicly, "Israeli hasbara blamed Arab intransigence and ongoing belligerency for the diplomatic impasse and for Israel's apparent 'obstinacy' in the face of international pressure." However, among the Israeli high leadership, no such conclusions had been reached.[968]

As Israel pulled out all the stops to persistently convey, in the international arena, the notion that "civilian life under military rule was 'returning to normal,'" it yet had to account for a new refugee (and image) problem—that is, the plight of West Bankers who had fled to Jordan during the fighting and now wanted to return. In the words of Foreign Minister Abba Eban, stationed in New York, the American media was showing damning images of "our soldiers…driving back women and children.'" In response, isolated scenarios were constructed for media attention by *hasbara* personnel in which "the press published pictures of refugee children being carried across the Jordan by smiling Israeli soldiers" and the West Bank town of Qalqilyah was falsely presented as "a model of rehabilitation and coexistence with neighboring Israeli municipalities," its expelled residents now happily returned.[969] Special *hasbara* had to be formulated to rationalize ongoing acts of Palestinian resistance (the "terrorists" were actually partisans from bordering states, it was claimed—not despondent residents of the West Bank), the annual Christmas broadcast to the world from Bethlehem had to be cleansed of images of Israeli snipers on roofs, while the occupied territories were rechristened the "administered areas" and the resistance fighters "opposition elements," "saboteurs," and "infiltrators."[970] Practices such as indefinite detention without trial, warrantless house searches and demolitions, and other forms of collective punishment brought on the opprobrium of foreign observers and the realization, according to one Foreign Ministry official, that "slowly-slowly, an image is being created of Israel as a denier of rights."

The sprouting of settlements, the extraordinary restructuring of Jerusalem (described as "municipal fusion"), and the declaration of "closed military zones," which journalists were forbidden to enter, all raised doubts that Israel was simply acting for its own "security" and eagerly awaiting "peace."[971] Israel's recalcitrance regarding the implementation of UN Security Council Resolution 242 of November 22, 1967—which included stipulations that the Israeli military remove itself from newly occupied territories and achieve "a just settlement of the refugee problem"[972]—further undermined international belief in Israel's claims.

The 1973 conflict known as the Yom Kippur War took Israel, uncharacteristically, by surprise and dealt it some harsh military and political blows. The severity of the attack by Egypt and Syria on October 6 was, at first, publicly met with denial and irrational optimism by Israeli Defense Minister Moshe Dayan (echoed by Prime Minister Golda Meir as well as the IDF spokesman). "We will turn the area into a gigantic cemetery," Dayan assured journalists on the first day, and later at a press conference he confidently asserted, "The IDF will smite the Egyptians in Sinai hip and thigh. The war will end in a few days, with our victory."[973] Journalists, influenced by these statements and still imbued with the indomitable IDF aura of 1967, repeated the same message, so that by the time the truth set in—and the tide ultimately turned—Israelis felt lied to and betrayed. Contributing to the dawning reality check was the fact that Arab states now countered Israeli *hasbara* with effective initiatives of their own. Notably, these included disseminating "pictures of the hundreds of Israeli prisoners of war captured in the first two days. These were given to international news services, via whom they made their way to Israeli television for the evening news on Sunday night. They made extremely gloomy viewing as well as contributing to a 'sudden drop' of credibility in the IDF's own accounts of the war."[974]

The traumatic shocks Israel suffered during the 1973 war did restore somewhat its "underdog" status internationally, which won it greater sympathy.[975] At the same time, the information debacles of the war were followed, once again, by various attempts to create a viable and unified *hasbara* apparatus. Turf wars among ministries, personal ambitions of individuals, commissions of inquiry whose recommendations went unheeded, advisory reports that fell through the cracks, conflicting analyses of the core problems, and simple lack of political will all contributed to a series of fits and starts—and stops—that led to the long-anticipated establishment in 1974, and then, within a year, demise, of a Ministry of Information.[976]

Whatever hearts and minds Israel had won for being attacked and beleaguered in the 1973 war were dramatically lost in the wake of Israel's 1982 invasion of Lebanon and its role in the massacres at the Sabra and Shatila refugee camps. The unimaginable brutalities inflicted on civilians were globally televised, and the notion that Israel was "defending itself" defied credulity—even for many Israelis. In a desperate attempt to reconfigure *hasbara* strategies for the occasion, the World Jewish Congress assembled, a year later in Jerusalem, an array of renowned professionals from American and Israeli public relations and advertising firms, political life, academia, print and broadcast journalism, and think tanks. Situating it as "The 19th America-Israel Dialogue" and calling the meeting "Hasbara: Israel's Public Image: Problems and Remedies," the participants brainstormed about the problems and possibilities of *hasbara* from a wide range of vantage points. From a professor of law to a PR strategist for Pepsi-Cola, they pooled their expertise, sometimes rebutting one another, but the talk stayed focused on tactics and barely touched on the underlying realities of Israeli policy and behavior that had caused the crisis to begin with.[977]

Though the proceedings of the conference, published by the *American Jewish Congress Monthly* a year later, reveal nothing conclusive, the effects of the war on Israel's image and Israel's ensuing problem-solving exertions are portrayed in the 2016 documentary *The Occupation of the American Mind*. Cultural studies and communications scholar Sut Jhally comments in it that the result of this pivotal moment was an "occupation" of American media and minds "by a pro-Israel narrative that's deflected attention away from what virtually everyone recognizes as the best way to resolve this conflict: end the occupation and the settlements so that Palestinians can finally have a state of their own."[978]

Yet that potential resolution did not appear to occupy the minds of those at the conference. Participant Leon Wieseltier, editor of the *New Republic* magazine, simply pressed in a policy paper for a reemphasis on foundational Zionist aphorisms. These constituted, he said, "the basics about Israel: that the Jews are a people or a nation, that as a people or a nation they deserve a state, that the state should be exactly where it is right now, that the state should be strong and secure, that those who deny the legitimacy of the state or its strength or security cannot be dealt with (particularly the PLO), that the legitimacy of the Jewish national identity and the Jewish state are unimpeachable."

Positing these "basics" as axiomatic and thus exempt from scrutiny or revision has, indeed, become a staple of *hasbara* and the legal structures it has engendered in the years since then. As Wieseltier put it, "A consensus of some sort does exist in America.... This consensus was the product of decades of hard intellectual and political labor that developed an orthodoxy in the American perception of Israel. The most dangerous thing that can happen to Israel in the United States is the erosion of that orthodoxy."[979]

THE "NEW" PUBLIC DIPLOMACY: THE NETWORK APPROACH

Astoundingly, that seemingly impenetrable "orthodoxy" has indeed finally begun to erode, a process certainly catalyzed by the globally televised, tweeted, and Instagrammed images of the post-October 7 carnage in Gaza and the harsh repression of pro-Palestinian activism on US campuses. In addition, online journalism has increasingly freed reporters from some of the political constraints conventionally imposed by editors of mainstream corporate media.

In reaction, the structures that support that orthodoxy have regrouped as Israel searches for ways to combat what it calls its "delegitimization" by an array of forces, not least of which is the BDS movement. The inception points of *hasbara* messaging still lurch from ministry to ministry, often leading the *hasbara* apparatus's chief players to complain about lack of clarity and consistency in the themes they are expected to convey. At the same time, the on-the-ground managers and enactors of *hasbara* are far more decentralized—though still very strongly, if furtively, connected to the government and to each other.

Hasbara now operates on a global scale according to what is called the "new" public diplomacy, or "the network approach." This sort of operation has been characterized as one that

> is made up of actors with shared interests and values that cooperate to promote a common narrative.... Strategic narratives are stories about human action created by elites including government leaders, security experts, consultants, professors, think tanks, institutes, and universities, among others; and they are communicated to the public through speeches, press conferences, official documents, journalistic reports, films and documentaries....[980]

Sarvestani et al. emphasize that while informational materials, conferences, speeches, student workshops, and the like may still be initiated or sponsored by "some of the top nodes with the highest degree of centrality" who act as "hubs in the operation" (some salient examples of these are Israel's Ministry of Foreign Affairs, the IDF, and the Interdisciplinary Center Herzliya), the flow of activities occurs *indirectly* and *discreetly* in order to *avoid the impression of government oversight*, which to many might smack of state propaganda. Some of the actors, they say, "belong to the government, Israeli NGOs, or pro-Israeli American organizations but act as private bodies" to "increase the appearance of objectivity and non-state activity. This is especially the case with programs that target university and college campuses."[981] Network members situated furthest from the core may participate by posting comments en masse in response to online articles or social media feeds "during crises to buy time for Israel's army to accomplish its operations." Some of the participating organizations are "identity-oriented" (e.g., Taglit-Birthright Israel,[982] Masa Israel[983]), some are "task-oriented" (e.g., CAMERA,[984] AIPAC,[985] The Amcha Initiative[986]), some are "education-oriented" (e.g., Hasbara Fellowships,[987] Campus Watch[988]), and often they are a combination (e.g., Stand with Us,[989] Hillel,[990] the Anti-Defamation League[991]). The organization that *Jewish News Syndicate* has called "one of the most powerful voices for Israel in the United States" is Christians United for Israel (CUFI),[992] which on its website claims over ten million members.[993] Such networks, say Savestrani et al., "tend to group-think" and "message promotion is very controlled." In addition to advocacy, a goal is to enlarge the network by creating more relationships among government entities, NGOS, pro-Israel groups, and individuals.[994]

A prototypical instance of how this works is a program called Masbirim Israel, inaugurated by Israel's Ministry of Information and Diaspora Affairs in 2010. The concept was novel because ordinary citizens who travel abroad—at that time, three million annually—were essentially subcontracted by a government ministry to personally boost Israel's image in the world amongst newfound acquaintances in foreign locales. Volunteers from a broad cross-section of Israel's (Jewish) citizenry were trained using new media tools and workshops to be "nonofficial ambassadors" for Israel. A Hebrew-only training website (www.masbirim.gov.il) was launched, along with a Facebook page and Twitter account, equipping Jewish Israeli voyagers to "correct misperceptions" held by foreigners with confidence and fluency. They were supplied with upbeat information about Israel's vital, modern culture and the message that "the Israeli-Arab conflict is rooted in the refusal of Israel's Arab neighbors to accept its right to exist and is not due to Israel's government policies."[995]

Intelligence and security expert Shay Hershkovitz observes that individuals engaged in such ambassadorial roles are imbued with "the virtues of good citizenship. The state's rhetoric is based on an emotional and intimate linkage between the PR messages and the citizens' own personal feelings.... PR is presented as 'the mission of the Jewish-Israeli collective.'"[996] The use of a dispersed, online network of Israel defenders was actually piloted during the Mavi Marmara flotilla crisis of 2010, when the seemingly impromptu posts of grassroots social media users were found to carry greater clout than official justifications from Israeli government figures.[997] Later, El Al, Israel's national airline, offered incentives for flight attendants in the US "to engage in personal *hasbara*. These El Al Ambassadors use their free slots between flights to engage in small talk with local residents, sharing personal stories about living in Israel, while mentioning Israel's success in the fields of science and culture."[998]

The identity-based program Taglit Birthright Israel also builds an ever-expanding person-to-person web of connections—in this case, as they say on the group's website, by "offering a free, life-changing trip to Israel for young Jewish adults between the ages of 18 and 26 and, in doing so, transforming the Jewish future."[999] And it's not over when it's over: "We partner with and support many Jewish organizations—including Moishe House, Hillel, AIPAC, local federations and others—so that they can help trip alums continue their Jewish journey."[1000] Funded by the Israeli government and private donors (among them the late billionaire Zionist philanthropist Sheldon Adelson), the organization was originally conceived to alleviate the perceived problem of waning American Judaism stemming from intermarriage and diminishing synagogue attendance. However, its focus has shifted to buttressing identification with and fealty to the "Jewish nation"—while honing the logic of that nation's sole entitlement to that "birthright."

As Kiera Feldman wrote in a 2011 reflection for the *Nation* on her own Birthright trip, the outfit claims that it "invites travelers to 'explore Israel without being force-fed ideology,' but you don't have to be Althusser to know that ideology almost always calls itself nonideological." Mixed in with the Zionism is a lot of fun in the sun and camaraderie and the "safety" of traveling in an armed-guarded tour bus free of potential suicide bombers and Hamas kidnappers. Participants mingle and flirt daily with Israeli soldiers as they see the sights, ride camels, dance away the evenings, have hook-ups, and engage in "dialogues" about Israel and Jewish peoplehood. There's little mention of Palestinians except as terrorists to be eliminated, and that's infrequently challenged: as Feldman says, "It's hard to imagine the suffering of others when you're having the time of your life." And nuzzling with attractive IDF soldiers while learning your history has its own payoff: "After the 2006 Lebanon war," Feldman writes, "Brandeis researchers found that Birthright alumni were more likely than other young American Jews to view Israel's military conduct as justified."[1001]

A former student of mine—a Birthright alum who became active in her campus Students for Justice in Palestine—chose to subject her experience to a rigorous analysis. Growing up with a strong Jewish identity but feeling the lack of a Jewish community, it was the latter that she sought through Birthright. But "by the end of the trip," she said in a presentation, "the lines are very blurry. It feels like such a natural progression from community and religion and culture to nation." She spoke of the transcendence of lying under the stars in the Negev desert with her newfound friends and feeling "totally swept up": "When it is so seamless, so difficult to disconnect Israeli nationhood from Jewish identity, it creates people that are unable to think critically about political issues.... The single greatest accomplishment of trips like this is the illusion of dialogue and openness."[1002]

But the *hasbara* network's activities are hardly limited to ostensibly friendly, informal relations, and its tentacles distend in myriad, often clandestine configurations. For example, the Israel on Campus Coalition (ICC), whose self-professed mission is "to unite the many pro-Israel organizations that operate on campuses across the United States,"[1003] has endorsed the work of Canary Mission[1004]—a McCarthyite organization whose donors and staff are shrouded in secrecy, dedicated to profiling and smearing pro-Palestinian students and faculty in hopes of thwarting their future job prospects. According to the *Forward,* "ICC sits at the center of the organized Jewish community's pro-Israel apparatus. Its board includes…leaders of Hillel international and top Jewish foundations."[1005] The ICC has secretly monitored Open Hillel meetings, slandered Palestinian American poet Remi Kanazi in a paid Facebook "anonymous digital campaign," and maintained "a close working relationship.…with Israel's Ministry of Strategic Affairs, an Israeli agency tasked with opposing the BDS movement worldwide."[1006] According to journalist James Bamford, "data from the ICC's web of campus spies and high-tech Israeli surveillance equipment then flows to the Anti-Defamation League.…The ADL then uses the information…along with other data to create an annual report, "Anti-Israel Activism on U.S. Campuses."[1007]

ICC donors have included the real estate billionaire Adam Milstein, who cofounded the Israeli–American Council, has served on the boards of other pro-Israel organizations such as Stand with Us, Hasbara Fellowships, and the AIPAC National Council as well as the ICC, backed anti-BDS legislation, served prison time for a 2009 felony tax evasion conviction, and infamously tweeted in 2019, without supplying any evidence, that US Representatives Ilhan Omar and Rashida Tlaib were linked to the Muslim Brotherhood and that their values "clash[ed] with American values."[1008] Milstein reportedly funds Canary Mission (he has denied it), which is enmeshed in its own byzantine fiscal grid, through an Israeli front group, Megamot Shalom. The latter organization receives funds from the Jewish Community Foundation of San Francisco, which itself funnels donations from the pro-Israel, Bay Area Helen Diller Family Foundation so that donors can get a US tax break (which they could not get by contributing directly to a foreign charity).[1009]

At times, the "news" itself is financed by the Israeli government in direct coordination with willing civil society players, though again, steps are taken to camouflage this. In 2017, the Israeli media watchdog group The Seventh Eye reported that Israel's Strategic Affairs Ministry paid the Yedioth Ahronoth Group—which publishes a major Israeli newspaper and owns the news website Ynet—to publish articles aimed to "expose the lies of BDS;" the articles were then disseminated by members of the Pro-Israel Network both domestically and abroad. Material was additionally sold for placement on Israel's Channel 2 News and its website as well as the *Jerusalem Post* and the *Times of Israel,* both regularly read by foreign audiences.[1010]

In 2022, *Haaretz* told of another Seventh Eye exposé involving the Strategic Affairs Ministry and its *hasbara*-laundering pursuits via "seemingly private users" on social media, this time in conjunction with a body called Concert (formerly known as "Solomon's Sling," and since 2022 named "Voices of Israel"). Concert described itself as a "public utility non-profit organization," but *Haaretz* revealed that ministry officials "admitted that launching the initiative was in practice a way to transfer funds to pro-Israeli organizations working abroad, mainly in the United States, without tainting them with government affiliation.... If the funding came straight from the government, these organizations would have to declare these transactions and be registered as foreign agents in the United States."[1011]

In 2024, *Haaretz* reported on an investigation by the Israeli fact-checking organization Fake Reporter. It revealed that Israel's Diaspora Affairs Ministry had commissioned a political campaigning firm called STOIC to carry out "a large-scale influence campaign primarily aimed at Black lawmakers and young progressives in the United States and Canada," which was "intended to sway certain segments of public opinion on Israel's conduct" after October 7.[1012]

Another way that Israel has tried to influence the public has been through the Wikipedia website. In 2008, five members of an editing campaign spearheaded by the right-wing, pro-Israel group CAMERA (Committee for Accuracy in Middle East Reporting and Analysis) were penalized or banned after Electronic Intifada exposed their plan "to rewrite history on Wikipedia."[1013] In 2010, two right-wing groups in Israel offered courses in "Zionist editing" for the popular platform in the professed belief, as Ayelet Shaked of the Israel Sheli ("My Israel") movement put it, that those in Europe and the US never had a chance to hear "the correct arguments and explanations" about Israel.[1014] In 2013, a social media employee of the right-wing, pro-Israel institute NGO Monitor, concealing his affiliation, edited articles on the Israeli-Palestinian conflict that Wikipedia editors deemed, in their lingo, "POV-pushing" and for which he was "topic-banned." Previously, he had recommended commencing a "wiki war."[1015]

In June 2024, as the "definition wars" around the term "antisemitism" raged, the English Wikipedia community pronounced the Anti-Defamation League (ADL) "a generally unreliable source about the conflict" due to the 'unretracted misinformation" the group published as well as for the "habit on the ADL's part of conflating criticism of the Israeli government's actions with antisemitism."[1016] Rob Eshman, senior columnist for the *Forward,* advised that the ADL should seize this as an opportunity for "self-reflection." He wrote, "The Wikipedia editors also cited statements by Jonathan Greenblatt, the ADL's CEO, that accused student protesters of being 'campus proxies' for the Iranian regime, compared the kaffiyeh, or Arab headscarf, to the Nazi swastika, and compared anti-Israel protesters to white supremacists and Jan. 6 insurrectionists. Wikipedia editors pointed out that some ADL staffers opposed or even quit over these comments."[1017]

This is, of course, just the tip of the iceberg. And a recitation of interconnections such as these is virtually guaranteed, in some quarters, to garner a gasp and a scandalized exclamation that one is implying the existence of a worldwide Jewish cabal, much like that portrayed in the notorious forgery "The Protocols of the Elders of Zion."[1018] Therein, I would propose, lies another dimension of Zionist propaganda: wielding the idea that because one extremely noxious, antisemitic, fictitious, and flagrantly propagandistic text portrayed a Jewish conspiracy contrived for nefarious purposes, it is unthinkable that a network of influential and well-funded Jews and Christians could ever organize to protect their passionate common interest in a Jewish state, by whatever means necessary. This handy way of deflecting any suggestion that such a network exists, even though it is patently obvious that it *does* exist (and its members routinely celebrate their intertwined existence), is but one dimension of what has come to be known as "the weaponization of antisemitism."

USERS' GUIDES TO DEFENDING ISRAEL

Advice for students, politicians, pundits, media workers, "thought leaders," "influencers," and others defending Israel who may yet feel a little shaky about their arguments abounds throughout this network. But that advice is largely duplicative, descending as it does from professionals offering purportedly unshakable, focus-group tested catchphrases and rationales. These can be found in two how-to manuals that may be seen as umbrella guides for the rest.

One of them was written by Frank Luntz, the seasoned Republican pollster and political strategist who in the past famously supplied American legislators with tips on obstructing health care reform, workers' benefits, and environmental and finance regulations. In *Words That Work*, his 2007 source book on how to spin dystopic reality into persuasive, vote-generating affirmations, he was adamant that "what matters is not what you say, it's what people hear," and offered numerous examples of baseless statements that nonetheless "worked" on their audience and rational statements that didn't.[1019] In the oddly named *The Israel Project's 2009 Global Language Dictionary*, he proposes the same technique to rationalize virtually anything of which Israel is likely to stand accused.

Some of his standard suggestions are to "show empathy for both sides" and to "talk about '***working toward a lasting peace***' that '***respects the rights of everyone in the region***,'" assuring us, based on his vast experience, that "**The speaker that is perceived as being most for PEACE will win the debate**." [1020] (Italics, bold, and underlining in original.) He does not explain how the Israeli violence that has taken an enormous toll on Palestinian lives and infrastructure over many decades can be persuasively reconciled with this bromide. Luntz also urges (this is one of his traditional specialties) "reframing" any uncomfortable subject, as in this about Palestinian refugees: "Whenever 'right of return' is raised, we must immediately respond with '*No, you are talking about the right of confiscation. This is not about returning. It is about taking away and we will not accept it.*'" Of course, this must be followed up with the familiar refrain that the Jewish "refugees" who departed Arab countries for Israel surely merit, but have not received, similar compensation.[1021]

Much else in this supposed dictionary will sound familiar to anyone habituated to mainstream American news. Many talking points are simply old canards such as "Israel has the right to defend itself," shocked references to the Hamas charter, and rhetorical rejoinders such as, "What would you have done—or wanted your government to do—if you and your family were under rocket attack every day?" The reader is urged to remind their audience of the "culture of hate" fostered in Palestinian schools, in which children "sing songs about the destruction of Israel" and are indoctrinated into "hero worship for suicide bombings," and to ask withering questions that expose the illiberal illogic of the other side, sometimes in the form of alliterative jingles: *"Why is Hamas building bombs when they should be buying books?"*[1022]

A second guide, dated March 2002, is more plainly titled *Hasbara Handbook: Promoting Israel on Campus.* This booklet, it says, is "published and produced by WUJS, the World Union of Jewish Students." While there is overlap between the two guides, the *Hasbara Handbook* takes a more rhetorical approach, openly instructing on the arts of deceptive argument. Significantly, it says near the outset, "There are two major approaches to communication to use during Israel advocacy." These approaches—to be used in different situations— are *"point scoring"* and *"genuine debate."* (Italics in original.) Far more attention is devoted to the first, as, we are told, genuine debate "can backfire when used on people who are analysing arguments and trying to think deeply, and who really just want somebody to present arguments rationally to them."[1023] In short, this guide isn't designed for colloquy with those people. Instead, the reader is tutored in "basic propaganda devices" that can work on less intellectually sophisticated people—not, as in a university classroom, to recognize them as sleight of hand that malfeasants use to cheat at logic, but rather to be able to mobilize them tactically oneself.

When one is engaging with these more naïve people, *point scoring* is effective since their credulousness allows one to "give the appearance of rational debate, whilst avoiding genuine discussion." (Recall, here, the observation of the Birthright participant who said that the "single greatest accomplishment of trips like this is the *illusion* of dialogue and openness.") "Point scoring works because most audience members fail to analyse what they hear" and anyway, these people are "only paying partial attention." (On the other hand, point scoring should be avoided when "talking in serious academic circles" because it "can seem shallow.") Good venues for practicing point scoring include "talk radio, student newspapers, large panel discussions, and anything to do with television or the internet." Still, to avoid alienating audience members, "all point scoring needs to be disguised. To disguise point scoring, comments need to seem to be logical, and to follow from what was said before. Use phrases that subtly change the agenda or reframe the debate…." Some ways to do this might be to say, "Well, that's not really the right question…" or 'I really think that we would all be better served by looking forward instead of back at the things that happened over 50 years ago. The past is important to note, but we have to move on in an attempt for peace...."[1024]

Some of the more convoluted forms of sophistry that are recommended might indeed draw laughs from the "academic" set, but the gullibles are likely to be stopped in their tracks by faux-commonsensical statements such as, "Settlements have never been the main obstacle to peace. Before 1967 there were no settlements and still no peace agreement."[1025] Or there's this:

> Israel is constantly being accused of a disproportionate reaction. The question of proportionality is somewhat absurd. A proportional response to a bus bombing would be for Israel to place a bomb on a Palestinian bus. This is obviously unacceptable.... It is equally absurd to suggest that Israel must be wrong because more Palestinians have died than Israelis: as if it were a competition and were more Israelis to be killed Israel would become the good guys.[1026]

The impact of language is not neglected. "For the Israel activist," the guide says, "it is important to be aware of the subtly different meanings that well-chosen words give. Call 'demonstrations' 'riots,' many Palestinian organizations 'terror organizations,' and so on."[1027] Anyone who refers to Gilo (a post-1967 Jewish neighborhood built on occupied land) as a "settlement" should be accused of "name-calling." Instead, "Consider calling settlements 'communities' or 'villages.'" (Or "suburbs," when, like Gilo, it is so close that it virtually seems to sprout out of Jerusalem.) Other advice: "Enlisting celebrity support for Israel can help to persuade people that Israel is a great country.... A celebrity doesn't have to fully support Israel to be useful. Quotes can work as testimonial, even when they might be old or out of context." If a celebrity endorses, say, BDS instead, "Threats of tainting a celebrity's image will usually persuade them to back away from controversial political issues."[1028]

TANGLED UP IN PARADOXES

"A state's legitimacy is affected by perceptions of reality no less than by reality itself," write two Boston-based security experts in reference to what they—along with so many others—call "the delegitimization campaign against Israel."[1029] For many Israelis, this appears to hold true. In the vast literature by Jewish Israeli citizens and their supporters who rail against Israeli PR incompetence and failure to make the world love their country again, far more attention is paid to altering "perceptions of reality" than to reckoning with "reality." One might imagine that, after years of criticizing the strategies of the myriad ministries and directorates that have worked to boost Israel's popularity, some contemplation might be turned on "reality." This, however, rarely happens. Longtime *Haaretz* political journalist Akiva Eldar wrote in 2005:

> For 57 years, we've been told that the world is against us due to poor hasbara and unpolished (to put it mildly) spokespeople. We've heard that it would be a totally different picture if we only produced more explanatory movies about Arab terror and more documents proving the anti-Semitic incitement in their textbooks. We're told that our situation in the world would be completely different if we'd only send Bibi Netanyahu to explain in fluent American English to CNN viewers that the Palestinians brought the separation fence - pardon me, I mean the "security fence"—on themselves, and that this so-called "obstacle" isn't really bothering anyone.

Many of the complaints Eldar alludes to open with familiar litanies of what Israelis perceive as brute, senseless animus, as if airing them one more time might confirm their absurdity. Yet inexplicably, these affronts endure despite all the goodness Israel has shown the world. An oft-cited example of this complaint can be seen in a 2006 article by Israeli international relations expert Eytan Gilboa, titled "Public Diplomacy: The Missing Component in Israel's Foreign Policy." Gilboa first details some of the bashing to which Israel has been subjected since, he says, the Second Intifada in 2000:

> Israel is the only nation in the world whose right to exist is constantly being challenged, and whose ancient capital, Jerusalem, is unrecognized by all but a few states. Israeli leaders are often compared to leaders of Nazi Germany, and Israeli actions against the Palestinians are often described as Nazi-like policies. Conditions in Israel and the Palestinian territories

are often compared with those that existed in apartheid South Africa. The main goal of these comparisons is to demonize, dehumanize and de-legitimize Israel.

He goes on:

> The UN, and most other international organizations, has systematically discriminated against Israel and disproportionately attacked its policies.... Enemies, opponents and critics—some of whom are Jews and Israelis—portray Israel as the world's worst violator of human rights, UN resolutions and international law....[1030]

These certainly are harsh allegations and reflect the theme of the popular Israeli song "The Whole World Is Against Us" (see the epigraph to this chapter). But Gilboa does not subject the charges to an analysis that might refute them. Instead, he treats them as instances of irrational and infantile name-calling. Some helpful questions he could have raised are: In what ways is Israel *said* to be analogous to Nazi Germany and South Africa? Under scrutiny, examining the characteristics of each of those parties, *do the analogies hold up?* Why or why not? What human rights violations and laws has Israel been accused of violating, *and on what specific grounds?* Looking at the evidence, *why are these accusations unwarranted?* Why do *even some Jews and Israelis* believe these things? And what *is* it that arouses so many in this world to "*demonize, dehumanize and de-legitimize*" Israel?

Rather than posing such questions, Gilboa, like so many others airing this grievance, descends into what Freud called "the compulsion to repeat." If Israel would just seriously flex its *hasbara* muscles *one more time,* the job could finally be done right, and all might end well. "The Israeli government has failed to prevent the deterioration of Israel's image and reputation in the world," he argues, due mainly to "the lack of awareness and understanding of the critical role PD plays in contemporary international relations."[1031] The problem is that Israel *just doesn't get it.* So Gilboa offers an exposition, in professional jargon, of the New Public Diplomacy, replete with explanations of soft power, nation branding, and the like. But when the moment comes to reveal how Israel could effectively manifest these techniques, he reverts to enumerating the slights and denouncing the putatively biased, double-standards-bearing, hypocritical global media that inflames them.

Late in the article, he envisions factors that might explain Israel's repeated failures in public diplomacy. These range from the predictable (intractable antisemitism; the Arabs have done a slicker job with their propaganda) to the administrative ("Israeli leaders...have rarely addressed the issue in a systematic way"; Israel's coalition governments can "produce only inconsistent, confusing and wavering messages"); and from to the pecuniary (deficient budget allotments) to the heretical (there are Israeli academics residing in the UK, such as the historian Ilan Pappe, who openly support BDS, undercutting Israel's efforts to discredit it).[1032]

In fact, he considers everything except the obvious: that no fine-tuning of spin techniques can overcome the "negative image" generated by Israel's actual policies. Among the solutions he proposes are professional coordination of public diplomacy; increased funding for it; "refut[ing] misperceptions prevalent in the Arab world"; clever rebranding efforts; promoting a positive online "e-image"; utilizing NGOs such as CAMERA and Honest Reporting; and boosting "correct" language (e.g., rejecting the use of "the empty Arab term, 'West Bank'" for the biblically consistent "Judea and Samaria").[1033] In fact, all of these remedies have been tried over the years, and despite the gloom most Israelis feel about what they perceive to be their limited success, Israel has been able to coast upon them to a remarkable degree. But denying a reality that a globalized, cyber-connected world can increasingly see for itself cannot go on forever.

To be clear: Gilboa's piece is typical of a long stream of *woe is Israel* gripes aired by a range of Israelis who view, as the root cause of the problem, their government's inability to wield *hasbara* effectively. In addition to the timeworn ideas of reshuffling the responsibilities of the ministries once again, bolstering cultural diplomacy programs, or changing the subject from war and occupation to technology and innovation, some have suggested fanciful remedies—for example, "Make Zionism sexy again!" (to keep pace with the sexy anti-Zionists, who are popular because they "march alongside every trendy protest").[1034]

Over the years, a tiny minority of voices has suggested that Israel's policies are indeed the source of its "image problem." One was Abba Eban, notable among Israel's chief political figures for questioning the orthodoxy on the subject. On December 24, 1973, while he was foreign minister, he addressed the Knesset: "Once again, I feel a sense of intellectual frustration when the issue of how the government communicates is taken out of the context of the political reality. Because what really affects our image at the end of the day is not the skill of the policy advocate. It's not the salesman, nor the wrapper, but the goods themselves that matter...."[1035] More pointedly, in the summer of 1982, amid Israel's ferocious invasion of Lebanon, Eban published an op-ed in the *Jerusalem Post* in which he tried to delineate the lenses through which the world regarded Israel:

> The immediate association in recent weeks has been the crash of steel against buildings, the screams of bereaved and wounded, the children lining up for water denied by an Israeli 'blockade', the rat-infested garbage heaps, the collapse of those thin layers of civility which shelter human beings against their own human vulnerability. It is little short of idiotic to believe that this movement of opinion could have been arrested by technical means such as a transfer of responsibility for "hasbara" from one Cabinet desk to another, or the enlistment of people abroad skilled in the propagation of exaggeratedly favourable publicity for tooth-paste or automobiles. The erosion has occurred among the well-informed, not the ill-informed.[1036]

But Eban's compatriots were not persuaded, and the attempts to rectify what was essentially unrectifiable via spin went on year after year, war after war, checkpoint after checkpoint. In 2006, the Israel state comptroller published an investigative report on the *hasbara* apparatus that aired many of the structural criticisms leveled by Gilboa and others. This led to certain reforms of the system, most notably the creation of a new entity in the Prime Minister's Office nicknamed the "national *hasbara* headquarters." These changes did not, however, lead to a cessation of the complaints (or of the "image problem"), and in 2012 an Israeli think tank called Molad, The Center for the Renewal of Israeli Democracy, did what was essentially its own report on the report—and on the implementation of its conclusions. Titled "Israeli Hasbara: Myths and Facts," it reads—whatever its original aims—like a supportive job performance review of the new *hasbara* mechanism. While acknowledging the problems of the past, Molad's report glowingly observes that "significant improvements in recent years have made Israel's hasbara apparatus into one of the finest public diplomacy networks in the world."[1037]

Yet the basis of the analysis is technocratic rather than empirical. That is, Israel's *hasbara* is lauded for its adherence to the best practices of the public diplomacy profession, making it far superior to the shoddy productions of "the anti-Israel public diplomacy network." The stated conclusion of the study is "the 'hasbara problem' is a myth that diverts focus from Israel's real problems which are the results of problematic policy, not flawed hasbara of appropriate policy." This might have been welcome and useful news indeed if those problematic policies and their consequences had been studied in some detail. But the report simply follows in the footsteps of all those others who see merit through the professional lens of an efficiency expert rather than that of a quality control inspector.

The shrewdest analysis of the *hasbara* apparatus's flawed and self-defeating logic that I have seen comes from Dutch Moroccan anthropologist and Palestine scholar Miriyam Aouragh, who wrote in 2016:

> [H]asbara involves an inherent contradiction that is extremely difficult to overcome and which continues to destabilize its objectives.... It attempts to construct consensus through persuasion about its right to occupy and repress Palestinians. Yet, it does so while executing military campaigns in the oPt and maintaining segregationist policies for Palestinians inside Israel.... [E]ven if it suddenly wanted to, *hasbara* would not be able successfully to increase its moral authority—to make a "post-conflict" shift—as that would undermine the Zionist project itself.[1038]

And therein lies the crux of *hasbara*'s efficacy problem. What plays in Petah Tikva doesn't play in Peoria. In response to "recent images released by the army showing arrested Hamas terrorists stripped and blindfolded," Israeli journalist Yaakov Katz commented, "'To an Israeli audience this is great but to the rest of the world, it is awful.'"[1039]

As Giora Goodman has most adroitly put it: "Some things are very difficult, sometimes impossible, 'to explain.'"[1040]

EPILOGUE: WHAT THEY SAID THEY SAID ABOUT OCTOBER 7, 2023

APRIL 2025

The Hamas-led attacks of October 7, 2023, and Israel's ensuing devastation of Gaza, all took place as I was in the last stages of writing this book. Therefore, though references to those events appear at times in these pages, a thorough examination of the ways that *hasbara* has been applied to October 7 and its aftermath requires more than a small appendage to this volume. Fortunately, crucial parts of that examination have appeared in US independent media including *Mondoweiss*, Electronic Intifada, The Intercept, Drop Site News, *Democracy Now!*, *Jewish Currents*, Middle East Monitor, and the *Nation*, in foreign media such as Al Jazeera, the *Guardian*, *+972 Magazine*, and *Haaretz*, and in Internet-based media such as Middle East Eye and the interactive database project Hasbara Tracker.

One of the notable tactics used in the post-October 7 era by *hasbarists* and their colleagues in mainstream media and government has been attacking people not for what they say, but for what other people claim they said—or what these other people insist they *really meant*. For example, recently, against the backdrop of the ongoing war on Gaza and protests against it, accompanied by ongoing accusations from many (including antisemites) that the protesters were antisemitic, Senate Minority Leader Chuck Schumer (D-NY) put his two cents in. He asserted confidently in a *New York Times* interview, "When you use the word 'Zionist' for Jew—you Zionist pig—you mean you Jewish pig."[1041] He failed to clarify how he (or anyone) can divine when the word "Zionist" means "Jew" and when it means "Zionist." But it's curious that Schumer is not more sensitive to spurious renderings of others' meanings, since after he broke congressional ranks and said that "Palestinian civilians do not deserve to suffer for the sins of Hamas," Donald Trump proclaimed the senator no longer Jewish; not only was he now, according to Trump, Palestinian (an intended racist slur), he was even "a proud member of Hamas."[1042]

Back on October 15, 2023, when the Hamas-led attacks on Israel and the onset of Israel's war on Gaza were fresh in everyone's mind, a popular, tenured Cornell history professor named Russell Rickford gave a speech at a downtown rally in Ithaca, New York, where I live. In it, he attempted some things rarely heard in rally speeches: complexity and ambiguity. Speaking of "deep traditions of resistance" in a variety of cultures, he came to the present moment and acknowledged the "deep divisions among progressives within the left in the wake of the Hamas operation" that some call resistance to occupation and some call terrorist barbarity. "I *hate* violence, I *hate* violence," he reiterated. "I abhor the killing of civilians." That was one fundamental part of a complicated equation. But then, there was another part: "If you did to me what has been done to the people of Gaza, and what has been done to the Palestinian people systematically for 75 years, if you displaced me, if you dispossessed me, if you bulldozed my orchards, if you destroyed my water, if you prevented me from gaining access to health care, to electricity, if you destroyed my infrastructure, if you tried to destroy my culture, if you destroyed my olive groves, if you penned me in checkpoints, if you segregated me, if you degraded me, if you humiliated me, if you threatened my family, if you threatened my daughter, I who hate violence would take up arms." (Applause ensued.)

He went on, "What has Hamas done? Hamas has shifted the balance of power. Hamas has punctured the illusion of invincibility.... You don't have to be a Hamas supporter to recognize that Hamas has changed the terms of the debate.... Hamas has challenged the monopoly of violence."

Then came the part that would be fateful for Rickford: "And in those first few hours, even as horrific acts were being carried out, many of which we would not learn about until later, there are many Gazans of good will, many Palestinians of conscience who abhor violence, as do you, as do I, who abhor the targeting of civilians, as do you, as do I, who were able to breathe. They were able to breathe, for the first time in years. It was exhilarating. It was energizing. And if they weren't exhilarated by this challenge to the monopoly of violence, by this shifting of the balance of power, then they would not be human. I was exhilarated."

Well.

In *Words That Work,* his bestselling guide to manifesting a persuasive style that can camouflage a message's substance, the propaganda sage Frank Luntz (discussed here in Chapter 9) hammers home a key mantra: "What matters is not what you say, it's what people hear." *Saying what you mean* can be ineffective, often to the point of backfiring, once it gets warped in the coils of your audience's interpretive system. Instead, Luntz advises, use language that reflects your listeners' logic, however dissociated from your original meaning that may be. Since October 7, 2023 (and, I would add—not unrelatedly—the ascent of Donald Trump), it's become frighteningly clear that one can be condemned, denounced, censured, deported, detained, or fired from one's job when *what people hear* outstrips *what you said* in the first place.

On October 25, a headline in the *New York Post* read, "Cornell professor who found Hamas attack 'exhilarating' and 'energizing' now on leave of absence." Cornell President Martha Pollack and board of trustees chair Kraig Kayser issued a statement in which they said, "This is a reprehensible comment that demonstrates no regard whatsoever for humanity." A petition demanding Rickford's dismissal, co-written, according to the *Cornell Daily Sun,* by Jewish Cornell student leaders and Hillel, included the lines, "We are outraged that our professor has endorsed terrorism and is 'exhilarated' by a twenty-first-century massacre of Jewish men, women, children and babies. As a result of his decision to publicly endorse violence against Jews, we feel silenced and unsafe in his classes." US Senator Kirsten Gillibrand (D-NY) told a regional news organization, "As a person of authority at an educational institution, to celebrate murder, rape, and abducting children and slaughtering children, I think he should be fired."

Rickford also had many supporters, with competing petitions and a rally in his defense. Many defended him on freedom of speech grounds and assailed Cornell's academic freedom policy as hypocritical. Some argued that his words had been taken out of context. In the aftermath, he first tried to clarify: according to the *Ithaca Voice,* "Rickford said when he used the word 'exhilarating,' he was referring to the initial hours of Hamas' attack when they 'broke through the apartheid wall, that it seemed to be a symbol of resistance' to the 'destruction and devastation caused by Israeli policies[.]" But clearly no modification or explanation proffered to those who controlled Cornell would soften their stance, since they knew better than he did what he meant. Finally, facing a wall of willful incomprehension and the specter of unemployment, he issued a statement expressing regret for his "horrible choice of words."

Have I mentioned that immediately following Rickford's speech at the rally, I went over to him and told him that his words had expressed my own feelings more cogently than anything else I'd heard that week? I would be remiss not to.

***

Many others have also stepped forward to share their magical powers of detecting others' thoughts and secretly harbored inspirations. For instance, in his May 7, 2024, keynote speech at the Capitol marking the US Holocaust Memorial Museum's Days of Remembrance, President Joe Biden explained that on October 7, Hamas had been "driven by the ancient desire to wipe out the Jewish people off the face of the Earth."[1043] Responding in *Mondoweiss,* Robert Clines pointed out that that "ancient desire" has been the West's, rather than that of Hamas, and referenced the 2017 document issued by Hamas that states unequivocally that its ire is reserved for Zionist occupiers, *not* Jewish people.[1044]

In October 2024, just before the US presidential election and amidst blowback from the voting public regarding the Biden-Harris administration's ongoing arming of Israel in contravention of US and international law, Bill Clinton attempted damage control by telling us how Hamas *really* felt: "Hamas did not care about a homeland for the Palestinians. They wanted to kill Israelis and make Israel uninhabitable."[1045]

***

Framing the campus protests as expressions of antisemitism, rather than concern about enabling death and destruction in Gaza with American material support, was a standard feature of these renditions of the purported meanings of others.

The Anti-Defamation League (ADL) complained of "a steady stream of rhetoric from anti-Israel activists expressing explicit support for US-designated terrorist organizations, such as Hamas, the Popular Front for the Liberation of Palestine (PFLP), and others."[1046] No illustrative quotations or evidentiary sources were provided.

In the fall of 2023, Brandeis University barred its Students for Justice in Palestine chapter from conducting on-campus activities. The reason? According to a letter addressed to "the Brandeis Community" by its president on November 8, 2023, "This decision was made because SJP openly supports Hamas, which the United States has designated as a Foreign Terrorist Organization, and its call for the violent elimination of Israel and the Jewish people."[1047] According to the *Forward,* the students had "declared on social media that 'Palestinian resistance is a multifaceted struggle' that includes 'armed resistance.'"[1048] Translating that into "a call for the violent elimination of…the Jewish people" is yet a further instance of many *hasbarists'* addiction to the original Hamas Charter of 1988, whose antisemitic severity they love to hate and refuse to let go of—even though it was revised in 2017. Hamas's 2017 statement of principles explicitly says, ""Hamas affirms that its conflict is with the Zionist project not with the Jews because of their religion. Hamas does not wage a struggle against the Jews because they are Jewish but wages a struggle against the Zionists who occupy Palestine. Yet, it is the Zionists who constantly identify Judaism and the Jews with their own colonial project and illegal entity."[1049]

The *Times of Israel* headlined an April 25, 2024, article about the Columbia University encampment, "Jewish students horrified by 'Judenrein' on campus." It reported on Jewish students "fleeing" the campus, "fearing for their safety." One student, speaking on Zoom from the shelter of his parents' home in Houston, said, "[The protesters] got what they wanted. The campus is Judenrein now. It's occupied territory.…Jews are not allowed." Another Jewish student reported, "They say things like, 'Kill all the Jews,' and 'We want one Arab state.'.…It's like the Hitler youth." The author of the article doesn't mention any attempts she made to verify these allegations or whether any of her firsthand experience on-site confirmed them. Certainly, she does not let any of the protesters speak for themselves, nor does she quote any of their signs or handouts that might support or contradict the notion that a perilous animus toward Jewish students reigned at Columbia.[1050]

Renata Nyul, a spokesperson for Northeastern University, claimed that the student encampment on that campus had been dismantled after "virulent antisemitic slurs, including, 'Kill the Jews,'" were heard.[1051] Yet, according to *GBH News* in Boston, the protesters maintained that it was counter-protesters carrying an Israeli flag, not pro-Palestinian activists, who had used that language in order to goad them. One Zionist counter-protester allegedly called out, "Kill the Jews! Anybody on board? Anybody on board?" However, when that information was brought to the attention of Nyul, she dismissed the idea that the identity of the speaker of those "repulsive antisemitic comments" was relevant. That did not, of course, alter the penalty: tearing down the encampment.

These are the sorts of exculpatory pretexts behind what Stanley Cohen calls "interpretive denial" when manifested intentionally (see Chapter 4). Just as, in Schumer's personal dictionary, "Zionist" can only mean "Jew," and in Brandeisspeak "multifaceted struggle" including "armed resistance" can only mean "a call for the violent elimination of…the Jewish people," the specter of antisemitism is routinely hauled out as a straw person, an expedient substitute for perspectives that would be more difficult to impugn. The disingenuity behind this is clear. As the British Palestinian novelist Isabella Hammad pointed out in the *New York Review of Books*, "We do not have to guess or suppose" what the Palestinian solidarity activists are demanding,

> because the students have said so, emphatically, repeatedly, and at considerable risk and sometimes cost to themselves. Their first demand is that their universities disclose their financial investments. Their second is that the universities divest from arms companies associated with the Israeli state and from war profiteering more broadly. Anyone who has watched the videos or visited the campuses will hear these words: "Disclose; Divest; We will not stop; We will not rest."[1052]

***

On September 13, 2024, the *Detroit Metro Times* ran a story based on an interview that reporter Steve Neavling had done with Rep. Rashida Tlaib (D-MI). The article relayed Tlaib's concern about the decision by Dana Nessel, Michigan's attorney general, to criminally prosecute eleven University of Michigan protesters who had taken part in a campus Palestinian solidarity encampment. Tlaib suggested that pressure from the university's leadership had prompted the usual "Palestine exception" to free speech and protest:

> "We've had the right to dissent, the right to protest," Tlaib says. "We've done it for climate, the immigrant rights movement, for Black lives, and even around issues of injustice among water shutoffs. But it seems that the attorney general decided if the issue was Palestine, she was going to

treat it differently, and that alone speaks volumes about possible biases within the agency she runs."

The final quotes signal the endpoint of Tlaib's remarks. Following paragraph, no quotation marks, clearly Neavling's add-on: "Nessel is the first Jewish person to be elected Attorney General of Michigan."[1053]

CNN hosts Jake Tapper and Dana Bash nonetheless alchemized that into the "news" that Tlaib had questioned Nessel's ability to handle the case fairly *because Nessel is Jewish*. Tlaib had neither said nor indicated any such thing, and the article never claimed that she had. Still, Nessel herself gave the lie a boost with a post on X: "Rashida should not use my religion to imply I cannot perform my job fairly as Attorney General. It's anti-Semitic and wrong." Tapper, without doing any fact-checking, went on to prod Michigan's governor, Gretchen Whitmer, to weigh in on Nessel's charge. After some hesitation, Whitmer (also apparently skipping the verification process) issued a statement that said, "The suggestion that Attorney General Nessel would make charging decisions based on her religion as opposed to the rule of law is antisemitic." Meanwhile Bash, on her show *Inside Politics* (ditto about substantiation), averred that "Tlaib accused 'the state's Jewish attorney general' of 'letting her religion influence her job.'" Despite Neavling's best efforts to set the record straight, "tweeting at Tapper and Bash, and publishing an explicit fact-check report in the *Metro Times*," the false and inflammatory story went viral, with predictable input from the ADL's Jonathan Greenblatt and a flock of House Democrats about Tlaib's anti-Jewish "bias." Except for a feeble comment from Tapper that he "misspoke," neither apologies nor major retractions were heard from CNN.[1054]

By then, of course, Tlaib, the only Palestinian American in the US Congress, had plenty of "what they said she said" war stories to tell. Most infamous was her censure by the House of Representatives in November 2023 for referencing the expression "From the river to the sea, Palestine will be free" when calling for a ceasefire in Gaza. The resolution, passed by twenty-two Democrats along with most House Republicans, claimed the statement was actually "a genocidal call to violence to destroy the state of Israel and its people to replace it with a Palestinian state extending from the Jordan River to the Mediterranean Sea."[1055] Writing in the *Atlantic* (before the censure, but when the slogan was gaining popularity and wider recognition), Simon Sebag Montefiore informed his readers that it was actually "code," a "chilling phrase that implicitly endorses the killing or deportation of the 9 million Israelis."[1056] The American Jewish Committee characterizes the refrain as a "call to arms" for "erasing the State of Israel and its people,[1057] and Julie Rayman of the AJC told NPR that the expression produces "a feeling that the conflict has been exported and that Hamas is on the doorstep."[1058]

There was no indication that the critics had so much as considered Tlaib's explanation (reinforced by countless others, including the numerous Jews such as myself who had chanted it) that it is "an aspirational call for freedom, human rights and peaceful coexistence, not death, destruction or hate."[1059] Nor did they engage with the rational discourse of Ahmad Khalidi, a researcher at Oxford University, who asked, "Is 'free' necessarily in itself genocidal? I think any reasonable person would say no. Does it preclude the fact that the Jewish population in the area between the sea and the river cannot also be free? I think any reasonable person would also say no."[1060] But where are the reasonable people in Congress and in media? In the end, NPR[1061] and the *New York Times*[1062] short-circuited any real attempt at inquiry by opting for a "conflicting interpretations" perspective—to some, it's this, to others, it's that—which, like "conflicting narratives" and conflicting everything else (as discussed in Chapter 3), leaves us, as we began, in limbo, as if there are no sources available to be researched that might possibly give us a clue and steer the discussion in an illuminating direction.

Another notably nefarious act in the circus of recasting visions of hope and freedom as calls for mass anti-Jewish carnage was performed in December 2023. This was the grilling by Rep. Elise Stefanik (R-NY) of Harvard president Claudine Gay during a hearing held by the House Committee on Education and the Workforce called "Holding Campus Leaders Accountable and Confronting Antisemitism." Had this been testimony in a court of law, a defense attorney for Gay would certainly have objected that Stefanik was "leading the witness" with questions such as, "[Y]ou understand that the use of the term 'intifada' in the context of the Israeli-Arab conflict is indeed a call for violent armed resistance against the State of Israel, including violence against civilians and the genocide of Jews. Are you aware of that?"

Unfortunately, Gay seemed to possess neither the knowledge nor the wherewithal to correct Stefanik's mistranslation of "intifada," an Arabic word meaning "to shake off" or "dust off" that was, outside of Palestine, often used during the Arab Spring. As Daniel Lefkowitz, a professor of language and culture in the Middle East at the University of Virginia who has lived in Israel, commented in the *Forward,* it's had different manifestations, from "the First Intifada, a largely nonviolent Palestinian protest largely involving work stoppages, boycotts, and demonstrations" to the "Second Intifada, a far bloodier Palestinian uprising characterized by suicide bombings on buses and cafes…." How about Stefanik's framing of the concept? "'Intifada and genocide—to me that's an unreasonable stretch,' he said. 'I don't think there's any reasonable interpretation of 'intifada' where it means genocide.'"[1063]

Stefanik's aim was to illustrate that because Harvard's code of conduct mandated no disciplinary action for those using the term "intifada," Gay was at the helm of a lax operation that gave loose rein to genocide and antisemitism. The transcript of the interrogation reveals that Gay never actually accepted Stefanik's definition. Instead, she attempted to deflect by saying things like, "I have heard that term, yes." But Stefanik proceeded as if she had agreed: "Does that speech not call for the genocide of Jews and the elimination of Israel? You testified that you understand that that is the definition of 'intifada.'" Gay had not done this. However, neither had she outright rejected Stefanik's framing or refuted Stefanik's insistence that she had accepted it. The consequence was that Stefanik was now armed with a winning premise and Gay's defeat was assured. The points that Gay had been shakily trying to make about free speech and the role of context in meaning didn't matter anymore. The moral of the story hinged on what Stefanik said Gay said.[1064]

Not so incidentally, the *Jewish Telegraphic Agency* pointed out that Stefanik "has drawn condemnation for comments echoing the white supremacist 'great replacement theory,' which in its original form claims that Jews are orchestrating the mass immigration of people of color into Western nations to replace their white populations." The same article quoted Betsy Sheerr, a Democratic donor to Jewish and pro-Israel organizations, saying of Stefanik, "She has really turned into one of the propagators of some of the vilest antisemitism…. She doesn't call out anybody in her party…. [S]he's a very dangerous member of Congress."[1065]

***

Lastly, anyone who followed the news during that period will certainly recall two of the most incendiary accusations that would consign Hamas to a class of barbarism beyond the ambit of any sort of whataboutism (as if accounts of the violence of that day really needed an extra fillip). One of these claims was that Hamas had planned and carried out a widespread, systematic program of raping women as an instrument of terrorism. The other was that they had beheaded babies.

In both cases, a central point of contention was the matter of evidence. On the one hand, this was claimed to be definitively present, and on the other hand, it was denounced as fabricated and derived from unreliable narrators. To make the rape story acceptably plausible, there were ample appeals to the #MeToo movement and the newly credentialed maxim that one should "believe women" in defiance of a past when women's charges of rape were deemed too flimsy to weigh in on the scales of justice.

Yet in the case of October 7, women were not coming forward to say that they had survived rape. As Australian sociologist Randa Abdel-Fattah wrote for the Institute for Palestine Studies, "believe women" is a misleading proposition here because "the allegations of mass rape have come from the Israeli regime, not women."

Observers invested in conserving the story rationalized the absence of first-person testimonials by saying that many women who had been raped had died the same day, some burned beyond recognition, and others were presumed to be fraught with the age-old taboo against acknowledging such experiences. Many of the accounts on which commentators relied were delivered second-, third-, or even fourth-hand from "witnesses" whose testimony was problematic—either because they were deemed too many steps removed from the events that someone had ostensibly observed to be reliable, or because they had proven to be untrustworthy witnesses in the past, or because the first responders had not performed the most basic tasks necessary to preserve forensic evidence.[1066]

Of particular interest were volunteers from a group called ZAKA, described by *Haaretz* as an "ultra-Orthodox organization that retrieves human remains after attacks and disasters." However, in its exposé, *Haaretz* also makes it clear that ZAKA volunteers exploited their activities on October 7 for fundraising and publicity purposes. The nearly insolvent organization, according to the report, was grossly negligent in its collection and documentation of bodies and body parts, used corpses as props in videos for prospective donors, generated tales of gruesome scenes that were found to be false, hired a PR firm to photograph them in their work, covered dead bodies wrapped in IDF body bags with bags displaying their own logo, and, later, operated private tours of the devastated areas (designated "closed military zones" and barred to civilians) for donors. By the end of January, the group had reportedly raised $13.7 million.[1067] An *Intercept* article by Arun Gupta building on the *Haaretz* piece sums up that amidst these preoccupations, they "botched forensics that are central to Israel's claim that Hamas carried out a premeditated campaign of mass rape."

Still, ZAKA did perform an important service for Israel's PR machine. Eitan Schwartz, who works with the prime minister's National Information Directorate, explained to the Israeli news site *Ynet*,

> The testimonies of Zaka volunteers, as first responders on the ground, had a decisive impact in exposing the atrocities in the South to the foreign journalists covering the war.... The entire state of Israel was engaged in framing the narrative that Hamas is equal to ISIS and in deepening the legitimacy of the state to act with great force.... [They] caused a horror and revealed to the reporters what kind of human-monsters we are talking about.

Gupta points out that while Israeli media has debunked many of the lies that have circulated as justification for the war in Gaza, American media remains "credulous" and repeats what it is told.[1068]

Then, on December 28, the *New York Times* ran a story called "Screams Without Words: How Hamas Weaponized Sexual Violence on Oct. 7," which has since famously unraveled, revealing in its wake a trail of irresponsible reporting. One of the three journalists, Anat Schwartz, an Israeli filmmaker and former air force intelligence official with no previous reporting experience, conducted at first what might seem like due diligence in seeking corroboration of the stories she'd heard. She pursued "Israeli hospitals, rape crisis centers, trauma recovery facilities, and sex assault hotlines in Israel," but could find no one who knew of any such complaints from survivors of that day. Unable to extract the information she wanted at a holistic therapy facility, she insisted that the staff were conducting "a conspiracy of silence." One woman said Schwartz and Adam Sella, also on the byline, had pressed her for photos and videos she had in her possession, insisting on "how important it is for Israeli hasbara."[1069]

"At every turn," write the authors of an Intercept piece called "'Between the Hammer and the Anvil': The Story Behind the *New York Times* October 7 Exposé," whenever leads didn't pan out as hoped, "they turned to anonymous Israeli officials or witnesses who'd already been interviewed repeatedly in the press," still "relying overwhelmingly on the word of Israeli officials, soldiers, and Zaka workers" to validate their claims. Israeli authorities claimed that they were assessing forensic evidence that would confirm one of the more macabre accounts and were said to be looking at DNA from rape victims, but none of this materialized. So the team fell back on testimony from someone who had already been known to falsify stories and others with histories of dubious claims. Schwartz said it was "challenging" to respond to questions such as, "If this has happened in so many places, how can it be that there is no forensic evidence? How can it be that there is no documentation? How can it be that there are no records? A report? An Excel spreadsheet?" Afterward, the third writer on the "Screams" story, Jeffrey Gettleman, contended while participating in a panel discussion at Columbia University's School of International and Public Affairs that "evidence" was a legal matter; it was the role of journalists "to share the story in a way that makes people care," not to "prove an allegation" as a lawyer would.[1070]

Neither was "evidence" critical to the "beheaded babies" story. The IDF declined to investigate because, writes Hamza Yusef in Declassified UK, an independent media site, it "insisted testimonies from soldiers amounted to sufficient evidence" that forty decapitated babies had been found in the areas under attack in southern Israel. "What started as a claim from Israeli military and media circles that lacked certainty was instantly transformed into an established fact by virtually the entire British media," even though journalists on the scene and army personnel said they had encountered no such spectacle.[1071] Hamas denied the allegation, but that didn't count for anything among Israel's allies.

In the United States, CBS News and CNN promulgated the story, and President Joe Biden, taking Netanyahu's word for it, claimed publicly (against the advice of some of his staff) that he had seen photos of the horrors himself. Secretary of State Antony Blinken, too, expressed revulsion after viewing images shared with him by Netanyahu. He called them "new evidence of depravity and the inhumanity of Hamas—depravity and inhumanity directed at babies, at small children, at young adults, at elderly people, at people with disabilities." National Security Council spokesman John Kirby, "without confirming the authenticity of the images...said 'it's obvious what Hamas has proven willing to do to innocent Israeli civilians.'"[1072] Nonetheless, these officials, all key players in rationalizing continued US arms shipments to Israel, were not stirred enough by the verified images of tens of thousands of Palestinian children killed and maimed by the IDF to cease reiterating, "Israel has a right to defend itself."

***

Jennine Khalik, Palestinian Australian founder of an interesting database called Hasbara Tracker,[1073] which charts post-October 7 Israeli propaganda, maintains that merely *fact-checking* or *debunking* a false claim isn't enough. What's more enlightening and useful is documenting the trajectory from its genesis so that one can analyze its evolution and mutation along the trail of spokespeople, politicians, media outlets, and other actors in public discourse.[1074]

I very much agree with her argument. I would suspect that even some higher-ups in Israel's PR machine might have given it some thought after an AI bot designed to get out the Zionist message ran amok in January 2025—"inadvertently," in *Haaretz's* description, "contributing to the same denialism it was trained to counter." The *Haaretz* headline ran, "Hasbara Hitch: Pro-Israel Social Media Bot Goes Rogue, Calls IDF Soldiers 'White Colonizers in Apartheid Israel.'" In response to a report on X of a family killed on Kibbutz Nir Oz, the bot lectured, "The tragic event you mentioned did not occur on October 7. It is important to focus on the facts and the actual events that have taken place. The situation involving the hostages and the ongoing conflict with Hamas are complex issues that require careful consideration."[1075]

Touché.

ACKNOWLEDGMENTS

This book was over twenty years in the making. I am indebted to many people but would like to begin where the two primary topics of the book initially took hold in me. The first came from a group called Rhetoricians for Peace, formed within the Conference on College Composition and Communication (CCCC) during the run-up to the Iraq War in 2003. Our three years of conference workshops on propaganda and our 1984+20 Project furnished the springboard for my study of propaganda. I am especially grateful to Tom Huckin of RFP for introducing me to sources and materials that became germane to this book.

The other formative event was a 2004 gathering attended by a number of writers, scholars, activists, and journalists at the home of my good friends Barbara Bloch and Alissar Gazal in Sydney, Australia, at which Ilan Pappe was the honored guest. In preparation for that evening, I'd read his *History of Modern Palestine,* but I also felt propelled to a new level of involvement with Palestinian reality as the dynamic discussion in Barbie and Al's living room unfolded.

In 2013, I was denied a sabbatical to work on this book by the dean and the vice president for academic affairs at Long Island University, where I taught. (They insisted they did not have to give a reason.) A long battle ensued (which I lost—though I suppose I also won, because it was just the jolt I needed to leave LIU in a joyful burst of early retirement). Countless faculty supported me: the English department faculty committee who unanimously recommended that I receive the sabbatical and stuck their necks out further when we hit the big roadblock—thank you, Michael Bennett, Leah Dilworth, Jonathan Haynes, Maria McGarrity, Patrick Horrigan, John Killoran, and Bernard Schweizer; the department co-chairs, Vidhya Swaminathan and Patricia Stephens, who also unambiguously recommended that I receive the sabbatical and raised their voices in objection when all faculty decisions were ignored; the other colleagues who protested the administration's decision, many of whom were in gender studies:

Dawn Kilts, Janet Haynes, Susanna Jones, Carol Allen, Claire Goodman, Dalia Fahmy, Emily Drabinski, Katelyn Angell, Kimberly Jones, Rachel King, Sara Haden, Stacey Horstmann, Susan Thomas, Melissa Antinori, and Margaret Cuonzo; and the special interdisciplinary faculty committee that was appointed by the administration near the end as one final arbiter of my sabbatical fate, who again unanimously recommended that I be granted the sabbatical—Louis Parascandola, Barbara Parisi, Jose Sanchez, and Kevin Meehan—who were nonetheless, once more, roundly ignored by the administration.

Sabbaticals, tenure—there was certainly a cost to being an academic writing about Palestine then. In 2025, for campus supporters of justice for Palestine, the stakes are much higher: one can be beaten, arrested, deported, suspended, blacklisted, or fired. Between that, and the acquiescence of many campus leaders to Trumpian demands that threaten to turn universities into the antithesis of what are here for, I am finding more and more people who agree that there is a special circle of hell reserved for college administrators and trustees.

But back to the positive side: There are several others from outside LIU who stepped forward to offer help at that time. Some wrote articles about the abuse of academic freedom at LIU: Aaron Barlow of the American Association of University Professors (AAUP) in *Academe Blog;* Philip Weiss in *Mondoweiss;* and Jewish Voice for Peace in *Muzzlewatch.* Judith Butler brought the case to the MLA Committee on Academic Freedom and Professional Responsibilities, which touched me deeply. And Barbara Harvey, a labor lawyer and Palestine solidarity activist in Detroit, materialized to offer pro bono legal advice, moral support, and good company.

In addition, my wonderful friend and colleague Bronwyn Jones started a Change.org petition headlined, "Long Island University: Stop Stifling Academic Freedom," urging the LIU administration to revise its verdict. Though once again, they didn't budge, I cannot say how thankful I am to the 1,668 people all over the world who signed and commented on it, including people in Europe, Canada, Jordan, Lebanon, Morocco, Turkey, Colombia, Brazil, Israel, and Ramallah.

Huge thanks to Aneil Rallin, who invited me to give a talk on this project at Soka University of America in 2014, to Ian Barnard, who invited me to speak at Chapman University during that same visit to Southern California, and to all there who made my stay so delightful. Love and appreciation to Noura Hajjaj, who invited me to present a paper at the New York State Communications

Association Virtual Conference in October 2020 (and who brilliantly makes me Palestinian food without sesame, to which I am sadly allergic). The students under the trees at the Cornell Liberated Zone Teach-In, April 2024, were the first to hear some of the material in this book; their enthusiastic participation convinced me that perhaps I had something new to say.

I am grateful to Gideon Kouts, whose scholarship on Nahum Sokolow was vital to my research and who kindly answered further questions in an email exchange.

Thanks to Hannah Gignoux for her insightful reflections on her Birthright trip and to Sam Morris-Rosenstein for responding so helpfully to one chapter. (If only I'd thought of asking him sooner!) I was thrilled to finally put this book into the publishing hands of Michel Moushabeck from Interlink Books; in terms of finding the right "fit" for this work, I think I hit the jackpot.

Particularly supportive, helpful, and encouraging friends were Sherri Barnes and Jacquie Sue Morris. Patricia Stephens and Barbara Bloch reappeared at later stages to give helpful feedback and reinforcement on chapters in progress. Rebecca Manzi serendipitously dropped into my life at a crucial time in this book's development, sharing expert advice and knowledge, especially about the Jewish National Fund. Tony Iantosca, a treasured former student, brought her to Ithaca and deserves much credit for connecting us. I would also like to thank my partner, Jill Tripp, for giving me the space to write every day, along with the knowledge that despite my hermetic daytime existence, there was always food, wine, *Jeopardy*, our cats, and her love to look forward to when the day was done.

I am also more appreciative than I can say to many of the wonderful researchers on whose work this project depended. They were the ones who went into archives, were fluent in Arabic and Hebrew, and approached history, traditions, rituals, and what often passes for "common knowledge" from unconventional analytic angles. Some of them were already well-known to me, but I discovered a few gems along the way.

The three most enormous thank-yous go to Bronwyn Jones, Kerryn Higgs, and Stan Malinowitz, who generously and rigorously responded to drafts of chapter after chapter over a long period of time. They epitomize the smart, educated, compassionate reader I'd envisioned, who nevertheless didn't know much about the topic beforehand and asked just the right questions. Kerryn also performed the miracle of training me to summarize and write shorter sentences.

—Harriet Malinowitz, April 2025

ENDNOTES

CHAPTER 1: INTRODUCTION

1   George Orwell, *1984* (Plume, 1981) [Harcourt Brace & Co., 1949].

2   Jacques Ellul, *Propaganda:* The Formation of Men's Attitudes (Knopf, 1965).

3   Louis Althusser, "Ideology and Ideological State Apparatuses (Notes towards an Investigation)." *Lenin and Philosophy and Other Essays* (Monthly Review Press, 1971).

4   David Ben-Gurion, quoted in Anita Shapira, "Ben-Gurion and the Bible: The Forging of an Historical Narrative?" *Middle Eastern Studies* 33, no. 4 (1997): 651.

5   Dan Porat, "From the Scandal to the Holocaust in Israeli Education," *Journal of Contemporary History* 39, no. 4) (2004): 621.

6   Porat, "From the Scandal to the Holocaust in Israeli Education," 627.

7   Porat, "From the Scandal to the Holocaust in Israeli Education," 628.

8   Porat, "From the Scandal to the Holocaust in Israeli Education," 629.

9   Porat, "From the Scandal to the Holocaust in Israeli Education," 629.

10   Porat, "From the Scandal to the Holocaust in Israeli Education," 631.

11   See International March of the Living, www.motl.org.

12   Simha Flapan, *The Birth of Israel: Myths and Realities* (Pantheon Books, 1987), 8.

13   Benny Morris, "The New Historiography: Israel and its Past" in *1948 and After: Israel and the Palestinians,* ed. Benny Morris (Oxford University Press, 1990), 5.

14   Benny Morris, "Peace? No Chance," *The Guardian,* February 20, 2002.

15   Benny Morris quoted in "The Arabs Are Responsible," excerpts from a November 23, 2001, interview with the Israeli newspaper *Yediot Ahronot,* translated by the Middle East Media Research Institute (MEMRI) and posted on the website of Free Republic, December 10, 2001, freerepublic.com/focus/fr/587517/posts.

16   Morris in "The Arabs Are Responsible."

17　Nur Masalha, *The Politics of Denial: Israel and the Palestinian Refugee Problem* (Pluto Press, 2003), 62. (Note: IDF is the abbreviation for Israel Defense Forces.)

18　Nurit Peled-Elhanan, *Palestine in Israeli School Books: Ideology and Propaganda in Education* (I.B. Tauris, 2012), 223–24.

19　Peled-Elhanan, *Palestine in Israeli School Books*, 19.

20　Peled-Elhanan, *Palestine in Israeli School Books*, 219.

21　Peled-Elhanan, *Palestine in Israeli School Books*, 180.

22　Raoul Wootliff, "Final text of Jewish nation-state law, approved by the Knesset early on July 19," the *Times of Israel,* July 18, 2018, updated: July 19, 2018, www.timesofisrael. com/final-text-of-jewish-nation-state-bill-set-to-become-law/.

23　Ian McGonigle, *Genomic Citizenship: The Molecularization of Identity in the Contemporary Middle East* (MIT Press, 2021): 55, 59, DOI: doi.org/10.7551/ mitpress/14128.001.0001.

24　Raphael Falk, "Genetic markers cannot determine Jewish descent," *Frontiers in Genetics,* January 2015, Vol. 5, Article 462, DOI: 10.3389/fgene.2014.00462.

25　Nadia Abu El-Haj, *The Genealogical Science* (University of Chicago Press, 2012), 14.

26　"Untangling False Claims About Ashkenazi Jews, Khazars and Israel," published Feb. 28, 2024 on the website of the Anti-Defamation League (ADL), www.adl.org/resources/ article/untangling-false-claims-about-ashkenazi-jews-khazars-and-israel.

27　"75 percent of today's Jews have Middle Eastern origins, says DNA pioneer," November 13, 2014, www.worldjewishcongress.org/en/news/75-percent-of-today-s-jews-have-middle-eastern-origins-says-dna-pioneer.

28　Nadia Abu El-Haj, *Facts on the Ground: Archaeological Practice and Territorial Self-Fashioning in Israeli Society* (University of Chicago Press, 2001), 22–27.

29　El-Haj, *Facts on the Ground,* 92–3.

30　Keith Whitelam, *The Invention of Ancient Israel: The Silencing of Palestinian History* (Routledge, 1996), 35, 45, 57.

31　El-Haj, *Facts on the Ground,* 148–9.

32　El-Haj, *Facts on the Ground,* 165–66.

33　El-Haj, *Facts on the Ground,* 173, 167.

34　Yael Zerubavel, *Recovered Roots: Collective Memory and the Making of Israeli National Tradition* (University of Chicago Press, 1995), 8–10.

35　Zerubavel, *Recovered Roots,* 16.

36　Zerubavel, *Recovered Roots,* 27, 217

37　Zerubavel, *Recovered Roots,* 217.

38   Zerubavel, *Recovered Roots*, 218.

39   Zerubavel, *Recovered Roots*, 121.

40   Nachman Ben-Yehuda, *The Masada Myth: Collective Memory and Mythmaking in Israel* (University of Wisconsin Press, 1995).

41   Marek Dospěl, "The Histories of Flavius Josephus," Bible History Daily, September 4, 2024, Biblical Archaeology Society, www.biblicalarchaeology.org/daily/people-cultures-in-the-bible/people-in-the-bible/the-histories-of-flavius-josephus/.

42   Ben-Yehuda, *The Masada Myth*, 8–9.

43   Yigal Yadin, *Masada: Herod's Fortress and the Zealots' Last Stand*, Trans. Moshe Pearlman (Steimatzky Ltd., Tel Aviv, 1966), 197.

44   Yadin, *Masada*, 15.

45   Ben-Yehuda, *The Masada Myth*, 71–76.

46   Shmaria Guttman quoted in Ben-Yehuda, *The Masada Myth*, 77.

47   Ben-Yehuda, *The Masada Myth*, 80–1.

48   Josephus's rendition of Eleazar's speech, quoted in Yadin, *Masada*, 225–26.

49   Ben-Yehuda, *The Masada Myth*, 153.

50   Ben-Yehuda, *The Masada Myth*, 202.

51   Ben-Yehuda, *The Masada Myth*, 210.

CHAPTER 2: FOUNDATIONS

52   Hannah Arendt, *The Origins of Totalitarianism* (Harcourt Bruce & Company, 1976 [1951]), 7.

53   Aristotle, *Rhetoric*, trans. W. Rhys Roberts (Dover Publications, Inc, 2004), 5.

54   Jacques Ellul, *Propaganda: The Formation of Men's Attitudes* (Vintage Books, 1973).

55   Leonard W Doob, *Public Opinion and Propaganda* (Holt, 1948), 237.

56   Doob, *Public Opinion and Propaganda*, 237–8.

57   Doob, *Public Opinion and Propaganda*, 240.

58   Doob, *Public Opinion and Propaganda*, 240.

59   Doob, *Public Opinion and Propaganda*, 246.

60   Philip M. Taylor, *Munitions of the Mind: A History of Propaganda from the Ancient World to the Present Era* (Manchester University Press, 2003), 6.

61   Taylor, *Munitions of the Mind*, 14.

62   Beth S. Bennett and Sean Patrick O'Rourke, "A Prolegomenon to the Future Study of Rhetoric and Propaganda," in *Readings in Propaganda and Persuasion: New and Classic Essays.* Garth S. Jowett and Victoria O'Donnell, eds., Sage Publications, 2006, 51–71.

63   Bennett & O'Rourke, "Prolegomenon," 66.

64   Garth Jowett and Victoria O'Donnell, *Propaganda & Persuasion* (Sage Publications, 2019), 16.

65   Jowett & O'Donnell, *Propaganda & Persuasion*, 16.

66   Jowett & O'Donnell, *Propaganda & Persuasion*, 16.

67   Jowett & O'Donnell, *Propaganda & Persuasion*, 48; Taylor, *Munitions of the Mind,* 2–3, 111; Randal Marlin, *Propaganda and the Ethics of Persuasion* (Broadview Press, 2003), 15.

68   Taylor, *Munitions of the Mind*, 22–24.

69   Jowett & O'Donnell, *Propaganda & Persuasion*, 41.

70   Taylor, *Munitions of the Mind*, 41–45.

71   Jowett & O'Donnell, *Propaganda & Persuasion*, 43.

72   Jowett & O'Donnell, *Propaganda & Persuasion*, 52.

73   Jowett & O'Donnell *Propaganda & Persuasion*, 42.

74   Taylor, *Munitions of the Mind*, 52–9; 57–72; 73–5.

75   Taylor, *Munitions of the Mind*, 87–9.

76   Taylor, *Munitions of the Mind*, 92.

77   Taylor, *Munitions of the Mind*, 97–101.

78   Taylor, *Munitions of the Mind*, 113–21.

79   Ellul, *Propaganda*,117.

80   Taylor, *Munitions of the Mind*, 148; 158–60.

81   Lindley Fraser, *Propaganda* (Oxford University Press, 1957), 26.

82   Quoted in Marlin, *Propaganda and the Ethics of Persuasion*, 58.

83   Quoted in David Clampin, "Commercial Advertising as Propaganda in World War One," *British Library*, n.d., accessed February 6, 2016, www.bl.uk/world-war-one/articles/commercial-advertising-as-propaganda.

84   Harold D. Lasswell, *Propaganda Technique in World War I* (MIT Press 1971 [1927]), 82.

85   Gordon Williams, "'Remember the *Llandovery Castle*': Cases of Atrocity Propaganda in the First World War," in *Propaganda, Persuasion and Polemic*, ed. Jeremy Hawthorn (Edward Arnold Publishers, 1987), 19–34, 19.

86   "MEMO #3—THE LUSITANIA," accessed 17 January 2016, www.americanhistoryrules.com/unit6/ShouldAmericaEnterWWI/ memo3.htm. The memo was subsequently removed from

that website, but was accessed 20 December, 2021 at "Advise (sic) for President Woodrow Wilson—Manhasset Schools" in the PDF "WWi Memo PKT" (school assignment), www.google.com/url?sa=t&rct=j&q=&esrc=s&source=web&cd=&ved=2ahUKEw-i2sv_yr_P0AhWlmuAKHeeuCgMQFnoECAkQAQ&url=http%3A%2F%2Fwww.manhassetschools.org%2Fcms%2Flib8%2FNY01913789%2FCentricity%2FDomain%2F299%2FWWi%2520Memo%2520PKT.docx&usg=AOvVaw0OHNalHvxAoXHpcf1W0y8B.

87   "PRESS CALLS SINKING OF LUSITANIA MURDER: Editorials in New York Newspapers Agree Torpedoing Was Crime Against Civilization," 8 May 1915, *New York Times,* accessed December 29, 2024, www.nytimes.com/1915/05/08/archives/press-calls-sinking-of-lusitania-murder-editorials-in-new-york.html.

88   Richard Norton-Taylor, "Edith Cavell, shot by Germans during WWI, celebrated 100 years on," the *Guardian,* 12 October 2015, accessed December 29, 2024, www.theguardian.com/world/2015/oct/12/edith-cavell-nurse-shot-by-germans-wwi-celebrated.

89   Richard Norton-Taylor, "Edith Cavell, shot by Germans during WWI, celebrated 100 years on."

90   Marlin, *Propaganda and the Ethics of Persuasion,* 71.

91   Adolf Hitler, *Mein Kampf* (Jainco Publishers, 2007), 164.

92   Stuart Ewen *PR! A Social History of Spin* (Basic Books, 1996), 104–5.

93   Howard Zinn, *A People's History of the United States* (Harper & Row, 1980), 354.

94   Zinn, *A People's History,* 353–5.

95   Quoted in Zinn, *A People's History,* 356.

96   Jowett and O'Donnell, *Propaganda & Persuasion,* 97.

97   George Creel, *How We Advertised America.* (Forgotten Books, 2012 [Harper & Brothers, 1920]), 3–5.

98   George Creel, *How We Advertised America,* 6.

99   George Creel, *How We Advertised America,* 6–7.

100   George Creel, *How We Advertised America,* 6–7.

101   George Creel, *How We Advertised America,* 133–7.

102   George Creel, *How We Advertised America,* 71-22.

103   George Creel, *How We Advertised America,* 9–10.

104   George Creel, *How We Advertised America,* 213.

105   Stuart Ewen, *PR!,* 115.

106   Taylor, *Munitions of the Mind,* 216–19.

107   Quoted in Amos Elon, *Herzl* (Holt, Rinehart and Winston, 1975), 141–2.

108   Nahum Sokolow, *History of Zionism, 1600–1918* (Kindle Edition [Longmans, Green & Co., 1919]), 28–29.

109   Sokolow, *History of Zionism*, 44–45.

110   Walter Laqueur, *A History of Zionism* (Schocken Books, 2003 [1972]), 44.

111   Gideon Shimoni, *The Zionist Ideology* (Brandeis University Press, 1995), 12.

112   Maurice Samuels, *The Right to Difference: French Universalism and the Jews* (University of Chicago Press, 2016), 3.

113   Samuels, *The Right to Difference*, 14.

114   Arthur Hertzberg, ed., *The Zionist Idea: A Historical Analysis and Reader* (Atheneum, 1984), 21.

115   Laqueur, *A History of Zionism*, 23.

116   Laqueur, *A History of Zionism*, 16.

117   Laqueur, *A History of Zionism*, 6–19; Shimoni, *The Zionist Ideology*, 14–15.

118   Hertzberg, *The Zionist Idea*, 34.

119   Shlomo Sand, *How I Stopped Being a Jew*, trans. David Fernbach (Verso, 2014), 4–5.

120   David Biale, "A Journey Between Worlds: East European Jewish Culture from the Partitions of Poland to the Holocaust," in *Cultures of the Jews: A New History*, ed. David Biale (Schocken, 2002), 801–2.

121   Benny Morris, *Righteous Victims: A History of the Zionist-Arab Conflict, 1881–2001*, (Vintage Books, 2001 [1999]), 14; S. Ettinger, "Demographic Changes and Economic Activity in the Nineteenth Century," in *A History of the Jewish People*, ed. H.H. Ben-Sasson, trans George Weidenfeld and Nicolson Ltd. (Harvard University Press, 1976), 794–99, 885; Biale, A Journey Between Worlds, 803.

122   Morris, *Righteous Victims*, 14–15.

123   Laqueur, *A History of Zionism*, 59.

124   Laqueur, *A History of Zionism*, 60.

125   Laqueur, *A History of Zionism*, 119–21.

126   Emiliana P. Noether, "Guissepe Mazzini" in *Encyclopedia of 1948 Revolutions* (1999), revised James Chastain 23 October, 2004, www.ohio.edu/chastain/ip/mazzini.htm.

127   Quoted in S. Ettinger, "The Attitude of European Society in the Seventeenth and Eighteenth Centuries, in Ben-Sasson, ed., *A History of the Jewish People*, 745.

128   Dimitry Shumsky, "Kohn, Hans," trans. Rami Hann, YIVO Encyclopedia of Jews in Eastern Europe, August 18, 2010, accessed June 20, 2021, yivoencyclopedia.org/article.aspx/Kohn_Hans.

129   Krzysztof Jaskulowsky, "Western (Civic) versus Eastern (Ethnic) Nationalism: The Origins and Critique of the Dichotomy," *Polish Sociological Review* 171, no. 3 (Jan. 2010): 291.

130   Hans Kohn, "The Nature of Nationalism," the *American Political Science Review* 33, no. 6 (Dec. 1939): 1008.

131   Hans Kohn, "The Nature of Nationalism," 1002.

132   John Coakley, "National Identity and the 'Kohn Dichotomy,'" *Nationalities Papers* 46, no. 2 (2018): 252–3, doi:10.1080/00905992.2017.1360267.

133   John Coakley, "National Identity and the 'Kohn Dichotomy,'" 256–57.

134   Krzysztof Jaskulowsky, "Western (Civic) versus Eastern (Ethnic) Nationalism, 296–7.

135   John Coakley, "National Identity and the 'Kohn Dichotomy,'" 258.

136   John Coakley, "National Identity and the 'Kohn Dichotomy,'" 253.

137   Shabtai Teveth, *Ben-Gurion: The Burning Ground, 1886–1948* (Houghton Mifflin, 1987), 509–19.

138   Jewish Telegraphic Agency, "Latest Cable Dispatches" (December 23, 1935), 3, pdfs.jta.org/1935/1935-12-23_116. pdf?_ga=2.104777024.154488845.1602099804-1902729271.1598757350.

139   Quoted in Victor Kattan, "The Failure to Establish Democracy in Palestine: From the British Mandate to the Present Times," Jadaliyya, 2 April 2011, www.jadaliyya.com/Details/23862.

140   Quoted in Victor Kattan, "The Failure to Establish Democracy in Palestine."

141   Don Peretz, "Early State Policy towards the Arab Population, 1948–1955" in Laurence J. Silberstein, ed., *New Perspectives on Israeli History: The Early Years of the State* (New York University Press, 1991), 98.

142   "Basic Law: Israel - The Nation-State of the Jewish People." Unofficially translated by Susan Hattis Rolef, The Knesset, main.knesset.gov.il/EN/activity/Documents/BasicLawsPDF/BasicLawNationState.pdf.

143   Zeev Sternhell, *The Founding Myths of Israel: Nationalism, Socialism, and the Making of the Jewish State*, trans. David Maisel (Princeton University Press, 1998), 3.

144   Sternhell, *The Founding Myths of Israel*, 7.

145   Sternhell, *The Founding Myths of Israel*, 15.

146   Sternhell, *The Founding Myths of Israel*, 11.

147   Masha Gessen, *Where the Jews Aren't: The Sad and Absurd Story of Birobidzhan, Russia's Autonomous Region* (Nextbook/Schocken, 2016), 5–8.

148   Anny Wynchank, "In the Beginning Was a School: The Alliance Israélite Universelle and Its Legacy," *Jewish Affairs* (Chanukah 2013), www.sajbd.org/uploads/Articles/

Jewish-Affairs/Chanukah-2013.pdf, 25–32; Jonathan Frankel, "Jewish Politics and the Press: The 'Reception' of the *Alliance Israélite Universelle* (1860)," *Jewish History* 14 (2000): 29–50.

149   Gideon Shimoni, *The Zionist Ideology*, 63.

CHAPTER 3: "BALANCE" AND THE MANUFACTURE OF DOUBT

150   Quoted in Naomi Oreskes & Erik M. Conway, *Merchants of Doubt: How a Handful of Scientists Obscured the Truth on Issues from Tobacco Smoke to Global Warming* (Bloomsbury Press, 2010). A copy of the original memo can be found at www.industrydocuments.ucsf.edu/tobacco/docs/#id=rsdw0147.

151   Gary Bass, "Word Problem." *The New Yorker,* May 3, 2004.

152   Michel Foucault, "Truth and Power" in *Power/Knowledge: Selected Interviews & Other Writings 1972–1977*, ed. Colin Gordon (Pantheon, 1972), 131–33.

153   Charles King, *Gods of the Upper Air: How a Circle of Renegade Anthropologists Reinvented Race, Sex, and Gender in the Twentieth Century* (Doubleday, 2019).

154   Eric Alterman, "The Professors, The Press, The Think Tanks—And Their Problems." *Academe*, American Association of University Professors (May–June 2011).

155   Oreskes & Conway, *Merchants of Doubt*.

156   Ellen Willis, "Glossary for the Eighties" in *Beginning to See the Light: Pieces of a Decade* (Knopf, 1981), 145–46.

157   "At 81, Feminist Gloria Steinem Finds Herself Free of the 'Demands of Gender.'" Interview with Terry Gross, Fresh Air, National Public Radio, October 26, 2015, www.npr.org/2015/10/26/451862822/at-81-feminist-gloria-steinem-finds-herself-free-of-the-demands-of-gender.

158   Elissa Gootman, "Shelving of Panel on Mideast Roils School," *New York Times,* February 17, 2006, www.nytimes.com/2006/02/17/nyregion/shelving-of-panel-on-mideast-roils-school.html.

159   Byron Calame, "Picturing the Conflict: Perspective Versus Balance," *New York Times,* September 10, 2006, www.nytimes.com/2006/09/10/opinion/picturing-the-conflict-perspective-versus-balance.html.

160   Alan Dershowitz, "Brooklyn College Denies Equal Time to Pro-Israel Students," *Newsmax*, January 30, 2013, www.newsmax.com/alandershowitz/brooklyn-college-dbs-israel/2013/01/30/id/488151/.

161   Scott Jaschik, "Debate over panel at MLA raises issue of when balance matters," *Inside Higher Ed,* January 3, 2014, www.insidehighered.com/news/2014/01/03/debate-over-panel-mla-raises-issue-when-balance-matters.

162   Judy Frank, "WMass Jewish Voice for Peace denounces chancellor's BDS statement,"
       Amherst Bulletin, November 9, 2019, quoted in Jonathan Cook, *Mondoweiss,*
       November 12, 2019, "Israel is silencing the last voices trying to stop abuses against
       Palestinians," mondoweiss.net/2019/11/israel-is-silencing-the-last-voices-trying-to-
       stop-abuses-against-palestinians/; Subbaswamy, Kumble. "Statement of University of
       Massachusetts Amherst Chancellor Kumble Subbaswamy," University of Massachusetts
       News & Media Relations, October 21, 2019, accessed December 31, 2024, www.umass.
       edu/newsoffice/article/statement-university-massachusetts-amherst.

163   Barnabe F. Geisweiller, "The Creed of Objectivity and *The New York Times.*" *Truthout,*
       April 6, 2010, truthout.org/articles/the-creed-of-objectivity-and-the-new-york-
       times/; Peter Hart, "Former Times Gaza Reporter on Balance, Bronner and More,"
       Fairness and Accuracy in Reporting Blog, July 2, 2010, fair.org/uncategorized/
       former-times-gaza-reporter-on-balance-bronner-and-more/.

164   Francine Prose, "Texas schools are being told to teach 'opposing views' of the Holocaust.
       Why?" *Guardian,* October 19, 2021, www.theguardian.com/commentisfree/2021/
       oct/19/texas-holocaust-curriculum-schools-hb-3979.

165   Edwin Black, *The Transfer Agreement: The Untold Story of the Secret Pact Between the
       Third Reich and Jewish Palestine* (Macmillan, 1984); Rosalyn Baxandall, Linda Gordon,
       and Susan Reverby, eds. *America's Working Women: A Documentary History—1600 to
       the Present* (Vintage Books, 1976): 184–85; Anna Clark, "Magazine censored, editor
       dropped for covering Henry Ford's anti-Semitic newspaper," *Columbia Journalism Review*
       (February 4, 2019), www.cjr.org/united_states_project/dearborn-historian-indepen-
       dent-henry-ford.php.

166   Lorenzo Veracini, "Introducing Settler Colonial Studies." *Settler Colonial* Studies 1, no. 1
       (2011).

167   Patrick Wolfe, "Settler colonialism and the elimination of the native," *Journal of Genocide
       Research* 8, no. 4 (December 2006): 387–409).

168   See, for example, Steven Salaita, *The Holy Land in Transit: Colonialism and the Quest
       for Canaan* (Syracuse University Press, 2006); Salaita, *Inter/Nationalism: Decolonizing
       Native America and Palestine* (University of Minnesota Press, 2016); Nadia Abu El-Haj,
       "Reflection on Archeology and Israeli Settler-Nationhood," *Radical History Review,* Issue
       86 (Spring 2003): 149–163; John Collins, *Global Palestine* (Hurst & Co., 2011); Wolfe,
       "Settler colonialism and the elimination of the native"; David Lloyd, "Settler Colonialism
       and the State of Exception: The Example of Palestine/Israel." *Settler Colonial Studies* 2,
       no. 1 (2012): 59–80; Robert Warrior, "Canaanites, Cowboys, and Indians: Deliverance,
       Conquest, and Liberation Theology Today," *Christianity and Crisis,* September 11, 1989,
       reprinted at www.rmselca.org/sites/rmselca.org/files/media/canaanites_cowboys_and_
       indians.pdf; Robert Warrior with Jean M. O'Brien, "Introduction: Indigeneity, Palestine,
       and Israel," *Journal of the Native American and Indigenous Studies Association* (NAIS)1,
       no. 2 (Fall 2014): 105; Gershon Shafir, "Settler Citizenship in the Jewish Colonization
       of Palestine." *Settler Colonialism in the Twentieth Century,* eds. Caroline Elkins and Susan

Pedersen (Routledge, 2005), 41–57; Lana Tatour, "Citizenship as Domination: Settler Colonialism and the Making of Palestinian Citizenship in Israel," *Arab Studies Journal* 27, no. 2 (December 3, 2019): 8–39; Brenna Bhandar and Rafeef Ziadah, "Acts and Omissions: Framing Settler Colonialism in Palestine Studies," Jadaliyya, Jan. 14, 2016. www.jadaliyya.com/Details/32857.

169   Oreskes & Conway, *Merchants of Doubt*, 19.

170   Oreskes & Conway, *Merchants of Doubt*, 34.

171   Oreskes & Conway, *Merchants of Doubt*, 164.

172   Quoted in Oreskes & Conway, *Merchants of Doubt*, 149.

173   Oreskes & Conway, *Merchants of Doubt*, 179 (italics added).

174   Oreskes & Conway, *Merchants of Doubt*, 214–15.

175   Oreskes & Conway, *Merchants of Doubt*, 267.

176   John Bacon, "Lawyer: NYPD officer Daniel Pantaleo a 'scapegoat' in Eric Garner's death," *USA Today*, May 13, 2019, www.usatoday.com/story/news/nation/2019/05/13/eric-garners-death-officer-daniel-pantaleo-faces-hearing-monday/1186492001/.

177   Michael R. Sisak, "NYPD officer says he inflated charge against Eric Garner," Associated Press, May 22, 2019, accessed January 1, 2025, apnews.com/general-news-ce589240fb884eceab7eaba2bfdff9e2.

178   Jerry Markon and Tom Hamburger, "Unorthodox police procedures emerge in grand jury documents," *Washington Post*, November 25, 2014, www.washingtonpost.com/politics/seemingly-unorthodox-police-procedures-emerge-in-grand-jury-documents/2014/11/25/48152574-74e0-11e4-bd1b-03009bd3e984_story.html.

179   Yali Corea-Levy, "Making Sense of Reasonable Doubt: Understanding Certainty, Doubt, and Rule-Based Bias Filtering." American University Criminal Law Brief 8, no. 1 (2012): 48–62.

180   Emanuella Grinberg, "Why police-involved shooting trials rarely end in convictions for officers." CNN.com, June 23, 2017, www.cnn.com/2017/06/23/us/police-deadly-force-trials/index.html; Nick Wing, "When Killer Cops Go On Trial, Their Fate Is Mostly In White Hands," *Huffington Post*, December 16, 2016. www.huffpost.com/entry/police-shooting-juries-race_n_584ebcdbe4b0e05aded4a110; Christopher Wright Durocher, "Seeking Jurors Willing to Hold Police Accountable," *American Constitution Society,* December 9, 2016, www.acslaw.org/expertforum/seeking-jurors-willing-to-hold-police-accountable/; German Lopez, "Cops are almost never prosecuted and convicted for use of force," *Vox*, August 13, 2016.

181   German Lopez. "Police can use deadly force if they merely perceive a threat." *Vox*, August 13, 2016 (italics added).

182 Naomi Klein, "Introduction: The End of Israeli Exceptionalism," in *The Goldstone Report: The Legacy of the Landmark Investigation of the Gaza Conflict*, eds. Adam Horowitz, Lizzy Ratner, and Philip Weiss (Nation Books, 2011), xiii.

183 See, for example, Karl Vick, "Goldstone Rubs off Tarnish, and Israel Basks," Time. com, April 3, 2011, accessed May 8, 2023, world.time.com/2011/04/03/goldstone-rubs-off-tarnish-and-israel-basks/; Barak Ravid, "Israel to Launch Campaign Urging UN to Retract Goldstone Report," *Haaretz,* April 3, 2011, accessed May 6, 2023, www.haaretz.com/2011-04-03/ty-article/israel-to-launch-campaign-urging-un-to-retract-goldstone-report/0000017f-dbb5-db22-a17f-ffb5a84d0000; Peter Hart, "The Goldstone Report's Non-Retraction Retraction," FAIR (Fairness and Accuracy in Reporting), June 1, 2011, accessed May 6, 2023, fair.org/extra/the-goldstone-report8217s-non-retraction-retraction/.

184 See, for example, Noura Erekat, Roundup on the Goldstone Controversy," *Jadaliyya,* April 13, 2011, accessed May 8, 2023, www.jadaliyya.com/Details/23887; Richard Falk, "The Goldstone Report without Goldstone," *Journal of Palestine Studies* 41, no. 1 (2011); Ilan Pappe, "Goldstone's shameful U-turn, *The Electronic Intifada,* April 4, 2011, accessed May 13, 2023 electronicintifada.net/content/goldstones-shameful-u-turn/9294; Adam Horowitz, "Goldstone op-ed praises Israeli investigation of Gaza war ccrimes, but UN committee paints a different picture, *Mondoweiss,* April 2, 2011, accessed May 9, 2023, mondoweiss.net/2011/04/goldstone-op-ed-praises-israeli-investigation-of-gaza-war-crimes-but-un-committee-paints-a-different-picture/.

185 Richard Goldstone, "Reconsidering the Goldstone Report on Israel and war crimes" (Opinion), *Washington Post,* April 1, 2011, accessed April 23, 2023, www. washingtonpost.com/opinions/reconsidering-the-goldstone-report-on-isra-el-and-war-crimes/2011/04/01/AFg111JC_story.html.

186 Hina Jilani, Christine Chinkin, and Desmond Travers, "Goldstone report: Statement issued by members of UN mission on Gaza war," *Guardian,* April 14, 2011, accessed May 26, 2023, www.theguardian.com/commentisfree/2011/apr/14/goldstone-report-statement-un-gaza.

187 B'Tselem, "Human rights groups in Israel in response to Goldstone Report: Israel Must Investigate 'Operation Cast Lead,' September 15, 2009, accessed May 6, 2023, www.btselem.org/press_releases/20090915, [The organizations endorsing this statement are: Association for Civil Rights in Israel, Adalah, Bimkom, B'Tselem, Gisha, HaMoked, Physicians for Human Rights-Israel, The Public Committee Against Torture in Israel and Yesh Din]; International Federation for Human Rights (FIDH), "Shielded From Accountability: Israel's Unwillingness to Investigate and Prosecute International Crimes, no. 572a (September, 2011), accessed May 6, 2023, www.fidh.org/IMG/pdf/report_justice_israel-final.pdf; United Nations Human Rights Council, "Committee following up on 'Goldstone Report' says investigations by Israel and de facto Gaza authorities inadequate," September

21, 2010, accessed May 6, 2023, www.ohchr.org/en/press-releases/2010/09/committee-following-goldstone-report-says-investigations-israel-and-de-facto.

188   Alan Dershowitz, "The Case Against the Goldstone Report: A Study in Evidentiary Bias," *Digital Access to Scholarship at Harvard,* Harvard Library, January 27, 2010, accessed May 9, 2023, dash.harvard.edu/bitstream/handle/1/3593975/DershowitzGoldstone.pdf.

189   Yousef Munayyer, "A History of Impunity" in *Midnight on the Mavi Marmara,* ed. Moustafa Bayoumi (Haymarket Books, 2010), 182.

190   Robert Fisk, "Massacre in sanctuary," *Independent,* 18 April, 1996, accessed June 10, 2023, www.independent.co.uk/news/massacre-in-sanctuary-1305571.html.

191   Major-General Franklin Van Kappen (Military Adviser), "Report dated 1 May 1996 of the Secretary-General's Military Adviser concerning the shelling of the United Nations compound at Qana on 18 April, 1996," accessed June 10, 2023, web.archive.org/web/20070520003524/http://domino.un.org/UNISPAL.NSF/0/62d5aa740c14293b8 5256324005179be?OpenDocument.

192   "Response to UN Secretary's Report on Kana Incident—09-May-96," Israel Ministry of Foreign Affairs, Communicated by Foreign Ministry Spokesman, Jerusalem, 9 May 1996, accessed June 10, 2023, web.archive.org/web/20121008045443/ www.mfa.gov.il/MFA/Terrorism-%20Obstacle%20to%20Peace/Terrorism%20from%20Lebanon-%20Hizbullah/RESPONSE%20TO%20UN%20SECRETARY-S%20REPORT%20ON%20KANA%20INCIDENT.

193   Zeena Saifi, Eliza Mackintosh, Celine Alkhaldi, Kareem Khadder, Katie Polglase, Gianluca Mozzofiore and Abeer Salman, "'They were shooting directly at the journalists': New evidence suggests Shireen Abu Akleh was killed in targeted attack by Israeli forces," CNN, May 26, 2022, accessed June 3, 2023, edition.cnn.com/2022/05/24/middleeast/shireen-abu-akleh-jenin-killing-investigation-cmd-intl/index.html.

194   "Justice for Shireen: The Israeli investigation—Part 1," The Take, podcast of Al Jazeera, 2 September, 2022, accessed June 5, 2023, www.aljazeera.com/podcasts/2022/9/2/justice-for-shireen-the-israeli-investigation-part-1.

195   B'Tselem, "The killing of Shireen Abu Akleh," 21 July 2022, accessed June 3, 2023, www.btselem.org/firearms/20220721_killing_of_shireen_abu_akleh.

196   Zeena Saifi et al., "They were shooting directly at the journalists."

197   IDF Editorian Team, "Final Conclusions of Shireen Abu Akleh Investigation," May 9, 2022, accessed June 17, 2023, www.idf.il/en/articles/2022/final-conclusions-of-shireen-abu-akleh-investigation/.

198   B'Tselem, "The killing of Shireen Abu Akleh."

199   Committee to Protect Journalists, "Deadly Pattern: 20 journalists died by Israeli military fire in 22 years. No one has been held accountable," May 9, 2023, cpj.org/reports/2023/05/deadly-pattern-20-journalists-died-by-israeli-military-fire-in-22-years-no-one-has-been-held-accountable/.

200 "Justice for Shireen: The American Investigation—Part 2," The Take, podcast of Al Jazeera, September 5, 2022, accessed June 5, 2023, www.aljazeera.com/podcasts/2022/9/5/justice-for-shireen-the-american-investigation-part-2.

201 Quoted in David Holthouse, "State of Denial," *Intelligence Report*, June 3 (2008, Summer Issue). *Southern Poverty Law Center*, www.splcenter.org/fighting-hate/intelligence-report/2008/state-denial.

202 Holthouse, "State of Denial."

203 Marc A. Mamigonian, "Academic Denial of the Armenian Genocide in American Scholarship: Denialism as Manufactured Controversy." *Genocide Studies International* 9, no. 1 (Spring 2015): 61–82, www.utpjournals.press/doi/abs/10.3138/gsi.9.1.04; John Kifner, "Armenian Genocide of 1915: An Overview," *New York Times*. August 11, 2014, archive.nytimes.com/www.nytimes.com/ref/timestopics/topics_armeniangenocide.html?mcubz=0.

204 Stanley Cohen, *States of Denial: Knowing About Atrocities and Suffering* (Polity, 2001), 244.

205 Marc A. Mamigonian, "Academic Denial of the Armenian Genocide," no. 9.

206 Shelley Murphy, "Suit Challenges How Armenian Genocide is Taught." *Boston Globe*, Oct. 28, 2005. www.boston.com/news/local/massachusetts/articles/2005/10/28/suit_challenges_how_armenian_genocide_is_taught/ (italics added).

207 Randal C. Archibold, "Armenian Furor Over PBS Plan For Debate," *New York Times*, February 25, 2006, www.nytimes.com/2006/02/25/arts/television/armenian-furor-over-pbs-plan-for-debate.html.

208 Marc A. Mamigonian, "Academic Denial of the Armenian Genocide," 69.

209 Amnesty International, *Turkey: Article 301: How the Law on "Denigrating Turkishness" is an Insult to Free Expression*, January 3, 2006, EUR 44/003/2006. www.refworld.org/docid/44c611504.html.

210 Among them are www.lethistorydecide.org and www.FactCheckArmenia.com; in 2016 the latter advertised itself in skywriting over Manhattan (Sözeri). The website of the Turkish Coalition of America (www.tc-america.org) features, at the head of its "Issues and Information" page and just above the "List of Articles on the Turkish-Armenian Question," a lengthy piece by Justin McCarthy, a historian at the University of Louisville who has been characterized by numerous other scholars as a genocide denier. McCarthy makes great use of terms such as "Armenian-Muslim conflict," "two-sided conflict," and "two warring sides," and frames matters in the tradition of the official Turkish narrative, such as, "What must be considered by the serious historian is a simple question: 'Did the Ottoman Government carry out a plan to exterminate the Armenians?'— followed by paragraphs that each conclude in the incantatory refrain, "It was not genocide."

211 Walter Laqueur, *A History of Zionism* (Schocken Books, 2003), 584. Thanks to Haim Bresheeth-Zabner for drawing my attention to this passage in his book *An Army Like No Other* (Verso, 2020), 66.

212   Simha Flapan, "The Palestinian Exodus of 1948," *Journal of Palestine Studies* 4.

213   Walid Khalidi, "Why Did the Palestinians Leave, Revisited," *Journal of Palestine Studies* 34, no. 2 (Winter 2005): 43. "Why Did the Palestinians Leave?" originally published in *Middle East Forum,* American University of Beirut, 1959.

214   See, for example, Benny Morris, *The Birth of the Palestinian Refugee Problem Revisited* (Cambridge University Press, 2004); Simha Flapan, *The Birth of Israel: Myths and Realities* (Pantheon Books, 1987); Tom Segev, *A State at Any Cost: A Life of David Ben-Gurion*, trans. Haim Watzman (Farrar, Strauss & Giroux, 2019); Ilan Pappe, *The Ethnic Cleansing of Palestine* (Oneworld Publications Ltd, 2006).

215   Khalidi, "Why Did the Palestinians Leave, Revisited," 44.

216   Khalidi, "Why Did the Palestinians Leave, Revisited," 45.

217   Khalidi, "Why Did the Palestinians Leave, Revisited," 49.

218   Khalidi, "Why Did the Palestinians Leave, Revisited," 49.

219   Benny Morris, *The Birth of the Palestinian Refugee Problem Revisited*, 169.

220   Erskine Childers, "The Other Exodus," the *Spectator*, May 12, 1961, archive.spectator. co.uk/article/12th-may-1961/8/the-other-exodus, is a model of how one can take such investigation into one's own hands when stymied by "competing narratives." Describing his process of inquiry, he writes, for example, "Examining every official Israeli statement about the Arab exodus, I was struck by the fact that no primary evidence of evacuation orders were ever produced. The charge, Israel claimed, was 'documented'; but where were the documents? There had allegedly been Arab radio broadcasts ordering the evacuation; but no dates, names of stations, or texts of messages were ever cited. In Israel in 1958, as a guest of the Foreign Office and therefore doubly hopeful of serious assistance, I asked to be shown the proofs, I was assured they existed, and was promised them. None had been offered when I left, but I was again assured. I asked to have the material sent on to me. I am still waiting."

221   Anti-Defamation League, "Palestinian Refugees," ADL website, published September 1, 2016, accessed Feb. 13, 2022, www.adl.org/resources/glossary-term/palestinian-refugees.

222   Ben-Dror Yemini, "What About the Jewish Nakba?, BESA, May 31, 2009, accessed 13 February, 2022, besacenter.org/what-about-the-jewish-nakba/.

223   Avi Shilon, "It's time to stop keeping score: Both sides committed massacres in 1948," *Haaretz*, February 10, 2022, www.haaretz.com/opinion/.premium-it-s-time-to-stop-keeping-score-both-sides-committed-massacres-in-1948-1.10602748.

224   Glenn Kessler, "The dueling histories in the debate over 'historic Palestine,'" *Washington Post*, May 28, 2021, www.washingtonpost.com/politics/2021/05/28/dueling-histories-debate-over-historic-palestine/.

225   Moshe Arens, "The Nakba—perpetuating a lie," *Haaretz,* May 19, 2014, www.haaretz.com/opinion/.premium-the-nakba-perpetuating-a-lie-1.5248690.

226 Anne Irfan, "Nakba Denial and Other Attacks on the Palestinian Refugee Identity," Institute for Palestine Studies, December 15, 2021, www.palestine-studies.org/en/ node/1652248 (Blog).

227 Hagar Shezaf, "Burying the Nakba: How Israel systematically hides evidence of 1948 expulsion of Arabs," *Haaretz*, July 5, 2019, www.haaretz.com/israel-news/.premium. MAGAZINE-how-israel-systematically-hides-evidence-of-1948-expulsion-of- arabs-1.7435103.

228 Ilan Pappe, "Israel's latest attempt to erase Palestine," the *Electronic Intifada*, July 25, 2019, electronicintifada.net/content/israels-latest-attempt-erase-palestine/27941.

229 Justin McCarthy, "Let Historians Decide on So-called Genocide," *Turkish Daily News*, April 11, 2001. Located on site of Turkish Coalition of America, www.tc-america.org/ issues-information/armenian-issue/historians-decide-genocide-361.htm.

230 "The Trump Presidency" on *Last Week Tonight with John Oliver*, HBO, YouTube, November 13, 2017. https://www.youtube.com/watch?v=1ZAPwfrtAFY.

CHAPTER 4: "THE PICTURES IN OUR HEADS" AND THE MANUFACTURE OF DENIAL

231 Sharif Nashashibi, "Israel: A State of Denial," Al Jazeera, April 28, 2015, www.aljazeera. com/opinions/2015/4/28/israel-a-state-of-denial.

232 Eitan Bronstein, "The Nakba: Something That Did Not Occur (Although It Had to Occur)," *Zochrot*, August 2009, www.zochrot.org/publication_articles/view/50644/ en?The_Nakba_Something_That_Did_Not_Occur__Although_It_Had_to_Occur.

233 Quoted in Alasdair Soussi, "The mixed legacy of Golda Meir, Israel's first female PM," Al Jazeera, March 18, 2019, www.aljazeera.com/features/2019/3/18/the-mixed-legacy- of-golda-meir-israels-first-female-pm.

234 Morton A. Klein, "There Is No 'Occupation,'" *Jewish Journal*, May 16, 2002, jewishjournal.com/commentary/opinion/5989/.

235 Quoted in Mairav Zonszein, "Netanyahu to Gaza Flotilla: Did you mean to sail to Syria?," *+972 Magazine* (June 28, 2015), www.972mag.com/ netanyahu-to-gaza-flotilla-didnt-you-mean-to-sail-to-syria/.

236 Walter Rugaber, "The Watergate Mystery," *New York Times*, Nov. 1, 1972. www.nytimes. com/1972/11/01/archives/the-watergate-mystery-the-watergate-mystery-after-19- weeks-of.html.

237 Neil Macfarquhar, "Muslim Charity Seeks Dismissal of Charges of Terrorism," *New York Times*, December 12, 2006, www.nytimes.com/2006/12/12/washington/muslim-chari- ty-seeks-dismissal-of-charges-of-terrorism.html.

238 Quoted in Soussi, "The mixed legacy of Golda Meir."

239 E.R.F.S., "A Talk with Golda Meir," *New York Times*, August 27, 1972, www.nytimes.com/1972/08/27/archives/a-talk-with-golda-meir.html.

240 Dan Froomkin, "Anatomy of a Non-Denial Denial," the *Intercept,* September 26, 2014. theintercept.com/2014/09/26/deception-heart-john-brennans-non-denial-denial/.

241 Avner Cohen and Marvin Miller, "Bringing Israel's Bomb Out of the Basement: Has Nuclear Ambiguity Outlived Its Shelf Life?", *Foreign Affairs* 89, no. 5 (Sept/Oct 2010): 30–31.

242 Avner Cohen, *Israel and the Bomb* (Columbia University Press, 1998), 89.

243 Cohen, *Israel and the Bomb*, 85.

244 Cohen, *Israel and the Bomb*, 86.

245 Cohen, *Israel and the Bomb*, 91.

246 Cohen, *Israel and the Bomb*, 177.

247 Cohen, *Israel and the Bomb*, 188.

248 Cohen, *Israel and the Bomb*, 316-19.

249 Avner Cohen and William Burr, "Israel crosses the threshold," *Bulletin of the Atomic Scientists* 62, no. 3 (May/June 2006): 28, DOI: 10.1080/00963402.2006.11460984.

250 "Obama Ducks Question on Israeli Nukes," *Democracy Now,* February 10, 2009, www.democracynow.org/2009/2/10/headlines/obama_ducks_question_on_israeli_nukes.

251 Carol Cohn, "Sex and Death and the Rational World of Defense Intellectuals," in *Women on War,* ed. Daniela Gioseffi (Touchstone, 1988), 84.

252 Cohn, "Sex and Death," 88.

253 Cohn, "Sex and Death," 91.

254 Cohn, "Sex and Death," 88–89.

255 Cohn, "Sex and Death," 84.

256 Cohn, "Sex and Death," 97.

257 Greg Myre, "In Mideast Conflict, a War of Euphemisms," *Los Angeles Times,* August 25, 2002, www.latimes.com/archives/la-xpm-2002-aug-25-adfg-midspeak25-story.html.

258 Haim Bresheet-Zabner, *An Army Like No Other: How the Israeli Defense Forces Made a Nation* (Verso, 2020), 273.

259 Bresheet-Zabner, *An Army Like No Other,* 321.

260 Bresheet-Zabner, *An Army Like No Other,* 325–6.

261 Eyal Weizman, "The Art of War," *Frieze* 99, May 6 (2006), www.frieze.com/article/art-war.

262 "Media reporting on Palestine 2021," published by the Center for Media Monitoring (CfMM), quoted in Ahmet Gurhan Kartal, "UK report highlights 'euphemism' for Israeli aggression in media coverage," Anadolu Agency, May 27, 2021, www.aa.com.tr/en/europe/uk-report-highlights-euphemism-for-israeli-aggression-in-media-coverage/2255906.

263   Stanley Cohen, *States of Denial: Knowing About Atrocities and Suffering* (Polity, 2015), 137.

264   John Collins and Ross Glover, eds., *Collateral Language: A User's Guide to America's New War* (New York University Press, 2002).

265   Philip T. Neisser, "Targets," in Collins & Glover, *Collateral Language,* 144.

266   Laura J. Rediehs, "Evil," in Collins & Glover, *Collateral Language*, 65.

267   Rediehs, "Evil," 66.

268   "Israel's 'terrorism' designation an unjustified attack on Palestinian civil society—Bachelet," United Nations Human Rights, Office of the High Commissioner, n/d [website], accessed February 25, 2022, www.ohchr.org/EN/NewsEvents/Pages/DisplayNews. aspx?NewsID=27708&LangID=E.

269   "Israel/Palestine: Designation of Palestinian Rights Groups as Terrorist; Attack on the Human Rights Movement," Human Rights Watch News, October 22, 2021, accessed February 25 2022, www.hrw.org/news/2021/10/22/israel/palestine-designation-palestinian-rights-groups-terrorists.

270   James North, "The 'NYTimes' blackout of the Amnesty 'apartheid' report continues," *Mondoweiss,* February 18, 2022, mondoweiss.net/2022/02/the-nytimes-blackout-of-the-amnesty-apartheid-report-is-in-its-18th-day/.

271   Morton A. Klein and Liz Berney,"ZOA: U.S Shouldn't Call PFLP Front Groups 'Human Rights' Groups; Join Israel & Designate them Terrorist Groups," Zionist Organization of America [press release/website], Oct. 26, 2021; zoa.org/2021/10/10444214-zoa-u-s-shouldnt-call-pflp-front-groups-human-rights-groups-join-israel-designate-them-terrorist-groups/.

272   "Israel's 'terrorism' designation an unjustified attack," OHCHR.

273   Walter Lippmann, *Liberty and the News* (BN Publishing, 2007 [1920]).

274   Walter Lippmann, *Public Opinion* (The Free Press, 1922), 3–20.

275   Lippmann, *Public Opinion,* 8–9, 16.

276   Lippmann, *Public Opinion,* 59.

277   Reporters Without Borders, "Region performs poorly, Israel nose-dives," October 20, 2009, updated on January 25, 2016, rsf.org/en/middle-east-north-africa-0.

278   Rachel Shabi, "Special spin body gets media on message, says Israel," *Guardian,* January 1, 2009, www.theguardian.com/world/2009/jan/02/israel-palestine-pr-spin.

279   Rachel Shabi, "Winning the Media War," *Guardian,* January 10, 2009, www.theguardian. com/commentisfree/2009/jan/10/gaza-israel-media.

280   Chris McGeal, "Ban on foreign journalists skews coverage of conflict," *Guardian,* January 9, 2009, www.theguardian.com/world/2009/jan/10/gaza-israel-reporters-foreign-journalists.

281   Haviv Rettig Gur, "Coordination is putting Israel ahead in the media war," *Jerusalem Post,* December 30, 2008, www.jpost.com/international/coordination-is-putting-israel-ahead-in-the-media-war.

282   Foreign Press Assocation, "Statements 2008," December 28 and December 29, 2008, www.fpa.org.il/?categoryId=90291.

283   Human Rights Watch, "Israel: Allow Media and Rights Monitors Access to Gaza," January 5, 2009, www.hrw.org/news/2009/01/05/israel-allow-media-and-rights-monitors-access-gaza.

284   Human Rights Watch, "Israel: Allow Media."

285   Human Rights Watch, "Israel: Allow Media."

286   Peter Lagerquist, "Shooting Gaza: Photographers, Photographs, and the Unbearable Lightness of War," *Journal of Palestine Studies* 38, no. 3 (2009): 87–88.

287   Robert Fisk, "Keeping out the cameras and reporters simply doesn't work," *Independent,* January 5, 2009, www.independent.co.uk/voices/commentators/fisk/robert-fisk-keeping-out-the-cameras-and-reporters-simply-doesn-t-work-1225800.html.

288   Anti-Defamation League, "Key talking points on Israel's operation in Gaza, Washington, N.D." *Journal of Palestine Studies* 38, no.3 (2009): 356–357, doi.org/10.1525/jps.2009. XXXVIII.3.356.

289   "Israel: Toxic Environment." Reporters Without Borders, *World Press Freedom Index,* 2021, rsf.org/en/Israel.

290   Reporters Without Borders, "Israel's arguments for denying foreign reporters access to Gaza are spurious," May 19, 2021, rsf.org/en/news/israels-arguments-denying-foreign-reporters-access-gaza-are-spurious.

291   Amnesty International, "Israel and the Occupied Territories, Shielded from scrutiny: IDF violations in Jenin and Nablus," November 2002, 2, www.amnesty.org/en/wp-content/uploads/2021/10/mde151432002en.pdf.

292   Amnesty International, Shielded from Scrutiny," 3.

293   Amnesty International, "Shielded from Scrutiny," 4.

294   "Israel travel bans on Palestine journalists condemned by rights groups," *Middle East Monitor,* December 8, 2021, www.middleeastmonitor.com/20211208-israel-travel-bans-on-palestine-journalists-condemned-by-rights-groups/.

295   International Federation of Journalists, "Intimidation and Violence Against Palestinian Journalists Must End Now" (press release), July 2, 2014, www.ifj.org/media-centre/news/detail/category/press-releases/article/intimidation-and-violence-against-palestinian-journalists-must-end-now.html.

296   Noga Tarnopolsky and Rushdi Abu Alouf, "Journalist or Terrorist? Palestinian's Death at Gaza border a year ago still unresolved," *Los Angeles Times,* April 2, 2019, www.latimes.com/world/middleeast/la-fg-israel-gaza-yasser-murtaja-20190330-story.html;

"Israel to investigate killing of Palestinian journalist," *BBC News,* April 7, 2018, www.bbc.com/news/world-middle-east-43683184.

297 International Press Institute, "Patriotism, Pressure and Press Freedom: How Israeli and Palestinian Media Cover the Conflict from Inside," Report on IPI Mission to Israel, the West Bank & Gaza, February 12-19, 2003, 7–8, ipi.media/wp-content/uploads/2016/12/Patriotism_Pressure_and_Press_Freedom_IPI_Report.pdf.

298 Reporters Without Borders, "Destruction of Voice of Palestine's building. Reporters without Borders indignant at that new act of war against Palestinian media," January 19, 2002, rsf.org/en/destruction-voice-palestines-building-reporters-without-borders-indignant-new-act-war-against.

299 "Reporters Without Borders, "Israeli air strike destroys Turkish news agency's Gaza City Bureau," May 7, 2019, rsf.org/en/news/israeli-air-strike-destroys-turkish-news-agencys-gaza-city-bureau.

300 "Israel's attack on a press building in Gaza draws condemnations," *New York Times,* May 16, 2021, www.nytimes.com/2021/05/16/world/middleeast/israel-gaza-associated-press.html.

301 "'Silence the story': Israeli bombing of media offices condemned," Al Jazeera, May 15, 2021, www.aljazeera.com/news/2021/5/15/silence-the-story-israeli-strike-on-media-offices-gaza-condemned.

302 "Al Jazeera strongly condemns Israel's destruction of Gaza offices," Al Jazeera, May 15, 2021, www.aljazeera.com/news/2021/5/15/al-jazeera-strongly-condemns-israels-destruction-of-gaza-offices.

303 Shrouq Aila and Anna Therese Days, "Israel Destroyed Offices of More than 20 Palestinian Media Outlets in Gaza," the *Intercept,* May 18, 2021, theintercept.com/2021/05/18/gaza-journalists-israel-palestine-attacks/.

304 Aila and Days, "Israel Destroyed Offices."

305 Emerson T. Brooking and Eliza Campbell, "How to End Israel's Digital Occupation," *Foreign Policy,* December 3, 2021, foreignpolicy.com/2021/12/03/palestinian-israeli-occupation-social-media-censorship-facebook-silicon-valley/.

306 Palestine Legal and the Center for Constitutional Rights, "The Palestine Exception to Free Speech," 2015, 17, static1.squarespace.com/static/548748b1e4b-083fc03ebf70e/t/560b0bcee4b016db196d664b/1443564494090/Palestine+Exception+Report+Final.pdf.

307 Oded Yaron, "Israel buys social media monitoring system that can 'plant ideas' in online discourse," *Haaretz,* April 1, 2017, www.haaretz.com/israel-news/.premium-israel-buys-social-media-monitoring-system-that-can-plant-ideas-1.5454695.

308 Brooking & Campbell, "How to End."

309 Human Rights Watch, "Israel/Palestine: Facebook Censors Discussion of Rights Issues," October 8, 2021, www.hrw.org/news/2021/10/08/israel/palestine-facebook-censors-discussion-rights-issues.

310 Human Rights Watch, "Israel/Palestine: Facebook Censors Discussion of Rights Issues."

311 "Gantz: Extremists spread misinformation on Facebook and TikTok," *Jerusalem Post,* May 15, 2021, www.jpost.com/israel-news/gantz-extremists-spread-misinformation-on-facebook-and-tiktok-668230.

312 Yoni Kempinski, "Benny Gantz to Facebook and TikTok executives: You must take action," Israel National News, May 14, 2021, www.israelnationalnews.com/news/306224.

313 Usaid Siddiqui and Radmilla Suleymanova, "Israel, social media groups cooperating against Palestinians: NGO," Al Jazeera, May 21, 2021, www.aljazeera.com/news/2021/5/21/close-cooperation-between-israel-and-social-media-companies-ngo.

314 Brooking & Campbell, "How to End."

315 Adi Kuntsman and Rebecca L. Stein, "Another War Zone: Social Media in the Israeli-Palestinian Conflict," Middle East Research and Information Project, September 20, 2010, merip.org/2010/09/another-war-zone/.

316 Diana Allan and Curtis Brown, "The *Mavi Marmara* at the Frontlines of Web 2.0," *Journal of Palestine Studies* XL, no. 1 (Autumn 2010): 63.

317 Allan and Brown, "The Mavi Marmara at the Frontlines of Web. 2.0," 64.

318 Allan and Brown, "The Mavi Marmara at the Frontlines of Web. 2.0," 66. For the quote about the "team of Wikipedians," the authors cite Hasbara Fellowships Newsletter, IsraelActivism.com: The Official Website of Hasbara Fellowships, May 31, 2007, They also explain in a footnote that "'Hasbara-bots' is a slang term for individuals trained—by the Foreign Ministry's 'Internet Warfare Team,' by Hasbara Fellowships, or similar organizations—to disseminate pro-Israeli propaganda in online comment threads, in university-lecture Q&S session, on Wikipedia, and so on," 77.

319 Allan and Brown, "The Mavi Marmara at the Frontlines of Web. 2.0," 70.

320 Allan and Brown, "The Mavi Marmara at the Frontlines of Web. 2.0," 73.

321 Maysoon Zayid, "Google 'Palestine'—It Exists, And So Do Palestinians," the *Daily Beast,* June 4, 2013, updated July 11, 2017, www.thedailybeast.com/google-palestineit-exists-and-so-do-palestinians.

322 Nayeli Lomeli, "Fact Check: Google does not have a Palestine label on its maps," *USA Today,* May 21, 2021, updated May 22, 2021, www.usatoday.com/story/news/factcheck/2021/05/21/fact-check-google-maps-does-not-label-palestine/5145256001/.

323 Tom Suarez, "Palestinian cities are ghost towns between settlements, on Google Maps," *Mondoweiss,* June 3, 2019, mondoweiss.net/2019/06/palestinian-between-settlements/.

324 Reporters Without Borders, "WhatsApp blocks accounts of at least seven Gaza Strip journalists," June 3, 2021, updated June 7, 2021, rsf.org/en/news/whatsapp-blocks-accounts-least-seven-gaza-strip-journalists.

325 Louise Matsakis, "Venmo is halting some payments referring to Palestine," Rest of World, May 18, 2021, restofworld.org/2021/venmo-palestinian-relief/#:~:text=But%20a%20number%20of%20Venmo%20users%20have%20discovered,that%20include%20the%20words%20"%20Palestine%20Relief%20fund."

326 Omar Zahzah, "Social media giants repress Palestinian content," The Electronic Intifada, March 29, 2022, electronicintifada.net/content/social-media-giants-repress-palestinian-content/35096.

327 Amal Nazzal, "YouTube's Violation of Palestinian Digital Rights: What Needs to be Done," Al Shabaka, The Palestinian Policy Network, December 27, 2020, al-shabaka.org/briefs/youtubes-violation-of-palestinian-digital-rights-what-needs-to-be-done/.

328 Nazzal, "YouTube's Violation of Palestinian Digital Rights."

329 Nazzal, "YouTube's Violation of Palestinian Digital Rights."

330 Figures are from the "Report of the Independent Commission of Inquiry on the 2014 Gaza Conflict," United Nations Office for the Coordination of Humanitarian Affairs (OCHA), June 23, 2015, www.ochaopt.org/content/key-figures-2014-hostilities. .

331 Israel Defense Forces @IDF, Twitter, twitter.com/IDF/status/1393378525890158593

332 Peter Hart, "Why ABC Thought Suffering Palestinians Were Israelis," FAIR, July 10, 2014, fair.org/home/why-abc-thought-suffering-palestinians-were-israelis/.

333 Ella Lee, "Fact check: Photo shows airstrike in Gaza Strip, not Russian invasion of Ukraine," USA Today, February 24, 2022, www.usatoday.com/story/news/factcheck/2022/02/24/fact-check-gaza-strip-not-ukraine-pictured-explosion-photo/6922317001/.

CHAPTER 5: JEWISH NATIONALISM AND THE MANUFACTURE OF CONSENT

334 In Promises and Betrayals: Britain and the Struggle for the Holy Land, Dir. Arense Kvaale, YouTube, 2015. www.youtube.com/watch?v=Xo6YRCcajXM.

335 Mark Crispin Miller, "Introduction" in Propaganda by Edward Bernays (Ig Publishing, 1928), 11.

336 Edward Bernays, "The Engineering of Consent," The Annals of the American Academy of Political and Social Science, Vol. 250, Issue 1: 147.

337 Edward Bernays, Propaganda (Ig Publishing, 1928), 37.

338 Walter Lippmann, Public Opinion (The Free Press, 1922), 158.

339   Edward S. Herman and Noam Chomsky, *Manufacturing Consent: The Political Economy of the Mass Media* (Pantheon, 2002).

340   Quoted in Amnon Rubinstein, *From Herzl to Rabin: The Changing Image of Zionism* (Holmes & Meier, 2000), 10.

341   Rubinstein, *From Herzl to Rabin*, 11.

342   Quoted in Piterberg, Gabriel. *The Returns of Zionism: Myths, Politics and Scholarship in Israel* (Verso, 2008), 98.

343   Piterberg, *The Returns of Zionism*, 98.

344   Eli Kavon, "When Zionism Feared Yiddish," *Jerusalem Post*, May 11, 2014, www.jpost.com/opinion/op-ed-contributors/when-zionism-feared-yiddish-351939.

345   Rubinstein, *From Herzl to Rabin*, 11.

346   Lorenzo Veracini, "Israel-Palestine Through a Settler-colonial Studies Lens," *Interventions: International Journal of Postcolonial Studies*, 21, no. 4 (2019): 577, 575.

347   Veracini, "Israel-Palestine Through a Settler-colonial Studies Lens," 578.

348   David Day, *Conquest: How Societies Overwhelm Others* (Oxford University Press, 2008), 132–5.

349   Day, *Conquest*, 137–9.

350   Day, *Conquest*, 140–1.

351   Anita Shapira, "Ben-Gurion and the Bible: The Forging of an Historical Narrative?" *Middle Eastern Studies* 33, no. 4 (1997): 646–7. (Note: "Eretz Israel, or "Eretz Yisrael," is the Hebrew term favored by Zionists for "Land of Israel.")

352   Quoted in Shapira, "Ben-Gurion and the Bible," 651.

353   Quoted in Gideon Shimoni, *The Zionist Ideology* (Brandeis University Press, 1995), 387.

354   Nur Masalha, *The Bible and Zionism: Invented Traditions, Archaeology and Post-Colonialism in Israel-Palestine* (Zed Books, 2007), 54.

355   Masalha, *The Bible and Zionism*, 24, 28.

356   Masalha, *The Bible and Zionism*, 71.

357   Masalha, *The Bible and Zionism*, 71; Ilan Pappe, *The Bible in the Service of Zionism"* in *History, Archaeology and the Bible Forty Years After "Historicity," Changing Perspectives 6*, eds. Ingrid Hjelm and Thomas L. Thompson (Routledge, 2016): 211.

358   Quoted in Shapira, "Ben-Gurion and the Bible," 658.

359   Shapira, "Ben-Gurion and the Bible," 659.

360   Quoted in Shimoni, *The Zionist Ideology*, 385.

361   Masalha, *The Bible and Zionism*, 71.

362 Michael Prior, "The Moral Problem of the Land Traditions in the Bible" in *Western Scholarship and the History of Palestine*, ed. Michael Prior (Melinsende, 1998), 68.

363 Thomas L. Thompson, "Hidden Histories and the Problem of Ethnicity in Palestine" in *Western Scholarship and the History of Palestine*, ed. Prior, 34–5.

364 Quoted in Masalha, *The Bible and Zionism,* 50.

365 Moshe Dayan, *Living with the Bible* (William Morrow & Co., 1978), 6.

366 Dayan, *Living with the Bible,* 7.

367 Pappe, "The Bible in the Service of Zionism," 205. The source of the quote may have been Amnon Raz-Karkotzskin, who published an article in Hebrew in 2005 called "There is No God, But He Promised Us the Land" in *Mitaam,* an Israeli journal of literature and radical political thought. (See Edo Konrad, "Every day is land day, on both sides of the Green Line," +972, March 30, 2015, www.972mag.com/every-day-is-land-day-on-both-sides-of-the-green-line/.)

368 Moshe Machover, "Messianic Zionism: The Ass and the Red Heifer," in *Monthly Review,* February 1, 2020, monthlyreview.org/2020/02/01/messianic-zionism/.

369 Ben Evansky, "Israel's U.N. Ambassador gives the U.N. Security Council a history lesson on the Bible," *Fox News,* April 30, 2019, www.foxnews.com/world/israels-u-n-ambassador-gives-the-u-n-security-council-a-history-lesson-on-the-bible; *Jerusalem Post Staff,* "Israeli ambassador's 'Bible speech' at U.N. goes viral," May 18, 2019, www.jpost.com/diaspora/israeli-ambassadors-bible-speech-at-un-goes-viral-589986; Jonathan Ofir, "Israel's UN Ambassador waves a bible at the Security Council," *Mondoweiss,* May 2, 2019, mondoweiss.net/2019/05/israels-ambassador-security/.

370 Benjamin Beit-Hallahmi of Haifa University, 1992, quoted in Masalha, *The Bible and Zionism,* 21.

371 Masalha, *The Bible and Zionism,* 30–31.

372 Steven Salaita, *The Holy Land in Transit: Colonialism and the Quest for Canaan,* (Syracuse University Press, 2006), 55.

373 Quoted in Salaita, *The Holy Land in Transit,* 57.

374 Steven Salaita, *Inter/Nationalism: Decolonizing Native America and Palestine* (University of Minnesota Press, 2016), 161. (Note that "Naqab" is the Arabic name for what is "Negev" in Hebrew.)

375 Keith W. Whitelam, "Western Scholarship and the Silencing of Palestinian History" in *Western Scholarship and the History of Palestine*, ed. Prior, 18.

376 Edward Said, "Claims to the Holy Land and the Occupation of Palestine," YouTube, [name, date, and place of event unspecified], accessed December 21, 2024, www.youtube.com/watch?v=x2z7kEAy6mI.

377 Prior, "The Moral Problem of the Land Traditions in the Bible," 69.

378   Shlomo Sand, *The Invention of the Land of Israel*, (Verso, 2012), 15.

379   Michael Stanislawski, *Zionism: A Very Short Introduction*, (Oxford University Press, 2017), 5.

380   Anthony D. Smith, "The origins of nations," *Ethnic and Racial Studies,* Volume 12, No. 3 (July 1989).

381   Shlomo Sand, *The Invention of the Jewish People* (Verso 2009), 24–29.

382   Balashon, Hebrew Language Detective, "am, goy, leom and uma," June 13, 2016, www.balashon.com (blog).

383   Bernard Avishai, "Israel Passes a Law Stating What's Jewish About a 'Jewish and Democratic State.'" *The New Yorker*, 30 July 2018, www.newyorker.com/news/daily-comment/ israel-passes-a-law-stating-whats-jewish-about-a-jewish-and-democratic-state.

384   Sand, *Invention of the Jewish People,* 25.

385   Israeli Knesset, "Basic Law: Israel—the Nation State of the Jewish People," originally adopted 5778–2018. Noted at the top of the document: "This unofficial English translation of the basic law includes all the amendments adopted through May 1, 2022.... Special thanks to Dr. Sheila Hattis Rolef for the translation," accessed June 10, 2022, main. knesset.gov.il/EN/activity/Documents/BasicLawsPDF/BasicLawNationState.pdf. Note that "Basic Principles" are immediately established: "1. (a) The Land of Israel is the historical homeland of the Jewish People, in which the State of Israel was established. (b) The State of Israel is the nation state of the Jewish People in which it realizes its natural, cultural, religious and historical right to self-determination. (c) The realization of the right to national self- determination in the State of Israel is exclusive to the Jewish People."

386   Arthur Herzberg, "Introduction" in *The Zionist Idea: A Historical Analysis and Reader,* ed. Arthur Herzberg, (Atheneum, 1984), 32.

387   Rabbi Yehudah Alkalai, "The Third Redemption" in *The Zionist Idea,* 106.

388   Rabbi Zvi Hirsch Kalischer, quoted by Arthur Herzberg in *The Zionist Idea,* 109–10.

389   Moses Hess, "Rome and Jerusalem" in *The Zionist Idea,* 119.

390   Hess, "Rome and Jerusalem," 121–2.

391   Hess, "Rome and Jerusalem," 120.

392   Hess, "Rome and Jerusalem," 123–4.

393   Hess, "Rome and Jerusalem," 129–34.

394   Hess, "Rome and Jerusalem," 133–9.

395   Quoted in Walter Laqueur, *A History of Zionism: From the French Revolution to the Establishment of the State of Israel* (Schocken Books, 2003) [1972], 53.

396 Sand, *Invention of the Jewish People*, 72, 77; Laqueur, *A History of Zionism*, 54; Shimoni, *The Zionist Ideology*, 18, 57.

397 Sand, *Invention of the Jewish People*, 73.

398 Sand, *Invention of the Jewish People*, 72.

399 Shimoni, *The Zionist Ideology*, 32-8; Laqueur, *A History of Zionism*, 75–83.

400 Peretz Smolenskin, "It is Time to Plant," 1875-77, in *The Zionist Idea*, 146–7.

401 Moshe Leib Lilienblum, "Let Us Not Confuse the Issues," 1882, in *The Zionist Idea*, 170.

402 Moshe Leib Lilienblum, "The Way of Return," in *The Zionist Idea,* 170.

403 Lilienblum, "Let Us Not Confuse the Issues," and "The Future of Our People" in *The Zionist Idea*, 172–4.

404 Peretz Smolenskin, "Let Us Search Our Ways," 1881, in *The Zionist Idea,* 149.

405 Peretz Smolenskin, "The Haskalah of Berlin," 1883, in *The Zionist Idea*, 154.

406 Sand, *Invention of the Jewish People*, 85–8.

407 Sand, *Invention of the Jewish People*, 73.

408 Sand, *Invention of the Jewish People*, 88.

409 Shimoni, *The Zionist Ideology*, 19.

410 Sand, *Invention of the Jewish People*, 88.

411 Sand, *Invention of the Jewish People*, 89.

412 Simon Dubnow quoted in David Vital, *Zionism: The Formative Years* (Oxford University Press, 1982), 30.

413 Sand, *Invention of the Jewish People*, 88–95.

414 Michael Brenner, *Prophets of the Past: Interpreters of Jewish History*, trans. Steven Randall, (Princeton University Press, 2010 [first (German) edition, 2006]), 86.

415 Herzberg, "Introduction" in *The Zionist Idea,* 40.

416 Leo Pinsker, *Auto-Emancipation* in *The Zionist Idea*, 182.

417 Pinsker, *Auto-Emancipation*, 183.

418 Pinsker, *Auto-Emancipation*, 183–4, (italics added).

419 Pinsker, *Auto-Emancipation*, 184.

420 Pinsker, *Auto-Emancipation*, 184.

421 Pinsker, *Auto-Emancipation*, 192–6.

422 Pinsker, *Auto-Emancipation*, 194.

423 Pinsker, *Auto-Emancipation*, 197.

424 Hannah Arendt, *The Origins of Totalitarianism*, (Harcourt Brace & Company, New Edition with Added Prefaces, 1979), xi.

425 Arendt, *The Origins of Totalitarianism,* 7.

426 Ivan G. Marcus, "Jewish-Christian Symbiosis: The Culture of Early Ashkenaz" in *Cultures of the Jews: A New History,* ed. David Biale (Schocken Books, 2002), 458.

427 Sigmund Freud, *Group Psychology and the Analysis of the Ego,* (Bantam Books, 1960) [1921], 16.

428 Gustave Le Bon, *The Crowd,* (Penguin Books, 1977 [1895, 1960]), 29.

429 Le Bon, *The Crowd,* 32, 50.

430 Le Bon, *The Crowd,*114.

431 Gabriel Tarde, "The Public and the Crowd," in *On Communication and Social Influence: Selected Papers.* Ed. Terry N. Clark. (University of Chicago Press, 1969), 278.

432 Wilfred Trotter, *Instincts of the Herd in Peace and War,* (T. Fisher Unwin Ltd, 1916), 30.

433 Sigmund Freud, *Group Psychology and the Analysis of the Ego* (Bantam, 1960 [1921]).

434 Freud, *Group Psychology,* 41.

435 Freud, *Group Psychology,* 31.

436 Freud, *Group Psychology,* 59.

437 Amos Elon, *Herzl,* (Holt, Rinehart, & Winston, 1975), 223.

438 Elon, *Herzl,* 481.

439 Jacques Kornberg, "Theodore Herzl: A Reevaluation," *Journal of Modern History* 52, no. 2 (June 1980): 231.

440 Alex Bein, *Theodore Herzl: A Biography of the Founder of Modern Zionism* (Atheneum, 1970), 248.

441 Bein, *Theodore Herzl,* 519.

442 Louis Lipsky, "Introduction" in *The Jewish State*, Theodor Herzl (Dover Publications, 1988), 20.

443 Shlomo Avineri, *Herzl: Theodor Herzl and the Foundation of the Jewish State"* (Weidenfeld & Nicolson, 2013 [2008]), 84.

444 National Library of Israel, "Herzl, Zola, and Dreyfus," accessed September 21, 2022. web.nli.org.il/sites/NLI/English/digitallibrary/pages/viewer. aspx?presentorid=EDU_XML_ENG&docid=EDU_XML_ENG003220009.

445 Bein, *Theodore Herzl,* 116.

446 Bein, *Theodore Herzl,* 116.

447 Elon, *Herzl,* 128.

448   Laqueur, *A History of Zionism*, 401.

449   Avineri, *Herzl*, 66.

450   Avineri, *Herzl*, 71.

451   Henry J. Cohn, "Theodor Herzl's Conversion to Zionism," *Jewish Social Studies* 32, No. 2 (April 1970): 108.

452   Cohn, "Theodor Herzl's Conversion to Zionism."

453   Shlomo Avineri, "Herzl's Road to Zionism," *The American Jewish Year Book 1998*, 98: 10.

454   Cohn, "Theodor Herzl's Conversion to Zionism," 101.

455   Elon, 113.

456   Avineri, *Herzl*, 218–34.

457   Elon, 142.

458   Elon, 144.

459   Elon, 165.

460   Elon, 167, 140, 168, 147–8.

461   Theodor Herzl, *The Jewish State* (Dover Publications, 1988), 69, 76. Originally published in German as *Der Judenstaat,* Vienna, 1896.

462   Elon, 177.

463   Elon, 182, 184.

464   Elon, 182.

465   Elon, 207.

466   Elon, 205.

467   Elon, 185.

468   Elon, 186.

469   Kenneth Burke, *A Rhetoric of Motives* (University of California Press, 1969), 44.

470   Kenneth Burke, "Language as Action: Terministic Screens," in Kenneth Burke, *On Symbols and Society* (University of Chicago Press, 1989).

471   Shlomo Avineri, "Theodor Herzl's Diaries as a Bildungsroman," *Jewish Social Studies: History, Culture, and Society* 5, no. 3 (Spring-Summer 1999): 17–18.

472   Theodor Herzl, quoted in Avineri, "Herzl's Diaries as Bildungsroman," 3.

473   Avineri, "Herzl's Road to Zionism," 8.

474   Avineri, "Herzl's Road to Zionism," 4.

475   Avineri, "Herzl's Road to Zionism," 8.

476   Bein, 230.

477   Avineri, *Herzl*, 108.

478   Elon, 234.

479   Bein, 229.

480   Ben Ami, quoted in Bein, 231.

CHAPTER 6: "WE BOUGHT IT": ERSATZ NARRATIVES AND THE MANUFACTURE OF OWNERSHIP

481   Edward W. Said, *The Question of Palestine* (Vintage Books, 1992 [1979]), 68–69.

482   George Orwell, *1984* (Plume/Penguin, 1983 [1949]), 138.

483   "David Ben-Gurion," Wikiquote, en.wikiquote.org/wiki/David_Ben-Gurion. Note on page: "Attributed to Ben-Gurion in *A Call to Action: The Handbook to Unite and Ignite America's Betrayed and Imperiled Public* (2004) by A. T. Theodore, p. 6, but earlier published as a saying of *unknown* authorship in *Uncommon Sense: The World's Fullest Compendium of Wisdom* (1987) by Joseph Telushkin, p. 204.

484   Benny Morris, *Righteous Victims: A History of the Zionist-Arab Conflict, 1881–2001* (Vintage Books, 2001), 38.

485   For a comprehensive discussion of this subject, see Geoffrey C. Bowker and Susan Leigh Star, *Sorting Things Out: Classification and Its Consequences* (MIT Press, 1999).

486   Christina Joseph, "Move Over, Melvil! Momentum Grows to Eliminate Bias and Racism in the 145-year-old Dewey Decimal System," *School Library Journal*, August 18, 2021, accessed September 6, 2021, www.slj.com/story/move-over-melvil-momentum-grows-to-eliminate-bias-and-racism-in-the-145-year-old-dewey-decimal-system.

487   Benny Morris, *Righteous Victims*, 7.

488   Walid Khalidi, "Ottoman Palestine," excerpted from Part One of *Before Their Diaspora: A Photographic History of the Palestinians, 1876–1948 by Walid Khalidi*. Institute of Palestine Studies, digitalprojects.palestine-studies.org/resources/special-focus/ottoman-palestine.

489   Mazin B. Qumsiyeh, *Popular Resistance in Palestine: A History of Hope and Empowerment* (Pluto Press, 2011), 36; Ilan Pappe, *A History of Modern Palestine: One Land, Two Peoples* (Cambridge University Press, 2004), 20–21.

490   Nur Masalha, *Palestine: A Four Thousand Year History* (Zed Books, 2018), 225-6, 228.

491   Lester I. Vogel, *To See a Promised Land: Americans and the Holy Land in the Nineteenth Century* (Penn State University Press, 1993), 20, 27.

492   Gary Fields, *Enclosure: Palestinian Landscapes in a Historical Mirror* (University of California Press, 2017), 180.

493   Nadav Solomonovich and Ruth Kark, "Land Privatization in Nineteenth-century Ottoman Palestine," *Islamic Law and Society* 22, no. 3 (2015), 225, 228.

494   Masalha, *Palestine*, 221.

495   Noura Alkhalili, "Enclosures from Below: The *Mushaa'* in Contemporary Palestine, *Antipode* 49, no 5 (2017): 1106-7.

496   Masalha, *Palestine*, 219.

497   Khalidi, "Ottoman Palestine."

498   Pappe, *A History of Modern Palestine*, 24.

499   Masalha, *Palestine*, 219.

500   C. Ernest Dawn, review of *The Origins of Palestinian Nationalism* by Muhammad Y. Muslih, *American Historical Review* 95, no. 1 (February 1990): 219, doi.org/10.1086/ahr/95.1.219; Pappe, *A History of Modern Palestine*, 49.

501   George Bisharat, "Land, Law, and Legitimacy in Israel and the Occupied Territories," *American University Law Review* 43, no. 2 (Winter 1994): 492–3.

502   Ahmed H. Ibrahim, "Viewing the Tanzimat from Tulkarm," review of *Palestine and the Decline of the Ottoman Empire: Modernization and the Path to Palestinian Statehood* by Farid al-Salim, *Jerusalem Quarterly* 70 (Summer 2017): 133.

503   George Bisharat, "Land, Law, and Legitimacy in Israel and the Occupied Territories," 491–5; Pappe, *A History of Modern Palestine*, 24.

504   George Bisharat, "Land, Law, and Legitimacy in Israel and the Occupied Territories," 494–5.

505   Pappe, *A History of Modern Palestine*, 29–31.

506   Rashid Khalidi, *Palestinian Identity: The Construction of Modern National Consciousness* (Columbia University Press, 1997), 98.

507   Daniel Bitton, "Nation, Narration and Conflation: a mutual blind spot in historical narratives of the Israeli-Palestinian conflict," master's thesis, Department of Anthropology, McGill University, Montreal, December 2013, 21, escholarship.mcgill.ca/concern/theses/br86b666k.

508   Bitton, *Nation, Narration and Conflation,* 21.

509   Khalidi, *Palestinian Identity*, 112–13.

510   Bitton, "Nation, Narration and Conflation," 19; Alan Dershowitz, *The Case for Israel* (John Wiley & Sons, 2003), 6.

511   Dershowitz, *The Case for Israel*, 8.

512   Dershowitz, *The Case for Israel*, 23.

513   Dershowitz, *The Case for Israel, 6; 8; 20; 6.*

514   Haim Gerber, *Remembering and Imagining Palestine: Identity and Nationalism from the Crusades to the Present* (Palgrave Macmillan, 2008), 35.

515   Dershowitz, *The Case for Israel,* 23.

516   Mark Twain, *The Innocents Abroad,* or *The New Pilgrim's Promise* (Wordsworth Editions Limited, 2010), 303.

517   Twain, *The Innocents Abroad,* 304.

518   Twain, *The Innocents Abroad,* 43.

519   Twain, *The Innocents Abroad,* 51.

520   Twain, *The Innocents Abroad,* 53.

521   Twain, *The Innocents Abroad,* 97.

522   Twain, *The Innocents Abroad,* 121.

523   Twain, *The Innocents Abroad,* 319.

524   Masalha, *Palestine*, 219.

525   Marwan R. Buheiry, "The Agricultural Exports of Southern Palestine, 1885–1914," *Journal of Palestine Studies* 10, no. 4 (Summer, 1981), 65.

526   Buheiry, "The Agricultural Exports of Southern Palestine," 67.

527   Buheiry, "The Agricultural Exports of Southern Palestine," 68.

528   Buheiry, "The Agricultural Exports of Southern Palestine," 64–5.

529   Alexander Scholch, "The Economic Development of Palestine, 1856-1882," *Journal of Palestine Studies* 10, no. 3 (Spring 1981), 35–6.

530   Scholch, "The Economic Development of Palestine," 57, 49.

531   Scholch, "The Economic Development of Palestine," 49.

532   Scholch, "The Economic Development of Palestine," 51.

533   "Jaffa Orange," Bulletin of Miscellaneous Information (Royal Gardens, Kew) 1894, no. 88 (April 1894).

534   Buheiry, "The Agricultural Exports of Southern Palestine," 75-6.

535   Carol Bardenstein, "Threads of Memory and Discourses of Rootedness: Of Trees, Oranges and the Prickly-Pear Cactus in Israel/Palestine," *Edebiyat, The Journal of Middle Eastern Literatures* 8 (1998): 1, Harwood Academic Publishers.

536   Carol Bardenstein, "Threads of Memory and Discourses of Rootedness," 14.

537   Mark Levine, "Jaffa Oranges," review of *California Dreaming: Ideology, Society and Technology in the Citrus Industry of Palestine, 1890–1939* by Nahum Karlinsky, *Journal of Palestine Studies* 35, no. 4, (Summer 2006), 70.

538   *Jaffa, The Orange's Clockwork.* Documentary. Dir. Eyal Sivan, 2009. Momento Films, 5:45.

539 *Jaffa, The Orange's Clockwork.* Documentary, 14:35.

540 *Jaffa, The Orange's Clockwork.* Documentary, 15:45.

541 *Jaffa, The Orange's Clockwork.* Documentary, 30:10.

542 *Jaffa, The Orange's Clockwork.* Documentary, 30:50.

543 *Jaffa, The Orange's Clockwork.* Documentary, 27:06.

544 *Jaffa, The Orange's Clockwork.* Documentary, 48:34.

545 *Jaffa, The Orange's Clockwork.* Documentary, 32:54.

546 Said, *The Question of Palestine,* 9.

547 Masalha, *Palestine,* 308.

548 Anita Shapira, *Land and Power: The Zionist Resort to Force,* 1881–1948 (Stanford University Press, 1999), 42, 51.

549 Adam M. Garfinkle, "On the Origin, Meaning, Use and Abuse of a Phrase," *Middle Eastern Studies* 27, no. 4 (Oct. 1991): 540.

550 Diana Muir, "A land without a people for a people without a land," *Middle East Quarterly* 15, no. 2 (Spring 2008). On *Middle East Forum,* www.meforum.org/1877/a-land-without-a-people-for-a-people-without.

551 Leonard Fein, "Speech to Hadassah on Arab Israelis and the Zionist Enterprise," July 17, 2000. Berman Archive, Stanford University. www.bjpa.org/content/upload/bjpa/lfei/LFein%20Hadassah%20Arabs%20and%20Zionism%202000.pdf.

552 "Herzl and Zionism," Ministry of Foreign Affairs, Israel, July 20, 2004, www.gov.il/en/Departments/General/herzl-and-zionism, accessed December 11, 2022.

553 Ghada Karmi, *Married to Another Man: Israel's Dilemma in Palestine* (Pluto Press, 2007), 103–12.

554 Lawrence Davidson, *America's Palestine: Popular and Official Perceptions from Balfour to Israeli Statehood,* (University Press of Florida, 2001), 15–19.

555 Masalha, *Palestine,* 308.

556 Masalha, *Palestine,* 308.

557 Masalha, *Palestine,* 309.

558 Garfinkle, "On the Origin, Meaning, Use and Abuse of a Phrase," 539.

559 Garfinkle, "On the Origin, Meaning, Use and Abuse of a Phrase," 540.

560 Garfinkle, "On the Origin, Meaning, Use and Abuse of a Phrase," 545.

561 Garfinkle, "On the Origin, Meaning, Use and Abuse of a Phrase," 546.

562 Garfinkle, "On the Origin, Meaning, Use and Abuse of a Phrase," 539.

563 Garfinkle, "On the Origin, Meaning, Use and Abuse of a Phrase," 540-1.

564 Meir quoted in Garfinkle, "On the Origin, Meaning, Use and Abuse of a Phrase," 541.

565 Garfinkle, "On the Origin, Meaning, Use and Abuse of a Phrase," 541.

566 Garfinkle, "On the Origin, Meaning, Use and Abuse of a Phrase," 542.

567 Garfinkle, "On the Origin, Meaning, Use and Abuse of a Phrase," 548, Endnote # 15.

568 Yitzhak Epstein, "The Hidden Question," August 2007. From lecture delivered at the Seventh Zionist Congress in Basel 1905, Balfour Project, balfourproject.org/bp/wp-content/uploads/2014/05/Yitzhak-Epstein.pdf.

569 Shlomo Sand, *The Invention of the Land of Israel: From Holy Land to Homeland* (Verso, 2012), 199–200.

570 Garfinkle, "On the Origin, Meaning, Use and Abuse of a Phrase," 546.

571 Nur Masalha, *Expulsion of the Palestinians: The Concept of 'Transfer' in Zionist Political Thought, 1882–1948,* Institute for Palestine Studies, 1992, 2.

572 Israel Shahak, "A History of the Concept of 'Transfer' in Zionism," *Journal of Palestine Studies* 18, no. 3 (Spring 1989), 34.

573 Morris, *Righteous Victims,* 58.

574 Quoted in Masalha, *Expulsion of the Palestinians,* 11.

575 Masalha, *Expulsion of the Palestinians,* 13.

576 Quoted in Masalha, *Expulsion of the Palestinians,* 17.

577 Shahak, "A History of the Concept of 'Transfer' in Zionism," 23.

578 Shahak, "A History of the Concept of 'Transfer' in Zionism," 24.

579 Shahak, "A History of the Concept of 'Transfer' in Zionism," 24.

580 Shahak, "A History of the Concept of 'Transfer' in Zionism," 25.

581 Shahak, "A History of the Concept of 'Transfer' in Zionism," 25.

582 Quoted in Shahak, "A History of the Concept of 'Transfer' in Zionism," 26.

583 Herzl quoted in Benny Morris, *The Birth of the Palestinian Refugee Problem Revisited* (Cambridge University Press, 2004), 41.

584 Morris, *Righteous Victims,* 49.

585 Gerber, *Remembering and Imagining Palestine,* 33–34.

586 Shabtai Teveth, *Ben-Gurion: The Burning Ground 1886-1948* (Houghton Mifflin, 1987), 457.

587 Theodor Herzl, *Old New Land,* (Markus Wiener Publishers, 1987), 14–16.

588 Herzl, *Old New Land,* 85.

589 Herzl, *Old New Land,* 247.

590 Herzl, *Old New Land,* 248

591 Herzl, *Old New Land,* 272.

592 Herzl, *Old New Land,* 274.

593 Herzl, *Old New Land,* 190.

594 Herzl, *Old New Land,* 208.

595 Herzl, *Old New Land,* 68-9.

596 Herzl, *Old New Land,* 121.

597 Herzl, *Old New Land,* 121-4.

598 Dershowitz, *The Case for Israel,* 30.

599 Dershowitz, *The Case for Israel,* 30.

600 Adam Shatz, ed., *Prophets Outcast: A Century of Dissident Jewish Writing about Zionism and Israel* (Nation Books, 2004), 35.

601 Masalha, *Palestine,* 317.

602 Abigail Jacobson, "Sephardim, Ashkenazim and the 'Arab Question' in Pre-First World War Palestine: A Reading of Three Zionist Newspapers," *Middle Eastern Studies* 39, no. 2 (April 2003), 105.

603 Steven A Glazer, "Picketing for Hebrew Labor: A Window on Histradrut Tactics and Strategy," *Journal of Palestine Studies* 30, no. 4 (Summer 2001), 45.

604 Glazer, "Picketing for Hebrew Labor," 47.

605 Glazer, "Picketing for Hebrew Labor, 40.

606 Walter Laqueur, *A History of Zionism: From the French Revolution to the Establishment of the State of Israel,* Schocken Books, [1972] 2003, 217.

607 Bitton, *Nation, Narration and Conflation,* 24.

608 Jacobson, "Sephardim, Ashkenazim and the 'Arab Question' in Pre-First World War Palestine," 109–10.

609 Jacobson, "Sephardim, Ashkenazim and the 'Arab Question' in Pre-First World War Palestine," 110.

610 Jacobson, "Sephardim, Ashkenazim and the 'Arab Question' in Pre-First World War Palestine," 119.

611 Khalidi, *Palestinian Identity,* 114, 119.

612 Khalidi, *Palestinian Identity,* 121.

613 Khalidi, *Palestinian Identity,* 121-2.

614 Qumsiyeh, *Popular Resistance in Palestine,* 46.

615   Khalidi, *Palestinian Identity*, 125.

616   Khalidi, *Palestinian Identity*, 126–9.

617   Khalidi, *Palestinian Identity*, 133.

618   Khalidi, *Palestinian Identity*, 141.

619   Khalidi, *Palestinian Identity*, 142.

CHAPTER 7: THE JEWISH NATIONAL FUND AND THE MANUFACTURE OF ENVIRONMENTAL STEWARDSHIP

620   Rebecca Manski, "Bluing the Desert," *JNF eBook* Vol. 3, January 2011, 24, accessed February 14, 2022, bdsmovement.net/files/2011/02/JNFeBookVol3.pdf.

621   Meron Rapoport, "Gov't contract shows how Israel enlists forests to grab land from Bedouin citizens," in *+972*, September 22, 2022, accessed January 2, 2023, www.972mag.com/jnf-forests-israel-land-naqab/. Article published in partnership with *Local Call.*

622   Quoted in "The Jewish National Fund (JNF): A Parastatal Institution Chartered to Possess and Discriminate," *Al-Majdal Magazine*, no. 34 (Summer 2007), accessed October 31, 2001,www.badil.org/publications/al-majdal/issues/items/1253.html.

623   From letter cowritten by Eliezer Ben-Yehuda quoted in Benny Morris, *Righteous Victims: A History of the Zionist-Arab Conflict, 1881–2001* (Vintage Books, 2001), 49.

624   "JNF" stands for "Jewish National Fund," with affiliates in countries around the world (identified as JNF-USA, etc.). In Israel it is known by its Hebrew name, Keren Kayemeth LeIsrael (KKL). Often they are jointly identified as KKL-JNF.

625   Barbara Bloch, "When a forest becomes a means of destruction: The Jewish National Fund, Greenwashing and COP26," *Pearls and Irritations: John Menadue's Public Policy Journal*, Oct. 3, 2021, johnmenadue.com/when-a-forest-becomes-a-means-of-destruction-the-jewish-national-fund-greenwashing-and-cop26/; "We Are JNF," Jewish National Fund USA, 2021, www.jnf.org/menu-3/about-jnf.

626   "The First Decade: 1901–1910," "About KKL-JNF: Our History Decade by Decade," www.kkl-jnf.org/second_decade_1901_1910/.

627   Dan Leon, "The Jewish National Fund: How the Land Was 'Redeemed,'" *Palestine-Israel Journal of Politics, Economics & Culture* 12/13, no. 4.1 (2005): 121.

628   Walter Lehn, "The Jewish National Fund," *Journal of Palestine Studies,* 3, no. 4 (Summer, 1974): 81.

629   Yaara Benger Alaluf, "Why does the JNF still exist?" *+972 Magazine,* July 8, 2021, www.972mag.com/jnf-zionism-palestinians-dispossession/.

630   Uri Davis and Walter Lehn, "And the Fund Still Lives: The Role of the Jewish National Fund in the Determination of Israel's Land Policies," *Journal of Palestine Studies* 7, no. 4 (Summer, 1978): 17.

631 Alaluf, "Why does the JNF still exist?"

632 Daniel E. Orenstein, Steven P. Hamburg, "To populate or preserve? Evolving political-demographic and environmental paradigms in Israeli land-use policy," *Land Use Policy* 26 (2009): 986.

633 Leon, "The Jewish National Fund," 119.

634 Yoav Galai, "Narratives of Redemption: The International Meaning of Afforestation in the Israeli Negev," *International Political Sociology* 11, no. 3 (September 2017): 11.

635 "Second Decade: 1911–1920," "About KKL-JNF: Our History Decade by Decade," www.kkl-jnf.org/second_decade_1911_1920/.

636 Ilan Pappe, *The Ethnic Cleansing of Palestine* (Oneworld Publications, 2006), 227–230.

637 Jonathan Cook, "Canada Park and Israeli 'memoricide,'" The Electronic Intifada, March 10, 2009, electronicintifada.net/content/canada-park-and-israeli-memoricide/8126.

638 Uri Davis, "Apartheid Israel and the JNF of Canada: The Story of 'Imwas, Yalu, Beit Nuba and Canada Park," JNF eBook Vol. 2, May 2010, 33. www.stopthejnf.org/documents/JNFeBookVol2.pdf; *Canada Park – Park with No Peace*. Documentary. Produced by Neil Docherty. Correspondent Trish Woods. Aired by Canada's CBC network on "The Fifth Estate," Oct. 21, 1991, accessed on YouTube November 27, 2022, 2:28, 5:53, www.youtube.com/watch?v=0mK2ZbTCb7s.

639 *Canada Park – Park with No Peace*, 6:29.

640 "Italy Park - Alexander River: Rehabilitation for Coexistence," "Tourism and Recreation," KKL-JNF, www.kkl-jnf.org/tourism-and-recreation/forests-and-parks/italy-park/.

641 "Introduction to the British Park," Stop the JNF, www.stopthejnf.org/british-park-intro/.

642 Sarah Levy, "South Africans apologize over forest planted on Palestinian village," The Electronic Intifada, May 5, 2015, electronicintifada.net/content/south-africans-apologize-over-forest-planted-palestinian-village/14494.

643 "Martin Luther King Forest," Jewish Telegraphic Agency, archive, January 16, 1978, www.jta.org/archive/martin-luther-king-forest-2.

644 Coretta Scott King Forest, Jewish National Fund USA, support.jnf.org/site/PageServer?pagename=king.

645 "JNF Anti-Racism-Themed Forests Conceal Racist Massacre," Stop the JNF, July 5, 2021, www.stopthejnf.org/jnf-anti-racism-themed-forests-conceal-racist-massacre/.

646 "Israeli park commemorates SA Jews who opposed apartheid," South African Jewish Report Nov. 10, 2022, www.sajr.co.za/israeli-park-commemorates-sa-jews-who-opposed-apartheid/.

647 "American Independence Park—Friendship through Nature," KKL-JNF Tourism & Recreation, November 10, 2022, www.sajr.co.za/israeli-park-commemorates-sa-jews-who-opposed-apartheid/.

648 "Evangelical TV channel turns the Negev into a forest," *Middle East News Service* (press release), Feb. 16, 2011, www.scoop.co.nz/stories/WO1102/S00566/evangelical-tv-chan-nel-turns-the-negev-into-a-forest.htm; Jonathan Cook, "Jesus Recruited: God-TV Helps Israel Oust Bedouin," Middle East Monitor, May 4, 2014, www.middleeastmonitor.com/20140504-jesus-recruited-god-tv-helps-israel-oust-bedouin/.

649 Galai, "Narratives of Redemption" 279–82; Pappe, *The Ethnic Cleansing of Palestine,* 225–9; JNF 2013a quoted in Galai, 280.

650 Ravit Hananel, "Zionism and agricultural land: National narratives, environmental objectives, and land policy in Israel," *Land Use Policy* 27 (2010): 1168.

651 "Second Decade: 1911–1920," "About KKL-JNF: Our History Decade by Decade," www.kkl-jnf.org/about-kkl-jnf/our-history-decade-bydecade/second-decade-1911-1920/.

652 www.epa.gov/wetlands/why-are-wetlands-important.

653 Joel Greenberg, "Israel Restoring Drained Wetland, Reversing Pioneers' Feat," *New York Times,* Dec. 5, 1993, www.nytimes.com/1993/12/05/world/israel-restoring-drained-wet-land-reversing-pioneers-feat.html.

654 Alon Tal, *Pollution in a Promised Land: An Environmental History of Israel* (University of California Press, 2002), 29.

655 Tal, *Pollution in a Promised Land,* 81.

656 Orenstein and Hamburg, "To populate or preserve? Evolving political-demographic and environmental paradigms in Israel land use policy," *Land Use Policy* 26 (2009): 984.

657 Noam Levin, Eldad Elron, and Avital Gasith, "Decline of wetland ecosystems in the coastal plain of Israel during the 20th century: Implications for wetland conservation and management," *Landscape and Urban Planning* 92 (2009): 228–30.

658 K. D. Hambright & T. Zohary, "Lakes Hula and Agmon: destruction and creation of wetland ecosystems in northern Israel," *Wetlands Ecology and Management* 6 (1998): 87; Levin et al., "Decline of wetland ecosystems," 230.

659 Tal, *Pollution in the Promised Land,* 234.

660 Greenberg, "Israel Restoring Drained Wetland."

661 "About Hula Lake Park—An Example in 21st Century Eco-Tourism," KKL-JNF, "People and Environment," www.kkl-jnf.org/people-and-environment/sustainable-parks/hula-lake-park/hula-valley-eco-tourism/.

662 Noga Collins-Kreiner, Dan Malkinson, Zev Labinger, and Roy Shtainvarz, "Are birders good for birds? Bird conservation through tourism management in the Hula Valley, Israel," *Tourism Management* 38 (2013): 33–39.

663 "Forestry and Green Innovations: Turning the desert into a vibrant, green oasis," Jewish National Fund USA, www.jnf.org/our-work/forestry-green-innovations.

664 Pappe, *The Ethnic Cleansing of Palestine,* 227.

665   Joseph Weitz, *Forests and Afforestation in Israel,* trans. Shlomo Levenson (Masada Press, 1974), 15.

666   Weitz, *Forests and Afforestation in Israel,* 11.

667   Weitz, *Forests and Afforestation in Israel,* 24.

668   Weitz, *Forests and Afforestation in Israel,* 24.

669   Weitz, *Forests and Afforestation in Israel,* 19.

670   Weitz, *Forests and Afforestation in Israel,* 21.

671   Ben-Gurion quoted in Weitz, *Forests and Afforestation in Israel,* 195-6.

672   Ilan Pappe, "Introduction" to *Introducing the Jewish National Fund,* JNF eBook Vol. 1, Jan. 2010, 8.

673   Lea Wittenberg, "Israel wildfires: future trends, impacts and mitigation strategies," 19th EGU General Assembly, EGU2017, proceedings from the conference held 23–28 April, 2017 in Vienna, Austria, p. 17817.

674   Global Forest Watch: Israel, accessed Jan. 8, 2023, www.globalforestwatch.org/dashboards/country/ISR/?category=fires&location=WyJjb3VudHJ5IiwiSVNSIl0%3D.

675   Nili Liphschitz and Gideon Biger, "Past distribution of Aleppo pine (*Pinus halepensis*) in the mountains of Israel (Palestine)," *The Holocene* 11, no. 4 (2001): 434.

676   Liphschitz and Biger, "Past distribution of Aleppo pine": 431.

677   Fred Pearce, "In Israel, Questions Are Raised about a Forest that Rises from the Desert," *Yale Environment 360,* September. 30, 2019, e360.yale.edu/features/in-israel-questions-are-raised-about-a-forest-that-rises-from-the-desert.

678   "The First Decade: 1901–1910," "About KKL-JNF: Our History Decade by Decade," KKL-JNF, accessed Dec. 19, 2022, www.kkl-jnf.org/second_decade_1901_1910/.

679   Yoram Bar-Gal, *Propaganda and Zionist Education: The Jewish National Fund 1924–1947,* University of Rochester Press, 2003, 30.

680   Quoted in Bar-Gal, *Propaganda and Zionist Education,* 12; From JNF, *The JNF Box,* Jerusalem, JNF Head Office, 1921, 3-4 (Hebrew).

681   Bar-Gal, *Propaganda and Zionist Education,* 107.

682   Bar-Gal, *Propaganda and Zionist Education,* 107.

683   Bar-Gal, *Propaganda and Zionist Education,* 31.

684   "Blue Boxes," Jewish National Fund of Canada (website), n/d, jnf.ca/support/blue-boxes/

685   "How the Blue Box Was Born," *The Blue Box,* Keren Kayemeth LeIsrael (website), n/d, accessed December 15, 2022, www.kkl-jnf.org/about-kkl-jnf/the-blue-box/.

686   Bar-Gal, *Propaganda and Zionist Education,* 10–16.

687   Bar-Gal, *Propaganda and Zionist Education,* 18, 20.

688   Bar-Gal, *Propaganda and Zionist Education,* 15.

689   Bar-Gal, *Propaganda and Zionist Education,* x.

690   Michael Billig, *Banal Nationalism,* SAGE Publications, 1995.

691   Bar-Gal, *Propaganda and Zionist Education,* 108.

692   Bar-Gal, *Propaganda and Zionist Education,* 111.

693   Bar-Gal, *Propaganda and Zionist Education,* 120–1.

694   "Blue Box Bob," Facebook page, accessed Dec. 19, 2022, www.facebook.com/
        blueboxbob.

695   "About KKL-JNF 120th Anniversary Revival of the Zion Stamp," *WOPA+,* 2021,
        accessed Dec. 20, 2022, www.wopa-plus.com/en/stamps/product/&pgid=65499.

696   "JNF Stamps," The Central Zionist Archives, World Zionist Organization, accessed
        December 20, 2022, www.zionistarchives.org.il/en/Pages/Stamps.aspx.

697   Bar-Gal, "The Blue Box and JNF Propaganda Maps, 1930–1947," *Israel Studies,* 8, no. 1
        (Spring 2003).

698   Bar-Gal, *Propaganda and Zionist Education,* 39–40.

699   "Making the Desert Bloom Facilitators Guide," Jewish National Fund Tu BiShvat in
        the Schools, 2020/5780, jnf.blob.core.windows.net/images/docs/default-source/
        education-files/educators-guide_tbs-in-the-schools-mailings_update_2019_jnfusa-2.
        pdf?sfvrsn=5364f0ec_2; "#TreesAreTrending this Bu BiShvat: Catch the Tu BiShvat
        Spirit," January 31, 2020, Jewish National Fund, www.jnf.org/menu-3/press-releases/
        press-release-stories/january-31-2020; "Celebrate Tu BiShvat with JNF: Plant a Tree
        in Israel," Jewish National Fund, www.jnf.org/our-work/education-and-advocacy/
        kindergarten/celebrate-tu-bishvat. All accessed December 26, 2022.

700   Rebecca L. Stein, "Travelling Zion," *Interventions* 11, no. 3 (2009): 335–7.

701   Nadia Abu El-Haj, *Facts on the Ground: Archaeological Practice and Territorial Self-
        Fashioning in Israeli Society* (University of Chicago Press, 2001), 46–7.

702   Shay Rabineau, "Hiking in Israel: Why Are These Trails Different?" *Perspectives: The
        Magazine of the Association of Jewish Studies,* The Land Issue, Spring 2014.

703   Rebecca L. Stein, "Travelling Zion," 337–8.

704   Thomas Suárez, *Palestine Hijacked: How Zionism Forged an Apartheid State from River to
        Sea,* (Olive Branch Press, 2023): 80, 97–98, 108-9, 116–17, 142.

705   Devorah Brous, "Not Greening, but Weeding the Negev," *Haaretz* Mar. 10,
        2006, accessed January 17, 2023, www.haaretz.com/2006-03-10/ty-article/
        not-greening-but-weeding-the-negev/0000017f-e304-df7c-a5ff-e37ee8130000.

706   David Ben-Gurion, *Memoirs,* compiled by Thomas R. Bransten (The World Publishing
        Company, 1970), 133–50.

707 David Ben-Gurion, *Memoirs,* p. 142.

708 Quoted in Mansour Nasasra, "The Ongoing Judaisation of the Naqab and the Struggle for Recognizing the Indigenous Rights of the Arab Bedouin People," *settler colonial studies* 2, no. 1 (2012): 89.

709 "Community Building—The future starts here," JNF.org.

710 Chaim Chesler, "Strengthening the Periphery," the *Jerusalem Post* (daily edition), April 17, 2001.

711 Manski, "Bluing the Desert," 24.

712 Tom Pessah, "How colonialism and climate change displace the Negev's Bedouin," *+972 Magazine,* March 14, 2016, accessed January 2, 2023, www.972mag.com/how-colonalism-and-climate-change-displace-negev-bedouin/.

713 Devorah Brous, "Bedouin Woes," *Baltimore Jewish Times,* Vol. 289 no. 5 (March 31, 2006): 71.

714 Joseph Schechla, "The Invisible People Come to Light: Israel's 'Internally Displaced' and the 'Unrecognized Villages," *Journal of Palestine Studies* 31, no. 1 (2001): 23–4.

715 "Israel/OPT: Scrap plans for forced transfer of Palestinian Bedouin village Ras Jrabah in the Negev/Naqab," *Amnesty International,* News, May 22, 2022, accessed February 13, 2023, www.amnesty.org/en/latest/news/2022/05/israel-opt-scrap-plans-for-forced-transfer-of-palestinian-bedouin-village-ras-jrabah-in-the-negev-naqab/.

716 Negev Coexistence Forum for Civil Equality, "Mechanism for Dispossession and Intimidation: Demolition Policy in Arab Bedouin communities in the Negev/Naqab," (June 2019): 5, accessed March 12, 2023, www.dukium.org/wp-content/uploads/2019/07/Demolition-Report-Eng.2018-1.pdf.

717 Rafael Ben Ari, "The Unrecognized Bedouin Villages in the Negev—Facts and Figures," The Association for Civil Rights in Israel (ACRI), December 31, 2019, accessed February 21, 2023. www.english.acri.org.il/post/__148.

718 Dalia Hatuga, "In Protests, the Naqab Affirms Its Palestinian National Identity," *Jewish Currents,* February 16, 2022, accessed February 13, 2023, jewishcurrents.org/in-protests-the-naqab-affirms-its-palestinian-national-identity; ICAHD, "Displacements and demolitions in the Israeli Negev/Naqab," June 23, 2022, Israeli Committee Against House Demolitions (website), accessed February 13, 2023, icahd.org/2022/06/23/displacements-and-demolitions-in-the-israeli-negev-naqab/.

719 Shira Robinson, Review of *Palestinian Citizens of Israel: Power, Resistance and the Struggle for Space* by Sharri Plonski, *Journal of Holy Land and Palestine Studies* 18, no. 2 (2019).

720 Akevot Institute for Israeli-Palestinian Conflict Research, "Afforestation—a tool for landgrab," (January 19, 1987–June 29, 1987), accessed February 4, 2023, www.akevot.org.il/en/article/afforestation/?full.

721 Dalia Hatuga, "In Protests, the Naqab Affirms its Palestinian Identity."

722   Nasasra, "The Ongoing Judaisation of the Naqab," 84.

723   Nasasra, "The Ongoing Judaisation of the Naqab," 88.

724   Nasasra, "The Ongoing Judaisation of the Naqab," 91.

725   Nasasra, "The Ongoing Judaisation of the Naqab," 92-3.

726   Nasasra, "The Ongoing Judaisation of the Naqab," 95-7.

727   Dan Senor and Saul Singer, *Start-Up Nation: The Story of Israel's Economic Miracle* (Twelve/Hatchette Book Group, 2011 [2009]), 112.

728   "Turning the Desert Green," KKL-JNF, www.kkl-jnf.org/forestry-and-ecology/ afforestation-in-israel/turning-the-desert-green/, n/d, accessed March 5, 2023.

729   Arwa Aburawa, "JNF plants trees to uproot Bedouin," The Electronic Intifada, October 18, 2010, accessed Nov. 11, 2021, electronicintifada.net/content/ jnf-plants-trees-uproot-bedouin/9072.

730   Corey Balsam, "Tree Planting as Pedagogy," JNF eBook Vol. 4 (May 15, 2011), *Greenwashing Apartheid: The Jewish National Fund's Environmental Cover- Up*, published by International Jewish Anti-Zionist Network, accessed November 6, 2022, www.stopthejnf.org/download/jnf-e-book-vol-4-may-2011/. 94–5.

731   "Community Building—Our Blueprint Negev Strategy: Revitalizing Southern Israel," Jewish National Fund, copyright 2023, accessed December 27, 2022, www.jnf.org/ our-work/community-building/our-blueprint-negev-strategy.

732   "Community Building—The future starts here: Our case for population growth and regional economic development in Israel's north and south," Jewish National Fund, copyright 2023, accessed March 11, 2023, www.jnf.org/our-work/community-building.

733   Rebecca Manski, "Bluing the Desert," 25.

734   Rebecca Manski, "Bluing the Desert," 27, quote from Uriel Heilman, "The Negev's 21st century pioneers", *B'nai B'rith Magazine* (Winter 2008–2009), cited in Manski, www.urielheilman.com/0101negev.html.

735   "Our Vision: The Future is Beautiful," copyright 2023, by Jewish National Fund, accessed February 18, 2023, www.jnf.org/our-vision.

736   Community Building—Our Blueprint Negev Strategy.

737   "Fortified playground shows success of Negev revitalization efforts," press release, Jewish News Syndicate (JNS), September 19, 2022. "Media contact" listed is "Joseph JD Krebs, Jewish National Fund-USA," accessed January 1, 2023, www.jns.org/wire/fortified-playground-shows-success-of-negev-revitalization-efforts/.

738   Devorah Brous quoted in Manski, "Bluing the Desert," 35.

739   "Community Building—Our Blueprint Negev Strategy," JNF.

740 Jesse Benjamin, "Orwell's 'Green Patrol' and the Relentless Racialized Illogic of Ethnic Cleansing in the Name of Environmentalism," JNF eBook (Volume 4, May 15, 2011), *Greenwashing Apartheid: The Jewish National Fund's Environmental Cover Up,* 81–9, accessed February 14, 2022, stopthejnf.org/documents/JNFeBookVol4.pdf.

741 "Adalah demands Israel cancel illegal 'admissions committees' enforcing segregation in dozens of communities across the country," Adalah: The Legal Center for Arab Minority Rights in Israel, June 25, 2019, accessed March 10, 2023, www.adalah.org/en/content/view/9751.

742 "Adalah's Analysis of the New Israeli Government's Guiding Principles and Coalition Agreements and the Implications on Palestinians' Rights," Adalah: The Legal Center for Arab Minority Rights in Israel, January 10, 2023, position paper, accessed April 19, 2023. www.adalah.org/uploads/uploads/37_govt_position_paper_Eng_100123.pdf.

743 Rebecca Manski, "Bluing the Desert," 27.

744 "Israel 2040: KKL-JNF Builds the Land of Tomorrow," KKL-JNF, n/d, accessed Jan. 7, 2023, www.kkl-jnf.org/people-and-environment/community-development/israel-2040/.

745 "Israel 2040: KKL-JNF Builds the Land of Tomorrow."

746 Greg Dropkin, "Jewish National Fund works hand in glove with Israeli military," The Electronic Intifada, July 20, 2020, accessed Oct. 28, 2021, electronicintifada.net/content/jewish-national-fund-works-hand-glove-israeli-military/30716.

747 Note that announcing the search for "Israelis" for these positions gives the JNF the alibi of "open to all" in civic equality because Israel, unlike any other democratic country, distinguishes between its "citizens" and separate "nationalities"—Jewish, Arab, Druze, etc.—which are named on official identity cards. But the JNF, the non-governmental body that is executing the project, is only accountable to those with a "Jewish" national designation, which includes diaspora Jewish noncitizens of Israel.

748 Alan Rosenbaum, "Israel in 2040—Exciting, Innovative, and Strong," *Jerusalem Post,* Nov. 21, 2019, accessed Jan. 7, 2023, www.jpost.com/israel-news/israel-in-2040-exciting-innovative-and-strong-608554.

749 "Envision Tomorrow's Israel." Promotional flyer, JNFUSA, December 2020, zionistvillage.jnf.org/wp-content/uploads/2021/04/Envision_Form_2021_JNFUSA.pdf.

750 JNF On Demand: "How American College Students are Boosting Employment in the Negev," JNF-USA, YouTube, 2022, accessed March 21, 2023, www.youtube.com/watch?v=C3MhCY_Z234.

751 "Community Building—Our Blueprint Negev Strategy."

752 "Jewish National Fund-USA Launches Design Competition for $350 Million World Zionist Village in Be'er Sheva," PR Newswire, February 5, 2021, accessed December 29, www.prnewswire.com/news-releases/jewish-national-fund-usa-launches-design-competition-for-350-million-world-zionist-village-in-beer-sheva-301223072.html.

753 Eric Narrow, "A Task Force Growing New Communities and Creating a Lasting Change," *JNF* website, 2023, accessed February 4, 2023, www.jnf.org/menu-3/news-media/jnf-wire/jnf-wire-stories/a-task-force-growing-new-communities-and-creating-a-lasting-change.

754 Yael Levontin on IsraelCast, Episode 130 (podcast), hosted by Steven Shalowitz, December 12, 2021, accessed Dec. 27, 2022. www.jnf.org/menu-3/news-media/israelcast/yael-levontin.

755 "Galilee Culinary Institute by JNF," JNF website, 2023, my.jnf.org/gci; "About Jewish National Fund," *JNF* website, 2023, www.galileeculinaryinstitute.com/jnf; "Groundbreaking New Culinary Institute Announces Opening Date," JNF press release, March 8, 2023, www.prnewswire.com/news-releases/groundbreaking-new-culinary-institute-announces-opening-date-301765006.html, all accessed April 5, 2023.

756 Yael Levontin, *IsraelCast*, Episode 130.

757 "The Future of Food is in Northern Israel and Jewish National Fund Is Serving Up Some Culinary Delights," accessed April 5, 2023, www.jnf.org/menu-3/news-media/jnf-wire/jnf-wire-stories/the-future-of-food.

758 Gershon Shafir, "From Overt to Veiled Segregation: Israel's Palestinian Arab Citizens in the Galilee," *International Journal of Middle East Studies* 50 (2018)," 19.

759 Sam Bahour, "The Galilee First: Equal rights for Palestinian citizens of Israel is essential for peace and reconciliation," *Mondoweiss,* October 21, 2012, accessed March 25, 2023, mondoweiss.net/2012/10/the-galilee-first-equal-rights-for-palestinian-citizens-of-israel-is-essential-for-peace-and-reconciliation/.

760 Shafir, "From Overt to Veiled Segregation, 3-6; Ghazi Falah, "Israeli 'Judaization' Policy in Galilee," *Journal of Palestine Studies* 20, no. 4 (Summer 1991): 69–73.

761 Special Document: "The Koenig Report: Top Secret: Memorandum-Proposal—Handling the Arabs of Israel," *Journal of Palestine Studies* 6, no. 1 (1976): 191–3.

762 Falah, "Israeli 'Judaization' Policy in Galilee," 79–82.

763 Shafir, "From Overt to Veiled Segregation," 2, 7.

764 Shira Robinson, Review of *Palestinian Citizens of Israel: Power, Resistance and the Struggle for Space,*" IB Tauris 2018, *Journal of Holy Land and Palestine Studies* 18:2 (2019).

765 Falah, "Israeli 'Judaization' Policy in Galilee, 76–9; Shafir, "From Overt to Veiled Segregation," 6–7.

766 "Pre-State Israel: Stockade and Watchtower," Jewish Virtual Library, www.jewishvirtuallibrary.org/stockade-and-watchtower; "Tower and Stockade," Zionist Archives, www.zionistarchives.org.il/en/Pages/TowerStockade.aspx; "Stockade and Watchtower," Encyclopedia.com, www.encyclopedia.com/religion/encyclopedias-almanacs-transcripts-and-maps/stockade-and-watchtower, all accessed April 4, 2023.

767 Shafir, "From Overt to Veiled Segregation," 18.

768   Isabelle Humphries, "From Gaza to the Galilee: Same Policy, Same Agenda," the *Washington Report on Middle East Affairs,* September/October 2005, accessed April 5, 2023, www.wrmea.org/2005-september-october/special-report-from-gaza-to-the-galilee-same-policy-same-agenda.html.

769   Shafir, "From Overt to Veiled Segregation," 8, 10–11, 17–18, 19.

770   Oren Yiftachel and Naomi Carmon, "Socio-spatial mix and inter-ethnic attitudes: Jewish newcomers and Arab-Jewish issues in the Galilee," *European Planning Studies*, Vol. 5, no. 2 (April 1997): 8.

771   Shani Shiloh, "Settle the Hilltops—or Not," *Haaretz,* February 23, 2009, accessed April 5, 2023, www.haaretz.com/2009-02-23/ty-article/settle-the-hilltops-or-not/0000017f-e072-d804-ad7f-f1fa98a80000.

772   Shafir, "From Overt to Veiled Segregation," 10.

773   Falah, "Israeli 'Judaization' Policy in Galilee," 82

CHAPTER 8: THE "CAUSAL NEXUS": THE HOLOCAUST AND ISRAEL

774   Idith Zertal, *Israel's Holocaust and the Politics of Nationhood*, trans. Chaya Galai (Cambridge University Press, 2005 (Dvir Publishing House, 2002), 167.

775   Peter Novick, *The Holocaust and Collective Memory* (Bloomsbury, 2001), 69–70. First published by Houghton Mifflin as *The Holocaust in American Life,* 1999.

776   Yosefa Loshitsky, *Identity Politics on the Israeli Screen,* University of Texas Press, 2001.

777   Shabtai Teveth, *Ben-Gurion: The Burning Ground 1886–1948* (Houghton Mifflin, 1967), 717.

778   Teveth, *Ben-Gurion*, 850, 642.

779   Teveth, *Ben-Gurion*, 787.

780   Teveth, *Ben-Gurion*, 855.

781   Teveth, *Ben-Gurion*, 840–5.

782   Teveth, *Ben-Gurion*, 846.

783   Teveth, *Ben-Gurion*, 851.

784   Yosef Grodzinsky, *In the Shadow of the Holocaust* (Common Courage Press, 2004), 76, 112, 115.

785   Grodzinsky, *In the Shadow of the Holocaust*, 50–1.

786   Quoted in Grodzinsky, *In the Shadow of the Holocaust*, 96–8.

787   Grodzinsky, *In the Shadow of the Holocaust*, 135.

788   Grodzinsky, *In the Shadow of the Holocaust*, 179–80.

789   Grodzinsky, *In the Shadow of the Holocaust*, 198–208.

790 Grodzinsky, *In the Shadow of the Holocaust*,219. Violent German police raids in the DP camps were allegedly to crack down on black market activity.

791 Grodzinsky, *In the Shadow of the Holocaust*, 227.

792 Idith Zertal, *From Catastrophe to Power: Holocaust Survivors and the Emergence of Israel* (University of California Press, 1998), 48–58.

793 Zertal, *From Catastrophe to Power*, 83.

794 Zertal, *From Catastrophe to Power*, 82–92.

795 Zertal, *From Catastrophe to Power*, 240–1.

796 Giora Goodman, "'Operation Exodus': Israeli government involvement in the production of Otto Preminger's Film *Exodus, 1960*," *Journal of Israeli History* 33, no. 2 (2014): 211–12.

797 Amy Kaplan, *Our American Israel: The Story of an Entangled Alliance* (Harvard University Press, 2018), 66; Goodman, "'Operation Exodus,'" 213.

798 Goodman, "'Operation Exodus,'" 213–14.

799 Kaplan, *Our American Israel*, 65, 73.

800 Leon Uris, *Exodus* (Bantam Books, 1959 [Doubleday, 1958]), 307.

801 Kevin Mims, "Remembering 'Exodus,'" *Quillette,* September 4, 2023, quillette.com/2023/09/04/remembering-exodus.

802 Bradley Burston, "The 'Exodus' Effect: The Monumentally Fictional Israel that Remade American Jewry," *Ha'aretz,* November 9, 2012, www.haaretz.com/2012-11-09/ty-article/the-exodus-effect-of-leon-uris-on-u-s-jewry/0000017f-e8a2-da9b-a1ff-ecefad820000.

803 Kevin Mims, "Remembering 'Exodus.'"

804 Burston, "The 'Exodus' Effect."

805 Jenny Singer, "It was the million-selling novel that shaped a generation of Jews—does anybody still read it?", May 15, 2023, *Forward,* forward.com/culture/547036/exodus-leon-uris-israel/.

806 Kaplan, *Our American Israel*, 90.

807 Ruthie Blum Liebowitz, "Leon Uris 'Exodus' novel had nothing to do with reality, skipper said," *Jerusalem Post,* December 26, 2009, www.jpost.com/israel/leon-uris-exodus-novel-had-nothing-to-do-with-reality-skipper-said.

808 Jenny Singer, "It was the million-selling novel."

809 Jenny Singer, "It was the million-selling novel."

810 Alan Elsner, "Rereading Leon Uris' 'Exodus' a disquieting experience," *Jewish Journal,* April 18, 2013, jewishjournal.com/mobile_20111212/115763/.

811 Kaplan, *Our American Israel*, 67.

812   Goodman, "'Operation Exodus,'" 217.

813   Goodman, "'Operation Exodus,'" 218–20.

814   Goodman, "'Operation Exodus,'" 220–1.

815   Kaplan, *Our American Israel*, 60.

816   Kaplan, *Our American Israel*, 76.

817   Goodman, "'Operation Exodus,'" 223.

818   Tom Segev, *The Seventh Million: The Israelis and the Holocaust,* trans. Haim Watzman (Henry Holt 2001), 241, 249–50; Norman Finkelstein , *The Holocaust Industry: Reflections on the Exploitation of Jewish Suffering* (Verso, Second Edition, 2003), 151–2.

819   Segev, *The Seventh Million*, 191.

820   Segev, *The Seventh Million*, 206–8, 375.

821   Quoted in Segev, *The Seventh Million*, 208.

822   Segev, *The Seventh Million*, 192.

823   Segev, *The Seventh Million*, 213.

824   Segev, *The Seventh Million*, 215, 320.

825   Segev, *The Seventh Million*, 375.

826   Quoted in Segev, *The Seventh Million*, 314.

827   Segev, *The Seventh Million*, 369.

828   Zertal, *Israel's Holocaust and the Politics of Nationhood,* 174, 121, 186, 191; Segev, *The Seventh Million*, 460, 375.

829   Nurit Peled-Elhanan, "Holocaust Education and the Semiotics of Othering in Israeli Schoolbooks," Lecture derived from her book of the same name, on YouTube, accessed January 28, 2024. www.youtube.com/watch?v=1u3FEl4m9Tc.

830   Tom Segev, "Netanyahu's fairytale about Hitler and the mufti is the last thing we need," the *Guardian,* October 21, 2015, accessed February 17, 2024, www.theguardian.com/commentisfree/2015/oct/21/netanyahu-faitytale-hitler-mufti-holocaust.

831   Zertal, *Israel's Holocaust and the Politics of Nationhood,* 175.

832   Peter Beaumont, "Anger at Netanyahu claim Palestinian grand mufti inspired Holocaust," *Guardian,* October 21, 2015, accessed February 17, 2024, www.theguardian.com/world/2015/oct/21/netanyahu-under-fire-for-palestinian-grand-mufti-holocaust-claim; David Kaiser, "What Hitler and the Grand Mufti Really Said," *Time,* October 22, 2015, accessed February 17, 2024, time.com/4084301/hitler-grand-mufi-1941/; Rashid Khalidi, *The Hundred Years' War on Palestine: A History of Settler Colonialism and Resistance, 1917–2017,* (Henry Holt & Co.., 2020), 42–47, 66; Dina Porat, "Setting the Record Straight," October 21, 2015, accessed February 17, 2024, www.yadvashem.org/blog/setting-the-record-straight.html.; Segev, "Netanyahu's fairytale about Hitler and the

mufti"; Segev, *The Seventh Million,* 353; Nathan Yellin-Mor, *Israel, Israel,* excerpted in Lenni Brenner, ed., *51 Documents: Zionist Collaboration with the Nazis* (Barricade Books, 2002), 306-09; Zertal, *Israel's Holocaust and the Politics of Nationhood,* 100–03, 175.

833   Yf'aat Weiss, The Transfer Agreement and the Boycott Movement: A Jewish Dilemma on the Eve of the Holocaust," trans. Naftali Greenwood, *Yad Vashem Studies* XXVI, (Jerusalem 1998), 129–172. Accessed from Shoah Resource Center, The International School for Holocaust Studies, February 23, 2024 at www.yadvashem.org/odot_pdf/microsoft%20word%20-%203231.pdf; Segev, *The Seventh Million,* 18–22; Novick, *The Holocaust and Collective Memory,* 158; see also Edwin Black, *The Transfer Agreement: The Dramatic Story of the Pact Between the Third Reich and Jewish Palestine,* (Brookline Books, 1984).

834   Gulie Ne'eman Arad, "Israel and the Shoah: A Tale of Multifarious Taboos," *New German Critique,* no. 90 (Autumn 2003), 13–16.

835   Yechiel Klar, Noa Schori-Eyal, and Yonat Klar, "The 'Never Again' State of Israel: The Emergence of the Holocaust as a Core Feature of Israeli Identity and Its Four Incongruent Voices," *Journal of Social Issues* 69, no. 1 (2013), 133.

836   Gulie Ne'eman Arad, "The Shoah as Israel's Political Trope," Chapter Eight in *Divergent Jewish Cultures: Israel and America,* eds. Deborah Dash Moore and S. Ilan Troen (Yale University Press, 2001), 202–3. ProQuest Ebook Central, accessed January 24, 2024, ebookcentral.proquest.com/lib/cornell/detail.action?docID=3419904.

837   Ben M. Freeman, "Hamas's October 7 massacre shows that Never Again was a lie— opinion," *Jerusalem Post,* January 28, 2024, accessed March 2, 2024, www.jpost.com/opinion/article-784034; David Horovitz, "Hamas came for everyone it could kill in Israel on Oct. 7. Today, The Hague encouraged it," *Times of Israel,* January 26, 2024, accessed March 2, 2024 www.timesofisrael.com/hamas-came-for-everyone-it-could-kill-in-israel-on-oct-7-today-the-hague-encouraged-it/; Eva Blauch, "International Holocaust Remembrance Day in the shadow of Oct. 7," *Jerusalem Post,* January 25, 2024, accessed March 2, 2024, www.jpost.com/judaism/article-783642#google_vignette; "Remarks by President Biden on the October 7th Terrorist Attacks and the Resilience of the State of Israel and its People," Tel Aviv, Israel, The White House, October 18, 2023, accessed January 28, 2024, www.whitehouse.gov/briefing-room/speeches-remarks/2023/10/18/remarks-by-president-biden-on-the-october-7th-terrorist-attacks-and-the-resilience-of-the-state-of-israel-and-its-people-tel-aviv-israel/; Jason DeRose, "Holocaust Remembrance Day rings different after the Oct. 7 Hamas attack," *All Things Considered, NPR,* January 26, 2024, accessed March 2, 2024, WWW.NPR.ORG/2024/01/26/1227247649/HOLOCAUST-REMEMBRANCE-DAY-RINGS-DIFFERENT-AFTER-THE-OCT-7-HAMAS-ATTACK; Nick Watt, "October 7 was the deadliest day for Jews since the Holocaust. The Shoah Foundation is now documenting it," *CNN,* November 10, 2023, accessed March 2, 2024, www.cnn.com/2023/11/09/us/shoah-foundation-records-october-7-testimonies/index.html.

838 World Jewish Congress, "Remembrance of Kristallnacht is different this year," November 9, 2023 [mass email].

839 "Israel-Hamas war: Benjamin Netanyahu says 'Hamas are the new Nazis, they're the new ISIS and we have to fight them together," *Sky News,* UK, October 19, 2023, accessed March 2, 2024, news.sky.com/video/israel-hamas-war-benjamin-netanyahu-says-hamas-are-the-new-nazis-theyre-the-new-isis-and-we-have-to-fight-them-together-12987568.

840 Alternately, the word "sheep" rather than "lambs" is often used in this common expression.

841 Grodzinsky, *In the Shadow of the Holocaust*, 229.

842 Segev, *The Seventh Million*, 34.

843 Segev, *The Seventh Million*, 155–9, 167–86.

844 Sigmund Freud, "The 'Uncanny,'" first published in *Imago,* Bd.V., 1919, reprinted in *Sammlung.* Fünfte Folge, trans. Alix Strachey, accessed February 4, 2024 at web.mit.edu/allanmc/www/freud1.pdf.

845 Zertal, *From Catastrophe to Power,* 271–3.

846 Zertal, *Israel's Holocaust and the Politics of Nationhood,* 84–86.

847 Novick, *The Holocaust and Collective Memory*, 83–4.

848 Segev, *The Seventh Million*, 181.

849 Novick, *The Holocaust and Collective Memory*, 132.

850 "The six million" is more symbolic than numerically revealing, even as an approximation, especially as it has been contested on various grounds by Holocaust scholars and others. Nirit Anderson writes that while this number "has become hallowed and seared into everyone's consciousness, an iconic symbol of the Holocaust of the Jewish people," it's not clear how it's calculated. When did the Holocaust begin and end in regard to the death count? Are we including only those murdered, or also those who died of starvation and disease? In creating the President's Commission on Remembering the Holocaust in November 1978, President Jimmy Carter backed citing "eleven million" in order to include the many others targeted by the Nazis. These included trade unionists, gay people, people with disabilities, political activists—and most notably the Roma (known as gypsies, a once acceptable term now regarded as derogatory), whose murders were at least as proportionally high as those in the Jewish population and who, similarly to the Jews, were killed according to, as *Haaretz* has put it, an "eliminationist ideology." Elie Wiesel, chair of the commission, opposed including non-Jews in the count. As Mark Chmiel writes, "This conflation endangered the sanctity of what Wiesel was interested in promoting, namely, the essentially *Jewish* character of the Holocaust...." While there are various "origin stories" for the "six million" trope, Novick writes, "Although there is no detailed paper trail, it's generally agreed that the figure of eleven million originated with Simon Wiesenthal, the renowned pursuer of Nazi criminals. How did he arrive at

this number? The Israeli historian Yehuda Bauer reports that Wiesenthal acknowledged to him in a private conversation that he simply invented it." Nirit Anderson, "This Filmmaker Dares to Question the Figure of 6 Million Jewish Victims in WWII," *Haaretz,* January 16, 2022, accessed August 22, 2023, www.haaretz.com/israel-news/2022-01-16/ty-article-magazine/.highlight/this-filmmaker-dares-to-question-the-figure-of-6-million-jewish-victims-in-wwii/0000017f-e202-d7b2-a77f-e30759770000; Mark Chmiel, *Elie Wiesel and the Politics of Moral Leadership* (Temple University Press, 2001), 118–20; Novick, *The Holocaust and Collective Memory*, 215; "Holocaust Facts: Where Does the Figure of 6 Million Victims Come From?" *Haaretz,* January 27, 2022, originally published in August 2013, accessed August 22, 2023, www.haaretz.com/israel-news/2022-01-27/ty-article/6-million-where-is-the-figure-from/0000017f-da74-dea8-a77f-de761f480000?lts=1692728467744.

851   Zertal, *Israel's Holocaust and the Politics of Nationhood,* 95.

852   Zertal, *Israel's Holocaust and the Politics of Nationhood,* 108.

853   Segev, *The Seventh Million,* 328.

854   Quoted in Zertal, *Israel's Holocaust and the Politics of Nationhood.* Italics are Zertal's.

855   Segev, *The Seventh Million,* 343–61.

856   Hannah Arendt, *Eichmann in Jerusalem: A Report on the Banality of Evil,* Revised and enlarged edition, Penguin Books, 1994 [1964], first published in the US by The Viking Press, 1963.

857   Segev, *The Seventh Million,* 323–366; Idith Zertal, *Israel's Holocaust and the Politics of Nationhood,* 91–127; Novick, *The Holocaust and Collective Memory*, 134–142.

858   Daniel Maier-Katkin, "The Reception of Hannah Arendt's *Eichmann in Jerusalem* in the United States 1963–2011, *Journal for Political Thinking,* November 2011, accessed February 25, 2024 at HannahArendt.net, www.hannaharendt.net/index.php/han/article/download/64/84.

859   Segev *The Seventh Million,* 359–60.

860   Kathleen B. Jones, "Before and After *Eichmann in Jerusalem:* Hannah Arendt and the Human Condition," *Los Angeles Review of Books,* December 8, 2015, accessed February 25, 2024, lareviewofbooks.org/article/before-and-after-eichmann-in-jerusalem-hannah-arendt-and-the-human-condition/.

861   James E. Young, *The Texture of Memory: Holocaust Memorials and Meaning* (Yale University Press, 1993), 212.

862   Yad Vashem—The World Holocaust Remembrance Center, www.yadvashem.org.

863   Amos Goldberg, "The 'Jewish narrative' in the Yad Vashem global Holocaust museum," *Journal of Genocide Research* 14, no. 2, (2012): 189–92.

864   Segev, *The Seventh Million,* 425.

865 Young, *The Texture of Memory*, 246, 253.

866 Goldberg, "The 'Jewish narrative' in the Yad Vashem global Holocaust museum," 206–7.

867 Goldberg, "The 'Jewish narrative' in the Yad Vashem global Holocaust museum," 197, 207–8.

868 Goldberg, "The 'Jewish narrative' in the Yad Vashem global Holocaust museum," 207.

869 "In the Footsteps of Heroes: Monuments to Jewish Rebellion and Heroism at Yad Vashem, *Yad Vashem* website, accessed February 13, 2024, www.yadvashem.org/museum/art/articles/monuments.html.

870 Marek Edelman, *The Ghetto Fights: Warsaw 1941–43* (Bookmarks publishing 2014 [first published in Polish, 1945, English trans. first published in New York, 1946, first published in the UK by Turnaround, 1990]).

871 Itzhak Luden, "Marek Edelman, the Heroic Anti-Hero," *Jewish Currents*, October 7, 2015. Trans. from the Yiddish by Barnett Zumoff; published in the Yiddish *Forverts*, October 5, 2009, jewishcurrents.org/marek-edelman-the-heroic-anti-hero.

872 Hanna Krall, *Shielding the Flame: An Intimate Conversation with Dr. Marek Edelman, the Last Surviving Leader of the Warsaw Ghetto Uprising*, trans. Joanna Stasinska and Lawrence Weschler, (Henry Holt & Co, 1986 [1977]), 37.

873 Hanna Krall, *Shielding the Flame*, 10.

874 Hanna Krall, *Shielding the Flame*, 77.

875 International March of the Living Home Page: www.motl.org

876 Alan L. Nager, Phung Pham, & Jeffrey I Gold, "March of the Living, a Holocaust Educational Tour: Effect on Adolescent Jewish Identity, *Springer Science + Business Media,* New York, 2013, published online June 26, 2013, *J Relig Health* 52, no. 4 (Dec 2013):1402–14, doi: 10.1007/s10943-013-9749-3.

877 old.federationcja.org/en/genmtl/march-of-the-living/about-march-of-the-living/

878 "About March of the Living," Federation CJA, old.federationcja.org/en/genmtl/march-of-the-living/about-march-of-the-living/, accessed February 15, 2024.

879 Ariana Melamed, "It's Time to Abolish the March of the Living," *Haaretz,* April 13, 2018, accessed February 15, 2024, www.haaretz.com/opinion/2018-04-13/ty-article-opinion/.premium/its-time-to-abolish-the-march-of-the-living/0000017f-e125-d38f-a57f-e777afd00000.

880 "Thirteen Goals of the March of the Living," International March of the Living, www.motl.org/goals/, accessed February 15, 2024.

881 Finkelstein, *The Holocaust Industry*, 135–36.

882 Segev, *The Seventh Million*, 488.

883 Novick, *The Holocaust and Collective Memory*, 320, n. 59, 160.

884   "Oprah and Elie Wiesel at Auschwitz Death Camp" May 24, 2006 ("Announcements").
       International March of the Living, accessed September 9, 2006, www.motl.org/
       announcements/htm.

885   Avril Alba, "'Here there is no why'—so why do we come here? Is a pedagogy of atrocity
       possible?" *Holocaust Studies* 21, no. 3 (2015): 134, 131.

886   Jessica Lang, "What's Wrong With the March of the Living?" *Jewish Exponent,*
       April 16, 2015, 238, 2, accessed August 3, 2023, jewishjournal.com/commentary/
       opinion/170443/.

887   Boaz Evron, "The Holocaust: Learning the Wrong Lessons," in *Journal of Palestine
       Studies,* Vol. 10, No. 3 (Spring, 1981), p. 16.

888   Mark Chmiel, *Elie Wiesel and the Politics of Moral Leadership,* Temple University Press,
       2001, 29.

889   Alexander Cockburn quoted in Chmiel, *Elie Wiesel and the Politics of Moral Leadership*,
       52.

890   Deborah Lipstadt, *History on Trial* (HarperCollins, 2005), 173, 181.

891   Deborah Lipstadt, *Denying the Holocaust: The Growing Assault on Truth and Memory,*
       (Plume/Penguin, 1994 [1993]), xv.

CHAPTER 9: GREAT EXPLANATIONS: THE ARTS AND CRAFTINESS OF HASBARA

892   Ambassador Chas W. Freeman, Jr. (USFS, Ret), "Hasbara and the Control of Narrative
       as an Element of Strategy: Remarks to the Jubilee Conference of the Council on Foreign
       and Defense Policy," Moscow, Russia, 2012. Middle East Policy Council. https://mepc.org/
       speeches/hasbara-and-control-narrative-element-strategy/. Accessed July 15, 2023.

893   Dr. Shivi Greenfield, *Israeli Hasbara: Myths and Facts. A Report on the Israeli Hasbara
       Apparatus,* trans. Jason Rogoff (Molad: The Center for the Renewal of Israeli Democracy,
       December 2012), 29-31. www.molad.org/images/upload/files/49381451033828.pdf.

894   "The Whole World Is Against Us" (*Ha'Olam Kulo Negeinu*), hebrewsongs.com:
       Your Online Library of Hebrew Song Words, written 1969, accessed June 1, 2024,
       www.hebrewsongs.com/?song=haolam-kulo-negdeinu.

895   Ambassador Gideon Meir, Deputy Director-General for Media and Public Affairs, Israel
       Ministry of Foreign Affairs, "What 'Hasbara' Is Really All About," *Israel Missions Around
       the World,* May 24, 2005, embassies.gov.il/MFA/FOREIGNPOLICY/Issues/Pages/
       What%20Hasbara%20Is%20Really%20All%20About%20-%20May%202005.aspx.

896   Margalit Toledano and David McKie, *Public Relations and Nation Building: Influencing
       Israel* (Routledge, 2013), 2.

897   Fatemeh Shafiee Sarvestani, Saied Reza Ameli, and Foad Izadi, "Israeli public diplomacy toward the United States: a network and narrative approach," *Asian Journal of Communication* (2018), DOI: doi.org/10.1080/01292986.2018.1531898.

898   Giora Goodman, "'Palestine's Best': The Jewish Agency Press Relations, 1946-1947," *Israel Studies* 16, no. 3 (2011).

899   Shay Hershkovitz, "Masbirim Israel: Israel's PR Campaign as Glocalized and Grobalized Political Prosumption," *American Behavioral Scientist* 56, no. 4 (2012): 527.

900   Jonathan Cummings, *Israel's Public Diplomacy: The Problems of Hasbara, 1966-1975,* (Rowman & Littlefield, 2016), 5-8.

901   Garth Jowett and Victoria O'Donnell, *Propaganda & Persuasion* (Sage Publications, 2019), 16.

902   Joseph S. Nye, Jr., *Soft Power: The Means to Success in World Politics* (Public Affairs, 2004), ix-x.

903   Nye, *Soft Power,* 2-17.

904   Jan Melisson, "The New Public Diplomacy: Between Theory and Practice," in Jan Melisson, ed., *The New Public Diplomacy: Soft Power in International Relations* (Palgrave Macmillan, 2005), 3-27.

905   Nicholas Cull, "Public Diplomacy Before Gullion: The Evolution of a Phrase," *CPD Blog.* USC Center on Public Diplomcy, USC Annenberg, April 16, 2006, uscpublicdiplomacy. org/blog/060418_public_diplomacy_before_gullion_the_evolution_of_a_phrase/.

906   James S. Nye, Jr., "Public Diplomacy and Soft Power." *The Annals of the American Academy of Political and Social Science* 616 (March 2008): 104.

907   Melissa Aronczyk, *Branding the Nation: The Global Business of National Identity* (Oxford University Press, 2013), 16.

908   Anholt, Simon, "Nationbrands: Austrade Simon Anholt Interview," June 4, 2009, YouTube, accessed August 8, 2016, www.youtube.com/watch?v=2vMmbv8cul0.

909   Wally Olins, *Brand New: The Shape of Brands to Come* (Thames & Hudson, 2014), 140-46.

910   Kendrick, Alice, Jami A. Fullerton and Sheri J. Broyles, "Would I go? US citizens react to a Cuban tourism campaign," *Place Branding and Public Diplomacy* 11 (2015): 249-262.

911   Quoted in Mandy Katz, "The re-branding of Israel: from war planes to women: why at 60 Israel's image is taking off in new directions," *Moment* magazine, May 1, 2008. www. thefreelibrary.com/The+re-branding+of+Israel%3a+from+war+planes+to+women%3a +why+at+60...-a0205033077.

912   "What is BDS?" BDS Movement, accessed June 8, 2024, bdsmovement.net.

913   Nathaniel Popper, "Israel Aims to Improve Its Public Image," *Forward,* October 14, 2005, forward.com/news/2070/israel-aims-to-improve-its-public-image/.

914   "Christopher Reeve: Israel is at center of world research on paralysis," ISRAEL21c Staff, July 27, 2003, updated September 13, 2013, www.israel21c.org/christopher-reeve-israel-is-at-center-of-world-research-on-paralysis/.

915   Dan Senor & Saul Singer, *Start-Up Nation: The Story of Israel's Economic Miracle*, (Twelve/Hatchette Book Group, 2009).

916   Viva Sarah Press, Executive Producer, *Where will YOU eat your apple and honey this Rosh Hashana?* An Israel21c Production, September 15, 2014, updated July 14, 2015, 2 mins., 6 secs., www.israel21c.org/where-will-you-eat-your-apple-and-honey-this-year/.

917   Esther Alloun, "Veganwashing Israel's Dirty Laundry? Animal Politics and Nationalism in Palestine-Israel," *Journal of Intercultural Studies* 41, no. 1 (2020): 30-32.

918   For some examples, see Sarah Schulman, "Israel and 'Pinkwashing,' *New York Times*, November 22, 2011, www.nytimes.com/2011/11/23/opinion/pinkwashing-and-israels-use-of-gays-as-a-messaging-tool.html; Maya Mikdashi, "Gay Rights and Human Rights: Pinkwashing Homonationalism," *Jadaliyya*, December 16, 2011, www.jadaliyya.com/pages/index/3560/gay-rights-as-human-rights_pinkwashing-homonationa; Kathleen Peratis, "For Gay Palestinians, Tel Aviv is Mecca." *Forward*, February 24, 2006, forward.com/articles/1125/for-gay-palestinians-tel-aviv-is-mecca/; Jasbir Puar, "The Golden Handcuffs of Gay Rights: How Pinkwashing Distorts Both LGBTIQ and Anti-Occupation Activism," *Jadaliyya*, Feb. 7, 2012, www.jadaliyya.com/pages/index/4273/the-golden-handcuffs-of-gay-rights_how-pinkwashing; Brian Schaefer, "Gay Pride Takes Center Stage on Israel Pilgrimages," *Haaretz*, June 8, 2014, www.haaretz.com/travel-in-israel/gay-tel-aviv/tel-aviv-pride/.premium-1.597586; Harriet Malinowitz, "Torches and Metonyms of Freedom," "Queer and Now" special issue of *The Writing Instructor*, March 2015, parlormultimedia.com/twitest/malinowitz-2015-03.

919   "Tel Aviv Declared World's Best Gay Travel Destination," *Haaretz*, January 11, 2012, www.haaretz.com/israel-news/travel/2012-01-11/ty-article/tel-aviv-declared-worlds-best-gay-travel-destination/0000017f-df28-df9c-a17f-ff3837f60000.

920   Rhys Crilley and Ilan Manor, "Un-nation Branding: "The Cities of Tel Aviv and Jerusalem in Israeli Soft Power" in *City Diplomacy: Currrent Trends and Future Prospects*, eds. Sohaela Amiri and Efe Sevin, (Palgrave Macmillan, 2020 [eBook]). DOI, doi.org/10.1007/978-3-030-45615-3_7.

921   Ron Schleifer, "Jewish and Contemporary Origins of Israeli *Hasbara*," *Jewish Political Studies Review* 15, no. 1-2 (Spring 2003).

922   Cummings, *Israel's Public Diplomacy*, 5-6.

923   Cummings, *Israel's Public Diplomacy*, 7.

924   Yitzhak Grinbaum quoted in Gideon Kouts, "From Sokolow to 'Explaining Israel': The Zionist 'Hasbara' First 'Campaign Strategy Paper' and Its Applications," *Revue Européenne des Études Hebraiques, n*o. 8 (2016): 108. [Published by Intstitut Europeén He'braqiques (IEEH).]

925   Toledano & McKie, *Public Relations and Nation Building*, 31.

926   Toledano & McKie, *Public Relations and Nation Building*, 32.

927   Sokolow quoted in Kouts, "From Sokolow to 'Explaining Israel,'" 127.

928   Sokolow quoted in Kouts, "From Sokolow to 'Explaining Israel,'" 120, 123.

929   Sokolow quoted in Kouts, "From Sokolow to 'Explaining Israel,'" 126-7.

930   Cummings, *Israel's Public Diplomacy*, 20.

931   Cummings, *Israel's Public Diplomacy*, 23-4.

932   Toledano & McKie, *Public Relations and Nation Building*, 80-81.

933   Toledano & McKie, *Public Relations and Nation Building*, 70.

934   Cummings, *Israel's Public Diplomacy*, 24; Goodman, "Palestine's Best," 3; Margalit Toledano & David McKie, "Social integration and public relations: Global lessons from an Israeli experience," *Journal of Public Relations Research,* 33(4), January 2007, 392.

935   Toledano & McKie, *Public Relations and Nation Building*, 55.

936   Cummings, *Israel's Public Diplomacy*, 24-5.

937   Goodman, "Palestine's Best," 2.

938   Goodman, "Palestine's Best," 4-6, 13.

939   Goodman, "Palestine's Best," 14-16.

940   Goodman, "Palestine's Best," 19.

941   Shay Hazkani, *Dear Palestine: A Social History of the 1948 War* (Stanford University Press, 2021).

942   Shay Hazkani, *Dear Palestine*, 106, 119-120.

943   Shay Hazkani, *Dear Palestine*, 106.

944   Shay Hazkani, *Dear Palestine*, 80-82.

945   Shay Hazkani, *Dear Palestine*, 80-83.

946   Shay Hazkani, *Dear Palestine*, 96.

947   Shay Hazkani, *Dear Palestine*, 97.

948   Shay Hazkani, *Dear Palestine*, 111.

949   Cummings, *Israel's Public Diplomacy*, 32-34.

950   Quoted in Cummings, *Israel's Public Diplomacy*, 28.

951   Cummings, *Israel's Public Diplomacy*, 24-36.

952   Cummings, *Israel's Public Diplomacy*, 137-161.

953 Rachel Shabi, "Special Spin Body Gets Media on Message, Says Israel," *Guardian*, January 2, 2009. www.theguardian.com/world/2009/jan/02/israel-palestine-pr-spin; Adi Kuntsman and Rebecca L. Stein, "Another War Zone: Social Media in the Israeli/ Palestinian Conflict," *Middle East Research and Information Project*, September 2010, accessed July 31, 2024, www.merip.org/mero/interventions/anotherwarzone. Accessed July 31, 2024.

954 Meron Medzini, "Reflections on Israel's Public Diplomacy," *Bulletin du Centre de recherche francais à Jerusalem*, 23 (2012), accessed August 5, 2023, journals.openedition. org/bcrfj/6829.

955 Yousef Munayyer, "The Long Arm of Israeli Repression," *Foreign Policy*, November 5, 2121. foreignpolicy.com/2021/11/05/the-long-arm-of-israeli-repression/.

956 Alex Kane, "Israel's Scheme to Defund the BDS Movement," *In These Times*, November 11, 2019, inthesetimes.com/features/BDS-movement-Israel-Palestine-activists-boycott-occupation.html.

957 Prime Minister's Office, "Six Months of the War on the Global Public Diplomacy Front: The National Public Diplomacy Directorate Presents Its Activity in the International Arena after Six Months of the War," accessed April 28, 2024, www.gov.il/en/pages/explanation100424.

958 *Times of Israel Staff*, "Public Diplomacy Directorate Said Crumbling after Departure of Chief and Most Staff," the *Times of Israel*, June 24, 2024, www.timesofisrael.com/public-diplomacy-directorate-said-crumbling-after-departure-of-chief-and-most-staff/.

959 Benny Morris, *Israel's Border Wars 1949-1956: Arab Infiltration, Israeli Retaliation, and the Countdown to the Suez War* (Clarendon Press, 1993), 236-262; Avi Shlaim, *The Iron Wall: Israel and the Arab World* (W.W. Norton & Co., 2000), 91-92.

960 Doug Rossinow, "The dark roots of AIPAC, 'America's Pro-Israel Lobby': The group was formed to spin positive PR after Israeli atrocities." Reproduced on Weblog of Habib Siddiqui, *Washington Post—Blogs*, March 6, 2018, drhabibsiddiqui.blogspot. com/2018/03/the-dark-roots-of-aipac.html; John J. Mearsheimer and Stephen M. Walt, *The Israel Lobby and U.S. Foreign Policy* (Farrar, Straus and Giroux, 2007), 118.

961 Cummings, *Israel's Public Diplomacy*, 49.

962 Meron Medzini, "Reflections on Israel's Public Diplomacy."

963 Cummings, *Israel's Public Diplomacy*, 52.

964 Cummings, *Israel's Public Diplomacy*, 51.

965 Cummings, *Israel's Public Diplomacy*, 54.

966 Giora Goodman, "Explaining the occupation: Israeli hasbara and the occupied territories in the aftermath of the June 1967 war," *Journal of Israeli History*, 36:1, 2017, 71.

967 Goodman, "Explaining the occupation," 73.

968   Goodman, "Explaining the occupation," 74.

969   Goodman, "Explaining the occupation," 74-76.

970   Goodman, "Explaining the occupation," 77-79.

971   Goodman, "Explaining the occupation," 80-83.

972   The Security Council of the United Nations, "Resolution 242 (1967) of 22 November 1967," *UN Peacemaker,* peacemaker.un.org/sites/peacemaker.un.org/files/SCRes242%281967%29.pdf.

973   Quoted in Cummings, *Israel's Public Diplomacy*, 119.

974   Cummings, *Israel's Public Diplomacy*, 121.

975   Cummings, *Israel's Public Diplomacy*, 130-31.

976   Cummings, *Israel's Public Diplomacy*, 137-56.

977   *Hasbara: Israel's Public Image: Problems and Remedies, The 19th America-Israel Dialogue, The American Jewish Congress Monthly* 51 no. 2-3, 1984, www.readthemaple.com/content/files/content/upload/bjpa/the_/the-2019th-20american-israel-20dialogue-hasbara-20israel-s-20public-20image-20problems-20and-20remedies-201984-20vol-2051-20no-202-3.pdf.

978   *The Occupation of the American Mind,* dir. Loretta Alper, Jeremy Earp, 2016, 84 min., Media Education Foundation.

979   Leon Wieseltier, "Firming Up the Consensus of Support for Israel," *Hasbara: Israel's Public Image,* 28.

980   Sarvestani et al., "Israel Public Diplomacy Toward the United States," 4-5.

981   Sarvestani et al., "Israel Public Diplomacy Toward the United States," 8, 12.

982   www.birthrightisrael.com

983   www.masaisrael.org

984   www.camera.org

985   www.aipac.org

986   amchainitiative.org

987   hasbarafellowships.org

988   www.meforum.org/campus-watch

989   www.standwithus.com

990   www.hillel.org

991   www.adl.org

992   cufi.org

993 Sean Savage, "How CUFI has awakened the 'sleeping giant' of Christian Zionism," *Jewish News Syndicate*, March 9, 2021, www.jns.org/how-cufi-has-awakened-the-sleeping-giant-of-christian-zionism/; "Mission," Christians United for Israel, cufi.org/about/mission/. Both accessed July 28, 2024.

994 Sarvestani et al., "Israel Public Diplomacy Toward the United States," 7-8, 12-16.

995 Shay Hershkovitz, "Masbirim Israel: Israel's PR Campaign as Glocalized and Grobalized Political Prosumption," *American Behavioral Scientist* 56, no. 4 (2012): 518-19.

996 Herhkovitz, "Masbirim Israel," 523.

997 Karolina Jędrzejewska, "Hasbara: Public Diplomacy with Israeli Characteristics," *Torun International Studies* 1, no. 13 (2020): 112.

998 Miriyam Aouragh, "Hasbara 2.0: Israel's Public Diplomacy in the Digital Age, *Middle East Critique* 25, no. 3 (2016): 283-4.

999 Taglit Birthright Israel, accessed July 17, 2024, www.birthrightisrael.com.

1000 Birthright Israel Foundation, accessed July 20, 2024, birthrightisrael.foundation/faqs/.

1001 Kiera Feldman, "The Romance of Birthright Israel," the *Nation,* June 15, 2011, accessed July 20, 2024, www.thenation.com/article/archive/romance-birthright-israel/.

1002 Hannah Gignoux, Birthright Presentation, Ithaca College Students for Justice in Palestine, April 11, 2018, accessed July 17, 2024, www.facebook.com/watch/live/?ref=watch_permalink&v=1885202131512272&rdid=pIsC44C00IUeQk2N.

1003 *Israel on Campus Coalition,* "About Us," israelcc.org/about-us/.

1004 canarymission.org

1005 Josh Nathan-Kasis, "Shadowy Blacklist of Student Activists Wins Endorsement of Mainstream Pro-Israel Group," the *Forward,* October 3, 2017, forward.com/news/383938/shadowy-blacklist-of-student-activists-wins-endorsement-of-mainstream-pro-i/.

1006 Josh Nathan-Kazis (the *Forward*) and Justin Elliott (ProPublica), "Pro-Israel Group Secretly Ran Misleading Facebook Ads to Target Palestinian-American Poet," *Haaretz*, September 12, 2018, www.haaretz.com/us-news/2018-09-12/ty-article/pro-israel-group-secretly-targeted-palestinian-american-poet/0000017f-f014-d497-a1ff-f29435e90000.

1007 James Bamford, ""Israel's War on American Student Activists," the *Nation,* November 17, 2023 , https://www.thenation.com/article/world/israel-spying-american-student-activists/.

1008 Ron Kampeas, "Prominent Pro-Israel Donor Pulls Out of AIPAC Conference After Saying Two Muslim Lawmakers 'Clash' with American Values," *Jewish Telegraph Agency,* March 19, 2019, www.jta.org/2019/03/19/israel/prominent-pro-israel-donor-pulls-out-of-aipac-conference-after-saying-muslim-lawmakers-clash-with-american-values.

1009 James Bamford, "Who Is Funding Canary Mission? Inside the Doxxing Operation Targeting Anti-Zionist Students and Professors," the *Nation,* December 22, 2023, www.thenation.com/article/world/canary-mission-israel-covert-operations/.

1010 Itamar Benzaquen, "The Israeli government is paying for anti-BDS journalism," *The Seventh Eye*, December 20, 2017, accessed July 30, 2024.

1011 Rafaella Goichman, "This anti-BDS Initiative Failed. So Israel Throws Another $30 Million at It," *Haaretz*, January 26, 2022. www.haaretz.com/israel-news/2022-01-26/ty-article-magazine/.premium/this-anti-bds-initiative-failed-so-israel-throws-another-100-million-nis-at-it/0000017f-db50-df9c-a17f-ff58b4110000. See also Itamar Benzaquen and The Seventh Eye, "The new hasbara campaign Israel doesn't want you to know about," January 25, 2022, +*972 Magazine*. www.972mag.com/hasbara-funding-foreign-agents/.

1012 Omer Benjakob, "Israel Secretly Targeted American Lawmakers With Gaza War Influence Campaign," *Haaretz*, June 5, 2024, www.haaretz.com/israel-news/security-aviation/2024-06-05/ty-article-magazine/.premium/israel-secretly-targeted-american-lawmakers-with-gaza-war-influence-campaign/0000018f-e7c8-d11f-a5cf-e7cb62af0000.

1013 "EI exclusive: a pro-Israel group's plan to rewrite history on Wikipedia," Electronic Intifada, April 21, 2008, accessed July 19, 2024, electronicintifada.net/content/ei-exclusive-pro-israel-groups-plan-rewrite-history-wikipedia/7472.

Alex Beam, *Boston Globe*, "War of the virtual Wiki-worlds," Electronic Intifada, May 6, 2008, accessed August 5, 2024, electronicintifada.net/content/war-virtual-wiki-worlds/9713.

1014 Rachel Shabi and Jemima Kiss, "Wikipedia editing courses launched by Zionist groups," *Guardian*, August 18, 2010, accessed July 19, 2024, www.theguardian.com/world/2010/aug/18/wikipedia-editing-zionist-groups.

1015 Oded Yaron, "Aligning Text to the Right: Is a Political Organization Editing Wikipedia to Suit Its Interests?" *Haaretz*, June 17, 2013, accessed July 19, 2024, www.haaretz.com/2013-06-17/ty-article/.premium/the-israeli-editing-wars-on-wikipedia/0000017f-f95b-d044-adff-fbfbb3b30000.

1016 "Wikipedia and the Israeli-Palestinian Conflict," Wikipedia, accessed July 19, 2024, en.wikipedia.org/wiki/Wikipedia_and_the_Israeli–Palestinian_conflict#:~:text=The%20Israeli–Palestinian%20conflict%20has%20been%20covered%20extensively%20on,the%20conflict%20differs%20significantly%20between%20the%20encyclopedia%27s%20language-versions.

1017 Rob Eshman, "Wiklpedia Called the ADL 'Unreliable.' It's a Wake-up Call the Civil Rights Organization Badly Needs," *Forward*, June 19, 2024, forward.com/opinion/625117/wikipedia-adl-unreliable-jonathan-greenblatt/.

1018 United States Holocaust Memorial Museum, "Protocols of the Elders of Zion," Holocaust Encyclopedia, accessed July 31, 2024, encyclopedia.ushmm.org/content/en/article/protocols-of-the-elders-of-zion.

1019 Frank Luntz, *Words That Work* (Hyperion, 2007).

1020 Frank Luntz, *The Israel Project's 2009 Global Language Dictionary* (The Israel Project, 2009), 4, 7-9. (Italics, bold, and underlining in original.) Internet Archive, accessed July 31, 2024, archive.org/details/sf-israel-projects-2009-global-language-dictionary_202402/mode/2up.

1021 Frank Luntz, *TIP's 2009 Global Language Dictionary*, 75-76. (Italics in original.)

1022 Frank Luntz, *TIP's 2009 Global Language Dictionary*, 104, 84, 37. (Italics and bold in original).

1023 *Hasbara Handbook: Promoting Israel on Campus*, World Union of Jewish Students, March 2002, Jerusalem, 8-11, accessed July 31, 2024. (Italics in original.) www.middle-east-info.org/take/wujshasbara.pdf.

1024 *Hasbara Handbook: Promoting Israel on Campus*, 8-9.

1025 *Hasbara Handbook*, 98.

1026 *Hasbara Handbook*, 87.

1027 *Hasbara Handbook*, 22.

1028 *Hasbara Handbook*, 24-25.

1029 Matthew S. Cohen and Chuck D. Freilich, "War by other means: the delegitimization campaign against Israel," *Israel Affairs* 24, no. 1 (2018): 4.

1030 Eytan Gilboa, "Public Diplomacy: The Missing Component in Israel's Foreign Policy," *Israel Affairs* 12, no. 4 (October 2006): 715.

1031 Eytan Gilboa, "Public Diplomacy," 716.

1032 Eytan Gilboa, "Public Diplomacy," 735-38.

1033 Eytan Gilboa, "Public Diplomacy," 738-42.

1034 Blake Flayton, "Make Zionism Sexy Again," *Sapir: A Journal of Jewish Conversation* 4, Winter 2022. sapirjournal.org/aspiration/2022/02/make-zionism-sexy-again/.

1035 Abba Eban quoted in Cummings, *Israel's Public Diplomacy*, 129.

1036 Quoted in Ben White, "Abba Eban's comments on the idiocy of hasbara just as true three decades later," Electronic Intifada, February 18, 2013 [blog], accessed January 14, 2014, electronicintifada.net/blogs/ben-white/abba-ebans-comments-idiocy-hasbara-just-true-three-decades-later. Original appeared in Abba Eban, "A negative balance," the *Jerusalem Post*, August 13, 1983.

1037 Dr. Shivi Greenfield, *Israeli Hasbara: Myths and Facts. A Report on the Israeli Hasbara Apparatus*, trans. Jason Rogoff (Molad, The Center for the Renewal of Israeli Democracy, 2012), 5, accessed March 16, 2024, www.molad.org/images/upload/files/49381451033828.pdf.

1038 Miriyam Aouragh, "Hasbara 2.0: Israel's Public Diplomacy in the Digital Age," *Middle East Critique*, 25, no. 3 (2016).

1039 Tasha G. Oren, *Demon in the Box: Jews, Arabs, Politics, and Culture in the Making of Israeli Television* (Rutgers University Press, 2004); Jitka Panek Jurkova, "The Domestic Dimension of Israeli Public Diplomacy," *Polish Political Science Yearbook* 47, no. 2 (2018): 249; Ruth Marks Eglash, "Israel losing the hasbara battle because of a broken public relations playbook, experts say," *Jewish Insider*, March 21, 2024, jewishinsider. com/2024/03/israel-hasbara-public-diplomacy-war-gaza-hamas/.

1040 Giora Goodman, "Explaining the Occupation," 86.

1041 Philip Montgomery, "'The Interview': Chuck Schumer on Democrats, Antisemitism and His Shutdown Retreat," *New York Times,* March 16, 2025, www.nytimes.com/2025/ 03/16/magazine/chuck-schumer-interview.html. Accessed March 16, 2025.

1042 Alena Botros, "Trump once again likens Chuck Schumer to Palestinian people while doubling down on his Gaza takeover proposal," *Fortune.com,* February 6, 2025. fortune. com/2025/02/06/trump-gaza-takeover-proposal-chuck-schumer-palestinians/. Accessed March 20, 2025.

1043 "Here's what Biden said in his remarks at the Holocaust remembrance ceremony," *New York Times,* May 7, 2024. www.nytimes.com/live/2024/05/07/us/biden-holocaust. Accessed March 17, 2025.

1044 Robert Clines, "The 'ancient desire' to kill Jews is not Hamas's. It's the West's," *Mondoweiss,* May 18, 2024. https://mondoweiss.net/2024/05/the-ancient-desire-to-kill-jews-is-not-hamass-its-the-wests/. Accessed May 19, 2024; "Hamas in 2017: The document in full," *Middle East Eye,* May 2, 2017. www.middleeasteye.net/news/hamas-2017-document-full. Accessed March 17, 2025.

1045 Quoted in Ben Samuels, "Could Harris' approach to Arab-American voters cost her the White House?' *Haaretz,* October 31, 2024. www.haaretz.com/israel-news/haaretz-today/ 2024-10-31/ty-article/.highlight/could-harris-approach-to-arab-american-voters-cost-her-the-white-house/00000192-e362-dd31-a9be-fb6b0f100000 Accessed Oct. 31, 2024.

1046 Anti-Defamation League Center on Extremism, "Anti-Israel Activism on U.S. Campuses, 2023-2024" [Report], ADL website, published Sept. 16, 2024, updated February 7, 2025. www.adl.org/resources/report/anti-israel-activism-us-campuses-2023-2024. Accessed March 18, 2025.

1047 Office of the President, Ron Liebowitz, Brandeis University, "A space for free speech, not hate speech," November 8, 2023. www.brandeis.edu/president/past/liebowitz-letters/2023-11-08-free-speech-not-hate-speech.html. Accessed March 17, 2025.

1048 Rabbi Seth Winberg, "I'm a rabbi at Brandeis. Its decision voiding recognition for its Students for Justice in Palestine chapter was the right move," *Forward,* November 14, 2023. forward.com/opinion/569676/brandeis-hillel-students-for-justice-palestine/. Accessed March 17, 2025.

1049 "Hamas in 2017: The document in full."

1050 Cathryn J. Prince, "As Columbia anti-Israel encampment endures, Jewish students horrified by 'Judenrein' campus," the *Times of Israel,* April 25, 2024. www.timesofisrael. com/as-anti-israel-encampment-at-columbia-endures-jewish-students-lament-judenre-in-campus/. Accessed March 18, 2025.

1051 Sam Turken, "Northeastern protestors reject university's reasoning for clearing pro-Palestinian encampment," *GBH News,* Boston, April 29, 2024. www.wgbh.org/news/local/2024-04-27/northeastern-protestors-reject-universitys-reasoning-for-clearing-pro-palestinian-encampment. Accessed March 18, 2025.

1052 Isabella Hammad, "Acts of Language," the *New York Review of Books,* June 13, 2024. www.nybooks.com/online/2024/06/13/acts-of-language-isabella-hammad/. Accessed June 25, 2024.

1053 Steve Neavling, "Tlaib slams Nessel for targeting pro-Palestinian students at U-M: 'A dangerous precedent,'" *Detroit Metro Times,* September 13, 2024. www.metrotimes.com/news/tlaib-slams-nessel-for-targeting-pro-palestinian-students-at-u-m-a-dangerous-precedent-37343930. Accessed March 21, 2025.

1054 Natasha Lennard, "CNN Anchors Won't Stop Lying About Something Rashid Tlaib Never Said," the *Intercept,* September 24, 2024. theintercept.com/2024/09/24/cnn-rashida-tlaib-dana-nessel-antisemitism/. Accessed March 21, 2025.

1055 Kayla Guo, "House Censures Rashida Tlaib, Citing 'River to the Sea' Slogan," *New York Times,* November 7, 2023, updated November 8, 2023. www.nytimes.com/2023/11/07/us/politics/tlaib-censure-house-israel-gaza.html. Accessed November 8, 2023.

1056 Simon Sebag Montefiore, "The Decolonization Narrative Is Dangerous and False," the *Atlantic,* October 27, 2023. www.theatlantic.com/ideas/archive/2023/10/decolonization-narrative-dangerous-and-false/675799/. Accessed November 4, 2023.

1057 American Jewish Committee, "The Translate Hate Glossary: AJC's glossary of antisemitic terms, phrases, conspiracies, cartoons, themes, and memes." American Jewish Committee [website], February 2021, p. 10. www.ajc.org/sites/default/files/pdf/2021-02/AJC_Translate-Hate-Glossary-2021.pdf. Accessed November 5, 2023.

1058 Joe Hernandez, "How interpretations of the phrase 'from the river to the sea' made it so divisive," npr.org, November 9, 2023. www.npr.org/2023/11/09/1211671117/how-interpretations-of-the-phrase-from-the-river-to-the-sea-made-it-so-divisive.

1059 Kayla Guo, "House Censures Rashida Tlaib."

1060 Karoun Demirjian and Liam Stack, "In Congress and on Campuses, 'From the River to the Sea' Inflames Debate," *New York Times,* November 9, 2023. www.nytimes.com/2023/11/09/us/politics/river-to-the-sea-israel-gaza-palestinians.html. Accessed November 9, 2023.

1061 Joe Hernandez, "How interpretations of the phrase 'from the river to the sea' made it so divisive."

1062 Karoun Demirjian and Liam Stack, "In Congress and on Campuses."

1063 Mira Fox, "So what does 'intifada' actually mean?," the *Forward,* December 15, 2023. forward.com/culture/573654/intifada-arabic-israeli-hamas-war-meaning-linguistics/. Accessed March 26, 2025.

1064 "ICYMI: Stefanik Demands Answers from Harvard President Claudine Gay on Harvard's Failure to Condemn Antisemitism and Anti-Israel Attacks on Campus." [Press release] *Stefanik.house.gov,* Dec. 5, 2023. stefanik.house.gov/2023/12/icymi-stefanik-demands-answers-from-harvard-president-claudine-gay-on-harvard-s-failure-to-condemn-antisemitism-and-anti-israel-attacks-on-campus. Accessed March 24, 2025.

1065 Ron Kampeas, "'Is that really her?' Liberal Jews say Elise Stefanik, hailed as a hero of the House antisemitism hearings, has baggage of her own," *Jewish Telegraphic Agency,* Dec. 11, 2023. www.jta.org/2023/12/11/politics/is-that-really-her-liberal-jews-say-elise-stefanik-hailed-as-a-hero-of-the-house-antisemitism-hearings-has-baggage-of-her-own. Accessed March 6, 2025.

1066 Masha Gessen, "What We Know About the Weaponization of Sexual Violence on October 7th," the *New Yorker,* July 20, 2024. www.newyorker.com/news/the-weekend-essay/what-we-know-about-the-weaponization-of-sexual-violence-on-october-7th. Accessed March 11, 2025; Randa Abdel-Fattah, "A Critical Look at The New York Times' Weaponization of Rape in Service of Israeli Propaganda," *Institute for Palestine Studies,* January 14, 2024. https://www.palestine-studies.org/en/node/1655054. Accessed January 4, 2025.

1067 Aaron Rabinowitz, "Death and Donations: Did the Israeli Volunteer Group Handling the Dead of October 7 Exploit Its Role?, *Haaretz,* January 32, 2024. https://www.haaretz.com/israel-news/2024-01-31/ty-article-magazine/.premium/death-and-donations-did-the-volunteer-group-handling-the-october-7-dead-exploit-its-role/0000018d-5a73-d997-adff-df7bdb670000?lts=1706986320414. Accessed March 31, 2025.

1068 Arun Gupta, "American Media Keep Citing Zaka – Though Its October 7 Atrocity Stories Are Discredited in Israel," the *Intercept,* February 27, 2024. theintercept.com/2024/02/27/zaka-october-7-israel-hamas-new-york-times/. Accessed March 31, 2025.

1069 Jeremy Scahill, Ryan Grim and Daniel Boguslaw, "'Between the Hammer and the Anvil': The Story Behind the *New York Times* October 7 Exposé," the *Intercept,* February 28 2024. theintercept.com/2024/02/28/new-york-times-anat-schwartz-october-7/. Accessed March 29, 2025.

1070 Scahill, Grim, and Boguslaw, "Between the Hammer and the Anvil."

1071 Hamza Yusef, "'Beheaded Babies' – How UK Media Reported Israel's Fake News as Fact," Declassified UK, January 4, 2024. www.declassifieduk.org/beheaded-babies-how-uk-media-reported-israels-fake-news-as-fact/. Accessed October 7, 2024.

1072 "Netanyahu Shows Blinken Horrific Pictures of Infant Victims: PM Office," France 24, December 10, 2023. www.france24.com/en/live-news/20231012-netanyahu-shows-blinken-horrific-pictures-of-infant-victims-pm-office. Accessed March 31, 2025.

1073 Hasbara Tracker: Tracking Israel's Propaganda, hasbaratracker.com.

1074 "Tracking Israel's lies: MEMO in Conversation with Jennine Khalik," Middle East Monitor, June 19, 2024. www.middleeastmonitor.com/20240619-tracking-israels-lies-memo-in-conversation-with-jennine-khalik/. Accessed March 15, 2025.

1075 Omer Benjacob, "Hasbara Hitch: Pro-Israel Social Media Bot Goes Rogue, Calls IDF Soldiers 'White Colonizers in Apartheid Israel,'" *Haaretz,* January 29, 2025. www.haaretz.com/israel-news/security-aviation/2025-01-29/ty-article/.premium/pro-israel-bot-goes-rogue-calls-idf-soldiers-white-colonizers-in-apartheid-is-rael/00000194-ae81-def2-afdc-eeab470d0000. Accessed March 7, 2025.

INDEX

ABOUT THE AUTHOR

Harriet Malinowitz, a retired professor of English, specializes in writing, rhetoric, Palestine studies, and women's, gender, and sexuality studies. She is the author of *Textual Orientations: Lesbian and Gay Students and the Making of Discourse Communities* as well as articles and reviews in *Mondoweiss, Common Dreams, Slate, The Women's Review of Books, Radical Teacher, College English, The Right to Literacy,* and elsewhere. She co-founded a Palestine film series at her local independent cinema, is a member of Jewish Voice for Peace, and has worked with Palestine solidarity groups in the Hudson Valley and Central New York. She lives in Ithaca.